This book is due for return on or before the last

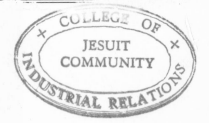

THE CONTRACT OF EMPLOYMENT

THE CONTRACT OF EMPLOYMENT

M. R. Freedland

of Gray's Inn, Barrister,
Fellow of St. John's College, Oxford.

CLARENDON PRESS · OXFORD
1976

Oxford University Press, Ely House, London W. 1

GLASGOW NEW YORK TORONTO MELBOURNE WELLINGTON
CAPE TOWN IBADAN NAIROBI DAR ES SALAAM LUSAKA ADDIS ABABA
DELHI BOMBAY CALCUTTA MADRAS KARACHI LAHORE DACCA
KUALA LUMPUR SINGAPORE HONG KONG TOKYO

ISBN 0 19 825306 0

© *Oxford University Press 1976*

*Printed in Great Britain by
Billing & Sons Limited, Guildford and London*

To my
Mother and Father

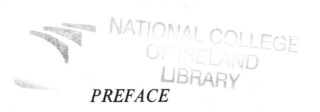
PREFACE

The present work is an adaptation and extension of my doctoral thesis, which was entitled 'The Application of General Contract Principles to the Termination of the Employment Relationship' and which was presented in August 1970. The main adaptation has consisted in the addition of material on the formation, structure, and breach of the contract of employment. A systematic exposition of all aspects of formation and definition of the contract of employment would have made an already expansive text over-lengthy; and considerations of space have also necessitated a reluctant exclusion of some historical aspects of the subject—above all, the extremely interesting Poor Law cases on the contract of employment from about 1750 to 1834. Discussion has, on the other hand, been added of the relevant issues raised by the Industrial Relations Act 1971. The repeal of that Act by the Trade Union and Labour Relations Act 1974 has been described in an Appendix; this seemed preferable to a hasty rearrangement of the main text, and avoided a premature consignment to oblivion of matters of lasting interest arising under the 1971 Act. At the time of writing this Preface, there are before Parliament the Trade Union and Labour Relations (Amendment) Bill, the Employment Protection Bill and the Sex Discrimination Bill. None of these proposals for legislation, as so far formulated, seems likely to have any fundamental effect upon contracts of employment, though important new statutory rights affecting employment are likely to be created. There may also be further progress with the EEC Draft Directives on the protection of employees in take-overs and mergers and on collective dismissals. Hence the area of individual employment law is full of potential developments; but the contractual framework which this book describes seems likely to retain its essential characteristics unchanged for some years to come. The law described in this book is that of England and Wales, and it is stated as it stood on 16 September 1974, which is the date upon which the Trade Union and Labour Relations Act 1974 came into full effect. A short Postscript deals with the most recent developments in the area of formation of contractual terms; as to cases decided too recently for inclusion in the text, the reader is referred to notes by the author on *Sanders* v. *Earnest Neale Ltd.*, *Hare* v. *Murphy Bros. Ltd.*, and *Chappell* v. *Times Newspapers Ltd.* published or to be published in the Industrial Law Journal during 1975.

The completion of the book gives me the opportunity to acknowledge the help which I have had in writing not only this book but the thesis which preceded it. My thanks go first of all to Otto Kahn-Freund who supervised my doctoral studies and whose intellectual example, kindness, and encouragement I have been most privileged to enjoy. I am no less indebted to Roger Rideout, with whom I first studied Labour Law, at whose suggestion I embarked upon research work in that subject, and from whose good advice I have benefited at various stages of the present work. Among those who read parts of the thesis or the present work in draft, I should like especially to thank Guenter Treitel and Paul Davies. I owe thanks also to Don Harris and to Paul O'Higgins for the encouragement which they as the examiners of my thesis gave me towards further efforts in the project of writing this book. In the course of so doing, I have had the advantage of discussing aspects of the subject-matter with the late Geoffrey Clark, Harry Kidd and Steve Anderman. I have received invaluable help at the proof-reading stage from Paul Brodestsky and Jaques Parry. Among those who have kindly helped me with the typing and production of both thesis and book, I should like to thank in particular Mrs. Wilbery, Mrs. Bryant, and Mrs. Beattie of the Oxford University Law Faculty Office. I am indebted to the Industrial Society for the opportunity to make use of their library and information services.

I am grateful also to the Secretary and Delegates of the Oxford University Press for the helpfulness of the staff of the Press during the preparation of this work. My last, but by no means least, acknowledgement is of my wife's patient encouragement.

St. John's College, Oxford   M.R.F.
30 April 1975

CONTENTS

NOTE ON ABBREVIATIONS

The following abbreviated modes of citation are used in text and footnotes:

1963 Act	Contracts of Employment Act 1963
1965 Act	Redundancy Payments Act 1965
1971 Act	Industrial Relations Act 1971
1972 Act	Contracts of Employment Act 1972
NIRC	National Industrial Relations Court
Royal Commission	Royal Commission on Trade Unions and Employers' Associations 1965–1968 (Chairman: Lord Donovan) whose report is published as Cmnd 3623 (HMSO 1968)
TULRA 1974	Trade Union and Labour Relations Act 1974

Table of Statutes and Statutory Instruments

Table of Cases

INTRODUCTION

The purpose of this introduction is both to describe the scope of the work which follows and at the same time to acknowledge its limits and limitations. This book consists of a detailed examination of the common law of the contract of employment—an area where, despite the marginal impact of many statutory provisions, the legal ground-rules are still the judge-made ones. As will appear in later pages, writers on the law and sociology of employment have demonstrated extensively the social irrelevance of this 'law of master and servant', and its failure to express the realities of the contemporary employment relationship. However, the importance of laws is not determined by their social adequacy. The law of the contract of employment, although obsolete in some respects and misconceived in others, has a critical role not only in individual employment law but in collective labour law also. As a conceptual starting-point, the contract of employment still preserves a central position in a rapidly developing part of the law. This work advances no greater claim for the contract of employment than that it is of considerable *legal* significance; in the ensuing chapters its social utility is frequently doubted.

If we regard the law of contracts of employment as an apparatus for processing individual employment disputes, then that law should be studied primarily in terms of its social effectiveness. This approach is considered by Wedderburn and Davies, who say that 'Legal processing of individual employment disputes in the English system rests naturally upon the enforcement of the individual contract of employment.'[1] On that basis, one should concentrate on the litigation upon contracts of employment which occurs before County Courts,[2] less frequently before the High Court, and perhaps occasionally before magistrates' courts.[3] We should establish what

---

[1] Wedderburn and Davies, *Employment Grievances & Disputes Procedures in Britain* (Berkeley, Calif., 1969) p. 21. It is, however, a theme of their work that the legal method and the legal training are not appropriate for the treatment of employment grievances and disputes.

[2] See the sample figures given by Wedderburn and Davies, op. cit., p. 38.

[3] Formerly under the Employers and Workmen Act 1875; and under s. 4 (now repealed) and s. 5 of the Conspiracy and Protection of Property Act 1875

is the distribution of the case-load between the different aspects of the contract of employment, for instance remuneration, dismissal, terms of notice; and should inquire what are the factors influencing the choice between litigation in the courts, resort to voluntary procedures[1] or applications to Industrial Tribunals for redundancy payments,[2] in respect of unfair dismissal[3] and statutory rights relating to trade union membership and activity,[4] or under the Contracts of Employment Act 1972[5] for enforcement of the right to particulars of terms and conditions of employment. Inquiries of that type would be useful indeed, and the establishing of a system of remedies for unfair dismissals has produced a heightened awareness of individual employment law as a mechanism for supplementing the working of our system of industrial relations.[6] But the importance of the law of the contract of employment lies elsewhere than in the handling of individual employment grievances, however regrettable that may be.

The only significant recent example of the use of the law of contracts of employment as part of a system of industrial relations seems to have been the practice in the coal-mining industry of bringing actions upon contracts of employment as test cases for the resolution of collective disputes, and as an instrument of industrial discipline.[7] Evidence given by representatives of the Coal Board to the Royal Commission showed that this practice had itself fallen into disuse because it was no longer an acceptable part of the machinery of employment relations in the industry.[8] There is admittedly a

---

(criminal prosecutions), and under the Truck Acts 1831–1940 (civil and criminal proceedings).

[1] The choice between voluntary procedure and the statutory process concerning dismissal is considered by Anderman, *Voluntary Dismissals Procedure & the Industrial Relations Act* (P.E.P. Broadsheet No. 538) (1972).

[2] Under the 1965 Act, s. 21.

[3] Under s. 22 and s. 106 of the 1971 Act. See Appendix Para. 2.

[4] Under s. 5 and s. 106 of the 1971 Act.

[5] Which consolidates the Contracts of Employment Act 1963 with the amendments made by the 1965 Act and the 1971 Act.

[6] An approach anticipated by the late G. de N. Clark in his innovatory writings on this topic—see 'Arbitrary Dismissal and Reinstatement' (1969) 32 MLR 532 and *Remedies for Unjust Dismissal—Proposals for Legislation* (P.E.P. Broadsheet No. 518) (1970).

[7] Cf. *National Coal Board* v. *Galley* [1958] 1 WLR 16, *National Coal Board* v. *Hughes* (1959) 109 LJ 526, and, among cases before nationalization, cf. *McCarthy* v. *Penrikyber Colliery Co. Ltd.* [1939] 1 KB1 (minimum wages legislation); *Hampton* v. *West Cannock Colliery Co.* [1932] 2 KB 293 (checkweighing legislation).

[8] *Royal Commission Minutes of Evidence* No. 4 p. 170 question 810.

steady flow of claims in the inferior courts for compensation under contracts of employment—for unpaid remuneration, holiday pay and sick pay, for damages for wrongful dismissal, and for inadequacy of notice of dismissal.[1] But such claims do not amount to the use of the law of the contract of employment as part of the apparatus of industrial relations, and they do not identify the importance of this branch of the law.[2]

What then is the importance of the law of contracts of employment? Kahn-Freund, writing in 1954, suggested that it was important as a legal framework for rights and obligations created by systems of industrial relations.[3] His concern was with the disparity between this legal framework and the factual situations; with the fact, for instance, that the contract of employment indicated a relationship entirely of subordination and took no adequate account of participation by employees in the control of working conditions; with the fact that the individual contract of employment imposes an atomized view of a reality which can be understood only in collective terms. Rideout, writing in 1966,[4] concluded that the contract of employment was unacceptable even as a legal framework, because the law of contract in general has so arbitrary a bearing on the needs of the employment relationship; because the law of the contract of employment seemed unable to shake itself free from the restrictions imposed on it by nineteenth-century judges; because of the failure of the Contracts of Employment Act 1963 to establish an important social role for the legal contract of employment; and because of the increasing impact of public law concepts of tenure in employment with which contractual thinking was inconsistent.

Fox has recently offered an even more fundamental critique of the contract of employment.[5] He shows how even during the nine-

---

[1] See Wedderburn & Davies, op. cit. p. 38. The *Civil Judicial Statistics* are uninformative on this point.

[2] In an attempt to alter this situation somewhat, by enabling breach of contract questions to be considered together with claims for redundancy payments and for remedies for unfair dismissal, section 113 of the 1971 Act provided that the Lord Chancellor had the power by affirmative resolution procedure to make an order conferring jurisdiction on Industrial Tribunals in respect of damages for breach of contracts of employment, damages being defined by Section 113(8) to include contractual debts. See Appendix, para 10.

[3] Chapter II of *The System of Industrial Relations in Great Britain* ed. Flanders and Clegg (Oxford, 1954) p. 45.

[4] (1966) 19 Current Legal Problems 111.

[5] Alan Fox, *Beyond Contract: Work, Power and Trust Relations* (London 1974) pp. 181–90.

teenth century, when the contractual framework of employment was most firmly established, there was a great inconsistency at the heart of the theoretical structure. For whereas general principles of freedom of contract were rigorously applied to give the employer the opportunity to treat labour as a pure market commodity, those principles gave way to older, almost feudal, notions of hierarchical duty when it came to regulating the extent of the employee's obligation to obey the employer. This theoretical inequality, this disparity of concepts was, Fox argues, a defect striking at the core of legal thinking about the contract of employment.

None the less, it is possible to identify an area of importance for the law of the contract of employment and to do so consistently with these telling criticisms of this branch of the law. The law of the contract of employment combines an apparatus for the regulation of the individual employment relationship—an apparatus admittedly now somewhat rudimentary and obsolescent—with a body of legal theory which is necessary for the working of many other parts of our system of Labour Law. The clearest example is the use of contractual concepts in the Redundancy Payments Act 1965—in order to define, for instance, dismissal, misconduct, continuity of employment, and hours of work. Other examples are not lacking; thus the classification of contracts of employment, in the sense of the distinction between them and contracts for services, has traditionally been and remains crucial in the application of statutes; not only within the area of Labour Law itself—in, for instance, the Trade Disputes Act 1906, the Contracts of Employment Act 1963, and latterly the Industrial Relations Act—but also in the adjacent areas of the law concerning safety at work and compensation for injury and the law concerning social security. Indeed, so significant has the classification of contracts of employment been that it gives rise in itself to a more elaborate body of law than that concerning the interpretation and effect of those contracts.[1] Furthermore, the concept of breach of the contract of employment has played a critical part in the development of the law concerning industrial conflict, whether at common law, under the Trade Disputes Acts, or in the Industrial Relations Act.

The law of the contract of employment thus deserves a systematic analysis not only as a process of adjudication in itself but also as a necessary element in various other aspects of Labour Law. This

---

[1] See below, p. 8.

book will thus attempt to formulate and suggest a coherent system of principles drawn together from judgments delivered in diverse contexts; principles perhaps unconsciously shaped by their practical effect in the particular circumstances in which they were formulated. This influence from consequences is perhaps most obvious when, for instance, the emergency powers of the Secretary of State for Employment in relation to industrial conflict depended upon the definition of breach of contracts of employment, as occurred in the *Secretary of State for Employment* v. *ASLEF* cases.[1] The influence is more complex when entitlement to redundancy payment depends upon the definition of consensual termination of the contract of employment, as occurred in *Marriott* v. *Oxford & District Co-operative Society Ltd.* (No. 2).[2] These situations are mentioned not as instances where principles have been fashioned in order to achieve a particular result, but in order to indicate the diversity of applications from which this system of principles is to be constructed.

In describing the principles of the contract of employment which serve this multiple function in our Labour Law, two particular emphases or definitions of the subject-matter have been adopted in this work. Firstly, the focus of attention is concentrated upon those principles which deal with developments supervening after the formation of the contract. It is in relation to that dynamic element in the employment relationship and the law governing it that the most interesting features of judicial reasoning in this area seem to occur; in relation, that is, to the different modes of termination of the contract of employment. An attempt will be made to survey these modes of termination systematically. But perhaps now equally important are those developments in the operation of the contract of employment which do not necessarily involve termination or constitute alternatives to termination—breach, variation, and suspension. An examination of these variants in the working of the contract is necessary to complement a survey of termination of the contract and receives a prominent place in this work.

The second emphasis of this work is upon the relationship between the principles of the law of the contract of employment and the general principles of the law of contract. For it is clear that some of the reasoning by which the principles of the law of the contract of employment have been evolved resorts to principles common

---

[1] [1972] ICR 7; (No. 2) [1972] ICR 19.
[2] [1970] 1 QB 186.

to the law of contracts in general. An examination of this interaction between the general and particular principles is thought to be instructive for the following reasons. It is tentatively suggested that the body of supposedly general principles of the law of contract can be divided into two broad types. There is a type of truly general principle of the law of contract, derived from the experience of no one particular species of contract. On the other hand there is a type of principle which is offered as if it were truly general but is in reality a generalization from judicial rulings in relation to certain specific kinds of contract. The principles of the truly general kind tend to be concentrated upon the formation of contracts. That is as one might expect, for the rules about formation have the function of defining the limits of the legal concept of contract. Thus the doctrines of consideration, privity, and intent to create legal relations are perhaps the most authentically general principles of contract law. By contrast, the principles associated with the variation and termination of contracts have less claim to a real generality; they are far more obviously generalizations of case-law relating to particular kinds of contract. Thus the characteristics of the contract of sale are stamped indelibly upon the principles of rescission of contracts for breach—in the distinction, for instance, between conditions and warranties—and the law of frustration is especially associated with contracts for the hire of goods, the provision of services, or the carriage of goods.

Thus there is an orientation of the supposedly general principles governing variation and discharge of contracts towards certain major types of commercial contract. For this reason, it is possible to see the application of these principles to the contract of employment as a process of interaction between Commercial Law and Labour Law; between the law governing mercantile transactions and the needs of the employment relationship. Clyde Summers considered[1] that the main justification for an attempt to relate the law of collective agreements to the law of contracts at large was that a new light might thereby be cast upon the general principles themselves, particularly in that it might become apparent that collective agreements were a less esoteric type of contract than was generally assumed. If similar results follow from the carrying out of the same type of study in relation to the contract of employment, that is an added bonus;

[1] Summers, 'Collective Agreements and the Law of Contracts' (1968) 78 Yale Law Journal 525 ff.

but perhaps there is in any event some special insight to be gained into the law concerning the formation, operation, and discharge of contracts of employment by considering how far it can truly be seen as an application of general contractual principles.

Chapter One

FORMATION AND STRUCTURE

SECTION 1 : THE FORMATION OF THE CONTRACT AND OF ITS TERMS

A. *The Formation of the Contract itself*

The formation of the contract of employment does not in itself present very great complications. The difficulties associated with formation relate to the formation of particular terms rather than to the question of whether a contract of employment has been brought into existence at all. This is leaving aside problems of distinguishing between contracts of service and for services, issues which are not separately discussed in this work because they are very fully treated elsewhere.[1] For the purpose of this work, a purely descriptive definition of the contract of employment will be adopted. That is to say, the contract of employment is that form of contract for personal service which the courts recognize as expressing the social relationship of employer and employee, as opposed to the other relationship of employer and independent contractor. This distinction is regarded as synonymous with the distinction between the contract of service and the contract for services respectively. At various points in this work, we shall touch upon aspects of the structure of the contract of employment which might be helpful in formulating an analytical definition of the contract;[2] but this writer

---

[1] See particularly Atiyah, *Vicarious Liability* (London 1967) Chapters 3–8; and the recent cases of *Ready Mixed Concrete (South East)* v. *MPNI* [1968] 2 QB 497; *Willy Scheidegger Swiss Typewriting School* v. *M.Soc.Sec.* (1968) 5 KIR 65; *Market Investigations Ltd.* v. *M.Soc.Sec.* [1969] 2 QB 173; *Construction Industry Training Board* v. *Labour Force Ltd.* [1970] 3 All ER 220; *Challinor* v. *Taylor* [1972] ICR 129; *Maurice Graham Ltd.* v. *Brunswick* (1974) 16 KIR 158.

[2] See pp. 19–21—the distinction between the single continuing contract and the series of exchanges of value on agreed terms; pp. 21–23—the distinction between the contract of employment and the 'service and pay' relationships; pp. 27–32—the principle of co-operation as a means of deciding whether there is a continuing obligation to employ; pp. 96–98—suspension by reason of unavailability of work (lay-off) and the termination of the contract of employment; pp. 148–9—contract of employment for the duration of a specific task; pp. 213–14—amenability of operatic artistes to criteria for dismissal applicable to employees

hesitates to offer a complete definition based solely upon the structural characteristics of the contract, or to assert that such a definition would be preferable to the present elaborate case-law.

The contract of employment may be formed by:—

(a) express written agreement, or
(b) express oral agreement, or
(c) conduct.

No formal requirements normally attach to the making of the contract, and non-compliance with the obligation to give particulars of certain terms which is imposed by Section 4 of the 1972 Act does not bear upon the validity or enforceability of the contract itself.[1]

As far as formation by express agreement is concerned, an aspect deserving special attention is the situation where the agreement is for employment to commence at a date later than that of the agreement itself, as in *Hochster* v. *De la Tour*,[2] a leading case upon anticipatory breach. The issue is whether there can be said to be a contract of employment in being before the actual employment has begun. If it is said there is no contract of employment in force, the alternative analysis is that there is a contract to enter into a contract of employment at a later date. The distinction is important where consequences are attached to the length of the period of contractual service. The view of this writer is that there can be said to be a contract of service in being and in force after the initial agreement has been made, but that we should not regard the employee as 'employed under' that contract until the commencement date fixed for employment thereunder. This approach would normally avoid anomalies in calculating periods of contractual service, whilst avoiding over-elaborate concepts of contracts to enter into further contracts. A corresponding analysis might be useful to deal with the period after actual service has ended but during which the former employee remains under obligations concerning trade competition and trade secrets.[3]

As far as formation by conduct is concerned, the problems arising

---

generally; pp. 303–5—frustration of short-term contracts of employment for a specific purpose.

[1] Cf. *Parkes Classic Confectionery Ltd.* v. *Ashcroft* (1973) 8 ITR 43 (change in terms of employment). Requirements of writing are made by the Merchant Shipping Act 1970 s. 1, and for apprentices.   [2] (1853) 2 E & B 678.

[3] Cf. *General Billposting Co.* v. *Atkinson* [1909] AC 118, which concerned the survival of obligations continuing after the period of actual service.

are of two types. Firstly, there is the broad problem of how specific terms are to be ascertained when the contract is formed by conduct. It has long been a striking fact that so complex and comprehensive a contract as the contract of employment may be concluded by the mere conduct of starting work at the employer's direction.[1] However, the difficulties raised by that method of formation relate to the ascertainment of specific terms; there is little difficulty in holding that the contract itself is formed in that informal way.

Two aspects of formation by conduct require particular attention. The obligation to give particulars of terms of employment imposed by Section 4 of the 1972 Act will normally result in the employer presenting the employee with a formal statement of terms at some time after the contract has been formed by conduct. It might be argued that the change in the nature of the contractual relationship thus brought about is so fundamental as to necessitate the conclusion that a new and different contract comes into force at that point. This writer prefers the view that there is a single contract of employment in force throughout—unless the presenting of formal particulars is taken by the employer as the opportunity to effect fundamental changes in the terms of the bargain which the employer and employee must have assumed while that bargain was still informal. Where a single contract remains in force throughout, it would be on the terms implied by common law, and such terms as can be inferred from conduct, unless and until those implied terms are superseded by terms evidenced by statutory particulars.

The other aspect of formation by conduct which requires attention is, this time, truly a problem of formation of the contract itself as opposed to the formation of particular terms of it. The problem is that it is possible to regard the mere conduct of exchanging service for remuneration as not amounting to the formation of a contract of service. That is because the arrangement may be seen as lacking that element of mutual obligation in respect of future services which is necessary to the existence of a contract of service. (The element of mutual obligation is discussed later in relation to the structure of the contract of employment.)[2]

We find examples of this refusal to infer a contract of service from conduct in cases where an employee has worked for his employer

---

[1] See Tillyard, *The Worker and the State* (3rd edn. 1948) p. 3 for a classic exposition of this model of the contract of employment.

[2] Below, pp. 19–21.

for a short period after the withdrawal by the employer of the previous terms and conditions of employment and the imposition of new terms. This was the situation considered by the Court of Appeal in *Marriott* v. *Oxford & District Co-operative Society Ltd.* (No. 2).[1] Further examples are now to be found in cases where an employee works for a short time for a new employer following the acquisition of an enterprise by that new employer—the situation in *Ubsdell* v. *Paterson*[2] and *Cartin* v. *Botley Garages Ltd.*[3]

In these cases, the courts have tended to avoid the conclusion that there is a contract of service, in order to protect the employee from the loss of the right to redundancy payment which would result from his accepting re-engagement with his existing employer or with the transferee of the employer's business. Thus Sir Samuel Cooke in *Ubsdell* v. *Paterson*:

The mere fact that an employee for a short period accepts wages on the same basis as his wages under his contract with the previous employer is by no means necessarily conclusive evidence that there has been an offer by conduct by the new employer to re-engage the employee on all the terms and conditions of the previous contract, or that the employee has accepted such an offer.[4]

Although the decisions concerned are appropriate in the context of the statutory right to redundancy payment, they are less easy to defend in terms of contractual theory. It is, in the view of this writer, a confusion of ideas to deny the existence of a contract of employment merely because the employment is for a short term and precarious. Neither of those factors is inconsistent with the existence of the contract of employment.

B. *The Formation of the Terms of the Contract*

The rules governing the creation of contractual obligations are normally considered under the heading of formation of contract. But in considering the formation of particular terms of the contract it is important to avoid a misleading emphasis upon the initial formation of the contract. Many of the particular obligations within the contract may be established or re-established during the continuance of the employment relationship. In that case, the establishment of

---

[1] [1970] 1 QB 186; *Shields Furniture Ltd.* v. *Goff* [1973] ICR 187; *Sheet Metal Components Ltd.* v. *Plumridge* [1974] ICR 373.
[2] [1973] ICR 86.   [3] [1973] ICR 144.   [4] [1973] ICR 86, 89C.

the particular obligation has also to be regarded as a variation of the contract as a whole and will be considered as such at a later stage in this work.[1] For the purposes of the present discussion, the point is that the formation of terms of the contract of employment is a dynamic and cumulative process which is perhaps not properly described as formation of the contract of employment.

In order to understand the legal issues concerning the establishing of obligations under contracts of employment, and in order also to identify the changes which are occurring in this process, it is useful to distinguish between the sources of contractual terms and the methods whereby those terms are established as part of the contract. The sources may be described thus:

(a) terms settled between employer and employee (which may include the adoption of a standard form of agreement such as a set of works rules);[2]
(b) collective agreements;[3]
(c) custom and practice;[4]
(d) terms presumptively implied under rules of the common law;[5]
(e) terms imposed by or under statute (e.g. terms embodying Wages Council Orders);
[(f) statutory written particulars of terms of employment.][6]

The methods whereby those sources are used to establish contractual obligation are as follows:

(a) direct agreement, e.g. by the signing of a complete written agreement;
(b) agreement by reference to other sources;[7]
(c) agreement by agency;[8]

---

[1] See below, pp. 42–53.

[2] For an important instance where works rules were said not to constitute contractual terms although the employee undertook to comply with them, see *Sec. of State for Employment* v. *ASLEF* (No. 2) [1972] ICR 19, esp. per Lord Denning M.R. at 54B.

[3] In their normative rather than procedural aspect—see Kahn-Freund, *Labour and the Law* (London, 1972) pp. 124–8. See below, pp. 48–51 and Appendix, para. 5.

[4] Cf. *Sagar* v. *Ridehalgh & Son Ltd.* [1931] 1 Ch. 310. Also, for a description of custom and practice in operation, see W. Brown (1972) 10 British Journal of Industrial Relations 42 'A Consideration of "Custom and Practice" '.

[5] See esp. *Lister* v. *Romford Ice & Cold Storage Co. Ltd.* [1957] AC 555 and *O'Brien* v. *Associated Fire Alarms Ltd.* [1968] 1 WLR 1916.

[6] In brackets because their status as sources is debatable—see below, p. 13.

[7] *National Coal Board* v. *Galley* [1958] 1 WLR 16 provides an excellent example.

[8] Cf. *Edwards* v. *Skyways Ltd.* [1964] 1 WLR 349—though the formation of terms of the contract of employment by agency will be relatively uncommon.

(d) acceptance in practice—as where a working practice, never expressly agreed upon, is accorded contractual force;

(e) judicial rule-making—where a term is held to be implied by law;

(f) application of statute law—where statutory provision takes the form of implying a term into the contract;

(g) issuing and acceptance of statutory particulars of terms of employment.[1]

By the use of that scheme of analysis the following recent changes can be observed in the patterns whereby obligations under the contract of employment are established. First and most obvious of these changes is the impact of the requirement upon the employer to issue written particulars of certain terms of employment, a requirement now embodied in the 1972 Act. The written particulars neither in themselves constitute contractual terms nor even necessarily provide conclusive evidence of those terms, as is demonstrated by the existence of the right to apply to an Industrial Tribunal for the rectification of the written particulars.[2] Yet, though initially neither a source of contractual obligations nor a mode of establishing them, they have become both of these things in the practice of Industrial Tribunals which have needed to ascertain contractual obligations in issues arising under the 1965 Act. Thus the Industrial Tribunals and the courts on appeal from them have often so readily accepted the statutory particulars as embodying the terms of the contract as to create a situation in which the particulars are effectively acting as a source of contractual obligations.[3] Perhaps this is really an estoppel rather than a source of terms in the ordinary sense; but we are probably justified in classifying it with the other sources by reason of the way it operates in judicial practice.

The written particulars are also often allowed to operate as a method of establishing contractual obligations. This occurs when they

---

[1] For the sense in which this operates as a mode of incorporation, see below, pp. 13–14.

[2] 1972 Act, Section 5.

[3] Cf. the decisions on quantum of the 'week's pay', e.g. *Pearson* v. *William Jones Ltd.* [1967] 1 WLR 1140; *Minister of Labour* v. *Country Bake Ltd* (1968) 3 ITR 379; *Tarmac Roadstone Holdings Ltd.* v. *Peacock* [1973] ICR 273. But contrast a judgment of Lord Parker C.J. where this kind of reasoning is carefully avoided; *Turriff Construction Co. Ltd.* v. *Bryant* (1967) 2 ITR 292 at 294. See now *Gascol Conversions Ltd.* v. *Mercer* [1974] ICR 420 (statutory particulars took the form of a written contract of employment which fixed a normal working week of 40 hours; held not variable by practice or by local agreement for a 54-hour week).

refer to a collective agreement, and the provisions of the collective agreement are more likely to be treated as incorporated into the individual contract than would have been expected in the absence of the linking device of the reference in the written particulars. In *Camden Exhibition & Display Ltd.* v. *Lynott* (1965),[1] a majority of the Court of Appeal allowed that process of incorporation via the written particulars to go to the lengths of including (as an individual obligation not to ban overtime) a provision in the collective agreement which was clearly intended[2] as a collective procedural provision that the naitonal level agreement would not itself place upper limits upon overtime. Furthermore, in *Joel* v. *Cammell Laird Ltd.*[3] the process of incorporation by reference in written particulars resulted in the inclusion of a provision from a collective agreement requiring the employee to be transferable between two ship-repairing yards, despite the fact that job definition and geographical mobility are not among the particulars required to be notified to the employee. The Industrial Tribunal did, however, recognize that there were present in that case the further elements of knowledge of, and acceptance of, that term by the employee, and these further elements were treated as necessary to the process of incorporation. But elsewhere, Industrial Tribunals and courts have freely treated reference to the collective agreement in the written particulars as in itself sufficient to result in establishment of contractual obligations.[4]

Finally, the role of the statutory particulars in establishing contractual terms was extended in a new direction in that part of Section 20 of the 1971 Act which deals with grievance procedure. Section 20(2) (b) and (c)[5] appeared to place the employer under an obligation to provide a grievance procedure, for they required the employer to specify a recipient of applications for redress of grievances concerned with the employment, and to indicate either directly or by reference to another document the steps consequent upon such an application; and the employer is not in this case, as he is in relation to certain other terms, allowed simply to declare the absence of a

---

[1] [1966] 1 QB 555.   [2] Ibid. at 568 B (Russell L.J.).
[3] (1969) 4 ITR 206.
[4] e.g. in cases concerning geographical mobility, although particulars do not have to specify geographical scope—cf. *Murray* v. *Cape Insulation Ltd.* (1966) 1 ITR 476; *Sharma* v. *Versil Ltd.*—referred to in the report of the above case at (1966) 1 ITR 479–80; *Stevenson* v. *Tees-side Bridge & Engineering Ltd.* [1971] 1 All ER 296 at 298e–g.
[5] Now appearing as s. 4(2) (b) and (c) of the 1972 Act. See Appendix, para 4.

contractual term of the type concerned.[1] Hence only by instituting such a grievance procedure can the employer comply with his obligations to issue written particulars. And although Section 20 does not itself require that the employee's entitlement to a grievance procedure shall be a contractual right, it is very likely that the entitlement will be regarded as contractual in character.[2] If so, the written particulars will have become the source of a mandatory term of the contract of employment.

The growing significance of the statutory written particulars is not the only changing aspect of the law and practice by which terms of employment are established. Three others may be tentatively suggested. Firstly, it is thought that proved customs are of declining significance as a source of contractual obligations. The 'reasonable, certain and notorious' custom,[3] based as it is in the idea of recognition of local traditional laws, must be an archaism in the context of employment relationships. The 'custom and practice' which forms so significant a part of the regulation of employment in such industries as engineering[4] cannot at all be identified with the type of custom which will be recognized as giving rise to contractual terms. Industrial 'custom and practice' is typically an inchoate collection of deliberately unarticulated rules whose function is to provide the context and traditions within which a particular dispute will be pursued, rather than the solution to disputes. As such, 'custom and practice' would frequently be the opposite of 'certain and notorious' and should not be identified with legally admissible custom. It seems unlikely that recognition of the practice of deductions for defective work from weavers' wages in Lancashire,[5] as a proved custom, could so easily recur in relation to the employment practices of today.

However, the second change is the growth in importance of

---

[1] 1972 Act s. 4(3) applies to all the particulars except those required by s. 20 of the 1971 Act (now s. 4(2) of the 1972 Act).

[2] It is possible that the effect of this provision is to incorporate, into individual contracts of employment, 'no-strike' obligations associated with grievance procedures; and this may have been part of the object of the legislation. See Hepple and O'Higgins, *Encyclopedia of Labour Relations Law* (London, 1972) paras 1–130; *Individual Employment Law, an Introduction* (London, 1971) paras 6–11. See Appendix, para. 5.

[3] See Allen, *Law in the Making* (6th edn. 1958) pp. 126 ff.

[4] See W. Brown, 'A Consideration of "Custom and Practice" ' (1972) 10 BJIR 42.

[5] As in *Sagar* v. *Ridehalgh & Son Ltd.* [1931] 1 Ch. 310.

practice as a mode of establishing contractual obligations. By contrast with custom as a source of obligations, there is no requirement that the practice be collectively observed, nor that it should be of long standing. It is rather the case that the conduct of the particular employer and employee towards each other is quite readily treated as the best indication of their mutual obligations. The clearest examples occur in relation to the geographical scope of employment: the strongest instance is one where a practice of employing in one particular place was held to override the employee's undertaking on his application form that he would be willing to work anywhere in Great Britain[1]; the job concerned, though originally not geographically restricted, had acquired a particular location as the result of practice. This process could be described as one of estoppel by conduct, or as the effect of one party's permitting the other to rely on his conduct as indicating their mutual agreement. This process is comparable with that of incorporation of exception clauses in contracts by virtue of the course of previous dealings in which such clauses had always been incorporated,[2] but with the radical difference that in the case of employment, the process occurs during the existence of a continuing contract. Here again, the establishment of the terms of the contract of employment has to be viewed as a dynamic process not limited to the moment of formation of the contract itself.

The increased importance of conduct as a method of establishing terms of the contract of employment brings with it the third and final change in the approach to these issues. This is that increasing use is being made of the device of explaining the actual conduct of the parties as non-obligatory in character and hence as not giving rise to contractual rights or duties. We can see this occurring in a decision normally cited in connection with the relationship between collective agreements and individual contracts of employment, that of *Young* v. *Canadian Northern Railway Company* (1930)[3] where the issue was whether a collective agreement concerning the order in which employees would be made redundant was incorporated into the individual contract of employment. The principal ground for holding that the agreement was not so incorporated was

---

[1] *McColl* v. *Norman Insurance Co. Ltd.* (1969) 4 ITR 285.
[2] Cf. *McCutcheon* v. *David MacBrayne Ltd.* [1964] 1 WLR 125; *Hollier* v. *Rambler Motors Ltd.* [1972] 2 QB 71.
[3] [1931] AC 83 (PC).

that its implementation in fact by the company was not conclusive of its establishing contractual liability, because the implementation did not have to be explained in terms of the employer's regarding himself as under a contractual obligation: 'The fact that the railway company applied the agreement to the appellant is equally consistent with the view that it did so, not because it was bound contractually to apply it to him, but because as a matter of policy it deemed it expedient to apply it to all.'[1]

The recognition of non-obligatory arrangements concerning terms and conditions of employment has recently occurred in relation to overtime working. Let it be stated at once that there is nothing surprising in the recognition of the voluntary character of overtime working. Clearly, the original conception of overtime working is as work which the employee is requested to do over and above his contractual stint and for which he is remunerated at a higher rate because of the additional and voluntary character of the work. It was to distinguish between compulsory basic hours and voluntary overtime in that sense that the 1963 Act defined 'normal working hours', in a situation where overtime was worked, as the 'fixed' number of hours for which the basic rate was paid.[2] That simple distinction between compulsory basic hours and voluntary overtime is, however, complicated by the existence of situations in which some or all of the overtime becomes compulsory, so that that work is 'overtime' only in the sense that it is paid at an enhanced rate. It was in an attempt to meet that situation that the 1963 Act went on further to define 'normal working hours', in a situation where the compulsory hours included an element paid at overtime rates, as the 'fixed' number of hours including the overtime element.[3] Because the concept of the 'fixed' number of hours was here being used in the sense of 'compulsory' whereas earlier it was used in the sense of 'remunerated at basic rates', the statutory definition of 'normal working hours' is inherently confused and has caused endless difficulty of application.[4] But the concept of voluntary overtime is neither

---

[1] Ibid., pp. 88–9.

[2] 1963 Act Sched. 2 Para. 1 (1), now replaced by the same provision in 1972 Act Sched. 2 Para 1(1).

[3] 1963 Act Sched. 2 Para. 1(2) now replaced by the same provision in 1972 Act Sched. 2 Para 1(2).

[4] See *Redpath Dorman Long (Contracting) Ltd.* v. *Sutton* [1972] ICR 477; *Tarmac Roadstone Holdings Ltd.* v. *Peacock* [1973] ICR 273 and also below, pp. 51–53.

novel nor difficult, though it has to be distinguished from the compulsory working at overtime rates of which the *ASLEF* case recently provided an instance.[1] There, a works rule that 'Staff . . . may be rostered up to nine hours per day, the time worked in excess of the normal working day being paid for at the appropriate overtime rate' was held to result in a contractual obligation to work up to nine hours per day, despite the overtime element of remuneration as to the ninth hour. That case also provided the contrasting instance of truly voluntary overtime working in relation to work on Sundays or rostered rest days.

Hence the notion of voluntary overtime does not in itself represent an innovation in the methods of establishing contractual terms. But the Industrial Tribunals and the courts on appeal from them have been required to decide whether agreements and arrangements concerning overtime result in compulsory or in voluntary overtime. Here they have taken the moderately radical step of explaining agreements for overtime working as non-obligatory in character.[2] They have tended in particular to treat site-level collective agreements which provide for overtime working over and above nationally agreed basic working weeks as if the more localized agreements resulted in entirely extra-contractual arrangements—as 'in the nature of a gentlemen's agreement for ironing out local difficulties'.[3] Wedderburn has castigated the Divisional Court for pursuing this kind of reasoning with an insensitivity to the importance of localized collective bargaining,[4] and this writer feels that the notion of non-obligatory and extra-contractual arrangements concerning individual employment is one which could easily become misleading and disruptive of the pattern of mutual contractual obligations. The principle applied in *Edwards* v. *Skyways Ltd.* (1964)[5] by Megaw J. (as he then was) is a useful one here, namely that an arrangement or agreement occurring in the context of a business relationship

---

[1] See *Secretary of State for Employment* v. *ASLEF* (No. 2) [1972] ICR 19.

[2] *Pearson & Workman* v. *William Jones Ltd.* [1967] 1 WLR 1140; *Darlington Forge Ltd.* v. *Sutton* (1968) 3 ITR 196; *Minister of Labour* v. *Country Bake Ltd.* (1968) 3 ITR 379; *Lynch* v. *Dartmouth Auto Casings Ltd.* (1969) 4 ITR 273; *Redpath Dorman Long (Contracting) Ltd.* v. *Sutton* [1972] ICR 477; *Tarmac Roadstone Holdings Ltd.* v. *Peacock* [1973] ICR 273; *Gascol Conversions Ltd.* v. *Mercer* [1974] ICR 420.

[3] *Loman and Henderson* v. *Merseyside Transport Services Ltd.* (1967) 3 KIR 726 per Lord Parker C.J. at p. 732. Cf. an *obiter dictum* of Lord Denning M.R. in *Gascol Conversions Ltd.* v. *Mercer* [1974] ICR 420, 425B–C.

[4] (1968) 32 MLR 99.   [5] [1964] 1 WLR 394.

should not easily be regarded as not intended to create legal relations. That principle was laid down in the case of an arrangement for the termination of contracts of employment and the making of payments in lieu of refund of pension contributions; but it has an important application to arrangements governing the continuing employment relationship.

SECTION 2: THE STRUCTURE OF THE CONTRACT

A. The Nature of the Structural Problem

Writers upon contractual theory are very prone to concentrate upon general contractual principles rather than upon specific types of contract. One unfortunate result is that the structure of each particular type of contract receives insufficient attention. The theory of contractual structure tends to be argued in relation to trivial and untypical agreements—such as the £100 reward for walking to York—rather than in relation to the contracts which are made significant by their daily occurrence in society and in commerce. Neither judicial nor academic authorities have examined at all fully the structure of the mutual obligations of the contract of employment. In that sense, the nature of that contract has not been systematically articulated. Yet a theory dealing with that structure is necessary in order to explain why there is a cause of action for wrongful dismissal or wrongful departure by the employee, what is the relationship between the employee's entitlement to remuneration and his right to damages for refusal to provide him with work, whether overtime working is an obligation upon the employee, and other crucial questions in the law of the contract of employment. We offer here an attempt to establish such a structure, and an examination of how far such questions are answered by general principles of the law of contract.

The basic problem concerning the structure of the contract of employment consists in deciding whether the law regards that contract as more than an exchange of work for remuneration, and if so, what is the nature of the additional element. There has to be an additional element of some kind if the law is to protect the employee's interest in the continuation of his employment and remuneration and the employer's interest in the continuance of the service he requires. This is the problem of deciding whether this contract is more than a series of exchanges of value on agreed terms—my work for your money at the rate of £x per week. Indeed, that might be better expres-

sed as the problem of explaining why the employee's services are regarded as rendered under a single continuing contract at all, for a series of exchanges of value on agreed terms cannot strictly speaking be regarded as constituting a single continuing contract, and only in a very special sense is it even a series of contracts. It is argued in the succeeding pages that the contract of employment does consist of mutual obligations reinforcing the basic process of exchange of work for remuneration. This gives the employment relationship its character of a continuing contract and is necessary to the explanation of much of the law concerning breach of that contract. Furthermore, the general principles of the law of contract do not give rise to a full understanding of this structural question; indeed, this is an instance where the examination of a particular type of contract demonstrates incompleteness in those general principles.

The structural issue, then, is how far the contract protects each party's interest in the due occurrence of the exchange or series of exchanges which form the basis of the contract. In the case of the contract of employment, the exchange is of service against remuneration; but there is more to the contract than this simple exchange, because the employee undertakes an obligation to make himself available to render service, while the employer undertakes to enable the employee to earn his remuneration. Each of these promises, however, is conditional upon the readiness and willingness of the other to perform his counter-promise. Hence the contract has a two-tiered structure. At the first level there is an exchange of work and remuneration. At the second level there is an exchange of mutual obligations for future performance. The second level—the promises to employ and be employed—provides the arrangement with its stability and with its continuity as a contract. The promises to employ and to be employed may be of short duration, or may be terminable at short notice; but they still form an integral and most important part of the structure of the contract. They are the mutual undertakings to maintain the employment relationship in being which are inherent in any contract of employment properly so called.

The formulation of the two-tiered structure clarifies certain crucial aspects of the law of the contract of employment. For instance, one set of rules has developed to regulate the employer's obligation to pay remuneration, and another has grown up concerning the employer's obligation to employ. Thus, the distinction between entire and divisible obligations relates to the former whilst the law concerning breach of contract and dismissal arises in the latter context. This kind of analysis could be facilitated by general contractual principles, since this type of structural issue is common to all types of contract, but in fact has to take place piecemeal, contract by contract. We proceed to develop the analysis in relation to the contract of employment and to suggest in what ways it throws light on the law concerning breach of that contract.

B. *The Employee's Action for Wrongful Dismissal*

The foregoing paragraphs suggested that for the purposes of an analysis of the structure of the contract of employment, the most important type of breach was that constituted by wrongful dismissal. For in allowing the employee an action for wrongful dismissal, the common law recognizes the employee's interest in the continuance of his employment and gives a particular legal expression to that interest. This sub-section examines the case-law in which that recognition occurred and was confirmed.

The action for wrongful dismissal was specifically recognized by 1800.[1] But there is evidence in the case-law of the middle of the nineteenth century that this particular species of breach of contract and the correlative obligation on the part of the employer were not finally accepted until different analyses had been tried and rejected. We can see the judges, in their handling of certain marginal cases, experimenting with an alternative approach which analysed the employment relationship as one of mere 'service and pay' whereby the employer was under no continuing obligation to employ, but only to pay remuneration accrued due.

Thus *Aspdin* v. *Austin* (1844)[2] concerned a contract which was for the manufacture of cement but was expressed as if the manufacturer were an employee and the purchaser his employer. The purchaser contracted to remunerate the manufacturer at a very substantial weekly wage for a fixed period of three years. Upon the termination of the contract by the purchaser within the three years, the manufacturer sued for damages, relying upon a right to damages for wrongful dismissal. The defence was that the 'employee' had no action for damages for wrongful dismissal, and that if he had a remedy at all, it was rather for recovery of contractual remuneration by virtue of his continuing availability for work. The argument

---

[1] *Robinson* v. *Hindman* (1800) 3 Esp. 235.   [2] 5 QB 671.

was upheld, and the plaintiff lost the action because the cause of action was held to have been misconceived. That decision was followed in *Dunn* v. *Sayles* (1844)[1] in the case of an agreement for the employment of a surgeon-dentist for five years, which was held to impose upon the employer only an obligation to pay wages and to give rise to no action for damages for wrongful dismissal. It will be apparent that this reasoning would, if widely accepted, have destroyed the action for damages for wrongful dismissal in all cases except those where the employer had given an express undertaking to continue to employ as well as an undertaking to pay wages.

However, the action for damages for wrongful dismissal was firmly established, and this challenge to it was rejected, by the judges advising the House of Lords in *Emmens* v. *Elderton* (1853).[2] Elderton had entered into a contract with a life assurance company of which Emmens was secretary, whereby he was paid a yearly retainer and agreed to act as attorney for the company when called upon to do so. It was the expectation of both sides that Elderton would receive a substantial amount of work from the company, for which he would charge item by item. As the result of disagreement, the company terminated this arrangement in the middle of a year. Elderton sued for damages for wrongful dismissal, alleging a promise to 'retain and employ' him. The defence was that there was no contract to 'retain and employ' at all, but only to pay the retainer, so that the claim was misconceived. This defence was rejected by a majority of eight to one of the judges advising the House of Lords.

Concealed among the highly technical points of pleading in this case was fundamental analysis by the judges of the structure of the contract of employment. A majority of them recognized that the ordinary contract of employment involved a duty upon the employer to maintain the employment relationship, and that this duty was the basis of a right of action in damages for wrongful dismissal. This duty did not involve a duty to provide actual work; thus in the present case they held that there was no duty to provide the attorney with specific items of work,[3] but that there was none the less an obligation to employ him in the sense of maintaining him in employ-

---

[1] 5 QB 685.

[2] 13 CB 495, affirming the decision of Exch. Chamber (6 CB 160), reversing that of Common Pleas (4 CB 479).

[3] See Crompton J. 13 CB 495 at 502, 506–7; Martin B. at 511; Wightman J. at 517; Coleridge J. at 529; Parke B. at 532.

ment.[1] Not only did the judges distinguish the duty to employ from the duty to provide actual work, but they also established that the duty to employ was separate from, and went beyond, the duty to pay for services already rendered. They recognized that the 'service and pay' relationship envisaged in *Aspdin* v. *Austin*[2] and *Dunn* v. *Sayles*[3] is typically transformed into a continuing contract of employment by virtue of the mutual obligations of the parties to maintain the employment relationship; it is that obligation on the part of the employer which enables the employee to recover damages for wrongful dismissal, and which caused the plaintiff and respondent to succeed in the present action. Thus Crompton J.: 'Wherever there is a contract for hiring or for employment on the one part and for wages or salary on the other, for a specified time, there is an engagement on the part of the employer to keep the employed in the relation in question during that time and not merely to pay him the wages for the services at the end.'[4] And elsewhere in his judgment: 'The question . . . is, whether there cannot be a breach of such a contract of employment and service as the present, by a dismissal . . . It seems to me quite too late to question the principle upon which so many actions have proceeded in modern times; and which is, that, after a dismissal, the servant or party employed may recover such damages as a jury think the loss of the situation has occasioned.'[5] The principle was thus established that wrongful termination of the contract of employment gives rise to an action for breach of an implied undertaking by the employer to maintain the employment relationship.

C. Breach of the Contract and Failure to Provide Work

It has been shown by what steps it was established that the contract of employment normally imposes upon the employer a duty to maintain the employment relationship. This duty is quite distinct from that of providing actual work, which is more specific and exists only in certain special circumstances. In this sub-section we consider when failure to provide actual work may constitute a breach of the contract of employment.

The cases in which it is recognized that the employee has an

---

[1] See Crompton J. ibid. at 504; Wightman J. at 517; Erle J. at 518; Coleridge J. at 530; Parke B. at 532.

[2] (1844) 5 QB 671 (above).   [3] (1854) 5 QB 685 (above).

[4] 13 CB 495 at 506. See also Wightman J. at 517; Erle J. at 518; Platt B. at 521; Parke B. at 531.

[5] Ibid. at 507–8.

interest in being given actual work to do are of several types. The first type of case is that in which the remuneration of the employee depends entirely on his being provided with work to do, as where he is paid entirely by piece-rates or by commission. In such a case the duty to provide actual work is necessary to give practical worth to the prior duty to maintain the employment relationship. Thus after the contrary view had been taken in cases in 1839[1] and 1843,[2] a line of authority beginning with *R. v. Welch* (1853)[3] established that the piece-rated employee or the employee paid entirely by commission will normally be held to be entitled to the provision of such work as to enable him to earn remuneration at a reasonable level.[4] That probably means the average level of remuneration which the employee had been receiving when work was being made available to him. There is authority to the effect that the same principle applies where the employee is remunerated partly by a fixed wage or retainer and partly on a commission.[5] But there are important decisions to the contrary where remuneration is mixed in this way.[6] In the case of employment at piece-rates subject to a guaranteed weekly minimum wage, it is unlikely that the employer would be held bound to provide piece-work to enable the employee to earn anything above the expressly guaranteed minimum. Perhaps even in that case, there might be such an obligation if the guaranteed minimum was very small in comparison with average piece-work earnings in the job concerned, and if it could be shown that the employer had work available but was withholding it from a particular employee.[7]

---

[1] *Sykes* v. *Dixon* 9 Ad & E 693.   [2] *Williamson* v. *Taylor* 5 QB 175.

[3] 2 E & B 357; also *Re Bailey, Re Collier* (1854) 3 E & B 607; *Whittle* v. *Frankland* (1862) 2 B & S 49; *Thomas* v. *Vivian* (1872) 37 JP 228; *Devonald* v. *Rosser & Sons* [1906] 2 KB 728—employees paid entirely at piece-rates; *Turner* v. *Goldsmith* [1891] 1 QB 544—employee paid entirely by commission; Lindley L.J. at 548— 'The company would not be employing the Plaintiff within the meaning of the agreement unless they supplied him with samples to a reasonable extent.' Compare the 'contractual right to work' as analysed by the Industrial Court in *Langston* v. *AUEW* (No. 2) [1974] ICR 510, 520 H–522 G (Sir John Donaldson).

[4] Dicta in *Puttick* v. *John Wright & Sons Ltd.* [1972] ICR 457 per Lord Thomson at 461 F–H suggest there can be a valid contract of employment without any such obligation on the part of the employer, but the court here tended to distort the theory on this point in order to preserve the employee's entitlement to redundancy payment.

[5] *Re Rubel Bronze & Metal Co. & Ors.* [1918] 1 KB 315; *Bauman* v. *Hulton Press Ltd.* [1952] 2 All ER 1121.

[6] *Ex parte Maclure* (1870) LR 5 Ch App 737; *Re Newman Ltd., Raphael's Claim* [1916] 2 Ch. 309.

[7] Cf. *Bauman* v. *Hulton Press Ltd.* [1952] 2 All ER 1121.

There are then the few special cases in which it has been held that even though the remuneration of the employee is not dependent upon his being provided with work to do, the failure to provide him with work is a breach of the employer's contractual duty because the employee is thereby deprived of publicity or of experience.[1] Furthermore, in *Hall* v. *British Essence Co. Ltd.* (1946)[2] Henn Collins J. indicated that[3] it was a breach of contract to suspend a director and general manager from his duties because of the injury to his reputation which would result among the traders who had dealt with him. But there is a conflict of authority upon the question whether the actor or author is precluded from claiming damages for loss of existing reputation as opposed to loss of possibility of enhancement of reputation.[4] In general, the cases where damages may be recovered for loss of publicity or experience are very much the exception rather than the rule. Such damages are refused in cases of wrongful dismissal under the ruling in *Addis* v. *Gramophone Co. Ltd.* (1909).[5] That rule was recently reaffirmed, whilst being held inapplicable to the contract of apprenticeship.[6] But it does not necessarily follow that damages for deprivation of actual work during the continuance of employment need be limited in the same way.

There is some slight authority also for a further and separate rule that where the employer contracts to appoint the employee to a specific job or a specific office, it is a breach of contract for the employer to deprive the employee of work in that job or office. This will apply even where the employer is willing to continue the payment of wages, and even though the employee cannot show a special interest in publicity or in experience. The authority is the decision in *Collier* v. *Sunday Referee Publishing Co. Ltd.*[7], though

---

[1] *Marbé* v. *George Edwardes (Daly's Theatre) Ltd.* [1928] 1 KB 269—£3,000 damages recovered by an actress for loss of reputation in not being allowed to act; *Herbert Clayton & Jack Waller Ltd.* v. *Oliver* [1930] AC 209—£1,000 damages recovered by an actor under the same head.

[2] 62 TLR 542.   [3] Ibid. at 543.

[4] *Marbé* v. *George Edwardes (Daly's Theatre) Ltd.* [1928] 1 KB 269 suggests that loss of existing reputation may be included. *Withers* v. *General Theatre Corpn.* [1933] 2 KB 536 holds that it is excluded. The view which includes such damages may be thought to conflict with *Addis* v. *Gramophone Co. Ltd.* [1909] AC 488. See below, pp. 247–9.

[5] [1909] AC 488.

[6] *Dunk* v. *George Waller & Son Ltd.* [1970] 2 QB 163; and cf. *Norton Tool Co. Ltd.* v. *Tewson* [1972] ICR 501 at 503 H–504 B.

[7] [1940] 2 KB 647, applying *Driscoll* v. *Australian Royal Mail Steam Navigation Co.* (1859) 1 F & F 458.

the point is a controversial one because it is generally thought that this decision is a direct application of the earlier cases where the employee could claim a special interest in publicity or experience. In fact the reports of the decision differ; it is the authorized report of the case which indicates that Asquith J. was deciding on the ground suggested here.[1] Although there is therefore only slender authority for this principle, the development is nevertheless an important one, because it tends to recognize the importance to the employee of being provided with actual work for its own sake. At the same time, that recognition is probably confined to white-collar jobs and is even associated with the proprietary concept of office-holding. Thus when Asquith J. made the point that the legal recognition of the interest in actual work was untypical, it is significant that he chose domestic employment to point the contrast with the ordinary rule: 'The contract of employment does not necessarily, or perhaps normally, oblige the master to provide the servant with work. Provided I pay my cook her wages regularly, she cannot complain if I choose to take any or all of my meals out. In some exceptional cases, there is an obligation to provide work.'[2]

It seems likely that the extent of the duty to provide actual work may increase in importance. This may turn out to be an instance where the structure of a type of contract—the contract of employment—is reshaped by social pressure. On the one hand, the development of theories of personnel management has caused a new importance to be attached to the employee's satisfaction with his job. On the other hand, the pattern of the labour market creates a variety of situations where individuals are employed though their labour may be surplus. The issue arose in the context of the Essential Work Order[3] system during the Second World War. Power was conferred upon National Service Officers to direct the reinstatement of persons dismissed where the requisite permission had been cancelled, or where an appeal to a local Appeal Board against a dismissal for serious misconduct had been successful.[4] That gave rise to litigation

---

[1] [1940] 2 KB 647, 651; contrast the report at [1940] 4 All ER 234, 236 F–G, where the wording is ambiguous and appears to suggest that it was an application of the rule in *Marbe* v. *George Edwardes (Daly's Theatre) Ltd.* [1928] 1 KB 269.

[2] [1940] 2 KB 647, 650. In *Langston* v. *AUEW*, Lord Denning M.R. said of this part of Asquith J.'s judgment, 'That was said 33 years ago. Things have altered much since then.' [1974] ICR 180, 190 B.

[3] Essential Work (General Provisions) (No. 2) Order 1942 (SR & O 1942, No. 1594).

[4] SR & O 1942, No. 1594 Article 5(3).

on the question whether the obligation to reinstate was satisfied by paying the employee wages without providing him with actual work. It was established that the employer's obligation was to provide work where available—which amounts to holding that work must not be distributed in a manner discriminatory against the particular employee.[1]

Reasoning of that kind could lead to the result that the employer's duty to maintain the employment relationship was seen not only as a bare duty to enable the employee to earn his remuneration but as a duty with a social dimension of ensuring the employee a function within the enterprise. In that event there would have been a change in the structure of the contract of employment. Lord Denning M.R. in *Langston* v. *AUEW* regarded it as arguable that such a change has indeed taken place, and that there may be a contractual right to work in this sense.[2] But when the point was argued before the Industrial Court in the same case, Sir John Donaldson indicated the Court's more cautious view that there was not normally a contractual right to work solely for the sake of the employee's job satisfaction.[3] The law is in a state of flux upon this question of social policy.

D. The Contractual Principle of Co-operation[4]

In considering the structure of the contract of employment, we have, so far, been considering the extent of the mutual obligations of employer and employee in respect of work, the provision of work, and the opportunity to earn remuneration. We now consider whether the general principles of the law of contract have any bearing upon these issues. The relevant general principle, and one which has recently been thrown into prominence in relation to contracts of employment by the *ASLEF* (No. 2) case,[5] is the 'principle of co-operation'; and this sub-section is concerned with the significance and usefulness of that principle in this area. This discussion relates not only to the employee's obligation of service but also to the previously considered obligation on the part of the employer to maintain the employment relationship.

---

[1] *Hodge* v. *Ultra Electric Ltd.* [1943] 1 KB 462.
[2] [1974] ICR 180, 190 F–G.   [3] [1974] ICR 510, 522 D.
[4] Patterson, 'Constructive Conditions in Contracts' (1942) 42 Columb. LR 903; Stoljar, 'Prevention and Cooperation in the Law of Contract' (1953) 31 CBR 231; Bateson, 'The Duty to Cooperate' [1960] JBL 187; Burrows, 'Contractual Cooperation & the Implied Term' (1968) 31 MLR 390.
[5] *Secretary of State for Employment* v. *ASLEF* (No. 2) [1972] ICR 19.

The history and status of the general contractual principle of co-operation are as follows. Patterson, writing in 1942,[1] showed how various particular rules of the law of contract supported an implicit requirement of co-operation between the parties; rules such as those whereby a party may be excused from performing a promise or condition by the prevention or hindrance of the other party, or that whereby one party is required to give notice to the other of a fact which is peculiarly within his knowledge and upon which the other party's duty of performance is conditional. Patterson agreed that these rules tended towards a general principle, a principle that contracts will be enforced in that way which will make them best serve their function in society (counterbalancing the negative rule against enforcement of contracts contrary to public policy). Stoljar[2] pursued this theme by the suggestion that there was a general requirement of co-operation which could be stated in two parts: both as (1) a duty not to prevent or hinder the occurrence of an express condition precedent upon which the performance by the promisor depends, with the sanction that if the promisor does so prevent, he will fall under an immediate duty (usually of payment) as if no condition had ever qualified his promise; and as (2) in appropriate circumstances, a distinctly positive duty; that is, a duty to take all such necessary or additional steps in the performance of the contract as will either materially assist the other party or will generally contribute to the full realization of the bargain, failure in this duty amounting to a breach of contract which will make the nonco-operative party liable in damages or will create a new defence for the benefit of the other. Stoljar's theme is that these contrasting consequences are nevertheless aspects of a common principle of co-operation of which the positive aspect had received insufficient recognition.

The general principle thus outlined is clearly relevant to problems concerning breach of contracts of employment, such as that of the extent of the employer's obligation to make work available or of the employee's obligation to exert himself positively in his employer's interest. But the general principle is useful to the resolution of such questions only to the extent that there are sub-rules about its applicability. Patterson recognized the need for such further rules and suggested that the answer lay in a process of holding

[1] (1942) 42 Columb. LR 903 at 931–42.
[2] (1953) 31 CBR 331 ff., esp. at 231–3.

the balance in the particular circumstances between the principle of co-operation and the countervailing principle that contractual rights should be restricted as far as possible to the express agreement of the parties.[1] Hence he concluded that the requirements of co-operation had so far chiefly affected the minor incidents of performance; though it could be extended further, by judicial good sense, without impairing the essential stability of transactions.

The extent of requirements of contractual co-operation was analysed by Burrows, writing in 1968.[2] He concluded firstly that the requirement seldom extends to the doing of a positive act which is not provided for in express terms; it is imposed only when there is something approaching a necessity for the act in order to render the express parts of the contract workable. Burrows goes on to assert that this restricted approach to a duty of co-operation is expressed in an almost complete absence of legal rules laying down broad moral principles, and a preference for the device of reliance on implied terms and the imputed intentions of the parties in particular situations. Finally Burrows considers the impact of the current tests for the implication of terms. He finds two tests: either that the term is so obvious that it must necessarily have been intended by the parties (the 'officious bystander' test)[3] or that the term is 'necessary for business efficacy'.[4] These tests, vague though they are, carry the particular emphases that, as to the 'officious bystander' test, the proposed term must be obviously fair to *both* parties, and that, as to the business efficacy test, there must be that combination of *laissez-faire* and smooth working of contracts which commercial men rely upon and require.

The following conclusions may be drawn about the usefulness, and the limits of the usefulness, of the principle of co-operation as thus outlined. The contractual requirement of co-operation may be helpful in establishing the content of particular contractual obligations where the basic structure of the contract concerned is not in doubt, but it cannot serve to dictate the structure of the contract itself. The two tests for implication of terms to which Burrows refers exemplify this point. It cannot be regarded as self-

---

[1] Op. cit. at 937–42. [2] (1968) 31 MLR 390–407 *passim.*
[3] So called from the characterization by MacKinnon L.J. in *Shirlaw* v. *Southern Foundries (1926) Ltd.* [1939] 2 KB 206 at 227 (affirmed [1940] AC 701).
[4] See Lord Wright in *Luxor (Eastbourne) Ltd.* v. *Cooper* [1941] AC 108 at 137.

evident what the parties intended, as is required by the 'officious bystander' test, unless and until the outline of their intentions is clear. And it cannot be decided what is 'necessary for the business efficacy' of the contract until the basic objects of the contract are known. This conclusion can be supported by applying it to the contract of employment, which provides good examples both of the usefulness of the principle and of its limitations. Thus while the principle has shown itself as useful in deciding the content of the employee's obligation to work, it produces circular and unsatisfactory discussions when the issue is whether the employer is under any obligation to provide a continuing opportunity to earn remuneration. Let us consider these two situations in turn.

The principle of co-operation could be, and in the second *ASLEF* case[1] was, convincingly used to produce the conclusion that the deliberate non-cooperation involved in a work-to-rule must be breach of contract. It is not in doubt that the employee in some sense agrees to serve the employer and it is not difficult to conclude that the employee cannot fulfil that obligation by pursuing the objective of disrupting the running of the employer's enterprise. That position was variously stated in the *ASLEF* case. Sir John Donaldson was thought to have overstated it when he referred to the 'breach of the fundamental obligation of every employee to behave fairly to his employer and to do a fair day's work'.[2] That is to impose a positive obligation of an excessively unspecific kind. Lord Denning M.R. spoke of a prohibition upon wilful disruption by the employee[3]; Buckley, L.J. spoke of an implied term to perform the contract in such a way as not to frustrate its commercial objective.[4] Roskill L.J. defined the obligation as an 'implied term that each employee will not, in obeying his lawful instructions, seek to obey them in a wholly unreasonable way which has the effect of disrupting the system, the efficient running of which he is employed to ensure'.[5] The last of those formulations could be criticized in so far as it refers to the *effect* of disrupting rather than the *object* of disrupting; for it seems to this writer that, useful as the principle of co-operation is in identifying the objection to deliberate disruption, it should not

---

[1] *Secretary of State for Employment* v. *ASLEF* (No. 2) [1972] ICR 19. See Appendix, Para. 7, where the role of breach of contract in the law of industrial conflict after the repeal of the 1971 Act is discussed.
[2] Ibid. at 30 H—see the criticism by Roskill L.J., ibid. at 73 B.
[3] Ibid. at 56 B–D.　　　　　　　　　[4] Ibid. at 62 C–D.
[5] Ibid. at 72 H.

be used to require that the employee must objectively safeguard the enterprise from disruption resulting from his manner of working.

However, although the principle of co-operation makes a useful contribution to the establishing of the scope of the employee's obligation to work, it leads to unsatisfactory circular arguments when it is invoked to decide whether an employer is under a continuing obligation to employ. This has occurred in relation to agency arrangements or similar arrangements contemplating a series of particular commercial transactions over a period of time, where the courts have considered as a matter of construction whether they can imply a term either on the one hand permitting the employer to discontinue his business without liability for so doing, or on the other hand obliging the employer to enable the person employed to have the opportunity of earning commission throughout the stated period.[1]

The courts have sometimes approached this issue by asking if a term can be implied that the employer is obliged not to prevent the other from performing his part of the contract, thus invoking directly the general principle of co-operation.[2] That principle, useful as it may be to identify the question at issue in such cases, becomes merely a disguise for creative interpretation of contracts by the courts when it is relied upon to supply the answer as well. This may be demonstrated by reference to two cases where that general principle and the tests for implication of terms were so relied upon. In *Southern Foundries Ltd.* v. *Shirlaw* (1940)[3] it was decided that a company bore towards its managing director an obligation to maintain the contractual relationship which was not limited by their

---

[1] Scrutton J. in *Lazarus* v. *Cairn Line Ltd.* (1912) 17 Com. Cas. 107, 113 (refusal to imply a term requiring the business to be kept open) and *French & Co. Ltd.* v. *Leeston Shipping Co. Ltd.* [1922] 1 AC 451; cf. *Hamlyn & Co.* v. *Wood & Co.* [1891] 2 QB 488. Also Kennedy L.J. in *Measures Bros. Ltd.* v. *Measures* [1910] 2 Ch. 248, 260; Scrutton L.J. in *Reigate* v. *Union Manufacturing Co. Ltd.* [1918] 1 KB 592, 605 (refusal to imply a term entitling the employer to discontinue his business without liability). Cf. *Ogdens Ltd.* v. *Nelson* [1905] AC 109 (arrangement for sale and purchase of tobacco from one source exclusively). See *Bowstead on the Law of Agency* (13th edn. 1968) (ed. Reynolds and Davenport) pp. 198–200; Powell, *Law of Agency* (2nd edn. 1961) pp. 380–5.

[2] Cockburn C.J. in *Stirling* v. *Maitland* (1864) 5 B & S 840, 852; *Rhodes* v. *Forwood* (1876) 1 App. Cas. 256, 272; *Southern Foundries (1926) Ltd.* v. *Shirlaw* [1940] AC 701 at 717; Lord Wright in *Luxor (Eastbourne) Ltd.* v. *Cooper* [1941] AC 108, 134–42; Devlin J. in *Mona Oil Equipment Co. Ltd.* v. *Rhodesia Railways Ltd.* [1949] 2 All ER 1014, 1016–18.

[3] [1940] AC 701.

making provision in their articles for the removal of directors from office by a company which had acquired a controlling interest in Southern Foundries. In *Luxor* (*Eastbourne*) *Ltd.* v. *Cooper* (1940)[1] it was decided that an agent who had been promised commission upon the sale of two cinemas to purchasers introduced by him was not thereby guaranteed the opportunity to earn that remuneration if the owners chose to dispose of the property themselves or through other channels. Each of these contrasting decisions represents a crucial judicial choice about the structure of the contractual arrangement, which could be rationalized by reference to the principle of co-operation, but could not be dictated by it. The same is true of decisions concerning the essential structure of contracts of employment themselves.

SECTION 3: THE FORMATION AND STRUCTURE OF THE CONTRACT AND THE GENERAL PRINCIPLES OF THE LAW OF CONTRACT

In the preceding sections we have considered the law concerning the formation and structure of the contract of employment, making occasional reference to the relationship between that law and the general principles of the law of contract. In this section we re-evaluate the matters discussed earlier by looking at them from the standpoint of the general contractual principles themselves. The same issues are approached in the order and according to the headings normally used in expositions of general contractual principles. The question to be considered is the degree of conformity with the general principles of the rules concerning the particular contract.

A. Offer and Acceptance, and Consideration

The first area of general contractual principle which is relevant to the matters considered in this chapter is that of offer and acceptance and consideration. The problem of *unilateral contracts*, which is discussed[2] as a matter of general contractual principle under those heads of offer and acceptance and consideration, is a more generalized version of the problem of the structure of the contract of employ-

---

[1] [1941] AC 108.
[2] See Treitel, *Law of Contract* (4th edn., London, 1975) pp. 28–32, 89–90.

ment which was considered at the beginning of this chapter.[1] In each case, the issue is that of whether and how the interest in the opportunity to earn remuneration or enjoy some other agreed benefit is to be protected. In the case of the contract of employment, it is treated as axiomatic that the contract is bilateral rather than unilateral,[2] but there has been insufficient examination of that bilateral structure. The structure of the contract of employment is in fact that of a series of unilateral contracts connected by a bilateral contract: that is to say, a series of unilateral contracts for the exchange of service and remuneration connected by bilateral promises to maintain the service relationship over a period of time.

What may be said of the usefulness of the general contractual principles in this connection? At least until recently, their usefulness was severely limited because they considered only the simplest and barest type of contractual arrangement and tried to construct a complete system out of those examples. As a result, the general contractual principles concerning unilateral contracts have been theoretical; they have not been related to the more complex contractual arrangements which arise for consideration in practice—the contracts of sale, hire-purchase, guarantee, or what you will. One admittedly isolated recent development encourages the view that there may in future be a greater interaction between this area of general contractual principles and the rules relating to particular contracts. In *United Dominions Trust (Commercial) Ltd.* v. *Eagle Aircraft Ltd.* (1967)[3] there arose for consideration a recourse agreement[4] between a finance company and a company from whom they were purchasing an aircraft. Two members of the Court of Appeal were prepared to decide the effect of this agreement by analysing its structure and deciding whether the constituent parts of the structure were in themselves unilateral or bilateral contracts or obligations.[5] This distinction was recognized as a method not only of characteriz-

---

[1] Above, pp. 19–21.

[2] Cf. Lord Esher M.R. in *Kearney* v. *Whitehaven Colliery Co.* [1893] 1 QB 700 at 711: 'Now the contract here is a contract of employment. The consideration on the one side is "If you will enter into my employment, I will make you one, two or more several promises." The consideration on the other side is, "If you will take me into your employment, I will make you one, two, or more several promises." '

[3] [1968] 1 WLR 74.

[4] i.e. an arrangement whereby the finance company was protected in the event of default by the company hiring from them.

[5] See per Lord Denning M.R. at 80 D–81 C and Diplock L.J. at 82 F–85A.

ing simple stereotyped examples, such as the £100 for walking to York, but as a useful way of breaking down complex contracts encountered in practice. That is an advance in terms of general contractual principles; and one which has important implications for the analysis of the contract of employment, because that contract is itself a complex accumulation of obligations.

B. *Certainty and Intention to Create Legal Relations*

The second area of general contractual principle which is relevant to the matters discussed in this chapter is that of intention to create legal relations and certainty of contractual terms. We have seen earlier how the courts have recognized that overtime working may be non-obligatory and hence extra-contractual in character.[1] In so doing, they have come close to applying the concept and terminology of 'intention to create legal relations' to this area. The difficulty about doing that was identified by Megaw J. (as he then was) in *Edwards* v. *Skyways Ltd.*[2] when he asserted that in the context of a commercial and contractual relationship there should be a strong presumption in favour of a uniform intention to create legal relations extending to any particular part of the total contractual arrangement.[3] The point is that the doctrine of intention to create legal relations helps to decide whether an agreement creating a social or commercial relationship is of a contractual and justiciable character *as a whole*. That is quite different from the question of whether a particular part of the total arrangement is of the same level of obligatoriness as the rest. The doctrine of intention to create legal relations has not developed in a form which makes it suitable for dealing with the latter type of question. The present law is unsatisfactory unless we consider the obligatoriness of each part of an arrangement as a distinct issue. The problem can then be seen as it should be, as one concerning the structure and interrelationship of the contractual arrangements, rather than the extent to which use of the legal process was intended in relation to each part of them.

The question of what is a valid term of the contract of employment often depends not only upon the obligatoriness of the item of agreement concerned but also upon its precision; upon whether it is sufficiently coherent and exact as to permit and justify enforcement as a contractual term. To what extent does the general contractual

---

[1] Above, pp. 17–19.   [2] [1964] 1 WLR 349.   [3] Ibid. at 355.

doctrine concerning certainty of terms provide an adequate criterion for the decision of such cases? There are two respects in which the general contractual doctrine is perhaps ill adapted to the needs of the contract of employment. Firstly, the general contractual doctrine states and requires that an agreement must satisfy the requirement of certainty as to at least its major terms, if it is to constitute a legally binding contract at all. No doubt a rule of *de minimis non curat lex* would readily be applied to prevent this rule from achieving absurd proportions; but the fact remains that the general contractual doctrine, like that concerning intention to create legal relations, deals with contracts as entireties and causes them to stand or fall as a whole. There is no adequate guidance to be found as to how that doctrine, with its undifferentiated effect upon the whole agreement, is to be applied to a composite contract such as the contract of employment. These difficulties are increased in the typical situation where the contract of employment has been operative and acted upon for a substantial period before its legal effect falls to be decided. It is recognized that the courts will redouble their efforts to make sense of commercial documents where the parties have acted upon the agreement apparently contained in them.[1] But that in itself creates the danger that the courts may feel obliged to treat each item of the agreement as enforceable merely because the only alternative is that of accepting that there is no valid contract in force.

We can see this problem touched upon, though ultimately evaded, in relation to the contract of employment in *National Coal Board* v. *Galley* (1957).[2] The employer alleged that the employee was in breach of his contract of employment in refusing to work on Saturdays. The obligation to work on Saturdays was claimed to derive from a collective agreement providing that employees of the type concerned should work 'such days . . . in each week as may reasonably be required by the management in order to promote the safety and efficient working of the pit and to comply with statutory requirements'. It was argued for the employee that this agreement was void for uncertainty. In the Court of Appeal the view was taken that the defendant was in the difficulty that 'he is asserting that the agreement as a whole exists while seeking to deny the enforceability of clause 12 [the clause quoted above]. If clause 12 is too vague to be enforceable, the whole agreement is not legally binding on either

---

[1] Cf. Denning L.J. in *Nicolene Ltd.* v. *Simmonds* [1953] 1 QB 543 at 552.
[2] [1958] 1 WLR 16.

side.'[1] In the event, and partly perhaps because of that difficulty, clause 12 was held enforceable. But the Court of Appeal were in fact underestimating the difficulty to which they referred. If clause 12 was unenforceable, this should on their view have meant not only that the collective agreement was not a legally binding contract but that the individual employment agreement which incorporated it by reference was also not a legally binding contract. It will be clear that if the general contractual doctrine produces this difficulty it is ill adapted to the situation of the contract of employment (and no doubt to that of other complex contracts), where some distinction between severable and non-severable items of agreement would seem to be required.

The second difficulty concerning the application of the general contractual doctrine to the contract of employment is that ascertainability is treated under that doctrine as the equivalent of certainty. That is understandable enough where the result of uncertainty is the destruction of the contract as a whole. Thus the general contractual doctrine would seem to be that where agreement has been positively postponed on crucial matters there is no contract; yet where the agreement has been brought to the point that the matters outstanding can be settled either by reference to well-established customary meaning attached to trade terms or by the application of a concept of reasonableness, the contract will be treated as valid. But whereas the ascertainability of terms in commercial agreements refers to general trade practice or to acceptable arbitration, the apparent ascertainability of terms and conditions of employment is frequently in fact a reference to a further stage of the collective bargaining process. To treat such a matter as ascertainable may be to override the collective bargaining process. For example, in *National Coal Board* v. *Galley*, it was argued for the defendant that the collective agreement provided for discussion between the representatives of the two sides in the event of complaints about the amount of time worked or the distribution of duties, and that this rendered the agreement concerning hours incomplete and unenforceable. But the Court of Appeal regarded that provision as indistinguishable from the provision for further agreement of prices between the parties which was held to be capable of ascertainment in *Foley* v. *Classique Coaches Ltd.*[2] The objection to that reasoning in the context of a contract of employment incorporating the results

---

[1] Per Pearce L.J., ibid. at 24.   [2] [1934] 2 KB 1.

of collective bargaining is that it treats a procedural term of the collective agreement—determining the method of processing future disputes—as if it were a normative term affecting the individual contract. The same distortion occurred in *Camden Exhibitions Ltd. v. Lynott*,[1] arrived at by a different process of reasoning. Moreover, such reasoning treats as if they were concrete obligations, statically determined, precisely those parts of their agreement which the parties have committed to the flexible and dynamic process of collective bargaining. Whilst all this perhaps tends to exaggerate the practical difficulties which have in fact arisen in this area, it serves to identify a kind of inappositeness which results from applying the general contractual principle in the context of the employment relationship.

C. Express and Implied Terms and Co-operation

The next main aspect of general contractual principles to be touched upon in the course of the discussion of the formation and structure of contracts of employment was that concerning express and implied terms[2] and the closely connected question of contractual co-operation.[3] The earlier discussion of those matters involved some consideration of the relevant general contractual principles, and it is sufficient at this point briefly to reiterate the conclusions there reached concerning those general principles and to add some reference to the distinction between terms implied in fact and terms implied in law. Firstly, as to the process whereby terms may be incorporated into contracts, the case-law concerning contracts of employment suggests that the general contractual principles could usefully be supplemented by a distinction between sources of contractual terms and methods whereby they may be incorporated into contracts.[4] The law concerning terms of contracts of employment perhaps suggests the incompleteness of the general contractual principles in a situation where the formation of terms is a complex, and above all dynamic, process. Secondly, on the subject of the contractual principle of co-operation, it was shown in relation to the contract of employment how that principle may be very useful in working out the detailed nature of contractual obligations whose existence is clearly established, but that it readily results in circularity of argument or in resort to rather unsatisfactory criteria such as the 'officious bystander'

---

[1] [1966] 1 QB 555 (see above, p. 14).   [2] Above, pp. 11–19.
[3] Above, pp. 27–31.   [4] Above, pp. 11–13

test when it is attempted to use it to decide the basic structure of a whole type of contract.

Finally on the subject of express and implied terms, the distinction, which is advanced as a matter of general contractual principle,[1] between terms implied in law and terms implied in fact, may be criticized as largely illusory in relation to contracts of employment. The argument in favour of the distinction is that it enables the courts to choose which of two processes is the more appropriate for establishing contractual terms other than express terms. On the one hand, terms are implied in law by the recognition of legal duties derived from the judges' views of the social and commercial requirements of the situation.[2] On the other hand, terms are implied in fact by the ascertainment of the intention of the parties by reference to their conduct and the context in which they made the contract. It is certainly important to the understanding of the process of implying terms to realize that it has a prescriptive as well as a descriptive element. But it is less obvious that it is possible or useful to attempt to maintain a rigid distinction between the two elements. That is demonstrated by reference to the contract of employment, where the universality of the employment relationship militates against a rigid distinction of this kind. For on the one hand, terms 'implied in fact' into one contract tend to be treated as if they had established norms for all contracts.[3] On the other hand, terms 'implied in law' must, if they are to be realistic, be based upon the normal practice of the employment relationship.[4] Thus the two categories converge upon each other.

More important in practice than the distinction between terms implied in fact and terms implied in law is the related question of how far the implying of terms into contracts is a matter of fact and how far a matter of law. Upon this depends the extent of jurisdiction of an appellate tribunal entrusted with appeals on points of law. Such has been the jurisdiction of the Divisional Court and lately

---

[1] See Treitel, *Law of Contract* (4th edn. 1975) pp. 131–2.

[2] e.g. terms relating to frustration—see McNair, *Legal Effects of War* (4th edn., Cambridge 1966) pp. 166–77 for discussion of theories relating to frustration.

[3] Cf. the sequence of cases concerning implied rights to payment during sickness: *Marrison* v. *Bell* [1939] 2 KB 187; *Petrie* v. *MacFisheries Ltd.* [1940] 1 KB 258; *Hancock* v. *BSA Tools Ltd.* [1939] 4 All ER 538; *O'Grady* v. *M. Saper Ltd.* [1940] 2 KB 469; *Orman* v. *Saville Sportswear Ltd.* [1960] 1 WLR 1055.

[4] Cf. *Lister* v. *Romford Ice & Cold Storage Co. Ltd.* [1957] AC 555 per Viscount Simonds at 577–9 (practice relating to motor insurance).

the jurisdiction of the Industrial Court in appeals from decisions of Industrial Tribunals in matters concerning redundancy payments, which have raised many issues of construction of contracts of employment.[1] The Court of Appeal ruled in *O'Brien* v. *Associated Fire Alarms Ltd.*[2] that the appellate jurisdiction was in this respect a broad one. Lord Denning M.R. said, 'I have always understood that the question whether a term is to be implied in a contract is a question of law for the court and not a question of fact. The primary facts, of course, and the surrounding circumstances have to be found by the tribunal of fact. But, that being done, the implication of a term is an implication of law.'[3] This ruling came as a much-needed corrective to the earlier tendency of the Divisional Court to treat the decisions of Industrial Tribunals concerning the terms of contracts of employment as unreviewable determinations of fact. This ruling also overrides the theoretical distinction between terms implied in fact and terms implied in law.

If the arguments advanced in this section are accepted, it may well be felt that in their present state of development general contractual theories will derive more from the particular law concerning the contract of employment than they can themselves contribute to an understanding of that contract. This is especially the case if the claims advanced in this chapter for the importance of structural analysis of particular contracts are accepted.

---

[1] See Appendix, para. 1.

[2] [1968] 1 WLR 1916. Later cases considering the particular implied term there under discussion (geographical mobility) are: *Ingham* v. *Bristol Piping Co. (Erection) Ltd.* (1970) 5 ITR 218; *Mumford* v. *Boulton & Paul (Steel Construction) Ltd.* (1971) 6 ITR 76; *Stevenson* v. *Tees-side Bridge & Engineering Ltd.* [1971] 1 All ER 296.

[3] [1968] 1 WLR 1916 at 1923 B–C.

Chapter Two

VARIATION

INTRODUCTION

The law concerning the variation of the contract of employment is a topic which receives much less attention than it deserves. In the general principles of the law of contract the topic of variation usually appears in the context of a highly technical distinction between varying the terms of a contract and replacing a rescinded contract by a new contract on different terms.[1] That distinction derived its importance from the statutory requirements for formalities in relation to contracts for the sale of goods worth more than £10.[2] With the abolition of those formal requirements, the topic of variation of the terms of contracts has been still further neglected. In relation to the contract of employment in particular, the law of variation had received very little attention indeed before it was thrown into some prominence by case-law arising under the 1965 Act.[3] Even since that time, the topic has not been as fully analysed as it might usefully be.

The law concerning the variation of the contract of employment acquires this high degree of importance because the mutual rights of employer and employee to terminate the contract of employment so often hinge upon their mutual rights to vary the terms of the contract. For example, an insistence by one party upon a variation of terms and conditions of employment will, if outside the contractual rights of that party, very often justify a termination of

---

[1] See Treitel, *Law of Contract* (4th edn. 1975) pp. 66–7, 72, 73–5.

[2] A requirement imposed originally by Section 17 of the Statute of Frauds 1677, re-enacted by Sale of Goods Act 1893, s. 4. The requirement was abolished by the Law Reform (Enforcement of Contracts) Act 1954. While the requirement applied, parol words were capable of rescinding, but not of varying, a contract caught by the provision.

[3] The starting-point was the succession of decisions in *Marriott* v. *Oxford & District Co-operative Society Ltd.* (No. 1)—(1968) 3 ITR 121; (No. 2)—[1969] 1 WLR 254, [1970] 1 QB 186. The problem is, with hindsight, apparent in, e.g. *Whiles* v. *Harold Wesley Ltd.* (1966) 1 ITR 342; *Spillane* v. *Wilson Lovatt (London) Ltd.* (1967) 2 ITR 40.

the contract by the other party.[1] If, on the other hand, the variation is within the contractual rights of the party imposing it, the refusal of the other party to accept it may in turn constitute a ground for termination of the contract by the first party.[2] This is the chief but not the sole example of how the law concerning variation has to be applied before the legal effect of the termination of the contract can be decided. The 1965 Act and the unfair dismissal provisions of the 1971 Act have in their different ways attached new importance to the termination of the contract of employment. By so doing, they have necessitated a new formulation of the law of variation of the contract of employment.[3]

Moreover, this new concern with variation of terms and conditions of employment is not confined solely to the province of legal theory. Such variation is important also in the theory of industrial relations. A general trend in relations betweeen employers and employees in Britain is away from the very extensive rights of control over employees once conceded to employers. Instead there are increasing claims by and on behalf of employees for participation on the workers' side in the regulation of terms and conditions of employment.[4] One aspect of this situation is indicated by the observation of Turner that

The great majority of strikes constitute reactions to or protests against some change in the work context: they are refusals to continue to work on the same terms as previously when the conditions previously assumed no longer apply. As such they very commonly amount to a demonstration against some managerial action (which is not to say that the action was necessarily wrong), or against a managerial assumption that men will continue to work on the same pay and conditions when the content or context of the job has changed.[5]

The law concerning contractual variation provides the description in legal terms of the balance between managerial prerogative and the rights of employees in relation to the terms on which they work.[6]

---

[1] See below, pp. 242 ff.

[2] e.g. *Stevenson* v. *Tees-side Bridge & Engineering Ltd.* [1971] 1 All ER 296.

[3] Cf. *U.K. Atomic Energy Authority* v. *Claydon* [1974] ICR 128.

[4] See for instance Flanders, 'Collective Bargaining; a Theoretical Analysis' (1968) 6 BJIR 1 at 17–23.

[5] *Is Britain Really Strike Prone?* (Cambridge, 1969) pp. 21–2.

[6] There is also the possibility that an employee's refusal to accept an employer's attempt to impose a variation of contractual terms will constitute a

The law of variation of terms and conditions of employment is best considered in three parts. The first part concerns the scope for variation within the original contract of employment—that is to say, the inherent flexibility of the contract. The second part is a statement of the conditions for a lawful variation of contractual terms by agreement subsequent to the making of the original contract. The third part is an examination of the difficult but potentially important distinction between varying the terms of a contract and replacing one contract by another on different terms.

SECTION 1: VARIATION UNDER PROVISIONS CONTAINED IN THE ORIGINAL CONTRACT

A. The Scope of Provisions for Variation Normally Occurring

This is a question of the extent of the legal recognition of managerial prerogative. For even when the processes of negotiation and consultation are well developed, the rules of work are essentially the employer's rules, and the right to vary the terms and conditions of employment will be reserved to the employer rather than the employee.[1] In considering the extent to which this type of managerial prerogative operates in practice, and is protected in law, it is useful to distinguish between the different main types of terms and conditions of employment which may be in issue. The main terms of employment to be discussed in this connection are:

(a) the place of work;
(b) the job specification;
(c) the hours and times of work.

In so far as general tendencies can be detected, they are to be found especially with regard to the impact of collective bargaining upon the individual contract of employment.

1. The Place of Work. The scope of the employer's prerogative to vary the place of work has been the subject of many difficult disputes in the administration of the 1965 Act. The disputes arise

---

'substantial reason' for dismissal within the meaning of the unfair dismissal provisions (1971 Act s. 24(1)(b)). Cf. *Knighton* v. *Henry Rhodes Ltd.* [1974] IRLR 71.

[1] The various ways in which employees assert their own control over working conditions do not normally seek to alter the rules of work themselves—cf. William Brown, 'A Consideration of "Custom and Practice"' (1972) 10 BJIR 42 ff.

where employers, unable to provide further employment for a given employee in the place where he has been working, have offered employment elsewhere and have sought to deny liability for a redundancy payment on the basis of such an offer. The drafting of the Act is such that a series of distinct issues may be raised where the employee refuses that offer and claims a payment. The problem may be treated as one of whether the situation comes within the definition of 'redundancy' in Section 1(2) of the Act—whether in particular the place in which the employee is offered further work can be regarded as within the geographical scope of his original job.[1] The same matter can, on the other hand, be treated in terms of the question of whether there has been a dismissal within Section 3(1) of the Act.[2] If the employer was offering the employee work at a place which was within the geographical area contemplated by his contract of employment, it can be said that a termination of employment resulting from the unwillingness of the employee to move is neither a termination of the contract of employment by the employer within Section 3(1)(a), nor a termination by the employee in circumstances such that the employer's conduct entitled him so to terminate, within Section 3(1)(c) of the Act. If, however, it is held that there has been a dismissal by reason of redundancy, then the issue of geographical mobility becomes one of whether the employee has unreasonably refused an offer of employment suitable in relation to him within Section 2(4) of the Act.[3] A discretion is thereby conferred upon the Industrial Tribunals as to how far they will, as a matter of policy, insist that the employee must be prepared to be geographically mobile, and will hold that an employee who does not show the required mobility cannot claim a redundancy payment.[4] It was recorded by Wedderburn and Davies that these three questions—of dismissal within Section 3(1); of redundancy within Section 1; and of the unreasonable refusal of suitable employment within Section 2(4)—have dominated the work of the Industrial Tribunals, and represented over 75 per cent of all the issues argued in a sample of

---

[1] *McCulloch Ltd.* v. *Moore* [1968] 1 QB 360; *Sutcliffe* v. *Hawker Siddeley Aviation Ltd.* [1973] ICR 560; *U.K. Atomic Energy Authority* v. *Claydon* [1974] ICR 128.

[2] e.g. *Charles* v. *Spiralynx (1933) Ltd.* (1970) 5 ITR 82.

[3] e.g. *Jones* v. *Aston Cabinet Co. Ltd.* [1973] ICR 292 (burden of proof placed on employer but shown to be of limited significance).

[4] See Fryer, 'The Myths of the Redundancy Payments Act' (1973) 2 ILJ I.

989 Tribunal decisions concerning redundancy payments which was analysed for this purpose.[1]

It is therefore clear that the question of geographical mobility straddles across the three central areas of the redundancy payments jurisdiction. If the issue of geographical mobility arises by way of the statutory definition of 'redundancy', or by way of that of 'dismissal', the scope of the employer's legal right to vary the terms of the individual contract of employment is then the decisive factor, because it operates to define the geographical limits of the job which is embodied in the contract. In *O'Brien* v. *Associated Fire Alarms Limited* (1968)[2] the Court of Appeal made it clear that there was no question of any presumption of mobility in favour of the employer. The Industrial Tribunal had found that two electricians and their mate were obliged to be mobile within a radius of at least 120 miles despite some seven years in the employment concerned during which they had worked within commuting distance of their homes. The Divisional Court abdicated any responsibility for laying down guiding principles, by treating the matter as one of fact alone in which they could not interfere with the Tribunal decision. The Court of Appeal, holding the implication of a term into a contract to be a question of law for the Court[3], took notice of the absence of any positive evidence of any term entitling the employer to call upon the employee to move, and held that there was no ground upon which they could make an implication to that effect.[4]

O'Brien's case effectively destroyed the idea of any presumption in favour of mobility beyond the area within which the employee can commute to work. A group of cases concerning steel erectors

[1] Wedderburn and Davies, *Employment Grievances and Disputes Procedures in Britain* Chapter XIII—'The Industrial Tribunals and the Law' at p. 263.

[2] [1968] 1 WLR 1916.

[3] Lord Denning M.R. at 1923 B; Salmon L.J. at 1925 B; Edmund Davies L.J. at 1927 E–F; cf. *Abernethy* v. *Mott Hay & Anderson* (1973) 8 ITR 228 where Sir John Donaldson said on a point of the same kind, 'In our judgment the tribunal's conclusion [against a term obliging the employee to do site work] was a mixed finding of fact and law. In so far as it was a matter of fact it was amply supported by the evidence and in so far as it was a matter of law it was correct.' (at p. 231 C). (Decision affirmed [1974] ICR 323.)

[4] Lord Denning M.R. at 1923 D–G; Salmon L.J. at 1925 F–1926 H; Edmund Davies L.J. at 1927 E. But contrast Sir John Donaldson, 'It is without doubt the law that there is no dismissal where both parties to a contract of employment freely and voluntarily agree to vary its terms. This happens whenever there is an increase in rates of pay or a promotion'—*Sheet Metal Components Ltd.* v. *Plumridge* [1974] ICR 373 at 376 E–F.

help to identify more precisely the factors which will be treated as determining the employee's obligations of mobility. It is clear that the practice between the employer and the particular employee— the extent to which the employee has been continually given work in one area near his home or has been moved about the country— will be the critical factor. In *Ingham* v. *Bristol Piping Co. Limited* (1970)[1] and in *Mumford* v. *Boulton and Paul (Steel Construction) Limited* (1970)[2] the Divisional Court and the Court of Appeal held against an implied term requiring the employee to be mobile throughout Britain; in *Stevenson* v. *Teeside Engineering Limited* (1970)[3] the Divisional Court held in favour of such a term. In the former two cases, the existence of any indications that the employee knew from the outset that he would be expected to be mobile was a matter of speculation only. In the latter case there were positive indications to that effect, in that evidence was given that the employee had been specifically asked whether he was prepared to work away from home and had answered affirmatively. Moreover, the court attached significance to the fact that the employee was, by the statutory particulars of his terms of employment, referred to the Memorandum of Agreement for the steel-erecting industry which at various points contemplated and made arrangements appropriate to 'away contracts'. (This was not, however, one of those relatively straightforward cases where the relevant and applicable collective agreement differentiates between mobile and static employees by providing an extra allowance for the 'travelling men', not merely for expenses attributable to actual travelling, but in respect of their being liable to be instructed to travel at the will of the employer.[4])

The decisive contrast between the cases under discussion seems to lie in the fact that in *Ingham's* case there was only very slight evidence that the employee had ever during the period of the relevant employment worked outside his commuting area, and that there had been no such outside working in *Mumford's* case, whereas in *Stevenson's* case it appeared that the employee had spent a considerable part of his time working away from home at various points during his employment. In *Stevenson's* case, the Court was readier than in the two earlier cases to find that an implied term requiring mobility of the employee was necessary to the business efficacy of the

[1] (1970) 5 ITR 218.   [2] (1971) 6 ITR 76.   [3] [1971] 1 All ER 296.
[4] e.g. *Bounds* v. *W. H. Smith & Co. Electrical Engineers* (1966) 1 ITR 53; *McCaffrey* v. *Jeavons & Co. Ltd.* (1967) 2 ITR 636.

contract of employment given the way the steel-erecting industry was organized. In *Ingham's* case, by contrast, the court had been disposed to regard occasional employment outside the commuting area as the kind of helpfulness one is entitled to expect from employees rather than evidence of an original obligation of mobility.[1] But this contrast must be read very much in the light of the different history of the employment in the two cases as far as actual past mobility was concerned. It was this latter distinction on the facts which was decisive and conditioned the court's reasoning on the other issues.[2]

The question of the extent of managerial prerogative to vary the place of employment arose in the application of the Reinstatement in Civil Employment Act 1944, and an instructive comparison may be drawn between the treatment of the problem under that Act and under the 1965 Act. The 1944 Act conferred a right to reinstatement 'in the occupation in which the applicant was last employed' before war service and 'on terms and conditions not less favourable' than those which would have been applicable but for interruption due to war service.[3] The tendency, in the Umpire's decisions applying that provision, was to hold that an employer could not satisfy his obligation by offering employment in a place different from that of the previous employment, unless he could show positive evidence that the employee had previously been a mobile employee.

Thus in *Gregory* v. *Corporation of London Cattle Market*,[4] a market constable employed at Islington Market before war service was offered reinstatement at Billingsgate Market, and it was held that the requirements of the Act were not satisfied, because no term in the original contract provided for this transfer. A case where express provision of that kind was made, and the Act was as a result

[1] (1970) 5 ITR 218 at 221 (Lord Parker C.J.).

[2] In *Sutcliffe* v. *Hawker Siddeley Aviation Ltd.* [1973] ICR 560, the NIRC applied *Stevenson's* case despite the fact that the employee—an aircraft electrician—had acquired a base during two years' employment. The trend appeared to be against allowing the employee to set up a custom localizing his employment. In *Litster* v. *Fram Gerrard Ltd.* [1973] IRLR 302, it was established that a term permitting transfer from one contract site to another will not justify transfer from one permanent depot to another.

[3] Section 1(1)(a) of the 1944 Act (subject to the qualification that the employer was obliged to reinstate only where it was 'reasonable and practicable' to do so). See Ball, *Statute Law relating to Employment* (3rd edn., London, 1949) pp. 192–3.

[4] Selected Decisions of the Umpire on Reinstatement in Civil Employment. Pamphlet No. 14, Case No. 23.

held to have been properly implemented, was that of *Gaunt* v. *Counter Products Ltd.*,[1] in which a commercial traveller was employed under a contract stating his area of work to be 'as laid down by [the employers] or varied from time to time by them'. In another decision a similar result was reached in the case of a school attendance officer, on the grounds that the employing local authority had a discretionary power to transfer the employee between their various districts.[2] Such a power would apparently not, however, be implied, or assumed to exist as a matter of course.

2. *The Nature of Work: the Job Specification.* The main tendency to be observed with regard to the employer's prerogative of requiring the employee to be occupationally mobile is that the scope of the prerogative can be enlarged in law as the result of the practices of collective bargaining, and in particular of productivity bargaining. It is common for collective agreements, especially those covering a wider area than a single plant, such as area or national agreements, to define job-categories and to specify occupations in fairly broad terms, perhaps in order to allow further differentials and narrower categories to be established in more localized negotiations. If such collective agreements are incorporated into individual contracts of employment, for example by reason of reference to them in written particulars issued in accordance with Section 4 of the 1972 Act, the result may be that the individual contract may be seen as having reserved to the employer a right to vary the job specification within fairly generous limits. The decision of an Industrial Tribunal in *Callison* v. *Ford Motor Co. Ltd.*[3] provides a good illustration of how the incorporation of successive collective agreements into a contract of employment may entitle the employer to vary the original job specification.

This possibility of a widening of managerial powers to vary the job specification as the result of incorporation of collectively bargained terms has been actually enlarged by the operation of Section 4 of the 1972 Act requiring written particulars of certain terms and conditions of employment[4] to be issued to employees of thirteen weeks' standing. In so far as the policy of Section 4 was to reduce the

---

[1] Pamphlet No. 17, Case No. 31.

[2] *Smith* v. *Bucks County Education Committee*. Pamphlet No. 8, Case No. 16.

[3] (1969) 4 ITR 74.

[4] Remuneration, intervals of payment, hours, holidays and holiday pay, incapacity for work and sick pay, pensions, length of notice, expiry date of fixed-term contracts (Section 4(1)).

uncertainties of employees as to their exact rights and duties under their contracts of employment, it defeats its own object when it provides that the obligation to give particulars can be discharged merely by referring to a document which is made reasonably accessible to the employee,[1] and that the obligation to inform the employee of changes in relevant terms within one month of the change[2] can be discharged in the same way.[3] By reason of these convenient opportunities for reference to other sources, the section appears to have resulted in a widening of the employer's right to vary the terms of the contract of employment in certain types of case. Furthermore, although the written particulars issued under Section 4 are not required to deal with the specification of the job, it seems none the less that the written particulars may act to bring about an incorporation into individual contracts of terms in collective agreements relating to *occupational* mobility, as was specifically held by an Industrial Tribunal in *Joel* v. *Cammell Laird Ltd.*[4]

It can thus be said that the incorporation of collective agreements into individual contracts has sometimes operated to widen managerial rights to vary the terms of those contracts. Productivity agreements are especially likely to have such an effect. For it is a particular feature of productivity agreements that they frequently impose extensive obligations of occupational mobility upon the employee, with corresponding obligations upon the employer in respect of retraining and offering suitable work where the agreement is a well-balanced one. This is, indeed, one of the central objectives of productivity bargaining, since the employee is thereby being paid an advantageous wage in return for the surrender of counter-productive limitations upon the scope of his job. However, the fact that occupational mobility is seen in such agreements as an advantage for which the employer has to bargain, should, as in the case of geographical mobility, point to the unreality of assuming that such mobility is part of the standard pattern of contracts of employment.

3. Times and Hours of Work. There is a considerable body of case-law, consisting both in common-law actions and in decisions under the 1965 Act, which deals with the scope and interpretation of provisions in contracts of employment which may have the effect of entitling the employer to vary the times and hours of work. The law upon this matter is in a state of some confusion and dis-

---

[1] Section 4(5).   [2] Section 4(4).   [3] Section 4(5).
[4] (1969) 4 ITR 206.

order, and clear principles are lacking in particular to deal with the relationship between individual contracts of employment and collective agreements in this respect. The problem concerning the relation between individual contracts and collective agreements may be stated as follows. Collective agreements frequently state heads of agreement concerning working hours which deliberately provide for flexibility. If a collective agreement is held to be incorporated into an individual contract of employment by reference, the question arises whether that flexibility is translated into the individual contract, so that one party or other has a wide contractual right to vary the hours of work. The proper resolution of these issues requires a practical understanding of the conventions of collective bargaining; and it may be suggested that the courts have on occasion demonstrated a less than complete grasp of the realities concerned.

It is useful to distinguish in this respect between contracts of employment where payment varies according to the number of hours or shifts worked, and those where it does not. The decision in *National Coal Board* v. *Galley*[1] concerned a case where it did not so vary.

Colliery deputies were there employed under contracts of employment which expressly incorporated the terms of national and local collective agreements currently in force. The relevant national agreement provided that the deputies should be paid an upstanding weekly wage—a wage, that is, which did not vary according to the time worked during each week. It also contained an agreement that deputies should work 'such days or part days of each week as may reasonably be required by the management in order to promote the safety and efficient working of the pit and to comply with statutory requirements.'

Upon the issue whether this provision entitled the employer to require the employees to work Saturday shifts, one argument of the employees was that they could not be regarded as having subjected themselves individually to so large a discretion on the part of the management.

Both at first instance and in the Court of Appeal, that argument was rejected and it was held that the men were individually bound by this clause in the national agreement. The reasons given were applications of general contractual principles which arguably represented an inappropriate approach to the problem. Finnemore J.

---

[1] [1958] 1 WLR 16. See the annotation by Kahn-Freund at (1958) 21 MLR 194.

at first instance held[1] that since the part of the agreement fixing wages was indubitably incorporated into the individual contracts by reference, the rest of the agreement was also incorporated, because the employee could not accept the national agreement in part and not in whole.[2] This type of argument is liable to ignore the distinction between the normative and the procedural aspects of collective agreements, as well as the distinction between the parts expressing understandings and intentions and those imposing obligations. In the Court of Appeal that decision was upheld, on the ground that, as the courts will where necessary imply a condition of reasonableness into contracts and treat them as workable on that basis,[3] it followed that where a contractual obligation was itself cast in terms of reasonableness, it was sufficiently precise to be enforceable.[4]

However, although it may be a proper policy on the part of the courts to give effect to contractual promises in as wide a range of circumstances as possible, it does not follow that they should treat clauses in collective agreements which are intended to preserve flexibility at the collective level as conferring a wide prerogative on management to vary the terms and conditions of individual contracts. It is true that on these particular facts there were probably good reasons for holding that the deputies were individually bound by the clause in the collective agreement.[5] It is true also that the main argument on behalf of the deputies was not so much that they were not bound to work such reasonable hours as might be required of them as that the hours actually required of them were not reasonable. Their main aim was to secure a judicial arbitration as to what were reasonable hours, rather than to deny the legal effect of the agreement.

However, it is suggested that even if the result reached was defensible on these grounds, the reasoning both at first instance and in the Court of Appeal was unsatisfactory. The general principle that a man shall not be allowed to approbate and reprobate, relied

---

[1] In an unreported decision.

[2] Compare the reasoning of the Industrial Tribunal in *Joel* v. *Cammell Laird Ltd.* (1969) 4 ITR 206.

[3] Pearce L.J. [1958] 1 WLR 16 at 24 citing *Hillas & Co. Ltd.* v. *Arcos Ltd.* (1932) 147 LT 503 and *Foley* v. *Classique Coaches Ltd.* [1934] 2 KB 1; cf. also *British Bank for Foreign Trade Ltd.* v. *Novinex Ltd.* [1949] 1 KB 623, *Powell* v. *Braun* [1954] 1 WLR 401; contrast *May & Butcher* v. *R.* [1934] 2 KB 17n.

[4] Pearce L.J. [1958] 1 WLR 16 at 24.

[5] This was, for example, the view taken by Kahn-Freund in his contemporary note at (1958) 21 MLR 194.

upon by Finnemore J., and the principle applied by the Court of Appeal, that the courts will, wherever possible, treat an agreement as a workable contract, take insufficient account of the industrial relations aspect of the issue. A proper treatment of this type of issue depends upon an awareness of the conventions within which the collective agreement is made, rather than an application of principles developed in relation to commercial contracts where the nature of the problem is very different. In particular, a collective agreement may contain undertakings to which very widely varying degrees and kinds of obligation are attached.

If we turn from the type of employment where the amount of pay does not vary with the number of hours worked to the cases where it does so vary, we come to the problem of the legal analysis of overtime working. The problem has been an important one because, from the time of the 1963 Act onwards, there has been a statutory definition of 'normal working hours'[1] (chiefly important for calculating redundancy payments) which has distinguished between different types of overtime arrangement. The statutory scheme, which was considered in the previous chapter,[2] proceeds in two stages. The first stage is to exclude hours paid at overtime rates from 'normal working hours'.[3] The second stage is to admit as an exception those hours which are paid at overtime rates but are within the 'number or minimum number of hours fixed by the contract of employment in the week'.[4]

If this scheme is applied to the different types of arrangement for overtime, it becomes clear that the problematical case is that where the employee is bound to work overtime at the instance of the employer but the employer is not bound to provide overtime. In the case where the employer is bound to provide overtime and the employee bound to work it, it is clear that the hours of overtime count as 'normal working hours' and that overtime here represents merely an enhanced rate of payment for certain hours.[5] In the opposite case where overtime is voluntary for both employer and employee, it is equally clear that the hours concerned are not 'normal working hours'; they are not contractually fixed hours.[6]

---

[1] Now contained in Para 1 of Sched. 2 of the 1972 Act.
[2] See above, pp. 17–18. [3] 1972 Act, Sched. 2, Para 1.
[4] Ibid. Para 1(2).
[5] *Armstrong Whitworth Rolls Ltd.* v. *Mustard* [1971] 1 All ER 598.
[6] *Redpath Dorman Long (Contracting) Ltd.* v. *Sutton* [1972] ICR 477.

The intermediate case is that where overtime is compulsory for the employee but not for the employer[1]; the effect of that situation is that the employer has the prerogative as a matter of contract to vary the number of hours worked (paying at overtime rates for the excess over a fixed number of hours). The view of the courts appeared at first to be that such hours could be part of 'normal working hours'; but they were decidedly reluctant to conclude that overtime was in any given case contractually obligatory upon the employer.[2] In *Tarmac Roadstone Holdings Ltd.* v. *Peacock*,[3] however, the Court of Appeal has ruled that in this intermediate situation the overtime cannot be part of 'normal working hours' because its amount is fixed *ad hoc* by the employer rather than being fixed *by the contract* as the statute requires. That represents a ruthlessly exact interpretation of the statutory words, in a situation where a more flexible approach would have been perfectly practicable. For although the contrary interpretation might make it difficult to say what were 'normal working hours' at the inception of the employment concerned, in actual cases under the 1965 Act the employee must have been working for the employer concerned[4] for at least two years, and it will normally be straightforward to determine what the pattern of overtime working was in his case. It is also relevant that contract law generally treats as contractually fixed and certain any quantity for which the contract provides a fixing method though it does not fix a quantum from the outset.[5]

The result of the recent case-law is that the statutory concept of normal working hours has now been systematically related to the different types of overtime arrangement. What remains less certain is the application of the three different legal stereotypes to factual situations—the real question with which this section is concerned. It is predicted that factual overtime situations will now, after the

---

[1] There is a further theoretical possibility of a situation where provision of overtime is compulsory upon the employer but overtime working is voluntary for the employee. But this situation appears not to arise in practice.

[2] Cf. *Pearson* v. *William Jones Ltd.* [1967] 1 WLR 1140; *The Darlington Forge Ltd.* v. *Sutton* (1968) 3 ITR 196; *Loman and Henderson* v. *Merseyside Transport Services Ltd.* (1967) 3 KIR 726; *Turriff Construction Co. Ltd.* v. *Bryant* (1967) 2 ITR 292; *Byrne* v. *Lakers (Sanitation & Heating) Ltd.* (1968) 3 ITR 105; *Lynch* v. *Dartmouth Auto Casings Ltd.* (1969) 4 ITR 273.

[3] [1973] ICR 273; cf. *Gascol Conversions* v. *Mercer* [1974] ICR 420.

[4] Though this could include employment with an associated company or the transferor of a business to the employer—1965 Act ss. 13, 48.

[5] e.g. *Hillas & Co. Ltd.* v. *Arcos Ltd.* (1932) 147 LT 503.

Tarmac Roadstone Holdings case, be presumed to be of the inter-mediate type—obligatory upon employee but not upon employer (and accordingly not to be part of 'normal working hours')[1]. In other words, a built-in contractual right on the part of the employer to vary the number of working hours will be more widely recognized than hitherto.

B. An Implied Provision for Variation by Proper Notice

Many or most contracts of employment contain their own provisions for agreed termination, in the shape of express or implied provision for termination by notice (or payment in lieu of notice). There is a widely held view that they also contain an equally wide provision for agreed *variation* upon notice of the length required to terminate the contract; or in other words, that a right to vary by notice can be implied into the contract where there is a right to terminate by notice. This represents an analysis of the law concerning variation of con-tracts which is partially, but only partially, correct. A more accur-ate result is reached by considering what is involved in a right to vary the terms of a contract. That right has two aspects; it involves both a right to demand the continuance of the contract on the new terms and conditions, and also the absence of liability for refusing to con-tinue it on the old terms.

It seems that the latter result, the absence of liability for termina-tion, will probably follow from a notice to vary the terms of a con-tract which is as long as the notice required to terminate the contract. The courts seem prepared to treat a notice of the requisite length, which says that employment will be available only on changed terms and conditions, as having the same effect, where the party receiving the notice is unwilling to accept the change, as an unconditional notice to terminate the contract.[2] We can see this view in operation in the analysis of a strike notice which was offered by Davies L.J. in *Morgan* v. *Fry*.[3] He suggested that such a notice amounted to an offer to continue the employment on different terms, and a notice to

---

[1] In *Gascol Conversions Ltd.* v. *Mercer* Lord Denning M.R. in an *obiter dictum* treated the words 'Employees will be expected to work overtime where necessary' as having a mutually non-obligatory effect; [1974] ICR 420, 424 H.

[2] Cf. *Santen* v. *Busnach* (1913) 29 TLR 214; *White* v. *Riley* [1921] 1 Ch. 1 (strike notices); and see below, p. 169.

[3] [1968] 2 QB 710. On strike notices and Section 147 of the 1971 Act see Foster (1971) 34 MLR 275 and (1973) 2 ILJ 28; O'Higgins (1973) 2 ILJ 152; Hepple & O'Higgins, *Individual Employment Law* (London, 1971) pp. 110–13.

terminate the employment if those terms were not acceptable to the employer; and it was his view that there was no illegality in such a notice if it was of the proper length.[1]

Moreover, a notice to vary the contract of the length requisite for a proper termination of the contract probably has the effect that if the employment continues after the expiry of the notice, the other party is thereafter bound by the new terms and cannot claim the previous rate of remuneration as a money debt; nor can he claim that the operation of the changed terms by the other party constitutes a breach of contract. It is true that the decision of the Court of Appeal in *Marriott* v. *Oxford & District Co-operative Society Ltd.* (No. 2)[2] was that the employee, by remaining in his employment for a short period after the employer has imposed changed terms and conditions, does not thereby forego his right to treat the action of the employer as a dismissal for the purposes of the 1965 Act. But nowhere have the courts gone to the further lengths of suggesting that the employee could both continue in his employment and claim the benefit of the previously existing terms and conditions. There is indeed positive authority for the view that the employee is in such a case bound by the new terms where he continues in the employment, for this was at issue in *Rowsell* v. *Metropolitan Water Board* (1915).[3] The plaintiff was employed upon seven days' notice and seven days' notice was given to discontinue overtime pay and the payment of travelling expenses. Having acquiesced in this change for seven years, the employee claimed arrears of those payments for that period. This claim was rejected, and Lord Reading C.J. laid it down that 'if he continues to serve, as he has continued to serve, the Metropolitan Water Board after they have given him a proper notice to alter the terms of the contract of employment which they had taken over, he cannot afterwards bring an action for the wages he has lost'.[4] However, it would seem that, in such a case, the inability of the employee to claim his former terms and conditions is caused by a waiver of them by him, rather than by the original contract of employment entitling the employer to vary its terms by notice. The extent to which a variation of terms and conditions of employment

---

[1] [1968] 2 QB 710 at 733 F–G; In *Horizon Holidays Ltd.* v. *ASTMS* [1973] IRLR 22, a strike notice was expressly conditional upon failure to reinstate certain employees. No objection was taken on this ground.

[2] [1970] 1 QB 186. Followed on this point in *Shields Furniture Ltd.* v. *Goff* [1973] ICR 187; *Maher* v. *Fram Gerrard Ltd.* [1974] ICR 31.

[3] (1915) 84 LJ(NS)KB pt. 2, p. 1869.   [4] Ibid. at 1874.

may acquire effect by reason of waiver or estoppel is considered later in the present chapter.[1]

Moreover, even if the employer has a right to rely in that special sense upon his notice to vary the terms of the contract, it seems clear that he cannot and does not have the further right to demand the continuance of the contract on the new terms, in the sense of treating it as a breach of contract in the employee to refuse to continue upon the new terms; nor can he deny that he has dismissed the employee where the latter refuses to continue the employment at all (assuming that the variation concerned has been a major one).[2] For these reasons the right, which it is often believed that the employer has, of varying the contract by a notice as long as that required to terminate the contract, is apparent rather than real, in the absence of a special provision in the original contract creating such a right.

SECTION 2: VARIATION BY SUBSEQUENT AGREEMENT

In relation to the legal principles governing the variation of contracts of employment by subsequent agreement, the following matters require particular examination. There would seem to be a general contractual principle that variation of contracts is subject to a requirement of consideration. The application of that principle to the contract of employment suggests that it is neither appropriate nor workable as a basis upon which to regulate variation of the terms of contracts of employment in particular. On the other hand, a requirement of consent to variation and of intention to vary is quite central to the regulation of contractual variation in this context, the main difficulty at the present day being the interpretation of the legal effect of collectively agreed subsequent variations of conditions of employment. It is to be considered in particular how the rules of waiver and equitable estoppel operate as limiting factors upon the requirements of consideration and of consent. It may be doubted whether the importation of these technicalities from the general principles of contract law serves a useful purpose in the context of the contract of employment. The examination of these matters enables general conclusions to be drawn concerning the proper role of the law of subsequent variation and its relationship with the law concerning termination itself.

[1] See below, pp. 59–60, 62–3, 66.
[2] *Sutcliffe* v. *Hawker Siddeley Aviation Ltd.* [1973] ICR 560.

A. The Requirement of Consideration

The general contractual principle that consideration is required to support a subsequent variation, or that a promise does not support a contractual variation where that promise is to do what one is already bound by contract with the promisee to do, itself originates in certain early cases concerning the contracts of employment of seamen, where the seamen were unable to recover wage increases promised in the course of voyages. Such a case was *Stilk* v. *Myrick*[1] where a seaman who had entered into a contract for a voyage (out and return) was held unable to recover additional wages promised for the return voyage. The report of Espinasse shows the decision to be based on the ground of public policy which had been applied in *Harris* v. *Watson*,[2] namely that it was against the general interest for seamen to be able to extort wage increases in mid-voyage by threats of refusal to proceed with the return voyage. But the report in Campbell shows the decision to be based upon the lack of consideration for the promise to pay additional wages. And in *Harris* v. *Carter*,[3] where a promise to pay additional wages to a seaman was similarly held to be unenforceable, the result was expressly based upon both grounds in the alternative. Comparison may be made with the case of *Frazer* v. *Hatton*[4] where a seaman contracted for a voyage on the terms of ship's articles which provided that 'The crew if required, [was] to be transferred to any other ship in the same employ.' The seaman was transferred into another vessel belonging to the same owners for the return part of the voyage. It was held that an agreement with the master of the latter vessel for higher wages for the return voyage was unenforceable, because of the provision for such variation in the original contract and the consequential absence of consideration for the subsequently agreed wage increase.

It may well be thought that a distinguishing feature of these cases was the agreement for the duration of a particular voyage, and that the requirement of consideration for variation does not arise in the same way where a contract for an indefinite period is terminable by notice. The principle was none the less applied in *Price* v. *Rhondda U.D.C.*,[5] a decision concerning the security of tenure of married

---

[1] (1809) 6 Esp. 129; 2 Camp. 317. See Treitel, *Law of Contract* (4th edn. 1975) p. 66.

[2] (1791) Peake 102.

[3] (1854) 3 E & B 559. So also *Hopkins* v. *M'Bride* (1901) 50 WR 255; *Harrison* v. *Dodd* (1914) 111 LT 47.

[4] (1857) 2 CB (NS) 512.   [5] [1923] 2 Ch. 372.

women teachers employed by a local authority, originally on the terms that their employment was terminable by one month's notice by the employing authority. A subsequent undertaking on the part of the employing authority to grant a minimum security of tenure to these teachers was treated as lacking in legal effect because the teachers had given no corresponding promise to remain in their employment for that length of time, and thus had given no consideration for this variation of the original contract.[1] The application in this type of case of a requirement of consideration for contractual variation was a retrograde step whose results are open to fundamental criticism.

The doctrine of consideration for variation is open to serious objections both on the ground that it gives rise to narrow and artificial technical distinctions, and on the wider ground that it takes no account of certain realities of the employment relationship. The narrowly technical distinctions arise by reason of a further rule that whereas consideration is required for variation, it is supplied automatically where there is a termination of one contract and replacement by another contract, even though the new contract represents a different balance of advantage from that expressed in the former contract. The difference between an agreement to rescind a contract and substitute a new one at a higher rate of pay, and a simple promise to pay higher wages for continuing to work, may not be easily visible to the naked eye.[2] This distinction is further considered in the following section of this work, as, whatever its artificiality, it may be a matter of some consequence in law. But it is clear that in so far as this distinction operates to modify the rule that consideration is required for contractual variation, it renders the rule itself a rather unsatisfactory one.

There is a further and fundamental objection to the operation of the doctrine of consideration in this context. It represents an oversimplified approach to the balance of interests which is involved in regulating the variation of the contract of employment. The contract of employment should not be regarded as expressing a static relationship where the equation contained in the original bargain must be maintained unchanged throughout the duration of the employment. In fact, the balance of interests may be altered in practice by negotiation and industrial action, by changes in the economic surroundings, and, over a longer period, by changes in social atti-

---

[1] See Eve J., ibid. at 385.   [2] See Treitel, op. cit., pp. 66–7.

tudes. For example, if *Stilk* v. *Myrick*[1] represents a view that it is improper extortion on the part of a seaman to obtain a wage increase by the threat of not working the return voyage, *Hartley* v. *Ponsonby*[2] signifies a judicial recognition that this aspect of the matter ultimately gives way to the interest of the seaman in extra compensation for working on an under-manned vessel. Thus also, the reasoning in *Price* v. *Rhondda U.D.C.*[3] was quite inappropriate because the promise by the employing authority to extend the minimum period of service no doubt represented a response to political pressures and opinions concerning the rights which should be accorded to married women teachers, and it was really beside the point to look for some additional undertaking by the teachers which could be balanced against this promise.

In the context of statutory remedies for unfair dismissal, the Industrial Court has recognized the importance of the element of variability in the bargain between employer and employee. In *Wallace* v. *Guy Ltd.*[4] the Court held that it had been unfair to dismiss a sheet-metal worker who refused to do pipe-bending work unless he was paid an additional 2p. an hour. In contractual terms the employer was within his rights; the employee was in effect attempting to insist upon a variation of contractual terms for which he was offering no new consideration beyond what he had already contracted to do. However, the Court found that it was customary in this firm for bonus rates for particular jobs to be negotiated between management and individual workers, and that it was unfair for the employer in those circumstances to dismiss an employee, who was asking a certain rate for a job, without any negotiation with him. This decision indicates the limitations of the contractual rules concerning variation of terms of employment, and shows how some other set of rules—in this case the law of unfair dismissal—was necessary in order to transcend those limitations.

B. Equitable Promissory Estoppel

It may be that the requirement of consideration for variations of

---

[1] (1809) 6 Esp. 129, 2 Camp. 317 (above); see Stoljar, 'The Modification of Contracts' (1957) 35 CBR 485 at 510–12—'Employment Contracts' where he argues that the requirement of consideration which was imposed by *Stilk* v. *Myrick* should be regarded as a narrowly limited rule against modification which appears oppressive or is achieved by some sort of duress.

[2] (1857) 7 E & B 872 (above). [3] [1923] 2 Ch. 372 (above).

[4] [1973] ICR 117.

contracts of employment could be modified by recourse to the doctrine of equitable promissory estoppel, so that a variation would thereby acquire a binding effect upon the party on whose part it represents a concession. This is not the place in which to attempt to state the results of all the discussion of that doctrine which has taken place in recent years. It will be sufficient to cite the statement of the principle in the Privy Council in *Ajayi* v. *R. T. Briscoe (Nigeria) Ltd.*:

The principle, which has been described as quasi-estoppel, and perhaps more aptly as promissory estoppel, is that when one party to a contract in the absence of consideration agrees not to enforce his rights, an equity will be raised in favour of the other party. This equity is, however, subject to the qualifications,

    (a) that the other party has altered his position,

    (b) that the promisor can resile from his promise on giving reasonable notice, which need not be a formal notice, giving the promisee reasonable opportunity of resuming his position,

    (c) the promise only becomes final and irrevocable if the promisee cannot resume his position.[1]

There are difficulties of both a technical and a fundamental nature in applying this doctrine to the variation of contracts of employment. It seems probable that the doctrine has only a suspensory effect, so that the variation will be ineffective for want of consideration at least in respect of the period following reasonable notice of an intention to reassert the former terms and conditions.[2] It is difficult to determine what would be required for a valid resumption of the *status quo ante* in the case of a contract of employment. Furthermore, the doctrine of equitable promissory estoppel is generally expressed in terms which suggest that it may apply only where the variation consists in a forbearance to enforce existing rights, and not where it consists in the granting of new rights.[3] If that is indeed the case, then it would result in a distinction which would be wholly artificial in the context of the relationship between employer and

---

[1] [1964] 1 WLR 1326 at 1330 (Lord Hodson).
[2] Cf. *Charles Rickards Ltd.* v. *Oppenhaim* [1950] 1 KB 616; *Tool Metal Manufacturing Ltd.* v. *Tungsten Electric Co. Ltd.* [1955] 1 WLR 761; *Ajayi* v. *R. T. Briscoe (Nigeria) Ltd.* [1964] 1 WLR 1326.
[3] Cf. the statement of the rule in *Ajayi* v. *R. T. Briscoe Ltd.* [1964] 1 WLR 1326 at 1330 quoted above. The rule in *Combe* v. *Combe* [1951] 2 KB 215 relates to the rather different point that the doctrine cannot be invoked to enforce a promise which does not take place in the context of, and as a modification of, an existing contractual relationship.

employee. If strictly applied, it could mean that the doctrine might apply to an undertaking by the employer to reduce the length of the basic working week, but not to an undertaking to raise the basic hourly rate. Yet it is very frequently the case that both these types of variation will have the same purpose and the same effect of raising the total weekly remuneration, and that the choice of mode in which to express the demand for that increase is dictated by conventions of collective bargaining.

A more fundamental objection to the use of the doctrine of equitable promissory estoppel to regulate the validity of variations of contracts of employment consists in the fact that the doctrine is itself subject to a test of whether it is equitable for it to be applied in a given case.[1] It is suggested that the application of this notion of equity to the variation of contracts of employment would be exceedingly difficult in view of the various kinds and degrees of pressure exerted by employers and employed upon each other in the course of settling and varying the terms and conditions of employment. The difficulty might not be insuperable; but it would involve the courts in arbitrations of disputes of *interest*.[2] If the courts are to fulfil that role, it is suggested that the doctrine of equitable promissory estoppel is not the heading under which they should do so. Like the older strict doctrine of consideration, it is not the right tool for the job of deciding when it is proper to give binding effect to changes in terms and conditions of employment.

C. The Requirement of Consent

Although the requirement of consideration does not seem useful as a test of validity of variation of contracts of employment, the requirement of consent has, by contrast, a critical role in this respect. The requirement of consent to contractual variation was affirmed in the decision of the Court of Appeal in *Marriott* v. *Oxford & District Co-operative Society Ltd.* (No. 2),[3] where it was held that the action

---

[1] Cf. *D. & C. Builders Ltd.* v. *Rees* [1966] 2 QB 617.

[2] Wedderburn in Aaron (ed.), *Dispute Settlement Procedure in Five Western European Countries* (UCLA 1969) argues that the distinction between disputes of right and of interest is unreal as regards collective disputes. But the distinction may have greater validity at the level of the individual contract.

[3] [1970] 1 QB 186 (annotated by the present writer at 33 MLR 93). Cf. *Scott* v. *Executors of A. E. Marchant* (1969) 4 ITR 319, 324 where the Tribunal pointed out that 'voluntary acceptance of new terms must be distinguished from taking Hobson's choice.' The 'Hobson's choice' point has been usefully reiterated in *Sheet Metal Components Ltd.* v. *Plumridge* [1974] ICR 373, 377 E.

of an employee in remaining at work for a period of a couple of weeks following the imposition by the employer of reduced remuneration and a lower status did not constitute a consent to a variation of the contractual terms and conditions. This is a matter of critical importance in distinguishing between variation and termination of the contract of employment at common law, because if it is held that the necessary element of consent is lacking for a valid variation, the attempt to impose the variation assumes the character of wrongful repudiation which entitles the injured party to treat the contract as terminated. The decision in *Marriott's case* deals with the further question of whether a short period of employment on the new terms has the result that this wrongful repudiation can no longer be regarded as a dismissal for the purposes of the 1965 Act. That aspect of the case is further considered below.[1]

The principle concerning consent to variation in *Marriott's case* has since been accepted and acted upon by the Industrial Court. This was in *G.K.N. (Cwmbran) Ltd.* v. *Lloyd*,[2] where the employee, a camshaft straightener in a foundry, remained at work for about four weeks after the termination of his original job. During that four-week period he was employed in a different foundry from previously, in an unskilled capacity as opposed to the previous semi-skilled capacity, with a reduction in wages of at least £7 per week. The Industrial Court treated this merely as further employment taken in mitigation of his loss rather than continuation of the previous employment. In *Shields Furniture Ltd.* v. *Goff*[3] the Court similarly held that three weeks' work and two weeks' paid holiday occurring after the employer had imposed changed conditions of employment was not 'so long an elapsed period of time that one ought to assume an agreed variation or replacement of the previous contract.'[4] Hence there is now an explicit doctrine that consent to variation is to be tested where appropriate by the length of time spent in the employment concerned after the imposition of the changed terms.

Although the decision in the *Marriott* (No. 2) case[5] represents a rule that a variation will be regarded as consensual only where the

---

[1] See below, pp. 190–1.   [2] [1972] ICR 214.
[3] [1972] ICR 214; cf. *Ubsdell* v. *Paterson* [1973] ICR 86, *Cartin* v. *Botley Garages Ltd.* [1973] ICR 144—the comparable situation upon transfer of a business.
[4] [1972] ICR 187, Sir John Brightman at 190 G–H.
[5] [1970] 1 QB 186 (above).

consent is a genuine one, it does not provide the complete answer to the question of the effect of an imposed, non-consensual, variation of terms. For in that case the question was not the effectiveness of the variation in pay and status, but the question whether it had resulted in a termination of the original contract. Nothing in the judgments in that case deals with the question whether the employer could have been sued upon an obligation to continue the employment on the old terms in respect of the period following the imposed variations during which the employee remained at work. It would in fact seem that if an employment relationship continues for a substantial period following the imposition of varied terms and conditions, it will be held that the party upon whom the variation was imposed has waived his right to insist upon the former terms and conditions. The element of consent will, in effect, be supplied by conduct.

An interesting decision in which the Ontario Court of Appeal took a contrary view was *Hill* v. *Peter Gorman Ltd.*[1]

A company which employed a number of salesmen and which remunerated them entirely by commission on their sales began to withhold ten per cent of those earnings as a reserve against non-payment of debts by customers. It was held by a majority of the Court that an employee whose employment was terminable by two weeks' notice on either side, but who remained in his employment for more than a year after this innovation, was entitled to reclaim the ten per cent deducted from his earnings, because by his periodical protests against the deduction he showed that he had never waived his right to payment in full. Mackay J.A. ruled that for the majority as follows: '[I]t cannot be said, as a matter of law, that an employee accepts an attempted variation simply by the fact alone of continuing in his employment. . . [W]hile refusing to accept it he may continue in his employment, and if the employer permits him to discharge his obligations and the employee makes it plain that he is not accepting the variation, then the employee is entitled to insist on the original terms.'[2]

It is, however, likely that an English court would take the view that the continuation of employment for such a period of time did result in a consent by conduct to the variation,[3] and that they would treat the issue as one of whether consideration was necessary and was present. This would, of course, bring them straight to an issue of

---

[1] (1957) 9 DLR 2d 124.

[2] Ibid. at pp. 131–2. The dissent of Gibson J.A. was based upon the view that variation may be effectively imposed by notice of the length required to terminate the contract.

[3] Cf. *Rowsell* v. *Metropolitan Water Board* (1915) 84 LJ(NS)KB pt. 2, p. 1869.

equitable promissory estoppel, with all the difficulties attendant upon the application of that doctrine in an employment context.[1] It is suggested that the approach of the Canadian court in that case is the preferable one; that it is more satisfactory to test the effectiveness of variations in employment according to whether there is a genuine consent to the variation, than according to whether there is consideration, or whether the need for consideration is met by the operation of an esoteric rule of law.

D. *Variation by Conduct*

The requirements for a valid variation of the contract of employment which have been discussed above lead to the general question, how far may the contract be effectively varied by conduct. To that general question, the only possible answer is that the law is at the moment in an uncertain state upon this point, but that there seems to be emerging a doctrine of variation by conduct for which, however, the conditions have not yet been systematically established. It may be useful to attempt to set out the different approaches to this question which are to be found in the cases.

Firstly, the conduct of the parties—in the sense of the working arrangements which they make and operate—may be seen not as producing a variation in existing terms of employment but as establishing what were the terms from the outset. The clearest example of this process occurs in cases such as *O'Brien* v. *Associated Fire Alarms Ltd.*,[2] and the case-law was discussed earlier in this work as a question of contractual formation.[3]

Secondly, the conduct of the parties may be seen as having no effect upon their mutual contractual rights by reason of a lack of intention to affect legal rights. That approach was discussed and criticized earlier in this work in connection with cases concerning collective agreements extending the normal working week beyond the length of the basic (normally 40-hour) week—cases such as *Turriff Construction Co. Ltd.* v. *Bryant*[4] and *Loman & Henderson* v. *Merseyside Transport Services Ltd.*[5] The artificial reasoning to which that approach may readily lead can be observed in the case of *Saxton* v. *National Coal Board*[6] where a mineworker, who had for many years

---

[1] See above, pp. 58–60.   [2] [1968] 1 WLR 1916.   [3] See above, pp. 15–16.
[4] (1967) 2 ITR 292 reversing a decision exactly comparable to that in *Chant* v. *Turriff Construction Co. Ltd.* (1966) 1 ITR 380.
[5] (1968) 3 ITR 108—Annotated by Wedderburn (1969) 32 MLR 99.
[6] (1970) 5 ITR 196.

worked as a continuous shiftman on a seven-day week, worked for five days each week during the last few months of his employment because the colliery had ceased production work. The Board contended that there had been a consensual variation of his contract of employment, such that his redundancy should be assessed on the footing that his contract of employment obliged him to work only for a five-day week at the time of its termination. That argument was rejected, and the assessment was based upon the seven-day week. The merits of the case were clear; thus Lord Parker C.J. said 'I dislike, I confess, the attitude of the Board in this case where . . . they are really making use of the employee's willingness to work, and to work for a lower wage, as a means of avoiding making a redundancy payment.'[1] The court was obliged to employ rather special pleading to reach the result they did, as may be seen from the statement of Lord Parker C.J. that 'Here was a man who was being called upon to co-operate to help his employers to run down this colliery, and one would think that in those circumstances it was difficult to say that he was working as he did otherwise than without prejudice.'[2] It is surely rather unreal to distinguish such arrangements according to whether they are 'without prejudice' or not.

Thirdly, the Divisional Court did in *Dorman Long & Co. Ltd.* v. *Carroll* (1945)[3] treat a variation in the actual conduct of the parties as *not* affecting their mutual contractual obligations by distinguishing between the substance of those obligations and the mere manner of their being carried out.

Colliery workers employed as fillers agreed, in 1943, to a scheme of reorganised working whereby they were to work an extra shift on Saturdays. After eighteen months and the passing of the most acute phase of the wartime emergency, the employees gave eight days' notice to terminate the extra shift (their employment itself being terminable upon fourteen days' notice). Their employers' claim for damages for breach of contract under the Employers and Workmen Act 1875 was rejected on the ground that there had never been a variation of the obligations of the employees in the first place, but merely 'an alteration of the method of carrying out the original agreement',[4] with the result that it was no breach of contract for them to revert to the original terms. It was also held that the agreement to work the extra shift was in any event terminable by reasonable notice and had been so terminated.

---

[1] Ibid. at p. 200.   [2] Ibid. at p. 200.   [3] [1945] 2 All ER 567.
[4] Ibid. at 599 A–B (Humphreys J.).

It would seem that the latter ground for the decision is more satisfactory than the former. Even if there was an underlying feeling, both before the magistrates and on appeal to the High Court, that the employees should not be penalized for their willingness to shoulder extra burdens in a time of emergency, it was still undesirable that this result should be achieved by resort to a supposed distinction between a variation in the method of working and a variation in the terms of work; a distinction which is unconvincing when applied to a change in the hours of work.

Fourthly (though this may be little more than another variant of the doctrine of lack of intention to affect legal relations), there are cases which have avoided a variation of contract by conduct, by admitting the possibility of discrepancy between the contractual obligations of the parties and their actual practice, and thus envisaging a dormant but none the less actual right to insist on the original obligations. We see this tendency in the reasoning of the Divisional Court in *Parkes Classic Confectionery Ltd.* v. *Ashcroft*[1] where an Industrial Tribunal was directed to reconsider a *de facto* reduction in the working hours of an employee and to decide into which of three possible categories it fell; that is to say, either

(a) a consensual variation of the contract; or

(b) an abandonment of any contractual term at all concerning normal working hours (an analysis which was criticized earlier in this work);[2] or

(c) (which illustrates the proposition advanced in this paragraph) that the parties had gone on with an effective contract specifying the original normal working week which was 'still legally in existence though not meticulously observed'. The Divisional Court appears not to have found this third alternative a very appealing one; it might well have been preferable if they had not felt obliged to consider that possibility at all.

There is encountered the same acceptance of discrepancy between contractual obligations and actual conduct in decisions of the Industrial Court concerning employees who have been given light or substituted duties by reason of ill health or disability. Thus in *O'Donnell* v. *George Wimpey & Co. Ltd.*[3] it was held of a 'general labourer' who had for a couple of years been treated as a light workman because of failing eyesight that 'the fact that in order to keep him in

---

[1] (1973) 8 ITR 43.   [2] See above, pp. 18–19.
[3] (1972) 7 ITR 343; cf. *Kyte* v. *Greater London Council* [1974] IRLR 8.

their employment and keep him in his job the respondents gave him work to do of a lighter nature than that of general labourer does not mean that at any time the nature of his employment with them ceased [*sic*].' A similar course was followed in *Runnalls* v. *Richards & Osborne Ltd.*[1] where a short-haul lorry driver was given a job driving on private roads because he had been disqualified for a year from driving on public roads. It was held that his contract of employment had not been varied by this change in practice. It is difficult to escape a sense that such decisions are hard cases giving rise to suspect law.

The foregoing paragraphs have described the grounds upon which the courts may refuse to recognize a contractual variation by conduct. To the extent that these hurdles are surmounted, there is an emergent doctrine of variation by conduct. Such a doctrine is closely allied to notions of waiver or of equitable estoppel; but here the waiver or the equity is to be found in *conduct*—in the cumulative effect of practice—rather than in specific acts or undertakings of the parties. Some such doctrine seems to be necessitated by the social operation of the employment relationship.

SECTION 3: VARIATION DISTINGUISHED FROM RESCISSION AND REPLACEMENT

The previous section of this chapter indicates the requirements for an effective variation of the terms of a contract of employment by subsequent agreement. If the change in the terms of employment fulfils certain conditions, then it will be regarded in law as being more than a simple *variation*; as being, in fact, a *rescission* of the existing contract and its replacement by a new contract upon different terms. In this way there arises a method of terminating the contract of employment—namely, a termination by a change in content— as part of a process of substituting a new contract for the old.

The distinction between variation, and rescission coupled with replacement, is one of the more esoteric aspects of the law of termina- tion of contracts, both as to contracts generally and as to contracts of employment in particular. It is true that the distinction was an important one for the purposes of applying the requirements of evidence in writing imposed on certain types of contract by Section

---

[1] [1973] ICR 225. Contrast *Weed* v. *A. E. Smith* (*Kettering*) *Ltd.* (1972) 7 ITR 352 where, however, the Court gives no reason for its view on this point.

4 of the Statutes of Frauds 1677 and by Section 4 of the Sale of Goods Act 1893. But it was partly because these provisions became enmeshed in a web of technicalities that they lost their usefulness and were amended and ultimately repealed.[1]

Again, it may be said that the distinction between variation and rescission plus replacement is sometimes one of substance when it comes to construing the mutual rights and obligations under a contract. If a contract containing a term (express or implied) dealing with a certain particular matter is varied by an agreement which replaces many of the old terms but says nothing about that particular matter, then the question whether that term continues to form part of the contract between the parties depends upon whether there has been a rescission and replacement of the old contract; for if so, that particular term in the original contract may be treated as having gone by the board.[2] This is indeed the most important single consequence of the distinction; but it may be regarded as an unnecessarily elaborate method of construction of the intentions of the parties, which could be considered in relation to the particular term without this intervening stage in the reasoning.

It was at one stage believed that the distinction between mere variation and rescission plus replacement was an important one for the purposes of applying the concept of dismissal as defined by Section 3(1) of the 1965 Act. It was thought that where an employer imposed a variation of terms upon the employee and the employee remained at work for a short time thereafter, the question whether he had been dismissed for the purposes of the Act depended upon whether there had been a rescission and replacement of the original contract. In *Marriott* v. *Oxford & District Co-operative Society Ltd.* the Divisional Court treated this as the central issue in the case, and remitted the matter to the Industrial Tribunal in order that they might give a decision upon this specific point.[3] The Tribunal held that there had indeed been a consensual variation as opposed to a rescission and replacement of the contract, and hence that there had not been a dismissal within the meaning of the Act; and the Divisional Court

---

[1] The scope of s. 4 of the Statute of Frauds 1677 was greatly reduced by s. 1 of the Law Reform (Enforcement of Contracts) Act 1954, and s. 4 of the Sale of Goods Act 1893 was repealed by s. 2 of the 1954 Act.

[2] This point is of some practical importance in relation to clauses concerned with restraints upon competition, upon promotion from one employment to another within an enterprise.

[3] *Marriott* (No. 1) (1968) 3 ITR 121.

upheld their view.[1] However, Lord Denning M.R. in the Court of Appeal,[2] with the agreement of his fellow judges, rightly held that the distinction was quite immaterial to the real issue. The question was whether the change in terms and conditions was consensual or not. If not, there was a dismissal by the employer for the purposes of the Act. But if the change had been agreed between the parties, then it would not have constituted a dismissal even if it had been a rescission and replacement of the contract, because, in the words of Lord Denning M.R., 'If the parties agree consensually to vary the terms of the contract of employment, or to rescind it and substitute a new contract of employment, the plain fact is that the contract is not terminated by the employers but by consent.'[3] So the distinction between variation and consensual rescission plus replacement turns out not to be an important one for the purposes of the application of the statutory definitions of dismissal contained in the 1965 and 1971 Acts.

There is an underlying explanation for the fact that this distinction between mere variation and rescission plus replacement is a relatively obscure one. Normally the law concerning the termination of the contract of employment is dealing with the termination of an employment *relationship*. The contract acts as the vehicle of legal rights and obligations upon the termination of employment. In this particular case of termination of the contract, the employment relationship continues, albeit on different terms. The termination of the contract is a phenomenon which is in this case visible only to the lawyer's eye and has no counterpart in the discontinuance of the social relationship of employer and employee. All this being so, the discussion of the distinction between mere variation and rescission plus replacement is still not lacking in justification. The application of this distinction, when properly understood, demands an analysis of what are the identifying features of the particular employment concerned—which is an instructive process. Moreover, the extent to which particular contractual terms are transmitted from one period of employment to the next is of some practical importance. It is useful to consider separately the treatment of the issue in general contract law and in relation to the contract of employment in particular.

---

[1] *Marriott* (No. 2) [1969] 1 WLR 254.
[2] [1970] 1 QB 186.   [3] Ibid. at 191H–192 A.

A. The Distinction in the Context of General Contractual Principles

The search for a general principle of contract law, whereby to decide whether there has been rescission and replacement, leads one to two decisions of the House of Lords which applied the distinction in connection with the requirement that contracts for the sale of goods worth over £10 be evidenced in writing. The decisions yield very little guidance concerning the principle to be applied in distinguishing between variation and rescission plus replacement; this is for good reasons which are themselves worthy of attention.

Morris v. *Baron & Co.*[1] concerned a large commercial contract for the sale of cloth. Disputes having arisen concerning delivery and payment, and legal proceedings having been commenced, a later agreement was reached by which the parties were to withdraw their action and cross-action, and certain concessions and allowances were to be made to the buyers. Upon the question whether this amounted to a rescission and replacement of the original contract, it was ruled that this depended upon the intention of the parties, and it was found that there had been the requisite intention to rescind the old contracts, and to replace them by an entirely new agreement.

Lord Finlay L.C. ruled that 'The evidence in this case points to the conclusion that the parties intended not merely to vary the original contract, but to set it aside and substitute another for it . . .'[2]

Viscount Haldane commented that 'What is, of course, essential is that there should have been made manifest the intention in any event of a complete extinction of the first and formal contract, and not merely the desire of an alteration, however sweeping, in terms which leave it still subsisting.'[3]

Lord Atkinson's formulation was that 'It is, I think, impossible to arrive at any rational conclusion as to meaning, aim and effect of this new arrangement other than this, that it was the clear intention of both the appellant and the respondents to put aside, in their future dealings, the original agreement and to treat it thenceforth as abandoned or non-existent.'[4]

Only Lord Dunedin had a more specific test to propose, which was that 'In the case [of variation] there are no such executory clauses in the second arrangement as would enable you to sue upon that alone if the first did not exist; in the [case of rescission] you could sue on the second arrangement alone, and the first contract is got rid of either by express words to that effect, or because, the second dealing with the same subject matter

---

[1] [1918] AC 1; cf. *Tallerman & Co.* v. *Nathan's Merchandise Prop. Ltd.* (1957) 98 CLR 93; *Don Lodge Motel* v. *Invercargill Licensing Trust* [1970] NZLR 1105.
[2] [1918] AC 1 at 12.　　　[3] Ibid. at 19.　　　[4] Ibid. at 33.

as the first but in a different way, it is impossible that the two should be both performed.'[1]

However, apart from this, the judgments offer no further guidance upon how the distinction is to be drawn.

A similar very general and vague treatment of the distinction between variation and rescission plus replacement by a new contract occurred in the later case of *British & Beningtons Ltd.* v. *N.W. Cachar Tea Co.*[2]

The case concerned a group of contracts for the sale of tea to be delivered at the Port of London. Delays having occurred in delivery as a result of congestion in the port, it was agreed that the buyers would accept delivery at provincial ports instead of London with an allowance per pound in return. It was held, following the earlier case, that the test for deciding whether this latter agreement had rescinded and replaced the earlier contract or merely varied it, was one of the intention of the parties; but that here the intention was merely to vary and not to rescind and replace it by a new contract.

Lord Sumner ruled upon the distinction between variation and rescission that 'The question is whether the common intention of the parties [when making the later agreement] was to "abrogate", "rescind", "supersede", or "extinguish" the old contracts by a "substitution" of a "completely new" and "self-contained" or "self-subsisting" agreement "containing as an entirety the old terms together with, and as modified by, the new terms incorporated".'[3]

However, there is, as in the earlier decision, little or no development of the question of how these concepts are to be applied.

It may be suggested that it was no accident that the House of Lords should on both occasions deal only cursorily with the requirement of intention to rescind. They were largely preoccupied with the great difficulties of deciding how to apply the Statute of Frauds, even given that one had established the nature of the transaction concerned; for the existing cases had reached a state of considerable complexity upon this point. But their decision upon the effect of the statute explains their difficulties concerning the definition of intention to vary. For they decided that where the later agreement did not comply with the statute, then, if it was a mere variation of the contract, it had no effect upon the original contract, which therefore survived intact. This was the result of the later case. But if the agreement amounted to a rescission and replacement then, even though

---

[1] Ibid. at 26.   [2] [1923] AC 48.   [3] Ibid. at 67.

unenforceable in itself if it did not comply with the statute, it was effective to rescind the original contract, and so left the old contract as no longer in force and the new contract as unenforceable. This had been the result in the earlier decision. This being so, the courts had in effect left themselves with two alternative methods of *defeating* the real intentions of the parties. They could either hold that their entire contractual arrangements were of no effect, or they could hold that their agreement to vary those arrangements was of no effect. The danger that a statute imposing requirements of form upon contracts may produce more injustice than it prevents is even greater in relation to the modification of contracts than in relation to their original formation. Hence the courts could hardly embark upon too close an analysis of the exact nature of the intentions of the parties, since whatever their intentions they were not going to be able to give effect to them. The matter was, understandably, left somewhat undefined.

Lord Devlin made a bold attempt in a later decision of a similar kind[1] to meet this difficulty, by declaring that the courts were, after all, consulting the intentions of the parties in a certain sense. He said of the result of the earlier two decisions:

[The parties] cannot have that which presumably they wanted, that is, the old agreement as amended; so the court has to make up its mind which comes nearer to their intention—to leave them with an unamended agreement or without any agreement at all. The House answered this question by distinguishing between rescission and variation. If the new agreement reveals an intention to rescind the old, the old goes; and if it does not, the old remains in force and unamended.[2]

Although this constitutes the best available justification of the earlier decisions, it is somewhat disingenuous in so far as it suggests that the courts were in those cases really able to follow the intentions of the parties themselves. The conclusion must be drawn that the distinction between mere variation and rescission plus replacement is not the subject of any satisfactory general contract principle because of the special context in which the problem arose.

If any suggestion may be made concerning the distinctions to be drawn from the facts of the cases, it is that one must consider the structure of the modified arrangements between the parties as a matter of drafting. If they have effected the changes by adding to,

---

[1] *United Dominions Corpn. (Jamaica) Ltd.* v. *Shoucair* [1969] 1 AC 340.
[2] Ibid. at 348 A–C.

subtracting from, or modifying the terms of the original contract, it is a mere variation. If, on the other hand, they have in effect drawn up a new agreement—if they have created a new repository for their mutual rights and obligations—then they have impliedly rescinded the original agreement. It was a test of this kind which was indicated by Lord Dunedin when he said in *Morris* v. *Baron & Co.*[1] that the question was whether the new agreement was such that it could be sued upon as an independent contract. On this view, the issue was hardly one of *intention* at all; the test becomes an objective one based upon the manner of drafting (to use that term in a wide sense) of the later modificatory agreement. As a matter of general contract principle, it seems more satisfactory to be able to point to some kind of objective test than to be forced back upon a very nebulous test of intention; it remains to compare this result with the effect of the authorities dealing with this problem in the context of the contract of employment.

B. *The Distinction as applied to Contracts of Employment*

In the context of the contract of employment, various different applications of the distinction between variation and rescission plus replacement have appeared from time to time. The case-law suggests that the general contractual principle should be regarded as modified by a concept of the identity of the particular employment itself, so that a change in terms of employment should be seen as involving the termination of one contract and its replacement by another where, but only where, there is a *change of job* involved.

The view was at one time taken that any and every change in the terms of a contract of employment resulted in its rescission and replacement by a new contract. However, this view was taken in the context of the application of the requirement formerly imposed by Section 4 of the Statute of Frauds that contracts not to be performed within a year of the making must be evidenced in writing. In *Williams* v. *Moss Empires Ltd.*,[2] the intentions of the parties in varying their contract could be fully implemented by the court if, but only if, the agreement to vary was seen as the formation of a new contract.

In that case, the employee was a music hall artiste employed under a written contract for a term of three and a half years at a yearly salary. Upon the outbreak of war, and in consequence of war-time conditions,

---

[1] [1918] AC 1 at 26. [2] [1915] 3 KB 242.

an agreement was made between theatre proprietors and the Variety Artistes Federation to distribute the risks of a falling-off in audiences between owners and artistes, and to distribute the same risks evenly as between artistes by substituting for existing salaries a scheme whereby the receipts of the halls were to be pooled for a twelve-week period, and fifty per cent. of them were to be divided among the artistes in proportion to their existing salaries. The plaintiff, not a member of the Federation, agreed verbally to his employers' applying the scheme, but then sought to recover his originally agreed salary in reliance upon the Statute of Frauds. It was held that he was now bound by a new contract, Sankey J. ruling that 'The result of varying the terms of an existing contract is to produce, not the original contract with a variation, but a new and different contract.'[1]

Clearly, upon the merits of the case the judge was under an incentive to take a wide view of the circumstances in which there could be said to be a rescission and replacement of the original contract.

In that case it was necessary, in order to achieve the desired result, to treat any and every modification of contractual terms as resulting in a new contract. The workings of the Statute of Frauds were, however, such that it could be necessary to take entirely the opposite view in order to prevent a fraudulent reliance upon the statute. Such a case was *Adams* v. *Union Cinemas Ltd.*[2]

A cinema manager had been employed since 1934 under an oral contract of employment which was not required to be evidenced in writing.[3] In 1937 he was promoted to the position of controller of a large number of cinemas and was told that he could make his arrangements for two years, this being qualified by the statement, 'You will see how you get on with the work.'

When this employment was terminated by the defendants upon one month's notice and the plaintiff sued for damages for wrongful dismissal, the defendants argued *inter alia* that the 1937 promotion had resulted in the termination of the existing contract, and its replacement by a new contract which could not be enforced because it was for a fixed term of two years, and was therefore required to be evidenced in writing. This argument was rejected on the ground that this was not a contract for two years, but was a mere variation

[1] Ibid. at 247–8.

[2] [1939] 1 All ER 169 (affirmed by CA [1939] 3 All ER 136 on other grounds).

[3] Because it was for an indefinite period. Such contracts were treated as falling outside s. 4 of the Statute of Frauds in that they might be performed within a year.

of the previous contract which could be enforced though not evidenced in writing. Stable J. indicated that variations of this kind should not be regarded as resulting in the formation of a new contract: 'I think that everyone would be astonished if they were told that, when an employee is put to more responsible work, or given a rise of salary, that constitutes an entirely new contract . . .'[1] However, it cannot satisfactorily be said as a general rule that a promotion does not involve the formation of a new contract. That would be too sweeping a view.[2] Hence it is clear that the cases which depend upon the Statute of Frauds seem generally to have resulted in a distortion of one kind or another of the law upon this point.

In some employment cases the distinction between variation and rescission has been a material one for the purpose of deciding whether a given term of the old agreement continued to apply after the making of the modifying agreement. The courts have wavered between the different tests of whether the new agreement represents a major departure from the pattern of the old contract in terms of content, or whether on the other hand it is inconsistent with the continued existence of the old contract in a structural or draftsman's sense.

Thus in *Meek* v. *Port of London Authority*[3] the plaintiffs were employed by the defendants from 1908 onwards, on contracts of which it was a custom, and assumed by the Court of Appeal to be a legally binding term, that the defendants would meet the income tax liability of those employees who were sufficiently well paid to incur such taxation. By the time, in 1912, that the plaintiffs had been promoted to a grade such that their incomes incurred tax, the employing authority had already given notice of the discontinuance of this practice. By virtue of the terms of the earlier statutory transfer of employment from private port employers, these plaintiffs were, it was held, entitled to claim that the terms of their original contracts of employment should not be changed. The question whether they had therefore become entitled to have their tax paid, depended upon whether the old contracts had continued in force, in which case they were so entitled, or whether on the other hand they had been rescinded and replaced by a new contract upon the promotion. It was held by the Court of Appeal that the promotion did result in a change of contract.

---

[1] [1939] 1 All ER 167 at 171 C–D.
[2] Cf. Pennycuick J. in *Re Mack Trucks (Great Britain) Ltd.* [1967] 1 WLR 780 at 780: 'It must frequently happen in the case of a long period of service with a single employer that employer and employee enter into a whole succession of new contracts, e.g. on promotion or for other reasons.'
[3] [1918] 2 Ch. 96.

In their view it was not as if there had been an automatic increment in salary and improvement in conditions growing out of the original contract; it was rather that the position of the employees had been changed by the employers voluntarily promoting them to a higher grade.

By contrast, a similar issue was handled in *S. W. Strange Ltd. v. Mann*[1] by considering whether the employers had replaced the original contract *as a document* and whether they had in a formal sense terminated one contract and replaced it by another.

The plaintiffs, a firm of bookmakers, sought to enforce against the former manager of one of their betting shops a restrictive covenant which had been contained in his original contract of employment. One issue was whether that covenant had survived an agreement between the parties, following earlier differences between them, that the defendant should relinquish the duties and responsibilities of manager in favour of another person and that the defendant should be appointed manager of the credit department. It was held that this agreement, recorded in a company minute, represented the cancellation of the old contract and the formation of a new agreement of which the restrictive covenant no longer formed a part.

The reason given was that a second agreement which is inconsistent with an earlier agreement abrogates the whole of the earlier agreement and not merely the inconsistent terms.[2] This was a point of construction of documents; the matter could as well have been based upon the fact that one appointment had been terminated and replaced by an inferior post.

It has been pointed out that it was at one stage thought that the distinction between variation and rescission plus replacement might be material for the purposes of the concept of dismissal in the Redundancy Payments Act 1965 in that a rescission and replacement might constitute a dismissal where a mere variation would not.[3]

In *Marriott v. Oxford & District Co-operative Society Ltd.* (No. 2) the Divisional Court,[4] regarding the distinction as relevant to their decision, took a very narrow view of the circumstances in which there could be said to be a rescission and a new contract rather than a variation. Lord Parker C.J. indicated that a change in terms amounted to a rescission and replacement of the contract only if it constituted so fundamental a variation that nobody could claim that the original contract was still in being.[5]

---

[1] [1965] 1 WLR 629.   [2] Stamp J., ibid. at 636 G–637 B.
[3] See above, pp. 67–68.
[4] [1969] 1 WLR 254 (reversed on other grounds by CA [1970] 1 QB 186).
[5] Ibid. at 259 C–D.

The Tribunal could not be said to have erred in law in holding that the demotion from foreman to supervisor and the reduction of £1 per week was not so fundamental a change. This reasoning was potentially dangerous to many claims for redundancy payments, though it would now seem not to be a relevant issue in those claims nor in claims for unfair dismissal.

It is suggested that decided cases have thus signally failed to agree upon a test for rescission and replacement of the contract of employment and have, furthermore, failed to indicate whether the courts should take a wide or a narrow view of the application of that concept. There is neither a ruling principle nor a guiding presumption. This difficulty can best be resolved if it is once realized that the real problem is the identification of the job. The Court of Appeal in *Meek* v. *Port of London* (above) held, in effect, that if a promotion constituted a change from one job to a better job, then, but only then, it represented the cancellation and replacement of the contract of employment. The Divisional Court in *Marriott* v. *Oxford & District Co-operative Society Ltd.* (No. 2) were surely wrong in holding that the demotion and consequential reduction in wages did not amount to the disappearance of one job and its replacement by a different and inferior post.

This distinction between variation and rescission and replacement is necessarily an amorphous and meaningless one if it is defined only by reference to general contractual principles. To the limited extent to which it can serve a useful purpose, the distinction needs to be related to the particular context of the employment relationship, and to be applied in terms of the identifying features of the particular job concerned.[1] The effect upon the transmission of contractual terms from one period of employment to the next will then be this. If the change in terms and conditions of employment is not great enough to have changed the whole nature of the employment concerned, any terms not specifically varied will automatically remain in being and in force. If, on the other hand, the whole nature of the employment has been changed, none of the previous terms of the contract retain their effect automatically; they do so only to the extent that they are expressed or implied in the new contract of employment which is taken to have been formed.

---

[1] *Chapman* v. *Goonvean and Rostowrack China Clay Co. Ltd.* [1973] ICR 310 shows a similar need to isolate the identifying features of the particular job in relation to the statutory concept of redundancy. Cf. *Johnson* v. *Nottinghamshire Combined Police Authority* [1974] ICR 170.

Chapter Three

SUSPENSION

INTRODUCTION

It is a matter of great practical importance that there should be clear rules of law concerning the duration of contracts of employment. For example—and this is less obvious than it might seem—a dismissal giving rise to the statutory rights to redundancy payment or to remedies for unfairness can occur only where there is a subsisting contract of employment at the time.[1] The main problem in formulating the clear rules lies in the need to distinguish between the situation where no contract of employment is in force and the situation where a contract subsists but in a suspended condition. Certain situations arise in the course of the employment relationship in which it can be said that the employment has been suspended. In these situations, there is a period during which there is a subsisting employment relationship, but the employee does not work and is not paid. Examples are periods of disciplinary suspension without pay; periods during which the employee is laid off by the employer because there is no work for him to do; periods of holiday[2]; periods of strike or lock-out; and periods during which the employee is absent as the result of sickness. We are here concerned with the analysis of those situations in contractual terms.

We may define the suspension of the *contract* of employment as that state of affairs which exists while there is a contract in force between the employer and the employee, but while there is neither work being done in pursuance of it, nor remuneration being paid.[3]

---

[1] Cf. *Puttick* v. *John Wright & Sons (Blackwall) Ltd.* [1973] ICR 457.

[2] Although holidays present the same kind of problem as the other instances of suspension, there is little or no legal authority concerning their effect in contractual terms. But compare the Commissioners' Decisions on termination and suspension of employment during holidays for the purposes of National Insurance Unemployment Benefit regulations; see especially R(U) 2/51; 20/51; 12/54; 1/62; 1/66; 2/66; 4/67; 8/68; 6/70.

[3] Cf. Hilary Magnus Q.C., Commissioner, in R(U) 11/72 at para. 24, speaking of suspension of employment by reason of a work-sharing agreement: 'What is in contemplation is a situation in which, by an act of the employer—albeit with the workman's consent—the workman is exceptionally and temporarily

Certain features of this concept should be especially noted. Firstly, suspension of the contract, as so defined, does not include a case in which no work is being done but in which remuneration continues to be paid. The contract would not be said to be suspended, in the sense in which that term is here used, during a period of paid holiday or paid sick leave. Contractual suspension connotes a period during which the employee is not in receipt of earnings and not entitled to earnings. Secondly, the contract of employment may be said to be suspended despite the fact that one or other party is in breach of contract by virtue of the suspension. For the contract is suspended in the sense here used whenever work is not being done and remuneration is not becoming due under the contract. The non-performance of work may be in breach of contract; hence, for example, it will be seen that a contract of employment may be suspended during a strike although the strike is a breach of contract on the part of the employee. It is possible, however, that this reasoning cannot be reversed; for it may be that, where no work takes place and the employer is none the less bound to pay remuneration but wrongfully withholds that remuneration, the employee may, rather than claiming damages, be able to claim the remuneration withheld, as a money debt *in specie*.[1] The correctness of this view is further examined in the course of this chapter[2]; but if it is right, then it follows that there can, strictly speaking, be no wrongful suspension of the contract of employment by the employer. If he purports wrongfully to suspend the contract, he can be obliged to pay wages as such, and there is then no true suspension of the contract at all. But the employee, on the other hand, cannot be specifically compelled to work; and, to that extent, the suspension of the contract of employment is a wider concept than the right to suspend the contract of employment.

Thirdly, suspension of the contract of employment is a narrower concept than suspension of the employment relationship. It is possible to say that the employment relationship subsists in certain cases in which the *contract* of employment has been terminated

---

relieved of his normal contractual obligation to work, and the employer is exceptionally and temporarily relieved of his normal contractual obligation to pay wages.'
[1] *Warburton* v. *Taff Vale Railway Co.* (1902) 18 TLR 420; and cf. Lush J. in *Hanley* v. *Pease & Partners Ltd.* [1915] 1 KB 698 at 705.
[2] See below, pp. 85–6, 92.

outright.[1] For example, it will be seen that there are instances of casual or intermittent employment in trades such as ship-repairing, where it can properly be said that the relationship of employment subsists between periods of actual work, but where the contractual relationship subsists only during the periods of actual work. The existence of an employment relationship at a particular time does not necessarily mean that there is a contract of employment in force at that time, as will be illustrated in the course of the succeeding discussion of the various cases of contractual suspension.

These comments upon the definition of suspension of the contract of employment enable us to identify the issues concerning contractual suspension. For in the course of defining the concept, it emerges that the law concerning contractual suspension must be considered in two stages:

(a) In what circumstances has one or other party a *right* to suspend the contract of employment; or in what circumstances is there a *lawful* suspension by subsequent agreement?

(b) How do we distinguish between those periods when there is a contract of employment in force, and those periods in which there is no subsisting contract, although there may still be an employment relationship?

In this chapter, these two issues are explored in relation to the main types of situation in which employment may be suspended. The types of situation to be considered are, in the following order:

(a) those in which the suspension of employment is a sanction imposed by the employer upon an individual; i.e. disciplinary suspension;

(b) those in which the employer suspends the employment because work cannot be made available or because it is not profitable to make work available; i.e. lay-off as the result of the unavailability of work:

---

[1] Cf. Mr. J. S. Watson, Commissioner in R(U) 4/67, 'I appreciate the force of the view that the word "employment" [National Insurance Act 1965 s.114(1)] does not refer exclusively and solely to the contract of service but embraces some wider conception of the relationship of employer and employee which may include some understanding or intention on the part of both that, although all legal obligations of a contract of service have been brought to an end, such termination is of a temporary nature, both parties fully intending to resume the contract of service when convenient such as after a period of holiday or other break in the employment.'

(c) those in which suspension of employment is imposed, usually by the employee, in the course of industrial action; i.e. strikes and lock-outs;

(d) those in which suspension results from the enforced unavailability of the employee for work; i.e. absence of the employee as the result of sickness or other incapacity.

SECTION 1: DISCIPLINARY SUSPENSION

A. The Extent of the Employer's Right of Disciplinary Suspension

The factual context in which the law concerning disciplinary suspension operates is indicated by the *Report of the National Joint Advisory Council on Dismissal Procedures*,[1] where the results are recorded of a research study conducted by Plumridge.[2]

It was disclosed that '29 of the 50 firms [who submitted information] used disciplinary suspension as a penalty less serious than dismissal but more so than a warning or reprimand. It was used frequently in some of those firms, in others only occasionally. In 20, the maximum was three days' suspension, but in others suspensions of 10–14 days had been imposed and there were isolated examples of three and four weeks' suspension. Within trade unions, differing attitudes [were found] towards this penalty, but not one shop steward in factories which used suspension wished to do away with it.'[3]

We begin by examining the extent to which this practice receives legal recognition.

The common law declares that a term entitling the employer to suspend the employment for disciplinary reasons will not be implied in the contract of employment in the absence of special evidence to support it. Indeed, in *Warburton* v. *Taff Vale Railway Co.*[4] it was held that where the rules of a railway company entitled the company to punish its servants by immediate dismissal *or* suspension, it was wrongful on the part of the company to suspend an employee for two weeks before dismissing him. This suggests that if an employer wishes to reserve the right to suspend employees during the course of a disciplinary procedure which may result in their ultimate dis-

---

[1] (H.M.S.O., 1967).

[2] A short account of which is given by its author in the journal Personnel Management September 1966 pp. 135 ff.

[3] *NJAC Report* at para. 30(c).   [4] (1902) 18 TLR 42 C.

missal, he must do so by an express term for that purpose. It is established, however, that where an employer is entitled to 'suspend' an employee, that includes a right to withhold wages as well as work. That was decided in *Wallwork* v. *Fielding*[1] in relation to a statutory power conferred upon a Watch Committee to suspend police officers, and Warrington L.J. commented, 'It would be a most extraordinary thing if suspension (assuming that there is power to effect suspension) were to be so one-sided that the servant were to be excused from performing his part of the contract while the employer was to remain liable to perform his.'[2] This reasoning may be criticized in that it may well be a serious punishment, especially for a professional employee, to be suspended from work on full pay, so that the courts should not assume as a matter of course that a right to withhold remuneration is included in an express provision for disciplinary suspension.

Although the common law does not provide for an implied right of disciplinary suspension, a suspension of employment may be lawful other than by virtue of a term in the original contract; it may be lawful by reason of an agreement reached subsequently to the original contract. Just as it was seen in earlier pages that a variation may be effective either by reason of provision in the original contract or by virtue of subsequent agreement, so a suspension of employment may avoid being a breach of contract in either of these two ways. That a suspension of employment may gain a lawful status upon the basis of agreement subsequent to the making of the original contract is indicated by the dissenting judgment of Du Parcq L.J. in the difficult case of *Marshall* v. *English Electric Ltd.*[3] The issue was whether a practice of disciplinary suspension which had for a long time existed at the factory of the respondents was permissible under the Essential Work Order[4] which allowed disciplinary suspension in scheduled undertakings where, but only where, suspension was 'in accordance with the conditions of . . . service'. It was held by a majority that this practice of suspension was permissible within the terms of that provision; but the implications of the decision are obscure because the judges differed from each other both on the legal nature of disciplinary suspension and on the meaning of 'conditions of service' in the Order. Lord Goddard C.J. held that the suspension took the

---

[1] [1922] 2 KB 66.   [2] Ibid. at p. 75.
[3] [1945] 1 All ER 653 at 657 F ff.
[4] Essential Work (General Provisions) (No. 2) Order 1942 (SR & O 1942 No. 1594) Art. 4(3).

form of dismissal coupled with a promise to re-engage, and that the practice of such dismissals and re-engagements could be regarded as a condition of service.[1]

Mackinnon L.J. reached the same decision by the different route of holding that there was an implied term in the original contract which provided for suspension and which was clearly a condition of service.[2] Du Parcq L.J. dissented on the ground that the practice was for suspension by *ad hoc* agreement, and that as such it could not be described as a 'condition of service' because that term connotes only that which is a right or obligation under the original contract and not that which is lawful only by reason of subsequent agreement. Thus he commented:

'The master's right to offer [the workman] the alternative of suspension, and the workman's right to accept or refuse the offer at his own pleasure form no part of the conditions of the service. Any contract may be varied by agreement between the parties, not because there is an implied term in the contract under which they are empowered to vary it, but because the parties remain free to make what new bargain they please.'[3]

This shows how, in cases where there cannot be said to be a right of suspension in the original contract of employment, a practice of suspension may still be treated as lawful by reason of agreements to suspend reached on each occasion. However, a practice of suspension should not be too readily justified in that way; there ought to be some evidence of a genuine consent on the part of the employees concerned.[4] In that case, the consent of the employees was in a sense deduced from the fact that they were liable to dismissal upon an hour's notice in any event, and to that extent had little to lose by suspension. It being the case today that employees generally have a greater contractual security of tenure, an *ad hoc* consent to suspension should not be too lightly imputed to them.

B. *Disciplinary Suspension and the Termination of the Contract*

The cases therefore show the circumstances in which a disciplinary suspension of employment may be lawful, either by virtue of provision in the original contract or by virtue of subsequent agreement.

---

[1] [1945] 1 All ER 653 at 656 E–H.   [2] Ibid. at 656 F–657 B.
[3] Ibid. at 658 A.
[4] Cf. *Powell Duffryn Wagon Co. Ltd.* v. *House* [1974] ICR 123 where the issue was whether the employees had genuinely agreed to the suspension of a guaranteed weekly wage arrangement.

However, they leave some room for doubt as to whether and when a lawful suspension of an employment operates as a termination of the contract of employment. It seems clear that if the suspension represents the exercise of a right conferred upon the employer by the provisions of the original contract, then it operates to suspend the contract rather than to terminate it. This is surely the proper role of contractual provisions for suspension, because the suspension then operates as a disciplinary sanction which leaves the contractual nexus intact and therefore does not impinge upon those incidental rights of the employee which depend upon the continuity of his contractual service. This view, that suspension of employment under a term in the original contract operates as a suspension of the contract rather than a termination of it, is supported by dicta in *Hanley* v. *Pease & Partners Ltd.* where Lush J. spoke of 'suspending' as meaning refusing to pay the employee for a given day without dismissing him, and electing to treat the contract as a continuing one (something which they had no right to do in this case).[1] Rowlatt J. referred to 'the implied power to punish the workman by suspending him for a certain period of his employment, the contract subsisting all the time',[2] and Atkin J. spoke of the 'power to suspend the contract in the sense which really means the fining of the employee in the sum of one day's wages for his previous default'.[3]

Similarly in *Wallwork* v. *Fielding*. Lord Sterndale M.R. ruled that a power of disciplinary suspension had the result that the contract was suspended with regard to its performance by both sides,[4] and Warrington L.J. commented that 'suspension suspends for the time being the contractual relation between the parties on both sides'[5]— without, apparently, terminating the contract itself. The same result seems to follow from the analysis by Scott L.J. in *Bird* v. *British Celanese Ltd.*[6] of the operation of a clause in a contract of employment which provided for disciplinary suspension. He remarked that 'The clause operates in accordance with its terms; the whole contract is suspended, in the sense that the operation of the mutual obligations of both parties is suspended; the workman ceases to be under any present duty to work, and the employer ceases to be under any

---

[1] [1915] 1 KB 698 at 704, 705. [2] Ibid. at 706.
[3] Ibid. at 706. [4] [1922] 2 KB 66 at 72. [5] Ibid. at 75.
[6] [1945] 1 KB 336. The contractual term in question was one whereby the employers were entitled 'temporarily to suspend the workman from his employment', the wording of the recognized practice being 'if he was guilty of misconduct or breach of duty or breach of an order'.

consequential duty to pay'; and that in this case the operation of the clause 'enabled the workman, when the suspension ended, to claim as of right to continue in his old job'.[1] Hence it was clearly his view that the contractual nexus survived unbroken throughout the suspension, in the shape of mutual contractual rights to a resumption of employment after the suspension.

Somewhat more doubtful is the position where suspension is lawful by reason of an *ad hoc* agreement rather than by virtue of a power in the original contract. In *Marshall* v. *English Electric Co. Ltd.*[2] Lord Goddard appeared to take the view that suspension of this kind involved a termination of the contract of employment. He said, 'In my opinion what is called suspension is in truth dismissal with an intimation that at the end of so many days, or it may be hours, the man will be re-employed if he chooses to apply for reinstatement', and later he described the practice as one of 'dismissal mitigated at the discretion of the employer by a promise to re-employ'.[3] Nor was Du Parcq L.J. convinced that there was any meaningful distinction between this type of suspension and summary dismissal with an offer of new employment.[4] Therefore this case provides no clear-cut answer to the question whether a suspension of this kind results in a severance of the contractual nexus. For if the employer 'dismisses with a promise to re-employ', and if the employee can be treated as having made a corresponding promise to return to work, then there is a contract of some kind in force during the suspension. If, on the other hand, the employer dismisses with a mere intimation of intention to re-employ or leaves open an offer to re-employ, then there is no standing contract in the suspension period.

It is hardly surprising that there was no final determination of this question in that decision, because the fact that the contract of employment was terminable upon an hour's notice on either side made it difficult to determine whether it had actually been terminated or not, and also because the employers did not in practice treat short periods of disciplinary suspension as affecting the question whether they would ultimately allow a pension to the employee concerned. Now that the normal pattern of manual employment in industry results in a legal entitlement on the part of the employee to greater security of tenure than formerly, and to incidental rights which may depend upon the preservation of continuity of contract, the issue may

---

[1] Ibid. at 341.   [2] [1945] 1 All ER 653.   [3] Ibid. at 655 E–F, F–G.
[4] Ibid. at 658 E-F.

be one of greater consequence; and it would be preferable if the contractual nexus were regarded as remaining unbroken during disciplinary suspension, even where that suspension is the result of an *ad hoc* acceptance by the employee of 'a merciful substitute for the procedure of dismissal, and a possible re-engagement'.[1]

If the employer purports to impose a period of disciplinary suspension upon the employee, and his doing so constitutes a breach of contract, then it would seem that the contract of employment is not *ipso facto* terminated. There will have been a wrongful repudiation of the contract which will entitle the employee to treat the contract as terminated if he so wishes; but if he does not so terminate the contract, then it will continue in force.[2] It would seem indeed that in a case where a disciplinary suspension is a wrongful act on the part of the employer the employee may be able to recover remuneration *in specie* for the period of suspension, and so produce the result that there has been no true suspension of the contract at all—for suspension of the contract connotes a period during which remuneration is not payable as well as one during which work is not done. Thus in *Warburton* v. *Taff Vale Railway Co.*[3] it was held, where the employee had been subjected to a wrongful disciplinary suspension, that he could recover his wages as such for the period of two weeks which was concerned. And in *Hanley* v. *Pease & Partners Ltd.*, where the employee claimed a sum equal to the wages for the day during which he had been wrongfully suspended, Lush J. commented that it was unnecessary to determine whether it was a claim for wages or for damages.[4]

However, it is suggested that a claim for wages *in specie* in respect of wrongful suspension may not be available to all employees. It may well be that in the case, for example, of hourly-paid employees and piece-rate workers, the earning of remuneration is conditional upon the actual doing of the work concerned, so that a wrongful suspension will be effective to the extent of preventing wages from being earned.[5] It will be seen in later pages that it is clear that re-

---

[1] Scott L.J. in *Bird* v. *British Celanese Ltd.* [1945] 1 KB 336 at 341.

[2] Cf. Sir Robert Micklethwait Q.C., Chief Commissioner in R(U) 11/72 at para. 17: 'We think it well arguable that there can be suspension by the employer where he lays off the employee in fact even though he has no legal right to do so. In such a case the employee could treat the suspension as a repudiation of the contract and refuse to be employed further, in which event there would be a termination of the employment.'

[3] (1902) 18 TLR 420.　　　　　　　　[4] [1915] 1 KB 698 at 705.

[5] But see Hepple & O'Higgins, *Encyclopedia of Labour Relations Law* at

muneration does not accrue after an outright wrongful dismissal;[1] but it is not at all clear how far it may be said that remuneration will accrue to the employee when he is wrongfully prevented from working during the continuance of the relationship. Upon this depends the question whether a wrongful suspension of employment results in a suspension of the contract of employment at all, or whether, by virtue of the remedies available to the employee, the contract continues in full operation save for the non-performance of work.

SECTION 2: LAY-OFF

Pursuing the distinction between the two issues of

(a) the extent of the right to suspend the employment relationship, and
(b) the question whether the suspension of employment results in a termination of the contract of employment,

we shall consider firstly the extent of the employer's right to subject the employee to temporary lay-off as the result of unavailability of work. The relevant matters are the rules of common law concerning the circumstances in which such a right may be an implied term of the contract or in which a suspension of this kind may be lawful by virtue of an *ad hoc* agreement; and the practice of guaranteed week agreements as modifying the common-law position. Secondly, the question of whether lay-off results in a termination of the contract of employment is examined; and, thirdly, special reference is made to the provisions of the Redundancy Payments Act 1965 which deal with lay-off and short-time.

A. The Employer's Right of Lay-off at Common Law

The entitlement of the employer to suspend employment by reason of the unavailability of work is a special aspect of the general question, what is the extent of the employer's obligation to provide work. That general question was examined in an earlier chapter as part of an inquiry into the nature of the cause of action for wrongful dismissal.[2] It was there argued that the contract of employment

---

p. 1092 note 33 and corresponding text, where it is argued that a custom to this effect might be challenged as unreasonable.

[1] See below, pp. 294–5. [2] See above, pp. 23–4.

necessarily imposes upon the employer some degree of obligation to maintain the employment relationship. We now consider those authorities which deal with the more particular question of temporary lay-off. The cases decided during the nineteenth century in which it was recognized that the employer necessarily comes under some kind of obligation to provide work, such that remuneration may be earned, nevertheless recognized that a wide prerogative to suspend employment could properly be implied, and that the existence of a wide power of suspension was not repugnant to the concept of a binding contract of employment. Thus in *Pilkington* v. *Scott* (1846)[1] it was held that the contract of employment of a glass-blower could not be regarded as void for want of mutuality by virtue merely of the fact that it entitled the employer to pay the employee 'a moiety of his wages during any depression of trade'. It was shown by *R.* v. *Welch*[2] that the courts would imply an even wider prerogative of reduction of work and earnings than was expressly reserved in the *Pilkington* case. It was there argued that the contract of employment of a piece-rate tin-plate worker was void for want of mutuality in that there was no express obligation upon the employer to provide any minimum amount of work. This argument was rejected on the ground that the employer was subject to an implied obligation to provide some amount of work; but Lord Campbell C.J. defined that obligation as one of finding 'reasonable employment according to the state of the trade'[3], thus recognizing the entitlement of the employer to reduce or suspend work during times of trade depression.

When a similar argument was raised in *Re Bailey*, *Re Collier*,[4] Lord Campbell C.J. offered a formulation of the implied obligation to provide work for a piece-rate coal-miner which probably allowed the employer an equally wide prerogative to suspend work. He

[1] 15 M & W 657. A similar argument of voidness for want of mutuality was raised in *Hartley* v. *Cummings* (1847) 5 CB 247, another case concerning a glass-blower, but the contract in that case did not give the employer a wide right of lay-off; on the contrary, it obliged the employer to provide alternative work when the specified work was not available, and it provided for a guaranteed minimum weekly wage during periods when the furnace was out. The argument of want of mutuality failed on this and other grounds.

[2] (1853) 2 E & B 357. (This was a prosecution of an employee under the Master and Servant Act 1823, where the magistrates held there was no contract of employment in force, and their refusal of jurisdiction was reviewed by the Court of Queen's Bench at the instance of the prosecuting employer.)

[3] Ibid. at p. 362.   [4] (1854) 3 E & B 607.

commented that '[T]here was an obligation on the part of the
employer, not merely to find them work day by day, but an obligation to continue the relation of master and servant; so that, if the
master causelessly refused to give the servant work whilst the
colliery was open, he would have broken his contract.'[1] This indicates a right on the part of the employer at least to suspend working
by imposing a temporary shut-down of the mine—perhaps by virtue
merely of bad trading conditions. An opinion of the same kind was
expressed by Crompton J. in *Whittle* v. *Frankland* (1862)[2] where he
suggested that the implied obligation to employ a piece-working
coal-miner was to find 'a reasonable amount of work if work is to
be had', or to provide work 'to a reasonable extent under surrounding circumstances'.[3] These formulae clearly allowed for lay-off by
reason of slackness in trade. It is not surprising to find that, in 1872,
there could be no objection on the ground of want of mutuality to
a contract which entitled an employer to lay off a furnaceman in the
event of 'unforeseen accident'.[4] However, it is regrettable that the
courts should, in 1899, have held that there was no want of mutuality,
and no unreasonable restraint of trade, in a contract which bound a
daily-rated glass-worker to work only for the one employer, while
obliging that employer only to give him a share of work equal to
that of other employees similarly employed, and therefore conferring
upon him an unlimited power to put the employee upon short-time
or to lay him off.[5]

The implied right of the employer to lay the employee off was
greatly limited by the decision of the Court of Appeal in *Devonald*
v. *Rosser & Sons*[6] which concerned the employment of piece-rate
workers in the tin-plate trade, and where it was held that, although
a custom of suspension in the events of breakage of machinery,
repairs, and failure of water or coal was a valid term of the contract
of employment,[7] nevertheless an alleged custom whereby the
employers were entitled to suspend for want of remunerative orders
for their products could not form part of the contract, because it
was not reasonable and would create an unacceptable element of

---

[1] Ibid. at pp. 618–19.   [2] 31 LJ (NS) MC 81.
[3] At p. 84 (*arguendo*). These dicta are not reported in the authorized report
2 B & S 49, which selects different passages from the arguments of counsel.
[4] *Thomas* v. *Vivian* 37 JP 228; see Cockburn C.J. at 229.
[5] *Phillips* v. *Stevens* 15 TLR 325.   [6] [1906] 2 KB 728.
[7] See Jelf J. at first instance—ibid. at 734.

uncertainty in the contract.[1] On the other hand, the decision in *Browning* v. *Crumlin Valley Collieries Ltd.*[2] affirmed an implied right upon the part of colliery employers to suspend the contracts of employment of coal-miners during a period of repairs required to put the mine into a safe condition. The period concerned was five weeks, and there was a further period of partial stoppage during which the employees were selectively employed. Very serious criticisms may be made of the decision. Firstly, the employers had not in fact suspended the employment of the miners concerned. It had been necessary for the men to go on strike in order to compel the employers to fulfil their obligations in respect of the safety of the mine. In these circumstances, the employers should not have been heard to allege, in effect, a right to suspend working in the interests of safety. Secondly, the decision of Greer J. was based upon the view that the dangerous condition of the mine was not the fault of the employers,[3] and that the risk of resulting loss of earnings was not one which it was intended that they should bear.[4] However, the facts of the case disclose that the unsafe condition of the mine was the result of movements of mineral strata which had required careful watching for many years, and which the employers had for a long time been attempting to counteract by inserting concrete girders. The finding of the judge might be compared to a hypothetical finding that the owner of a factory was not responsible to his employees for the shut-down of a building where the roof collapsed as the result of the gradual and perceptible erosion of the fabric by wind and rain. It is suggested that even if there can properly be implied into contracts of employment a term entitling the employer to suspend the employment in the event of a shut-down caused by the sudden and unforeseeable operation of *force majeure*, such a term should not lightly be extended to relieve the employer of the risk of having to pay wages during a period of repairs of more routine occurrence.

More recently, and on the basis of a full and careful examination of existing authorities, an Industrial Tribunal suggested that the implied right of the employer to lay the employee off should be regarded as limited according to the method of calculation of remuneration of the employee concerned.[5] Their view was that there

---

[1] Lord Alverstone C.J., ibid. at 741, Sir Gorell Barnes P. at 742, Farwell L.J. at 743.
[2] [1926] 1 KB 522.   [3] Ibid. at 527.   [4] Ibid. at 529.
[5] *Jones* v. *Harry Sherman Ltd.* (1969) 4 ITR 63.

could be no implied term for suspension as the result of unavailability of work in the case of an employee who was paid fixed remuneration calculated by the week or by a longer period. In other words, a right of suspension could be implied only in the case of employees whose wages were calculated on a daily or hourly basis, or by the piece, and who did not have a guaranteed minimum weekly wage. The Tribunal was at some pains to establish that the decision in *Browning* v. *Crumlin Valley Collieries Ltd.*[1] was not inconsistent with this view, and maintained that the pleadings in the case showed that the miners there were paid at a daily rate and that a minimum wage was guaranteed only to the extent of an arrangement which was itself dependent upon the number of shifts actually worked. The case before the Tribunal concerned the manager of a betting shop, who was paid a fixed weekly wage, and whose employers asserted a power to lay him off during a period in which horse-racing was cancelled by reason of a foot-and-mouth epidemic. It was held that the employers had no such power, and that the suspension was therefore a repudiatory breach of contract, which the employee was entitled to treat as a dismissal within Section 3(1)(c) of the 1965 Act. It is suggested that the Tribunal were correct in the view that a power of suspension by reason of unavailability of work is more likely to be inconsistent with the terms of employment of an employee who is paid a fixed wage calculated at weekly or longer intervals, than with those of an employee whose wages vary according to the amount of work done within a week. On the other hand, a right of suspension should not be readily implied in the latter type of case. The principle of *Devonald* v. *Rosser & Sons* should be strictly implemented, and the decision in *Browning* v. *Crumlin Valley Collieries Ltd.*, in so far as it is supportable at all, should be strictly confined.

More recently still in *Puttick* v. *John Wright & Sons (Blackwall) Ltd.*[2] the Industrial Court threw the law concerning lay-off into some confusion by recognizing that there could be, and that in the case before them there was, a contract of employment giving the employer an unlimited right to lay the employee off for periods when no work was available. The employee concerned was a boiler scaler and a casual worker of the kind known in the docks as a 'royal' or 'regular' employee. He would be notified by the employer's

---

[1] [1926] 1 KB 522 (above).
[2] [1972] ICR 457. See above, p. 24, note 4.

foreman the day before work on a job was due to start and laid off between jobs. He had been thus intermittently employed since 1948. By holding that a contract of employment subsisted during these periods of working and lay-off alike, the court seemed to disregard the argument based upon mutuality of contractual obligations. The employer's agreement to make available to the employee 'such work of that particular kind as from time to time comes to hand'[1] is a minimal obligation if the employer is in the nature of things the sole judge of what work is to be made available. It was a retrograde step to decide that any contract of employment could grant an unfettered discretion of this kind.

Thus far we have been considering rights of lay-off embodied in the main contract of employment. A suspension of employment by reason of the unavailability of work may be lawful other than by virtue of an implied term in the original contract. For example, the suspension of employment may take the form of the termination of the contract of employment by proper notice. And where it is neither the exercise of a right to suspend conferred by the original contract, nor a proper termination of the contract, it has been suggested that it may be lawful by virtue of a waiver by the employee of his rights to treat the contract of employment as repudiated, or to sue for damages for breach of contract. This analysis was advanced by Tillyard, writing in 1923,[2] at a time when suspension by reason of unavailability of work was a matter of very common occurrence in the engineering industry. By reason of the practice, widespread at that time, whereby workmen were employed upon terms of dismissal at very short notice or with no notice, it was difficult to distinguish between the termination and the suspension of the contract of employment, but Tillyard cites, in support of this analysis, a contemporary judgment of Atkin J. concerning the suspension of a munitions worker. Atkin J.[3] there held that the suspension of a munitions worker for a period of a week, on a system whereby suspension went in rotation among a body of employees, could not be regarded as an actionable breach of contract by the employer, the reason being that the employees concerned had acquiesced in it, and had not complained until two or

---

[1] Ibid. at 461 G–H (Lord Thomson).

[2] *The Worker and the State* (London 1923) pp. 14–17.

[3] The case is not named by Tillyard and this writer has been unable to discover any report of it; but the judgment is reproduced verbatim in Tillyard's text at 14–17.

three weeks after the suspension. It is suggested that, although the analysis in terms of waiver of the right to rescind and waiver of breach is necessary as a rationalization of that which occurs when the employee has accepted a period of suspension without protest, such acquiescence should not be too lightly attributed to an employee in such a way as to disentitle him from challenging the employer's right to such suspension.[1]

It should be added that where there is a wrongful suspension of this kind for which the employee is entitled to a remedy, it would seem that, as in the case of wrongful disciplinary suspension, the employee can probably create a situation in which there has been no true suspension of employment at all, by claiming wages *in specie* for the period concerned. Thus Atkin J., in the decision reported by Tillyard,[2] regarded the claim for wages as a valid alternative to the claim for damages for wrongful suspension, and Greer J. appears to have taken the same view in *Browning* v. *Crumlin Valley Collieries Ltd.*[3] The point is one of some theoretical interest.

B. The Effect of Provisions for Guaranteed Pay

Suspension of employment and short-time working by reason of the unavailability of work are of particular importance in relation to hourly-paid and piece-rate employees. For employees who are paid a remuneration calculated on a weekly or monthly basis are normally protected against short-term suspension or short-time working in that their remuneration will not generally be affected by the fact that work is not available for them. The hourly-paid and piece-rate employees who are liable to be affected by unavailability of work are, however, very often protected by guaranteed pay arrangements. These are, in essence, arrangements whereby the employee is entitled to a minimum weekly wage on the basis of his availability for work, and irrespective of the fact that actual work is not available. Such arrangements, where they exist, express the limitations upon the

---

[1] Cf. *Powell Duffryn Wagon Co. Ltd.* v. *House* [1974] ICR 123 concerning the suspension, by agreement, of a guaranteed weekly wage arrangement. See below, pp. 95–6.

[2] Op. cit., pp. 14–17 (above).

[3] [1926] 1 KB 522 at 530. The point did not arise in *Devonald* v. *Rosser & Sons* [1906] 2 KB 728 (above) where the claim was for damages alone. The NIRC in *Langston* v. *AUEW* (No. 2) would allow no blurring of this conceptual distinction: 'These additional sums are not wages or premium payments. They are damages for breach of contract by failing to allow him the opportunity of earning a like amount.' [1974] ICR 510, 522 G–H (Sir John Donaldson).

employer's right to suspend the employee, or to put him on short time by reason of the unavailability of work. Hence these arrangements must be studied together with the common-law rules concerning such suspension which were considered above.

The origins of a widespread practice of making guaranteed wage arrangements are to be found in the guaranteed wage provisions made by Essential Work Orders during the Second World War. The principal Essential Work Order[1] provided in Article 4 that there should be payable to persons employed in scheduled undertakings a minimum wage equal to the wage for normal working hours provided that the employee concerned was, during the normal working hours:

(i) capable of and available for work; and

(ii) 'willing to perform any services outside his usual occupation which in the circumstances he could reasonably be asked to perform during any period when work was not available for him in his usual occupation in the undertaking'.

Hence the employee was entitled to a guaranteed wage irrespective of the unavailability of actual work, provided that he was prepared to display reasonable occupational mobility.

This pattern of guaranteed wage provision has been reproduced, with variations, in a wide range of collective agreements. A report on guaranteed pay published in 1967[2] recorded that 'Guaranteed pay matters most in industries such as building and construction, because of the weather; for dock workers because of the casual nature, until recently,[3] of their employment; and in a wide range of manufacturing industries. Almost all the latter, e.g. engineering, chemicals, mining and textiles, have guaranteed pay arrangements of one kind or another.' Guaranteed pay provisions are also often contained in wages regulation orders made by Wages Councils. The making of such provisions falls within the powers of Wages Councils by reason of the terms of Section 11(1) of the Wages Councils Act

---

[1] The Essential Work (General Provisions) (No. 2) Order 1942 (SR & O 1942 No. 1594). Some industries were dealt with by special Orders containing variations on points of detail from the general Order.

[2] 'Guaranteed Pay in a Changing Situation'—Report No. 24 (June 1967) of the journal 'Incomes Data'. For more recent information see Incomes Data Studies Nos. 20 (January 1972) and 22 (February 1972).

[3] The reference is to the decasualization scheme implemented by the Dock Workers (Regulation of Employment) (Amendment) Order 1967 (S.I. 1967 No. 1252).

1959, which are that '. . . [A]ny wages council shall have power to submit to the Minister proposals . . . (a) for fixing the remuneration to be paid, *either generally or for any particular work*, by their employers to all or any of the workers in relation to whom the council operates.' The guaranteed pay clauses in the orders made by Wages Councils generally follow the pattern of the arrangements made by collective agreements.[1] That is to say, they usually adopt a variant upon the Essential Work Order formula, and provide that the receipt of guaranteed pay shall be conditional upon the employee being capable of and available for work, and upon his being willing to perform such duties outside his normal occupation as the employer may reasonably require if his normal work is not available.

In relating these guaranteed pay arrangements to the common law concerning suspension by reason of the unavailability of work, one matter requires particular comment. There are certain limitations upon the circumstances in which guaranteed pay arrangements apply; and where the guarantees do not apply, the employer is, in effect, entitled to suspend the employment. We therefore consider the limitation clauses to be found in guaranteed pay provisions, whether made by collective agreement or by wage regulation order.

Guaranteed pay arrangements generally contain limitation clauses for two purposes; firstly, that of suspending the guarantee as a sanction against industrial action, and secondly, that of suspending it in the event of stoppages of work produced by *force majeure* of which the employers are not willing to assume the risk. Most guaranteed wage arrangements are expressed to cease to apply, or to apply only in modified form, when work ceases to be available as the result of industrial action. The scope of escape clauses of this kind is a very contentious matter as between employers and employed, raising problems comparable to that of deciding what is the proper scope of the provision for disqualification from unemployment benefit where unemployment results from industrial action.[2]

---

[1] A random example of a typical guaranteed pay clause in a Wages Council Order is to be found in Part VII of the Schedule to the Wages Regulation (Laundry) Order 1973 (S.I. 1973 No. 1883).

[2] At present contained in s. 22(1) of the National Insurance Act 1965 and extending to employees losing employment by reason of a stoppage of work due to a trade dispute at their place of employment who are participating in, or financing, or directly interested in the dispute, or who belong to a grade or class of workers, members of which, employed at the place of employment of the claimants, were, immediately before the stoppage, participating in or financing or directly interested in the dispute.

Where guaranteed pay arrangements provide for their suspension when work is unavailable other than by reason of industrial action, they generally distinguish between unforeseeable *force majeure* on the one hand, and trade recession on the other. Thus they sometimes provide that they shall not apply in the event of fire, flood, national emergency, or breakdown of machinery; occasionally they do not apply in respect of lost time caused by failure of fuel or power supplies, or shortage of supplies. But they are rarely liable to be suspended on the ground merely of shortage of orders; indeed, it would to a great extent defeat their very purpose if they could be so suspended.[1] Thus, although many of them contain an escape clause in general terms in the event of 'circumstances outside the employer's control', this is generally understood as referring to hazards other than trade recessions or supply shortages, and is sometimes expressly so defined. It may be said in general that, in the drafting of their escape clauses, guaranteed pay arrangements reproduce the distinction, which was observed in the common law concerning suspension,[2] between unavailability of work resulting from emergencies and *force majeure*, and that resulting from lack of demand and adverse trading conditions. They reproduce, in other words, the result of *Devonald* v. *Rosser & Sons*[3] on the one hand and of *Browning* v. *Crumlin Valley Collieries Ltd.*[4] on the other.

The parallel between the common law of suspension and the practice of guaranteed pay arrangements goes still further. For just as the common law recognizes the possibility that suspension may be lawful by reason of *ad hoc* agreement, so also guaranteed pay arrangements often provide for their own suspension by mutual consent, in order to deal with the situation where short-time working is agreed in place of redundancies. And even where such provision is not made, it is not uncommon for employees to be regarded as having waived their right to guaranteed pay on a particular occasion. This provides a rationalization for the practice of periods of suspension and short-time working, which is well established, for example, in the motor industry in spite of the existence of nationally agreed guaranteed pay arrangements. In the case of *Powell Duffryn*

---

[1] Cf. Sir John Donaldson in *Powell Duffryn Ltd.* v. *House*. '[W]e can see no point in a guaranteed fall back wage if it is not to be paid at the one time when it is needed, namely, where there is insufficient work to enable the employees to earn more on time rates.' [1974] ICR 123 at 125 G.

[2] See above, pp. 89–90.   [3] [1906] 2 KB 728 (above).

[4] [1926] 1 KB 522 (above).

Ltd. v. *House*,[1] the Industrial Court had to consider an alleged agreement to suspend a guaranteed pay arrangement, and held that cogent evidence would be required to support the conclusion that such an agreement had been made for more than a short period, there being 'no reason why employees should forego their alternative rights'.[2] Hence the Industrial Court has recognized that guaranteed wage agreements are a protection against lay-off which effectively restricts the employer's power to suspend the contract of employment for economic reasons.

C. *Suspension by Reason of the Unavailability of Work, and the Termination of the Contract*

Having hitherto examined the extent of the employer's right to suspend employment by reason of the unavailability of work, we go on to consider here the effect of such suspension upon the contract of employment—the issue being whether the contract of employment continues in force during the suspension, or whether, on the other hand, it is terminated as the result of the suspension of work. This is in fact a specific aspect of a general issue concerning the structure of the contract of employment. The general issue is, how far can a series of exchanges of work against remuneration be linked together to form a single continuing contract of employment, and what form of standing obligations must be present to create that link between the successive periods of employment.[3] The particular problem is how far that continuing contract is compatible with periods of lay-off, of indeterminate length and frequency, imposed at the instance of the employer. The small amount of case-law which deals with this question is to be found in a decision of the Industrial Court concerning entitlement to redundancy payment, and in decisions of the National Insurance Commissioners on the question of whether employment has been 'suspended' or terminated, upon which entitlement to six-day periods of earnings-related supplement to unemployment benefit has been held to depend.[4]

In the case of short-time working, that is to say suspension of employment for some days in each week, it will normally be fairly clear that the contract of employment subsists throughout. But where the periods of suspension are more prolonged, the question

---

[1] [1974] ICR 123.   [2] Ibid. at 127 H.   [3] Cf. above, pp. 19–21.
[4] See National Insurance Act 1966 s. 3(1)(b) as interpreted in Commissioner's Decision R(U) 7/68.

will become one of greater difficulty. And where the employment is in its nature susceptible to frequent and substantial periods of suspension, it may become extremely hard to decide whether the employment takes the form of a single subsisting contract or, on the other hand, a series of intermittent contracts covering only those periods during which the employee is actually working. Thus, for example, in their decision R(U) 7/68, in which they laid down the rule, above described,[1] concerning the interpretation of the 1966 Act, the National Insurance Commissioners considered the case of a printer's warehouseman who was employed as a 'casual casual' in an employment pool run by the union SOGAT, the system being that he was allocated to various employers for shift work for single nights as and when such work was available. They held that he had no subsisting contract in between jobs, and so was not entitled to earnings-related supplement in respect of the period between jobs. Their decision was a straightforward one, because this employee was assigned at random to a large number of employers, and so could hardly be regarded as under a continuing contract with any of them. But if this pattern of intermittent employment had existed in relation to a single employer, the issue would have been a very difficult one.

In R(U) 11/72 a Tribunal of Commissioners did in such a situation make a finding of continuity, but they did not deal directly with the question of whether that meant *contractual* continuity (which had been expressly declared to be the criterion in R(U) 7/68). This concerned a lighterman employed on the building of London Bridge. The employer, faced with a problem of surplus labour, entered into a work-sharing arrangement with a group of nine employees whereby six would work at any one time. For each man, short periods of work were followed by short periods off work; but the alternation was not systematically scheduled, the foreman being responsible for deciding who worked on any day and for so notifying the men. It was part of the arrangement that each man, at the start of a period of non-working days, should be given his National Insurance cards and was entitled to seek employment, dropping out of the scheme if successful. The Tribunal decided that employment was suspended and not terminated during the intervening periods; and they seem to have taken the view that the contract of employment subsisted throughout, with the employer exercising a contractual right to

[1] See text at p. 96 n. 4.

suspend work and remuneration. If this view of their decision is correct, that result may be attributable to the fairly high element of predictability of resumption of work under this particular arrangement.

In *Puttick* v. *John Wright & Sons Ltd.*[1] the Industrial Court, dealing specifically with the contractual issue, held that a contract of employment had remained continuously in force despite an almost unlimited right of lay-off on the part of the employer. The decision concerned a boiler scaler who had been intermittently employed by the same employers since 1948.[2] The court took the view that the employer had undertaken only to make available to the employee such work of the particular kind as from time to time might come to hand, and that the employee had agreed to be temporarily suspended or laid-off for such periods as no work was in fact available. In this sense there could be, and was, a continuing contract of employment subsisting during periods of lay-off—a necessary conclusion if the employee was to be entitled to redundancy payment when made redundant during such a period of lay-off. The court did not need to go, and should not have gone, to the further lengths of implying that there can be a continuing contract of employment even where the employer is under no obligation of any kind to provide work.[3] This would be wrong in principle but was unnecessary to their decision; for even upon their own stated view of the facts the employer was under some kind of continuing obligation to make work available—though admittedly it would be hard to envisage an employee suing successfully for the breach of so loosely conceived and subjective an undertaking. This is a matter which the courts may well need to analyse more fully in future.

D. Statutory Provisions concerning Lay-off and Short-time Working

We conclude this account of the contractual analysis of lay-off and short-time working by drawing attention to two sets of provisions in the statutes concerning termination of employment; provisions which are necessary in order to correct anomalies which would arise if the rights of employees in relation to lay-off and short-time had been left to depend upon the contractual analysis alone.

The first such anomaly would consist in the possibility that an employer faced with a surplus of labour could by means of temporary

---

[1] [1972] ICR 457.   [2] See above, pp. 90–1.
[3] [1972] ICR 457 at 461 H–462 B.

suspension deliberately avoid terminating his employees' contracts of employment in order to avoid the liabilities attaching to such termination. For obvious reasons, it was thought necessary to make special provision against this contingency in relation to redundancy payments. If the 1965 Act made no special provision concerning short-time and lay-off, the position would be as follows. Where the employer has no right to suspend the contract, the employee is entitled to terminate the contract in response to the wrongful suspension, and to claim a dismissal within the meaning of the Act.[1] But where the suspension is within the rights of the employer and where, as was shown to be commonly the case, it does not take the form of a termination of the contract of employment, there would be no dismissal within the meaning of the Act, nor would the employee cause there to have been a dismissal by terminating the contract himself. It would therefore have been possible for the application of the Act to be avoided by means of short-time working and lay-off. The Act accordingly made further provisions whereby the employee might become entitled to a redundancy payment by reason of short-time or lay-off, even where the short-time or the lay-off was within the contractual rights of the employer. This is the effect of Section 1(1)(b) of the Act, whilst Sections 5–7 define the concepts of lay-off and short-time for the purposes of the Act, and prescribe the procedure which the employee must follow to entitle himself to a redundancy payment on this basis. However, although the Redundancy Payments Act 1965 causes short-time or lay-off to be treated as equivalent to dismissal for the purposes of redundancy payments even where they are within the contractual rights of the employer, it makes such exacting procedural requirements for such claims that these provisions do not seem to be of great practical usefulness. Their interest consists in the pattern whereby a reduction in work can be converted into a termination of employment, for the purpose of protecting the employee against avoidance of statutory obligations by the employer.

The second difficulty which would have arisen if statutory rights connected with termination of employment had been based upon a purely contractual treatment of periods of lay-off would have been this: that the period of continuous employment which controls the extent of the statutory rights would have been liable to be

---

[1] e.g. *Jones* v. *Harry Sherman Ltd.* (1969) 4 ITR 63 (Indust. Trib.); *Powell Duffryn Wagon Co. Ltd.* v. *House* [1974] ICR 123.

interrupted by lay-off periods during which there was no contract of employment in force. Schedule 1 of what is now the Contracts of Employment Act 1972, which has been used as the basis for all the assessments of the period of continuous employment, departs from the purely contractual criterion for continuity, by making provision for the inclusion of certain periods during which there is no contract of employment in force. The problem of lay-off is resolved by the inclusion of periods where the employee is 'absent from work on account of a temporary cessation of work'.[1] The interpretation of this new statutory concept has given rise to case-law which has established some important principles.

The concept of temporary cessation of employment has resulted in the recognition of a subsisting employment relationship during intervals between employment in trades where employment is of its nature intermittent, and where there is probably no contract of employment in force during the intervals; most notably the ship-building and ship-repairing trades. The decision of the House of Lords in *Fitzgerald* v. *Hall, Russell Ltd.*[2] established that this concept applied when there was a cessation in the work of the particular employee, and that it was unnecessary that there should be a total cessation by the employer of the type of work concerned. It was established by the Court of Appeal in *Thompson* v. *Bristol Channel Ship Repairers Ltd.*[3] that there may be a subsisting relationship even though the employee takes a short-term job elsewhere to bridge the gap between periods of employment with his normal employer. The Divisional Court in *Hunter* v. *Smith's Dock Co. Ltd.*[4] also established that a subsisting relationship can be recognized upon the evidence of hindsight, and that it was not necessary that there should have been mutual promises for the resumption of employment at the time when the cessation of work began.

Two decisions of the Industrial Court show that there will be held to have been a temporary cessation of work in the case of a genuine lay-off even though that lay-off occurs in the context or the aftermath of an industrial dispute. It was so held in *Clarke Chapman-John Thompson Ltd.* v. *Walters*[5] in relation to an interval of two weeks

---

[1] 1972 Act Schedule 1 Para. 5 (1)(b). The plaintiff in *Puttick* v. *John Wright Ltd.* [1972] ICR 457 was not saved by this provision because he had to show he had been dismissed *during* a period of lay-off, which meant showing a contract in force during the lay-off itself.

[2] [1970] AC 984.   [3] [1970] 1 Lloyd's Rep. 105.
[4] [1968] 1 WLR 1865.   [5] [1972] 1 WLR 378.

following the settlement of a strike, where the gap occurred because the employers had so planned their programme for resumption of work that they did not need the services of the employee concerned until the date on which he was in fact re-engaged. A comparable result occurred in *McGorry* v. *Earls Court Stand Fitting Co. Ltd.*[1] where a period of unemployment genuinely attributable to redundancy had commenced during a period when the employee was on strike (about proposed redundancies).

Although the above decisions give a wide scope to the concept of temporary cessation, it seems to remain an overriding requirement that there be no intention on the part of employer or employee for there to be a permanent termination of employment. A positive intention of permanent termination will negate a claim that continuity has subsisted, even although the employment was in fact later resumed. It was so held, for example, in *Newsham* v. *Dunlop Textiles Ltd.* (No. 2)[2] where a period of unemployment of five to six weeks resulted from a fire at the employer's mill, because, although the employers had been willing to keep the employment open till repairs took place, the employee had taken a positive decision to leave, and had withdrawn her contributions from the pension fund for that purpose. (She had then subsequently changed her mind.)

The requirement of lack of permanent intention to terminate becomes less clear when the employer's intention is in issue. On the one hand, in *Bunt* v. *Fishlow Products Ltd.*[3] the Divisional Court found against continuity where an employer had during a period of lay-off decided to effect a permanent dismissal of employees as the result of an industrial dispute and had then re-engaged the men after union intervention. On the other hand, in *McGorry* v. *Earls Court Stand Fitting Co. Ltd.*, to which reference was made above, the Industrial Court found in favour of continuity despite the fact that the relevant gap in employment followed an apparently absolute dismissal of the employees for redundancy. It would seem that the court must have regarded the employer's intention of permanent termination as qualified by a willingness to re-employ once the industrial dispute was settled; to this extent, a true intention of permanent termination might still negate continuity even after actual re-employment.

---

[1] [1973] ICR 100.   [2] (1969) 4 ITR 268.   [3] (1970) 5 ITR 127.

SECTION 3: STRIKES AND LOCKOUTS

As in the case of the types of suspension of employment so far discussed, a distinction may be drawn between the two issues of (a) whether suspension of employment during industrial action constitutes a breach of the contract; and (b) whether such suspension results in termination of the contract of employment. We consider firstly the issue of when such suspension constitutes a breach of contract.

A. The Right to Suspend the Contract during Industrial Action

It appears to have been assumed for many years that a strike preceded by due notice would not ordinarily constitute breach of the individual contract of employment because it would instead be treated as lawful termination of the contract.[1] The explanation of strike notices as notice to terminate contracts of employment has, in recent years, been regarded as unacceptable.[2] When this development first occurred, it appeared as a result that strike action must therefore constitute a breach of individual contracts of employment, whether accompanied by due notice or not.[3]

This situation, in which strikes had necessarily to be a breach of contract because they were not a lawful termination of contract, was modified by the ruling of two judges in the Court of Appeal in *Morgan* v. *Fry*[4] that a strike might be regarded as the lawful exercise of a right to suspend employment by way of industrial action. Very shortly before that decision, the judges of the Court of Session had rejected a similar argument that there might be an implied condition in the contract of employment of a draughtsman to the effect that a lock-out would not be treated as constituting a breach of contract.[5] They had awarded damages to the employee for lock-out in breach of contract by the employer. In rejecting the idea of an implied right of suspension by way of industrial action, the judges of the Court of Session did, however, address themselves particularly to the fact that

---

[1] See Foster, 'Strikes & Employment Contracts' (1971) 34 MLR 275 at 279.

[2] Donovan L.J. in *Rookes* v. *Barnard* [1963] 1 QB 623 at 676; Lord Devlin in the same case [1964] AC 1129, 1204; Lord Denning in *Stratford* v. *Lindley* [1965] AC 269. But cf. Foster, op. cit. at 279–81.

[3] This was the origin of Section 37 of the 1965 Act which redressed the balance as far as statutory continuity of employment was concerned.

[4] [1968] 2 QB 710 per Lord Denning at 728 B–C, and Davies L.J. at 733 F–G.

[5] *Cummings* v. *Charles Connell & Co. Ltd.* [1969] SLTR 25.

this was an exceptional contract of employment in that both sides undertook by it to continue the employment for eighteen months, making no provision for early termination. The view was taken that the employer's guarantee of employment would become worthless and that the employee would be subjected to an oppressive obligation if the implied term contended for was allowed in favour of the employer.[1] Hence the decision turns upon its own special facts.

In *Morgan* v. *Fry*, Lord Denning M.R., holding that a term allowing for suspension of employment by an employee during industrial action could be implied into the contract of employment, took the view that such a term must indeed be implied because the contrary argument would do away with the right to strike.[2] Davies L.J. agreed with Lord Denning M.R. in this view, though the force of his concurrence is weakened by the fact that he was elsewhere in his judgment inclined to view the strike notice as a termination of the existing contract and an offer to continue on different terms;[3] an analysis which is in fact inconsistent with the idea of suspension of employment under an implied right provided by the contract itself. Russell L.J. decided the case on different grounds and took a different view upon this point.[4]

The view of Lord Denning is questionable upon historical grounds, though defensible upon policy grounds. The idea of a right to suspend the employment by way of strike action had been expressly rejected in *Parkin* v. *South Hetton Coal Co. Ltd.* (1907)[5]:

Coal miners who had been dismissed by reason of a one-day strike over disputed piece rates sued for damages for wrongful dismissal and for unpaid wages. The County Court judge accepted their argument that a well-established custom of one-day strikes, over piecework calculations, had resulted in an implied right on their part to suspend the employment in this way. That argument was, however, rejected by the Divisional Court; and although it is true that the employees were here claiming a right to suspend their employment without prior notice, the rejection of that view by the judges in that court was couched in such general terms as to leave little room for the idea of an implied right of suspension by way of industrial action, even if such action were accompanied by prior notice.

Thus Darling J. said that the break in service was repugnant to the

---

[1] Ibid. at 31 (The Lord President, Lord Clyde).
[2] [1968] 2 QB 710 at 725 D–I.   [3] Ibid. at 731 F–732 A.
[4] Ibid. at 734 C–F.
[5] 97 LT 98 (affirmed on a different issue—98 LT 162).

very contract of service itself;[1] and for A. T. Lawrence J. the argument that the employees were entitled to suspend their employment was 'an extraordinary contention, and not in the least parallel to the right of employers to stop work when circumstances require it'.[2] Hence whatever the scope of 'the right to strike' at that period, the judges would not regard it as compelling them to take the view that it gave rise to an implied right of suspension of employment.

The decision in *Morgan* v. *Fry* was given almost exactly contemporaneously with the publication of the Report of the Royal Commission on Trade Unions and Employers' Associations (1968) which had deliberated upon the policy considerations affecting an implied right to suspend the contract of employment by way of strike action. Professor Wedderburn had argued in his evidence to the Commission that the difficulties attaching to a doctrine of suspension would be so great that it would be preferable to reform the law of tort in so far as it depended upon the contractual status of strikes, and to leave the law of contract unaltered in this respect.[3] He referred in particular to the difficulties of deciding whether such suspension would have to be preceded by notice, and how long the notice would have to be; and of deciding whether the doctrine would be defeasible in the event of grave breach, as is the corresponding right of the employee under French law.[4]

The Report of the Royal Commission accepted his views concerning the difficulties surrounding the doctrine of suspension and thought it inadvisable to introduce so fundamental a change in the law of contract. They preferred the idea that it should be accepted, wherever it was reasonable to do so, that a strike notice could operate as notice to terminate the contract; and that the consequential rupturing of periods of continuous service, for the purpose of calculating fringe benefits, should be avoided by formulating agreed definitions of periods of continuous service in such a way as to avoid this result.[5] It is the view of this writer that, although the difficulties in the way of such a doctrine of suspension were not insuperable, they were none the less sufficiently great as to require legislation for their

---

[1] 97 LT 98 at 101.   [2] Ibid. at 102.

[3] *Minutes of Evidence to the Royal Commission on Trade Unions and Employers Associations* (H.M.S.O. 1965–8)—Day 31—pp. 1287–9 (Written Evidence).

[4] Ibid., Para 61 of his Written Evidence; see Kahn-Freund & Hepple, *Laws against Strikes* (Fabian Society, 1972) pp. 36 ff. for a comparative discussion of unconstitutional strikes.

[5] Cmnd. 3623 at Paras 943–52.

STRIKES AND LOCKOUTS 105

removal, so that the judicial law-making of the Court of Appeal in *Morgan* v. *Fry* probably did not provide a workable basis for such a doctrine.

In Section 147 of the Industrial Relations Act, the legislators intended to embody the result of the judgments in *Morgan* v. *Fry* in statute law.[1] Their chosen method was not the creation of a positive right to suspend the contract of employment by way of strike action, but rather the removal of certain illegalities and contractual consequences from strike notice and strike action where the required conditions were satisfied.[2] Despite its ultimate repeal, Section 147 of the 1971 Act may possibly have abolished the common-law doctrine embodied in *Morgan* v. *Fry* and left the common law to reformulate itself as far as the contractual right to strike is concerned.[3]

B. *Suspension by way of Industrial Action and the Termination of the Contract*

The question whether a suspension of employment by reason of industrial action results in a termination of the contract of employment may be briefly considered. It has been shown that the prevailing view is that such suspension is not to be construed as the lawful termination of the contract by notice.[4] If the suspension can be regarded as the exercise of an implied right to suspend the contract of employment, then it is of the essence of such an implied provision that the contract of employment will continue in force during the period of suspension. If the industrial action concerned fell within Section 147, the result was the suspension of the contract of employment rather than its termination. In that situation, however, the employer retained such right as he has at common law to treat the strike as a ground for summary termination of the contract. That common-law right may possibly be qualified by the doctrine of lawful

---

[1] *H.C. Deb.* Vol. 812 Col. 365 (the then Solicitor-General, Sir Geoffrey Howe).

[2] See Foster, 'Strike Notice—Section 147' (1973) 2 ILJ 28; O'Higgins 'Strike Notices—Another Approach' (1973) 2 ILJ 152. In these articles, Foster relates Section 147 to various kinds of strike notices differentiated according to their legal characteristics, while O'Higgins prefers to take into account the different variants of industrial relations practice in the giving of strike notice.

[3] The problem of the effect upon the common law of the repeal of Section 147 is complicated by the fact that Section 147 legislated about the effect of strike *notices* for all purposes but dealt with actual strikes for the purposes only of certain specified proceedings and statutory provisions. See also p. 170 note 5 and Appendix, para. 8.

[4] See above, p. 102.

suspension propounded in *Morgan* v. *Fry*. The difficulty here is that it is unclear whether the doctrine in that case will have survived after Section 147 came into effect.[1]

If the suspension by way of industrial action *is* in breach of contract, it is not in itself a termination of the contract, and there will in that case not be a termination unless and until the employer acts upon the strike action, as a repudiatory breach of the contract entitling him to treat the employment as at an end. It was with this meaning that Sir John Brightman said in *Davis Transport Ltd.* v. *Chattaway* that, 'Just as a strike does not of itself amount to repudiation of a contract of employment, *with the result that a worker taking part in a strike puts an end there and then to his contract*, so also a lock-out does not amount to a like repudiation *and determination* on the part of the employer'[2] (emphases added). The point is not that the strike is not repudiatory, but that it is not as such a determination of the contract *per se*. This is illustrated by *Cardy* v. *City of London Corporation*,[3] where it was held that the period of continuous service of a local government employee had not been broken by a strike of a fortnight's duration. Sellers J. indicated that the employers were correct in conceding that the contract of employment had remained in force, because the wrongful repudiation constituted by the strike had never been treated by the employers as entitling them to terminate the contract.[4] He went on to hold that the continuity of service, which was a condition of the employees' entitlement to pension rights, did not require that there should have been actual working throughout the period concerned, so that the strike did not rupture continuity on the ground merely that it resulted in a period of suspension of employment.[5]

As a general principle, it would seem to be desirable that the contract of employment should be regarded as continuing during strike action. If a strike is regarded as an interruption in the continuity of employment, it may have a delayed effect upon the incidental rights of the employee which depend on seniority in the

---

[1] See text and note above at p. 105, n. 3; see also Appendix, Para. 8.

[2] [1972] ICR 267 at 271 B.   [3] [1950] 2 All ER 475.

[4] Ibid. at 476 H.

[5] To like effect is the decision of a majority of the House of Lords in *Price* v. *Guest, Keen & Nettlefold Ltd.* [1918] AC 760 applying a similar concept of continuous employment under the Workmen's Compensation Act 1906. In that case, the evidence was held to be unclear about whether the *contract* of employment had been terminated during the strike, and it was regarded as unnecessary to decide the point.

employment and may operate as a disproportionate sanction. If the employment is regarded as continuing, it should as far as possible be held that there is a *contract* of employment in force, for otherwise the contract of employment is in danger of becoming a narrow and legalistic concept, dissociated from the relationship of which it should be the legal expression. We proceed in the following pages to consider the statutory response to that very problem.

C. Suspension by way of Industrial Action and Statutory Continuity of Employment

The assessment of continuity of employment in purely contractual terms was considered impossible by the draftsmen of the 1963 Act (and the successive legislation concerned with continuity of employment[1]) in relation to strikes, just as we have seen it was considered impossible in relation to periods of lay-off.[2] In relation to strikes the legislation discounts the actual period spent on strike, but ensures that continuity is preserved so that the period accumulated before the strike is not lost.[3] Now that the proviso excluding strikes in breach of contract has been removed,[4] continuity is therefore maintained during any period of strike action connecting two periods which count on other grounds.

The decision of the Industrial Court in *Bloomfield* v. *Springfield Hosiery Ltd.*[5] indicates that the limiting factor on the statutory concept of continuity during strikes is the manifesting by either party of an intention permanently to terminate the employment relationship. At that point, the absence from work ceases to be attributable to the strike and continuity is lost. But that loss of continuity does not occur merely because the contract of employment is terminated during the strike. The person in question can still be regarded for the purpose of the statute as an 'employee'. Sir John Donaldson said of this that

'The fact that the employer terminates their contracts of employment does not take them outside this category, unless and until he engages other persons on a permanent basis to do the work which the strikers had been doing, or he permanently discontinues the activity in which they were

---

[1] i.e. the 1965 and 1971 Acts—the former for the purposes of qualification for and quantum of redundancy payment, the latter for the purpose of qualification for remedies for unfair dismissal.

[2] See above, pp. 99–101.   [3] 1972 Act Sched. 1, Paras. 6–7.

[4] 1965 Act s. 37.   [5] [1972] ICR 91.

employed. Similarly the fact that the striker takes other temporary employ-ment pending the settlement of the dispute does not prevent him claiming that he is taking part in a strike.'[1]

Thus on the facts of that case, continuity was not lost during a strike despite the fact that the employees were dismissed for striking. They were re-employed two weeks after that dismissal, and the point was that neither side had treated the dismissal as a permanent severance of relations. We thus have here the exact parallel of the law concerning 'temporary cessation', which it was argued earlier would be terminated only by a severance, intended to be permanent, of the employment relationship.[2]

SECTION 4: SUSPENSION DURING ABSENCE OF THE
EMPLOYEE AS THE RESULT OF SICKNESS OR INCAPACITY

A. The Extent of the Employer's Right to Suspend during Sickness

As in the case of the other types of suspension of employment, a distinction is drawn between the question what are the rights of the employer to suspend employment during sickness and the question whether the contract of employment is terminated during sickness; and the former question is considered first.

The question of how far the employer is entitled to suspend employment during the absence of the employee resulting from sickness or incapacity is another way of asking how far the employer is bound to continue to pay the employee during such absence. For employment is completely suspended (or even terminated) when the employee is absent and is not being paid during sickness; whilst if he is absent but is being paid then there is no suspension of employ-ment in the strict sense—there is a mere suspension of actual working. The common law concerning payment during sickness will be briefly described, and will be compared with the current practice of employers regarding payment during sickness. Two aspects of the common law concerning payment during sickness require particular comment. The first is the question of the extent to which the common law recognizes, or fails to recognize, social distinctions between

---

[1] Ibid. at 96 C–D.
[2] Moreover, the 'temporary cessation' may follow immediately upon a strike without an intermediate resumption of contractual working—see above at p. 101 where the case of *McGorry* v. *Earls Court Stand Fitting Co. Ltd.* [1973] ICR 100 is discussed.

different types of employment, and the effect of those distinctions upon the practice of payment during sickness. The second is the question of how far the common law regards the receipt of payments from other sources during sickness as preventing remuneration from continuing to be payable during sickness.

To consider, first, the extent to which the common law responds to social distinctions between different types of employment. A common-law presumption that remuneration continues to be payable during absence due to sickness in the absence of contrary indications in the contract has been built up on the basis of the decision in *Cuckson* v. *Stones*,[1] in which there was held to be such a right to continued remuneration in the case of a person employed for a fixed term of ten years as a master brewer responsible for the management of the employer's brewery and for instructing the employer himself in the running of the brewery. The ruling in that case was that,

'looking to the nature of the contract sued upon in this action, we think that want of ability to serve for a week would not of necessity be an answer to a claim for a week's wages, if in truth the plaintiff was ready and willing to serve had he been able to do so, and was only prevented from serving during the week by the visitation of God, the contract to serve never having been determined.'[2]

The later treatment of the *ratio* of that case as if it were applicable to all contracts of employment caused the common law concerning payment during sickness to become remote from the practice of employment in this respect. Schwarzer argued, in a learned article upon remuneration during sickness,[3] that the decision represents a judicial reaction to the pressing social problem of the impact of sickness upon the wage earner, and a limited encouragement of paternalism on the part of the employer—a harking back to an earlier period in which the judges had at times approached the relationship of master and servant as one in which the servant was part of the master's household, and as such was entitled to his protection in sickness and in health.[4] But this view neglects the evidence of the judgment of the court in the decision itself; for the court was at pains to stress that this was 'an agreement of a very

[1] (1858) 1 E & E 248.   [2] Ibid. at 256 (Lord Campbell C.J.).
[3] 'Wages during Temporary Disability—Partial Impossibility in Employment Contracts' (1952) 5 Stanford L.R. 30—republished in (1952) 8 Industrial Law Review.   [4] Schwarzer, loc. cit. Stanford L.R. pp. 33–6.

peculiar nature',[1] and the peculiarity consisted in the fact that the employee was a senior employee entitled to a particular security of tenure, and was able, moreover, to discharge a part of his managerial and organizational functions from the distance of his sick-bed. This was a case far removed from that of the manual industrial employee, who would have been most unlikely to succeed in such a claim at that date. Hence the decision could be satisfactorily applied only to employees of a comparable seniority and occupational level. The rule produced an acceptable result when applied in 1878 to a mercantile clerk employed at a salary of £120 per annum[2] and in 1902 when applied to an executive employed in the business of a piano manufacturer, the employee being also the holder of a share in the business as a condition of his obtaining the employment.[3] But in 1939, the rule was applied in *Marrison* v. *Bell*[4] to an outdoor salesman of fruit and vegetables. It appeared from this decision that the rule applied to wage earners as well as to salary earners, to manual employees as well as staff employees; and this produced a result quite at variance with the then current practice.

It may be thought that the courts were thus imposing a useful incentive towards improved provision of sick-pay schemes. But the gap between the common-law rule and the prevailing practice was too great. Lord Denning (as he now is) proposed a method whereby the rule could be harmonized with the social distinctions between different types of employment.[5] He suggested that the question of whether remuneration was payable for readiness and willingness to work if of ability to do so, or whether, by contrast, wages were payable only for actual work, must depend upon the type of employment concerned. Hence, he said, payment during sickness was progressively less likely as one went from cases of service agreements for terms of years, to other cases of payment by the month or at longer intervals, to payment calculated by the week, to payment calculated by the day, and finally to piece-rate wages.[6]

This realistic adaptation of the common-law rule to current

---

[1] 1 E & E 248 at 256 (Lord Campbell C.J.).
[2] *K.* v. *Raschen* (1878) 38 LT 38. It was held that the employee was not disentitled to continuance of remuneration by reason of the attributability of his illness (V.D.) to his own conduct, because that conduct had occurred before he entered into the employment and was not connected with the employment.
[3] *Warren* v. *Whittingham* (1902) 18 TLR 508.   [4] [1939] 2 KB 187.
[5] In a note on the decision in *Marrison* v. *Bell* (above) at (1939) 55 LQR 353.
[6] Ibid. at 354–5.

practice had in a sense come too late, in that the common-law courts, recoiling from the prospect, as they saw it, of a spate of actions for arrears of payment during sickness brought by manual employees, reacted to that possibility by entirely denying the existence of any such rule, and refusing to hold such payment to be due in the cases before them.[1] And although the presumption of payment during sickness was later vindicated in an isolated decision concerning the production manager of a dress factory,[2] it may be said that the common law has never quite resolved itself into a principle which is at once sufficiently well formulated to be useful, and at the same time sufficiently flexible to respond accurately to current practice.

The common-law rules concerning the continuance of remuneration during sickness are to some extent modified where the employee is in receipt of other benefits during sickness. It was established in *Niblett* v. *Midland Railway Co*.[3] that a contract of employment was not to be construed as entitling the employee to a continuance of wages during a period in which he was in receipt of sick pay from the company's friendly society, which he was required to join by the rules of the company. That case was justifiable on the ground that by making express provision for sick pay, the employer had given strong evidence of an intention that wages should be payable only during actual work.[4] More doubtful was the decision in *Elliott* v. *Liggens*[5] that the employers' liability for compensation to incapacitated workmen under the Workmen's Compensation Act 1897 had the result that the incapacitated employee was in receipt of a benefit provided by the employer which disentitled him from claiming a continuance of remuneration. It is something of an indictment both of the social attitudes of the time towards provision for sick employees, and of the preparedness of the judge to countenance such attitudes,

---

[1] *Petrie* v. *MacFisheries Ltd.* [1940] 1 KB 258 (fish-curer on weekly wages—express provision (though inadequately communicated) for half-pay during sickness on *ex gratia* basis). *Hancock* v. *B.S.A. Tools Ltd.* [1939] 4 All ER 538 (driller paid weekly wage consisting of minimum time rate plus piece-work supplement. Employment was expressed to be hourly; it was terminable by one hour's notice; and there was a custom of no payment except for actual work done). *O'Grady* v. *M. Saper Ltd.* [1940] 2 KB 469 (commissionaire—weekly wages—previously absent sick without pay).

[2] *Orman* v. *Saville Sportswear Ltd.* [1960] 1 WLR 1055.

[3] (1907) 96 LT 462.

[4] See Denning, loc. cit. (1939) 55 LQR 353 at 356.

[5] [1902] 2 KB 84. Approved in dicta in *Warburton* v. *Co-operative Wholesale Society Ltd.* [1917] 1 KB 663; Warrington L.J. at 667, Scrutton L.J. at 668; but Lord Cozens-Hardy M.R. *dubitante* at 665.

that Darling J. could defend this decision in these terms: 'The construction that we are putting upon the Act is not opposed to the interests of workmen in general, for, if the opposite construction were to prevail, the first act of every employer on hearing of an accident would be to discharge the workman from his employ so as to prevent him from setting up a claim to his wages in addition to his claim for compensation for his injury.'[1]

It was therefore a progressive step when the Court of Appeal in *Marrison* v. *Bell*[2] distinguished that decision, and held that remuneration might continue payable during sickness in spite of the receipt of benefits by the employee under the National Health Insurance Act 1936, on the ground that those benefits should be regarded as in their nature intended as a supplement to earnings to provide for the special needs arising during sickness, or at least as having been given independently of remuneration. It would seem appropriate to take that view of sickness benefit payable at the present day under the National Insurance Acts 1965–1973.

The common law concerning suspension of employment by reason of unavailability of work was shown to harmonize quite closely with the practice of guaranteed pay arrangements.[3] There was a well-marked parallel between rules of the common law and the formulation of guaranteed pay schemes in practice. By contrast, the common law concerning suspension of employment during sickness is rather different from the practice of sick-pay schemes. Firstly, the practice of sick-pay schemes leaves little room for any common-law presumption concerning continuance of remuneration during sickness. A large proportion of all employees are covered by some form of sick-pay scheme. The Report of the National Joint Advisory Council to the Ministry of Labour on Occupational Sick Pay Schemes in 1964[4] recorded that there had been no major change since 1961, when an inquiry conducted by the Ministry of Pensions and National Insurance had indicated that 57 per cent of employed men and 60 per cent of employed women were covered by some kind of formal or informal arrangement for sick pay. It seems very likely that the remainder who are not covered by such arrangements are made aware of this fact, to the point where a common-law presumption of continuance of remuneration can only be of marginal usefulness. This

---

[1] [1902] 2 KB 84 at 87.
[3] See above, p. 95.

[2] [1939] 2 KB 187 (above).
[4] (H.M.S.O., 1964) at paras 14 and 24.

would seem to have been all the more true since the 1963 Act required employers to give to all employees of thirteen weeks' standing a statement of written particulars of terms of employment including any terms and conditions relating to incapacity for work due to sickness or injury, and also any provision for sick pay.[1] The employer is moreover required to record expressly the absence of any such terms and conditions in any particular case.[2] This means that, whatever the imperfections of the system of written particulars, those particulars should provide some guidance as to what the contract of employment says about remuneration during sickness.

Secondly, the common-law rule is not in harmony with current practice in that sick-pay schemes rarely provide for a simple continuance of remuneration during sickness. They make more elaborate arrangements which have no counterpart in the common law. Thus provision is frequently made whereby the weekly amount of sick pay diminishes as the period of sickness continues.[3] Many schemes involve the payment of full basic pay for an initial period of sickness followed by a subsequent reduction.[4] Thus again, many schemes involve the deduction of National Insurance sickness benefit.[5] This is in contrast with the all-or-nothing result of the common-law decisions, whereby sick pay is either negated by the receipt of such benefit or else is unaffected by it. Furthermore, many schemes require a qualifying period of service, commonly of six or twelve months, before the employee becomes eligible for sick pay.[6] And some schemes impose a rule of waiting days before receipt of pay during a particular period of sickness,[7] being comparable in this respect to the rules for National Insurance sickness benefit.[8] But most important of all, most schemes provide that sick pay shall continue only for a limited period of time, some placing that limit within the discretion of the employer, and others setting fixed limits, generally between 9 and 26 weeks.[9] Hence the result of the current practice of sick-pay schemes is that they will, by contrast with the common-law rule, normally result in a suspension of employment after a period of sick pay has run out. It remains to consider at what

---

[1] Now 1972 Act s. 4 (1)(d)(ii).   [2] 1972 Act s. 4(2).

[3] *NJAC Report* Paras 40–7. Further information about the practice of sick-pay schemes is contained in Incomes Data Studies Nos. 26 (April 1972), 30 (June 1972), 47 (February 1973), 50 (April 1973).

[4] *NJAC Report* para 45.   [5] Ibid. para 43.

[6] Ibid. paras 57–8.   [7] Ibid. paras 59–61.

[8] National Insurance Act 1965 s. 19(6).   [9] *NJAC Report* paras. 48–56.

point that suspension takes the form of the termination of the contract of employment.

B. Absence due to Sickness and the Termination of the Contract

In analysing the extent to which the contract of employment subsists during unpaid absence due to sickness, we are not as in previous sections faced with a difficult distinction between lawful and wrongful suspension. This type of suspension will normally be lawful (in the sense of not being in breach of contract) on both sides. The contract of employment will in fact continue in force during a period of unpaid absence due to sickness until there occurs either an act of termination by the parties or either of them, or a termination under the doctrine of frustration. Termination by frustration in cases of sickness will be considered later in this work.[1] The doctrine of frustration has recently been seen as having a fairly closely restricted application to sickness cases.[2] There has been an insistence upon the impossibility of future resumption of work on anything like the previously existing basis before the doctrine will be held to have operated.

Where there has been no frustration of the contract, it may none the less be difficult to decide whether the conduct of the parties has amounted to a termination of the contract. The difficulty centres upon the fact that the parties may well during a long absence due to sickness allow the employment relationship to degenerate into a loose understanding that the employer will try to re-employ the employee in some capacity or other when he is able to work. Sometimes employers, particularly larger employers, formalize this practice by transferring employees absent and no longer in receipt of sick pay into a 'holding department'. The purpose of the practice is to enable the particular job of the employee to be filled for the remainder of his period of absence while keeping him 'on the books' of the firm and assuring him of preference over outsiders in allocation of a vacancy when he returns.

The disagreement to be found in the case-law about the contractual standing of such 'holding departments' exemplifies the whole difficulty of construing the contractual effect of arrangements obtaining during long periods of absence due to sickness. It was held by

---

[1] See below, pp. 303–10.
[2] *Marshall* v. *Harland & Wolff Ltd.* [1972] ICR 101; *Hebden* v. *Forsey & Son* [1973] ICR 607.

the Divisional Court in *O'Reilly* v. *Hotpoint Ltd.*[1] that the transfer of an employee into such a holding department did not constitute a termination of his contract of employment, with the result that the contract of employment remained in force throughout. They went on to hold that the refusal of the employers to find him work upon his return constituted a repudiatory breach of contract such that the employee was entitled to treat himself as dismissed and to claim a redundancy payment. In *Marshall* v. *Harland & Wolff Ltd.*, on the other hand, the Industrial Court regarded the 'holding department' as a convenient and proper method for the employer to keep sick employees 'on the books' whilst avoiding an unintended liability to redundancy payment in the event of a redundancy situation arising a long time after the employee has 'left the active list'.[2]

It was there said that 'The effect of such a transfer is that the employee ceases to be employed in any legal sense, but is on a list of men in respect of whom there is a voluntary arrangement between the employers and any relevant union, or the employees themselves, that all concerned will do their best to provide them with work as soon as they are again fit.'[3] This disagreement within the case-law may be resolved in future by reference to the precise terms of particular holding arrangements; but the underlying difficulty of relating actual practice to contractual patterns remains.

C. *Absence due to Sickness and Statutory Continuity*

As in relation to the types of suspension previously considered, the Contracts of Employment Act 1963 departed from a purely contractual assessment of continuity of employment by providing that weeks might count towards the period of continuous employment where the employee was incapable of work in consequence of sickness or injury.[4]

That description clearly includes weeks when there is no contract of employment in force. However, weeks in excess of twenty-six consecutive weeks of such absence do not qualify for the preservation of continuity under this head. They may, however, still qualify as weeks 'during the whole or part of which the employee's relations with the employer are governed by a contract of employment which normally involves employment for twenty-one hours or more

---

[1] (1970) 5 ITR 68.
[3] Ibid. at 109 G–H.
[2] [1972] ICR 101 at 109 F.
[4] Now 1972 Act Schedule 1 Para 5 (1)(a).

weekly.'[1] This makes it necessary to consider, in relation to absences due to sickness exceeding twenty-six weeks' duration, whether the contract of employment has subsisted. For shorter absences, the need to apply that test is avoided; but it is to be remembered that if the employment is terminated during a period of sickness, there will be a dismissal for statutory purposes only if there is a subsisting contract of employment.[2] The statutory concept of continuity of employment can operate only to bridge two contractual periods, and not to create something from which the employee can be 'dismissed' within the meaning of the statutes—such a thing must take the form of a subsisting contract of employment.

This section may be concluded by the observation that the common law concerning the suspension of employment is lacking in general principles dealing with the extent of the right of suspension, and with the effect of suspension upon the contract itself. The reason for this is that the law has developed separately in relation to the different types of suspension. If a systematic review of the law concerning different types of suspension gives rise to any general principle it is that if suspension of employment is seen as resulting in termination of the contract of employment, then it becomes necessary, in particular for statutory purposes, to recognize that there is none the less a subsisting relationship between the parties during periods of suspension.

---

[1] Ibid. Para 4.
[2] Cf. *Puttick* v. *John Wright Ltd.* [1972] ICR 457. See above, pp. 98, 100 n. 1.

Chapter Four

BREACH

INTRODUCTION

The topic of breach of the contract of employment does not call for
general theoretical treatment but presents a series of particular
problems of some interest and importance.

(a) Anticipatory Breach

Breach can be defined as any mis-performance or non-performance
of a contractual obligation except for non-performance resulting
from frustration of the contract; but that definition is incomplete
in that it fails to refer to renunciation of contractual obligations
before the due date for performance. It was in relation to the
contract of employment that the doctrine of anticipatory breach was
developed to give an immediate remedy to the employer for an
anticipatory repudiation by the employee. The relationship of this
anticipatory breach to ordinary breach of contract requires some
examination.

(b) Breach in the context of Industrial Action

Breach of the contract of employment has had a particular function
in the law of economic torts as a constituent element in the tort
liabilities attaching to industrial action. Under the Industrial
Relations Act 1971 it becomes a constituent of 'irregular industrial
action short of a strike'.[1] The application of the concept of breach
in this especially contentious context where the extensive indirect
consequences of tortious liability attach to breach has given a
particular significance to this part of the law of breach of contract
which justifies analysis.

(c) Effect of Breach upon Remuneration

The employer's most obvious remedy for breach of contract by the
employee is the self-help remedy of withholding remuneration. An

---

[1] See Appendix, para 7.

elaborate body of legal doctrine, frequently rendered obscure by its antiquity, attaches to this issue of the extent to which remuneration may be reduced on account of the employee's breach of contract.

(d) Damages for Employee's Breach of Contract

An account of the law concerning damages for breach of contract by the employer can most conveniently be given under the heading of remedies for wrongful dismissal. The awarding of damages against employees for breach of contract is one of the smaller and less active parts of the law of the contract of employment. But it is one whose historical growth is unexpectedly interesting for the extent of its departure from general contractual principles. It is also a part of the law of the contract of employment whose more active use may be possible in future. That is liable to occur as the extent of resources which employers expend in reliance upon the continuance of particular employees in employment tends to increase.

SECTION 1: ANTICIPATORY BREACH

One important form of breach of the contract of employment consists of non-fulfilment of the employer's obligation to employ or of the employee's obligation to continue in service. There is one complicated variant upon that type of breach which requires some examination, namely that breach which consists in anticipatory renunciation of the mutual obligations to maintain the employment relationship. The recognition of this type of breach occurred in *Hochster* v. *De la Tour* (1853)[1] where it was held that the plaintiff, engaged by the defendant for three months' service as a courier and notified before the engagement began that he would not be required, had an immediate action for damages for anticipatory wrongful dismissal, without the necessity to wait for the date on which the service should have begun. In this section, we consider the reasoning whereby anticipatory wrongful dismissal can be treated as immediate breach, and also the special conditions which attach to the concept of anticipatory breach.

The difficulty of principle which arises in relation to anticipatory breach is simply that of accepting that a contractual promise can be broken before it is due to be performed. Reluctant to advance directly to the radical proposition that the right of action for breach

[1] 2 E & B 678.

could be accelerated by the defendant's announcement of his future intentions, the judges reached the same result by reasoning which depended upon treating the contract as discharged by renunciation and the acceptance of renunciation. In a detailed study of this particular development, Neinaber has shown how the anticipatory wrongful dismissal was treated as an offer by the defendant to discharge the contract and a consent by the plaintiff to that discharge on the terms that he could claim damages for breach.[1] Neinaber criticizes this reasoning as both unnecessary in its elaboration, fictitious in its construction of the facts, and unfortunate in its consequences. The unfortunate consequences follow from the fact that, in order to establish a breach of contract, the plaintiff must also show that the conditions for discharge of contracts by repudiation and rescission have also been satisfied. That is to say, the wrongful repudiation must be a positive renunciation relating to a fundamental aspect of the contract and there must be an election by the injured party to treat the contract as discharged. It is thus possible that the employer might escape the consequences of anticipatory breach if he made an anticipatory announcement of an intention unilaterally to vary the terms and conditions of employment in a matter or to a degree which was not fundamental.[2]

Only the case of anticipatory wrongful dismissal has been considered by the courts; the doctrine of anticipatory breach might not extend to the prior announcement of a breach not amounting to a termination of employment.[3] Furthermore, it is possible that the requirement of renunciation might exclude the prior intimation of likely breach at some time in the indefinite future. In *Morton Sundour Fabrics Ltd.* v. *Shaw*[4] an employer was allowed in a redundancy payments case to rely on the argument that a warning of impending dismissal at a time not yet determined was not itself a dismissal.

[1] 'The Effect of Anticipatory Repudiation; Principle and Policy' [1962] CLJ 213.

[2] In *Maher* v. *Fram Gerrard Ltd.* [1974] ICR 31 the prior announcement of intention to transfer the place of employment was treated as immediate repudiation. But the place of employment is clearly one of the fundamental terms and conditions.

[3] In *Maher* v. *Fram Gerrard Ltd.* (above) the wrongful insistence upon the right to transfer the place of employment was deemed, by extension of the doctrine in *Marriott's Case* [1970] 1 QB 186, to be anticipatory wrongful dismissal. This reflects an increasing tendency to equate wrongful repudiation with wrongful dismissal. See below, pp. 237–8.

[4] (1967) 2 ITR 84.

Parallel reasoning could gravely and perhaps unjustly restrict the doctrine of anticipatory breach of contract. However, it could in such a case be argued that even if a party is free effectively to give a warning of lawful dismissal without actually dismissing, he is not free to give a warning of breach without thereby committing an anticipatory renunciation.[1]

Furthermore, complications arise from the fact that an anticipatory breach requires an election by the injured party to treat the contract as terminated. In the absence of such an election there is no breach.[2] In theory this precludes any claim by the injured party which at once relies on the anticipatory breach and yet seeks to keep the contract alive. However, it has been held that the right to sue for specific performance is not limited by this objection, so that the plaintiff may before the due date of performance obtain an order for specific performance on that due date.[3] If the objection to orders for the specific performance of contracts of employment turns out to be less absolute than was formerly supposed,[4] this rule may come to be applied to anticipatory wrongful dismissal or anticipatory refusal to let an agreed period of employment commence.

Another result of the requirement that the injured party must elect to determine the contract has been the notion that the injured party can subsequently rely on the actual breach of contract without showing any effort to mitigate his loss during the period of warning.[5] Thus in *Shindler* v. *Northern Raincoat Co. Ltd.*[6], the managing director then serving under a contract of service with the defendants was informed by them on 2 September 1958 that his service with them would terminate not later than 30 November 1958. It was held that the defendants could not, when sued for wrongful dismissal,

---

[1] This is the basis of the decision in *Maher* v. *Fram Gerrard* (above), which does very substantially restrict the doctrine of the *Morton Sundour Case* (above).

[2] This, at least, is the view to be derived from general contract principle. Some support is to be found in Lord Devlin's judgment in *Rookes* v. *Barnard* [1964] AC 1129 at 1207; '. . . it was said that BOAC could not have sued for an anticipatory breach unless they first elected to rescind, which they never did. I dare say that is right. . . .' But it is possible that the law of the contract of employment is moving towards a concept of termination by wrongful repudiation *requiring no election by the injured party*, which may extend to anticipatory breach. Cf. *Maher* v. *Fram Gerrard* (above) and see below, pp. 293–4, 323–4.

[3] *Hasham* v. *Zenab* [1960] AC 316—see Megarry (1960) 76 LQR 201.

[4] Cf. *Hill* v. *C. A. Parsons & Co. Ltd.* [1972] 1 Ch. 305. See below, pp. 277–8.

[5] *Tredegar Iron & Coal Co. Ltd.* v. *Hawthorn Bros.* (1902) 18 TLR 716.

[6] [1960] 1 WLR 1038 (Diplock J.).

complain of the plaintiff's failure to seek other employment before 30 November. This result is a just one when the service concerned is actually in progress at the time of the anticipatory repudiation, but it would seem doctrinaire if the same conclusion were reached as a matter of principle even where the employment had not yet commenced. In such a case, account should be taken of the extent of the would-be employee's opportunities to search for other employment. He might be precluded from so doing because he was still completing an earlier employment. But it would be contrary to the rationale of *Hochster* v. *De La Tour* itself—the avoidance of an incentive upon the employee to stand idle in order to obtain damages —if the employee were free to neglect opportunities of other employment as the arbitrary result of the principles concerning anticipatory repudiation. A doctrine of anticipatory breach is necessary to reinforce the protection of the parties' mutual interests in the continuance of employment but should not be taken to the point of sanctioning the under-exploitation of labour resources.

SECTION 2: BREACH IN CONTEXT OF INDUSTRIAL ACTION

We have so far discussed the concept of breach of the contract of employment primarily in the context of the relationship between the individual employer and employee. In order to give a complete picture of the concept, some reference must be made to its development in its other rôle, namely that of a constituent element in the torts concerned with industrial disputes and subsequently in the unfair industrial practices created by the Industrial Relations Act. Indeed, the law of breach of contract by the employee has arguably been more important and received more attention in its indirect operation in the law of tort than in its direct operation between the parties to the contract as such. This section accordingly attempts to state the law concerning breach of contract as it has developed in relation to industrial action in the context of economic tort law (including that of unfair industrial practices). We consider in turn the law relating to strikes and that relating to other types of industrial action.

In relation to breach of contract in strike situations, we consider firstly the notice to strike and secondly the strike itself. For many years, notice to strike seems to have been regarded as lawful notice to terminate the contract.[1] This was not the result of a special recognition of a right to strike; but a simple acceptance of the fact that many industrial workers were employed on very short terms of notice by either party to the contract. As termination by notice became a more momentous step involving a longer period of notice and perhaps more considerable effects on rights based upon seniority, that analysis became less compelling. It was established in *Rookes* v. *Barnard* (1963)[2] that even termination by notice could constitute breach of contract where it contravened a contractual obligation to refrain from industrial action; the right to terminate by notice could thus be qualified by an express undertaking imported from a collective agreement. Moreover it was indicated in dicta of Lords Donovan,[3] Devlin[4] and Denning[5] that it was in any event incorrect to construe strike notice as notice to terminate; it should be regarded as notice of impending breach, because it was not intended to result in a termination of the contract. The merits of this view are examined later in this work in connection with notice to terminate the contract of employment.[6] This analysis of the effect of strike notice— and, by implication, of the effect of the strike itself—necessitated an amendment[7] of the scheme in the Contracts of Employment Act 1963 for assessing the period of continuous employment,[8] which had proceeded on the assumption that a strike preceded by due notice did not constitute a breach of contracts of employment whilst other strikes did.

Once the view was taken that notice to strike was notice of impending breach, then it would have followed that the strike notice was itself a repudiation of the contract which would entitle the employer to dismiss the employee without notice and to sue for anticipatory breach of contract. This would be the case, it is thought, where the strike notice was conditional upon the employer's refusal to accede

---

[1] The history of this view of the law (which remained at the level of speculation and was never conclusively established by authority) is described by Foster, 'Strikes and Employment Contracts' (1971) 34 MLR 275 at 277–9.

[2] [1964] AC 1129.

[3] *Rookes* v. *Barnard* [1963] 1 QB 623 at 682–3. Foster op. cit. at 280–1 considers the possibility that Donovan L.J., as he then was, in fact favoured lawful suspension rather than breach as the correct analysis.

[4] Ibid. [1964] AC 1129 at 1204.

[5] *Stratford & Son Ltd* v. *Lindley* [1965] AC 269 at 285.

[6] See below, pp. 170–2.　　　　　　　　　　　　　[7] 1965 Act s. 37.

[8] Now contained in 1972 Act Schedule 1.

to demands, rather than absolute in character.[1] An alternative analysis was put forward in *Morgan* v. *Fry*[2] where it was suggested that notice to strike could be treated as notice to suspend the contract rather than to terminate or to break it. This analysis was examined above in connection with the suspension of the contract of employment, where it was suggested that the judges in *Morgan* v. *Fry* by no means provided a fully worked-out concept of a right to suspend the contract by way of strike action and were indeed at variance with each other and internally inconsistent at certain key points of the analysis.[3]

In the Industrial Relations Act, the policy of the legislators was to reproduce the effect of *Morgan* v. *Fry* by means of the negative provision that due notice by an employee of a strike should not in the absence of express provision be construed as notice of termination of or repudiation of the contract.[4] This had the effect that the notice is not an anticipatory breach either, because the whole concept of anticipatory breach depends upon being able to treat the notice as a repudiation; only if the repudiation is accepted is there an anticipatory breach. It probably also had the effect that the giving of notice to strike by the employee did not entitle the employer to dismiss him, the common law being amended in this respect.

The law concerning the effect of the strike itself upon the contract of employment is largely parallel to that relating to the strike notice, but certain differences and additional aspects exist. Since the view came to be taken that a strike would often or even typically constitute breach of contract rather than termination of the contract, there have been occasional suggestions of a distinction for the purposes of the law of tort between merely technical breach and substantial or serious breach. It was suggested first by Lord Devlin[5] and later by

---

[1] Cf. *Bowes & Partners Ltd.* v. *Press* [1894] 1 QB 202. The form which strike notices take has been examined by Hepple and O'Higgins in *Encyclopedia of Labour Relations Law* (London 1972) at paras 1–315 and further by O'Higgins at (1973) 2 ILJ 152–6. But the extent to which strike notices are conditional in character has perhaps received insufficient attention. See, however, Foster, op. cit. at 284.

[2] [1968] 2 QB 710.

[3] See above, pp. 102–3. Criticism of the decision along similar lines is advanced by Foster, op. cit. at 281–5; cf. Wedderburn (1968) 31 MLR 682; O'Higgins [1968] CLJ 223.

[4] Section 147 of the 1971 Act. See Foster, 'Strike Notices; Section 147' (1973) 2 ILJ 28 and O'Higgins, 'Strike Notices; Another Approach' (1973) 2 ILJ 152. See above, pp. 105–6 and Appendix, para 8.

[5] In *Rookes* v. *Barnard* [1964] AC 1129 at 1204, 1218–19.

Russell L.J.[1] that a strike might be viewed as a purely technical breach of contract where the true intention of the strikers was to terminate their employment but they gave a few days' too short a notice of their intention to do so. This was clearly regarded as a situation unlikely to arise in practice because the intention of strikers was *not* normally to be viewed as intention to terminate but rather as an intention to keep their contracts of employment alive for as long as their employer would tolerate the withdrawal of labour without dismissing them.[2] The possible distinction between merely technical and substantial breach appeared to have no place in the law of unfair industrial practices set up by the 1971 Act, where indeed the strike concept was so defined as not to require any element of breach of contract at all.[3]

The effect of the strike upon the contract of employment was altered by Section 147 of the 1971 Act, apparently in order to enact the result of the decision in *Morgan* v. *Fry*.[4] The section relieved a strike, preceded by due notice, of its character as a breach of contract for the purposes of a listed set of proceedings. The employer's power to dismiss for striking was expressly preserved, which was probably at variance with the doctrine propounded in *Morgan* v. *Fry*.[5] The relief from breach was expressly restricted so as to exclude cases where the employee is subject to a contractual no-strike obligation.[6] The restriction of these changes to the listed set of proceedings suggested that the common law remained operative and significant for other purposes, possibly for the purpose of seniority rights dependent upon contractual continuity.

The contractual standing of industrial action other than strike action is of some interest. It was given a new importance by the 1971 Act in that the definition of irregular industrial action short of a strike required that the action concerned should involve a breach of the contracts of employment of some at least of those concerned in it.[5] The concept of lawful suspension advanced in

---

[1] In *Morgan* v. *Fry* [1968] 2 QB 710 at 737 D–738 B.
[2] Lord Devlin [1964] AC at 1204.
[3] 1971 Act s. 167(1). See Appendix, Para 7.
[4] See the discussion of the effect of *Morgan* v. *Fry* upon the employer's right of summary dismissal by Foster at (1971) 34 MLR 283–4. It is arguable that s. 147, by preserving this right of summary dismissal, failed to provide for a contractual right to strike in any meaningful sense. See Appendix, Para 8.
[5] See above, pp. 102–3.
[6] See Appendix, para 5 (Restriction upon incorporation of no-strike obligations into individual contracts). [7] 1971 Act s. 167(1) and s. 33(4).

Morgan v. *Fry* would appear to have no application to forms of industrial action other than a complete withdrawal of labour for a continuous period; it seems most unlikely that it could apply to an intermittent withdrawal of labour such as would be involved, for example, in a series of one-day stoppages. The application of the concept of breach of contract to the refusal to work overtime and to the 'work-to-rule' has been considered in earlier chapters.[1]

Where industrial action takes the form of refusal to carry out a particular part of the working operation unless stated conditions are met, it appears from the authority of *Bowes & Partners Ltd.* v. *Press*[2] (which concerned a refusal by miners to descend the mine shaft in the same lift-cage as non-unionists) that the refusal will be regarded as tantamount to direct withdrawal of labour and as such will be treated not merely as breach but as repudiatory breach of the contract. It remains only to refer to the effect of refusal by employees to handle particular goods or provide services in favour of a particular customer of the employer—the practice known as 'blacking'. The only difficulty which stands in the way of a clear conclusion that such action will normally constitute breach of the contract of employment is the suggestion in *Thomson & Co. Ltd.* v. *Deakin*[3] that there will be no such breach where the employer refrains from making an issue of the threat of blacking by his employees. In such a case it is indeed a persuasive view that there is neither immediate breach of contract, nor even anticipatory breach in the threat; in that anticipatory breach would require an acceptance by the employer of the repudiation as a ground for terminating the contract. But this analysis must be limited to the case where the work is organized in such a way that the employees never reach the point of departing from their ordinary routine of work—as would be the situation where the contentious goods or work were diverted before reaching the employees concerned. For it is reasonably clear from subsequent decisions that where employees in fact refrain from handling blacked work which is presented to them in the ordinary course of their work, there is a breach of contract by them even though there has been no direct confrontation with the employer in relation to that particular item of work.[4]

---

[1] See above, pp. 13–14, 17–19, 30–1, 51–3.   [2] [1894] 1 QB 202.
[3] [1952] 1 Ch. 646 at 685 (Lord Evershed M.R.).
[4] *Stratford & Son Ltd.* v. *Lindley* [1965] AC 269 at 324 C–G (Lord Reid), 327 C–D (Viscount Radcliffe), 335 D (Lord Pearce), 338 B (Lord Upjohn), 342

In conclusion, it may be said that the concept of breach of contract undergoes substantial modification in the context of industrial action. It was first greatly extended, by reference to the presumed intention of the employee, to include strike notice. It was modified by a tenuous distinction between technical and substantive breach in the context of strike notice. The doctrine of suspension during strike action made substantial though rather ill-defined inroads upon the area of breach of contract. The common law was specially modified by statute; this being an absolute modification in relation to strike notice, but for specific proceedings in relation to strike action. Recently, in the *ASLEF* case[1] the concept of breach of contract was applied to a 'work-to-rule', with results which, however appropriate to the facts under consideration, should not readily be assumed to be directly applicable to cases of non-cooperative activity arising at an individual level. All this gives to the concept of breach of contract the appearance in this context of having been shaped by judicial and legislative concepts of the proper formulation of the law relating to industrial action. Although in abstract theory the concept of breach may be a constant factor about which the law of economic torts and unfair industrial practices could be pivoted, it has been found necessary to redefine the scope of breach of contract itself. The result, whatever its merits in a wider sense, is that the concept of breach of the contract of employment has a complex and extended meaning in the context of industrial action.

SECTION 3: THE EFFECT OF BREACH UPON ENTITLEMENT TO REMUNERATION

In this section, we discuss the question of how far an employee may be entitled to remuneration where a breach of contract on his part has rendered his work incomplete or in some other way defective. This will involve a discussion of the contractual principle concerning entire and divisible obligations, and that concerning substantial performance of entire obligations. That whole topic is a particularly significant one from the point of view of the interrelationship between

---

D-F (Lord Donovan); cf. *General Aviation Services* v. *T.G.W.U.* [1974] ICR 35 at 47 G–48 C (Sir John Donaldson) (refusal to cross picket lines—the suggestion of an implied term allowing for this was rejected).

[1] *Secretary of State for Employment* v. *ASLEF* (No. 2) [1972] ICR 19—see above, pp. 18, 30–1.

general contractual principles and rules special to the contract of employment. The topic is one to which we shall revert at other points in this work, particularly in order to consider whether there is a special doctrine of forfeiture of wages upon dismissal for misconduct[1] and in order to consider the restitutionary remedies of the dismissed employee.[2] But the discussion may appropriately be introduced in the context of breach of the contract of employment, especially as loss of remuneration is the most obvious potential consequence of breach of contract by the employee.

The contractual principle of entire obligations is an application of a more general rule as to conditions precedent. If an obligation is entire, then the performance of the counter-obligation in full is a condition precedent to its enforcement. The obligation is not divisible; it cannot be enforced *pro rata* to the incomplete performance on the other side of the contract, or divided up into smaller units corresponding to divided parts of performance on the other side.[3] If an employer's obligation to remunerate is entire, then remuneration is recoverable only in respect of complete periods of service. Thus if an employee is paid by wages calculated on a weekly basis and leaves or is dismissed in the middle of a week, then, if the obligation to remunerate him is an entire obligation, no remuneration is due to him in respect of the incomplete week. This rule does not require there to have been a breach of contract by the employee, but is best illustrated in situations where there has been such a breach.

The question of whether a contractual obligation is entire or divisible is a question of construction of the contract. But policy considerations enter into the process of construction, because too strict a construction of obligations as entire and indivisible may result in unjust enrichment of the person under the obligation— because it means that he may have the benefit of incomplete performance without paying anything for it. The application of this process of construction to contracts of employment depends upon judicial authorities of some antiquity; they suggest that an employer's obligation to remunerate was at one time regarded very generally as an entire obligation. The extent of that presumption merits detailed examination.

---

[1] See below, pp. 227 ff.   [2] See below, pp. 271–2; cf. also pp. 327–8.
[3] See Glanville Williams, 'Partial Performance of Entire Contracts' (1941) 57 LQR 373 and 490 at 373–4.

The leading authority in favour of construing the employer's obligation to remunerate his servant as entire is the case of *Cutter* v. *Powell* (1795)[1] where a sailor was employed as second mate for a voyage from Jamaica to England for the lump sum of 30 guineas, payable ten days after the arrival of the ship in Liverpool. The sailor died when the ship was about ten days short of home after six weeks of the voyage. It was held that no part of the agreed wage was recoverable by his estate. Stoljar has argued that there was a special element of public policy in this decision, in that the contract was regarded as oppressive upon the employer by reason of the unusually high wage rate.[2] But if this particular problem had been in the minds of the judges, then it is unlikely that they would have made no reference to it. At the same time, the decision has undoubtedly been accorded a greater status as laying down a general principle than it suggested or deserved. It was emphasized by the judges deciding the case that their decision was based upon the terms of this particular contract rather than upon general usage.[3] They gave a judgment which was expressly made liable to be reversed on production of evidence of a general usage treating contracts for the employment of seamen as divisible,[4] though such evidence was never in fact produced.[5] The position seems to have been that whilst the courts were prepared to implement strictly an express provision in the contracts of employment of seamen making the payment of wages entire by the voyage, there is no evidence to suggest that they applied a strong presumption of entirety. In the two leading cases concerning the wages of seamen decided in the middle of the nineteenth century, the harshness of the rule in *Cutter* v. *Powell* was much modified when it was held that if seamen were employed by the voyage but their wages were expressed to be calculated by the month ('at the rate of £20 a month' or '£20 per month') their wages accrued due at the end of each month.[6]

How far did the period following *Cutter* v. *Powell* produce a

---

[1] (1795) 6 TR 320. See Stoljar, 'The Great Case of *Cutter* v. *Powell*' (1956) 34 CBR 288.

[2] Loc. cit. at 292.

[3] Cf. 6 TR 320, 324 (Lord Kenyon C.J.), 324–5 (Ashurst J.), 326 (Lawrence J.).

[4] Ibid. at 327. Judgment was given for the defendant 'unless some other information relative to the usage in cases of this kind should be laid before the court before the end of this term'.

[5] Ibid. at 327.

[6] *Taylor* v. *Laird* (1856) 1 H & N 266; *Button* v. *Thompson* (1869) LR4 CP 330.

presumption against the apportionability of yearly wages? It was stated in an *obiter dictum* in *Cutter* v. *Powell* that 'with regard to the common case of a hired servant to which this has been compared, such a servant, though hired in a general way, is considered to be hired with reference to the general understanding upon the subject, that the servant shall be entitled to his wages for the time he serves, though he do not continue in the service during the whole year.'[1] In spite of this dictum, a number of cases decided in the early years of the nineteenth century suggest that where an employee was paid remuneration which was calculated at a yearly rate and paid by quarterly or longer intervals, the obligation to pay him was liable to be treated as entire by the quarter-year or a longer interval.[2] There is, however, good reason to think that these cases are not strong evidence of a general presumption against apportionment of yearly or quarterly wages. They were all cases of dismissal for misconduct, and it may well be that the judges in those cases were applying a rule that dismissal for misconduct resulted in the forfeiture of wages due but unpaid, rather than a rule that the wages were not apportionable in the first place.[3] No consistent distinction is made between the two rules in the language used in the cases.[4] It is notable that there are decisions of the same period which show considerable judicial inconsistency as to the apportionability of wages under yearly contracts. Thus, in a case in 1826, a jury was directed that a clerk employed by the year but apparently paid at intervals within the year could recover salary *pro rata* down to the time of dismissal if he had been wrongfully dismissed.[5] And in two decisions of the same period Lord Tenterden C.J. indicated that the remuneration of yearly-hired clerks might be apportionable.[6] In the light of those decisions and dicta the strength of the presumption against the

---

[1] 6 TR 320 at 326 (Lawrence J.) cited with approval in *George* v. *Davies* [1911] 2 KB 445, 449 (Lord Coleridge J.).

[2] *Spain* v. *Arnott* (1817) 2 Stark 256; *Turner* v. *Robinson* (1833) 5 B & Ad. 789; *Ridgway* v. *Hungerford Market Co.* (1835) 3 Ad. & El. 171; *Lilley* v. *Elwin* (1848) 11 QB 742.

[3] See below, pp. 227–9, where forfeiture of wages is discussed.

[4] In *Spain* v. *Arnott* (above) Lord Ellenborough expressed the matter in terms of entire contracts at p. 257; but in *Turner* v. *Robinson* (above) at p. 790 and in *Ridgway* v. *Hungerford Market Co.* (above) at p. 177, Lord Denman C.J. tends towards the terminology of forfeiture. However, in *Lilley* v. *Elwin* (above) Coleridge J. returns to the language of entire contracts at pp. 755 and 757.

[5] *Pagani* v. *Gandolfi* 2 C & P 370.

[6] *Huttman* v. *Boulnois* (1826) 2 C & P 510; *Atkin* v. *Acton* (1830) 4 C & P 208.

apportionment of wages may be doubted, even as regards the time
which would generally be thought to represent the heyday of such
a rule.

Subsequent developments indicate the absence of any general
presumption of entirety of remuneration under contracts of employment. Remuneration calculated and paid at yearly intervals has
ceased to be a significant phenomenon and later decisions concerning
the apportionability of remuneration payable at such long intervals
have generally related to the remuneration of directors of companies.
Here there is a conflict of authority as to whether remuneration 'at
the rate of £x per annum' is apportionable at common law.[1] Where
remuneration is expressed as a fixed sum 'per annum' or 'for each
year' (and assuming it is not paid at shorter intervals) then it would
seem that it is not, at common law, apportionable within the year.[2]
In *Moriarty* v. *Regents Garage Co. Ltd.*[3] the view was taken that
there could be apportionability in such a case only where a term
could be specially implied to that effect. There is no developed
approach at common law at all to the apportionability of remuneration calculated by the year and paid monthly or weekly, or calculated
by the week and paid weekly. There is no authority at common law
against apportionability in such cases, though the view does seem
to be widely held among employers that such remuneration is not
apportionable, so that if the employee leaves in mid-week or mid-
month or is dismissed for misconduct, no wages accrue due to him
in respect of the incomplete week or month. If such remuneration
is apportionable, then it is generally treated as apportionable by the
day, rather than *pro rata*. The contract is severable into daily units
rather than infinitely severable. But the common law offers little or
no clear guidance in this area.

The common law is more informative on the apportionability of
hourly and piece-rate remuneration, and here tends towards appor-

---

[1] *Boston Deep Sea Fishing & Ice Co.* v. *Ansell* (1888) 39 Ch.D. 339 is against
apportionment but was a case of dismissal for misconduct to which special
considerations may apply. *Swabey* v. *Port Darwin Co.* (1889) 1 Megone 385 is in
favour of apportionment but may be very inaccurately reported—see Lush J. in
Moriarty v. *Regents Garage Co. Ltd.* [1921] 1 KB 423, 435.

[2] *Salton* v. *New Beeston Cycle Co.* [1899] 1 Ch. 775; *Re Central Da Kaap
Gold Mines Ltd.* (1899) 69 LJ (NS) Ch. 18; *Re McConnell's Claim* [1901] 1 Ch.
728; *Inman* v. *Ackroyd & Best Ltd.* [1901] 1 KB 613. These cases were strongly
criticized at first instance in *Moriarty* v. *Regents Garage Co. Ltd.* [1921] 1 KB
423, 435–9 (Lush J.).

[3] [1921] 2 KB 766, reversing [1921] 1 KB 423.

tionment. Where the unit of calculation of remuneration is smaller or shorter than the interval of payment, as where pay is calculated on an hourly or piece-rate basis, it has been accepted (after a shift in judicial opinion) that the remuneration is apportionable by the smaller unit. The issue was fought out in a most important group of cases decided between 1870 and 1910. In the earlier of those cases, it was held that the general law rendered the contracts entire by the week.[1] The rule was even used to stultify a new statutory provision to protect female employees and young persons from inequitable terms in their contracts of employment imposing forfeitures of wages. The provision concerned was that of Section 11 of the Employers and Workmen Act 1875,[2] which protected female and young employees from certain forfeitures of 'wages due'. The decision in *Gregson* v. *Watson* (1876)[3] concerned a works rule imposing upon piece-rated women textile workers a forfeiture of wages for incomplete weeks of work where they left without giving fourteen days' notice. It was held that this rule did not contravene Section 11 because the remuneration was not apportionable within each week and accordingly the forfeiture did not relate to 'wages due' within the meaning of the statute.

A judicial retreat from that position occurred in *Warburton* v. *Heyworth* (1880)[4] where in a case on comparable facts the Court of Appeal held that the conclusion of the magistrates at first instance that the contract was an entire weekly contract was not an unassailable conclusion of fact, as it had been treated in earlier cases, but an inference of law from fact and an inference which they were prepared to reverse. The views taken in that case were reiterated in the important case of *Parkin* v. *South Hetton Coal Co. Ltd.*[5] where Darling J. said of the contract of employment of an underground mine-worker who was paid at piece rates, wages being ascertained and paid at fortnightly intervals: 'I do not think he was hired by the week or the fortnight to be paid wages at the end of the week or fortnight calculated for the week or fortnight, as in such a case as that of a man hired to drive a cart at £1 per week, who if he drives for a day or two and then goes away has not carried out his contract. I come to the conclusion that this man really was working on piece-

---

[1] *Walsh* v. *Walley* (1874) LR 9 QB 367; *Saunders* v. *Whittle* (1876) 33 LT 816.
[2] Repealed by the Statute Law (Repeals) Act 1973.
[3] 34 LT 143.   [4] 6 QBD 1.
[5] (1907) LT 98 (affirmed by CA–98 LT 162).

work.'[1] The recognition of the apportionability of piece-work wages was thus complete; and the same reasoning would seem applicable to hourly rates as to piece rates.

Problems of apportionment of wages or salaries have in the course of time come to concern relatively small sums of money because of the now general practice of paying wages or salaries at weekly or monthly rather than at yearly intervals. But incidental benefits may be payable at longer intervals and so raise more significant problems of apportionment. A case in point is that of holiday remuneration which is normally paid annually at the time of the annual holiday. The only common-law authority concerning holiday pay takes the extreme view that such remuneration does not accrue due at all unless and until a holiday is actually taken during the employment.[2] Upon that view, the dismissed employee has no claim in respect of paid holiday due to him (other than a possible claim in damages). This position hardly accords with the ordinary understanding of the employer's liability in respect of holiday pay. Sometimes provision is made in collective agreements for accumulation of holiday pay at a weekly rate; where that is done, it ought normally to follow that the employee is entitled to an apportionment of holiday pay on termination of employment. There has been a recent recognition of the importance of apportionment of holiday pay in that the 1971 Act amended Section 4(1)(d) of the 1963 Act by requiring that the particulars of entitlement to holidays, including holiday pay, should be sufficient to enable the employee's entitlement, including any entitlement to accrued holiday pay on the termination of employment, to be precisely calculated.[3] Hence, in the absence of a clear common-law rule, reliance is being placed upon specific contractual provision to deal with accrual of holiday pay.

The question of apportionment of remuneration is not clearly resolved by statute law despite the existence of a statutory provision of some obvious relevance. Section 2 of the Apportionment Act 1870 provides that, 'From and after the passing of this Act all rents, annuities, dividends, and other periodical payments in the nature of income . . . shall, like interest on money lent, be considered as accruing from day to day and shall be apportionable in respect of time accordingly.' Section 5 defines 'annuities' as including 'salaries

---

[1] 97 LT 98, 101.
[2] *Hurt* v. *Sheffield Corporation* (1916) 85 LJ(NS)KB pt. 2 p. 1684.
[3] Now 1972 Act s. 4(1)(d)(i).

and pensions'. But the scope of the application of that Act to contracts of employment is not clearly established. The Divisional Court in *Moriarty* v. *Regents Garage Co. Ltd.*,[1] whilst deciding that Section 2 applied to the remuneration of company directors, did not, as is commonly thought, regard it as applicable to wages as well as salaries. Indeed both judges recognized that there was a distinction between salary and wages—i.e. between the wages of superior and inferior servants—and regarded the Act as applicable only to the former.[2] It is quite unclear how far that social distinction survives in the present law. The history of this particular provision in the 1870 Act shows that it was intended to apply to the salaried holders of offices of profit,[3] and the whole context of the Act is that of proprietary rather than purely contractual interests. It is regrettable that the impact of statute upon this problem should be tangential and unsystematic as far as contracts of employment are concerned.

So far we have considered the effect upon the right to remuneration of the type of breach of contract which consists in the employee's failure to complete the promised period of service. Important also is the effect of the type of breach which consists in misconduct or the production of defective work. The law has developed somewhat differently in relation to misconduct on the one hand and defective work on the other. As far as misconduct is concerned, there have been attempts to persuade the courts to apply the doctrine of entire obligations to the contract of employment in such a way that it would be a condition precedent to the employee's right to wages, not only that he work for a complete period, but also that he commit no misconduct during that period. In *Button* v. *Thompson* (1869)[4] such an argument was rejected by a majority of the Court of Common Pleas. There a sailor was engaged under articles, in a standard form approved by the Board of Trade, for a voyage of up to twelve months at £5 10s. per month. He was left behind at an intermediate port as the result of his own negligence. During the voyage out, he had been guilty at various times of drunkenness and violent and insubordinate conduct. On return he sued for wages in respect of the completed months of the voyage, and it was held by a majority that the wages

---

[1] [1921] 1 KB 423.   [2] Lush J., ibid. at 429–30; McCardie J. at 444–5.

[3] It would appear that the word 'salaries' was inserted into the 1870 Act so as to enable the salaried holder of a private office to obtain the benefit of the Act, and in order to abolish the contrary ruling in *Lowndes* v. *Earl of Stanford* (1852) 18 QB 423 (which related to the Act of 1834).

[4] LR 4 CP 330.

became a debt due at the end of each month[1] (liable to forfeiture by statute in the event of desertion, but that had not occurred here). It was also held that the terms in the articles whereby the employee undertook to be of good conduct constituted a promise by the employee but not a condition precedent to the liability of the employer to pay wages, so that wages could not be withheld on that ground.

A similar result was reached in *Healey* v. *Société Anonyme Française Rubastic*[2] where a managing director, employed at a salary of £500 per annum payable monthly, was dismissed in October 1915, his salary having been paid up to the end of May 1915. The dismissal was justified in view of dishonest conduct which had occurred at times prior to May 1915. When the managing director claimed arrears of salary down to the time of dismissal, it was held that he was entitled to salary in respect of each completed month, i.e. down to the end of September 1915; and that the continuing concealment of prior misconduct during those months did not constitute the non-fulfilment of a condition precedent to the employer's liability for salary in respect of those months. Avery J. observed that the effect of permitting the doctrine of conditions precedent to be applied in this way would be to backdate the dismissal to the time of the original misconduct, and that he was not prepared to do.[3] It would none the less be consistent with that decision to withhold remuneration in respect of periods during which the employee had actually committed acts of dishonesty.

In *Secretary of State for Employment* v. *ASLEF* (No. 2)[4] Lord Denning M.R. suggested the same approach to periods during which the employee was wilfully disrupting the employer's enterprise: 'I ask: Is a man to be entitled to wages for his work when he, with others, is doing his best to make it useless? Surely not. Wages are to be paid for services rendered, not for producing deliberate chaos. The breach goes to the whole of the consideration.'[5] By implying that working-to-rule does *not* enable employees to earn their remuneration while achieving all the effects of industrial action, this dictum indicates the considerable practical importance of the effect of breach of contract upon entitlement to remuneration.

---

[1] *Cutter* v. *Powell* (1795) 6 TR 320 being distinguished on the express terms of the contract.
[2] [1917] 1 KB 946.   [3] Ibid. at 947.   [4] [1972] ICR 19.
[5] Ibid. at 56 D–E.

If we turn from the case of misconduct to that of defective work, the law of the contract of employment there depends upon the extent to which the doctrine of substantial performance of entire contracts applies to such contracts. The doctrine of substantial performance has developed in relation to contracts for constructional services—building, decorating, and equipping premises, and services of that kind. The doctrine has two separate aspects. On the one hand it prevents the recipient of such services, where the contract has been substantially performed, from relying on minor defects to relieve him from the entire obligation of payment. On the other hand, it entitles that person to set off, against the sum due, the cost of remedying the defects plus general damages for inconvenience. We shall consider whether anything in the law of the contract of employment corresponds to these two aspects of the rule concerning substantial performance.

The first aspect of the rule concerning substantial performance is best stated in the terminology of contracts for constructional services as a rule that defects in workmanship and departures from specification do not entitle the injured party to withhold payment, unless the defects are such as to bring about a total failure of consideration, or at least such as to negate substantial performance. The rule can be traced back to a case in 1794 concerning the erection of a booth on Bath race ground.[1] In *Dakin & Co. Ltd.* v. *Lee* (1916)[2] the rule was stated in such a way as to suggest that it might merely be of the '*de minimis non curat lex*' kind;[3] but in *Hoenig* v. *Isaacs* (1952)[4] and most recently in *Bolton* v. *Mahadeva* (1972)[5] it was emphasized that the failure in performance must be a substantial one, thus bringing the law concerning remuneration more into line with the law concerning rescission of contracts generally, where the relevant comparison is with fundamental breach as a ground for rescission. The rule is probably in that form applicable to contracts of employment and is comparable to the rule concerning withholding of remuneration on the ground of misconduct.

[1] *Broom* v. *Davies* (1794) 7 East 480 (note).
[2] [1916] 1 KB 566; [1916] 1 KB 577.
[3] See the statement of the rule by Lord Cozens-Hardy at 578–8. The headnote to the case states the rule in the wider terms in which it was put by Sankey J at first instance—ibid. at 574 But it is now recognized that the headnote is misleading as to what the Court of Appeal decided—Bankes L.J. in *Vigers* v. *Cook* [1919] 2 KB 475, 483; Cairns L.J. in *Bolton* v. *Mahadeva* [1972] 1 WLR 1009, 1012 B–C.
[4] [1952] 2 All ER 176.   [5] [1972] 1 WLR 1009.

The second and complementary rule which emerged from the cases on building contracts was a procedural one. Originally the procedure was that the injured party must, given that there had not been a total failure of consideration, pay the price and claim damages in a cross-action. But the courts then recognized a right in the defendant to set off his loss arising from the defects and omissions.[1] Although procedural provision is made in the Rules of the Supreme Court for setting off the defendant's claim against the plaintiff's as an integral part of the defence,[2] it remains a matter of law rather than procedure whether any particular type of claim can be set off, and there was disagreement among the judges in *Sagar* v. *Ridehalgh & Son Ltd.* (1930)[3] whether the employer was entitled to deduct from his workers' wages in respect of defective work, without an express term; that is, as a matter of common law. There is an argument in principle against such setting-off under contracts of employment, in that it would have the effect of raising the employee's implied duty of care to the level of a guarantee that each item of his work shall be free of defect—a promise which can more readily be imported into a contract for the performance of a single exactly specified job than into a contract for the performance of continuing services under the control and direction of the employer. On that view, the doctrine of substantial performance applies to contracts of employment in such a way as to require the employer to pay the agreed remuneration in full once the employee has substantially performed his obligation to serve—which he does by so proceeding that it cannot be said that he has committed any fundamental breach of his undertaking.

SECTION 4: DAMAGES FOR BREACH BY THE EMPLOYEE

Cases concerning the awarding of damages against employees for absence from work or departure from employment in breach of contract provide an interesting example of development of law by reason of historical factors peculiar to this particular type of contract. (Equally interesting is the body of principles governing

---

[1] *Thornton* v. *Place* (1819) 1 Moo & R 218 at 219—cf. Parke B. in *Mondel* v. *Steel* (1841) 8 M & W 858 at 870–1.

[2] RSC, O.18 r. 17.

[3] [1930] 2 Ch. 117, reversed [1931] 1 Ch. 310. The application of the rule was doubted by Farwell J. at first instance—[1930] 2 Ch. at 128–9 but held to apply by Lord Hanworth M.R. on appeal—[1931] 1 Ch. at 323–6.

damages for breach of contract by the employer. That is discussed later in this work under the head of Wrongful Dismissal.) The state of the law resulting from that historical development raises difficulties of principle which can be resolved only by deciding what should be the objectives of awards of damages against employees for breach of their contracts of employment.

The employer's right to damages for the wrongful departure of the employee or for misconduct by the employee has not been the subject of many decisions in the higher courts. As far as executive, commercial, and scientific employees are concerned, employers have generally sought to protect themselves, upon the departure of their employees, by means of injunctions to protect the goodwill of their businesses or their trade secrets, rather than by means of damages for wrongful departure. Such authority as exists concerning damages against employees for breach of the contract of employment deals almost entirely with claims against industrial employees for damages for wrongfully absenting themselves from work for limited periods of time, normally by way of industrial action. These actions were brought at first under the Master and Servant Act 1867 and later under the Employers and Workmen Act 1875. They reveal the absence during a long period of time of any systematic principle for the measure of damages, an absence explicable upon historical grounds. More recently there have been decisions in which there has developed something of a body of principles to deal with this question.

The absence of principles concerning the measure of damages in actions against employees under the Employers and Workmen Act 1875 is an indirect result of the criminal character of the jurisdiction against employees under the old Master and Servant Acts. The Master and Servant Act 1867 was an unsatisfactory compromise between, on the one hand, the position under the older Acts that breach of contract by a servant was a criminal offence punishable by imprisonment, and on the other hand, the demand of the trade union movement that it should be an entirely civil matter, as was breach of contract by the employer. A central feature of this compromise was the provision of Section 9 of the Act that the magistrates could, *inter alia*, award damages or compensation for breach of contract or, where no amount of compensation or damage could be assessed, or where pecuniary compensation would not meet the case, impose a fine upon the employee. The magistrates in applying this section seem to have treated it as if damages and fines were interchangeable at their discretion, and as if damages could be fixed arbitrarily like fines, rather than being assessed according to the loss caused by the breach of contract. This approach is well illustrated by a survey of cases decided by magistrates under the 1867 Act and recorded in the Reports of the Royal Commission on the Labour Laws[1] which dealt with the Master and Servant Acts and with the law concerning conspiracy. The survey discloses that magistrates would very often award damages of fixed sums resembling fines, such as 10s., £1, and £2.[2] In other cases *fines* were imposed for that sum of money which the employer had claimed as damages.[3]

The power of magistrates to fine employees for breach of contract did not survive the Employers and Workmen Act 1875. That Act conferred upon both the County Courts and the magistrates the jurisdiction to award damages for breach of the contract of employment. These provisions used quite frequently to be invoked as a sanction against industrial action, especially by the mine-owners and their successors the National Coal Board.[4] The County Courts and the magistrates, in applying the 1875 Act, to some extent perpetuated the confusion between damages and fines. Various examples are to be found of cases where 'damages' have been fixed without reference to actual loss. Thus in *Bowes & Partners Ltd.* v. *Press*,[5] some miners who had refused to descend a pit in the same cage as non-union workers and missed three days of work were held liable in damages of five shillings. It was intended to be an assessment of substantial rather than nominal damages, yet was one which clearly bore no relation to the actual loss on either side. Another instance of the assessment of damages in such actions as if they were fines occurs in *Ayling* v. *London & India Docks Committee*[6] where damages against an employee for three weeks' absence on strike were assessed at £1 on the ground that 'It has been usual in such cases to give the party complaining a week's wages. Therefore

---

[1] *First Report* (1874) Parliamentary Papers 1874 XXIV pp. 391 ff. *Second Report* (1875) PP 1875 XXI pp. 1 ff.

[2] e.g. the cases dealt with by the magistrates of Durham from 1870 to 1873— *First Report* pp. 20–1—and a case in 1874 in Marlborough Street Police Court— *First Report* p. 64.

[3] e.g. *Hodge* v. *Pike* (1873) Torquay Petty Sessions—*First Report* p. 62.

[4] The 1875 Act was itself repealed by the Statute Law (Repeals) Act 1973 implementing a recommendation made by *Law Commission Report No. 49* on the ground that the special jurisdictions concerned were 'seldom, if ever invoked' —ibid. p. 49. See above, pp. 2–3.

[5] [1894] 1 QB 202.   [6] (1893) 9 TLR 409.

the plaintiff is indebted to the defendants in the sum of 20s., which he has to pay as damages for not giving a week's notice.'[1] Grunfeld argued that it was preferable that the 1875 Act should be used in this way to impose a moderate disciplinary sanction rather than that it should be used for the large compensatory awards against employees which, as will be shown below, may follow from the principles laid down in more recent cases.[2] But he concedes that the method of fixing damages used in this case was an arbitrary one.[3]

Very often actions of this kind were in the nature of test cases, and the assessment of the actual loss would be a matter of little importance, since the employer was concerned primarily with establishing the illegality of the action taken. In more recent cases, there has been some development of principles for assessing damages, mainly because employers sought to place upon individual employees the liability for substantial losses resulting from collective action. In *Ebbw Vale Steel Iron & Coal Co.* v. *Tew*[4] and *National Coal Board* v. *Galley*[5] it was held by the Court of Appeal that an individual employee cannot be held liable for loss of output resulting from collective stoppage of work, except to the extent of the loss attributable to his individual absence from work, unless there is some special ground for doing so. In the latter case the court came close to recognizing that the loss caused by the collective stoppage could be attributed to the liability of the individual employee only as a matter of tort rather than contract.

Given that loss arising from concerted withdrawal of labour will not be attributed to the breach of any individual contract, the question remains whether the individual employee is contractually liable for stoppage of the work of other employees made inevitable by his own absence from work. In *National Coal Board* v. *Galley* the refusal by a deputy to work Saturday morning shifts had the actual result that no work was done by a group of coal-face workers on the occasions concerned until substitute deputies were employed. The Court of Appeal held that the deputy could not be held liable for loss of output but only for the cost of employing a substitute, in this case £3 18s. on each occasion.[6] This assessment was not strictly calculated in that on the relevant occasions no substitute

---

[1] Ibid. at 410 (the Judge of the City of London Court).
[2] *Modern Trade Union Law* (London 1966) p. 329.
[3] Ibid.   [4] (1935) 1 Law Journal Notes County Court Appeals 284.
[5] [1958] 1 WLR 16.   [6] See Pearce L.J. [1958] 1 WLR at 29.

was in fact employed, these being brought in only on later occasions. Hence the question is left open as to how extensive is the burden on the employer to prevent consequential loss by procuring substitute labour.

Where the loss caused by the withdrawal of labour is a clearly identifiable loss of output, and is not bound up with consequential stoppage of a process of work, then the decision in *Ebbw Vale Steel Iron & Coal Co.* v. *Tew* gives some guidance upon the method of assessing that loss. In that case the defendant was a coal-miner whose work consisted in the actual cutting of coal. The Court of Appeal affirmed that the basic principle was that of putting the employer in the position in which he would have been if the contract had been performed.[1] They rejected the claim advanced on behalf of the employer, that damages extended to the whole cost of overheads incurred in expectation of the work being done. They rejected on the other hand the argument for the employee that damages were limited to loss of net profit on coal sold. They adopted the compromise formula of taking the gross value of the expected output of the employee and deducting from it the wages and other expenses in fact saved by his absence.[2] However, the increased mechanization and sub-division of industrial processes has the result that such a calculation based on direct output can rarely be made and that a far more difficult assessment of value added by the work of the employee would have to be made in almost every case.

The assessment of damages against the employee for wrongful departure or other breach of contract has ultimately to be considered in terms of the purpose of the remedy against the employee. If such actions are brought as a sanction against industrial action, then it is the policy governing the intervention of the law in industrial relations which must decide whether damages should be substantial or not. In such cases, damages are not in any case serving the purpose of adjusting specific loss. On the other hand such actions may be seen as genuinely having the function of adjustment of loss where they are brought because a scientific or executive employee in a highly responsible position has seriously disrupted his employer's enterprise by his departure. If such cases were to come frequently before the higher courts, there might be a re-evaluation of the rule in *National*

---

[1] Per Roche L.J. (1935) 1 LJNCCA at 285–6, citing *British Westinghouse Ltd* v. *Underground Railways Ltd.* [1912] AC 673.

[2] Per Roche L.J. (1935) 1 LJNCCA at 287.

Coal Board v. *Galley* against recovery of loss consisting in consequential stoppage of work. In recent litigation arising out of a contract for an actor to play a leading part in a television film,[1] it was held that in claiming damages for wrongful repudiation by the actor, the employing company could, where they were unable to show what their profit on the film would have been, recover wasted expenditure; and that the recoverable expenditure could include expenses incurred *before* the contract was made provided it was such as would reasonably be in the contemplation of the parties as likely to be wasted if the contract was broken. It remains to be seen whether this radical approach to the adjustment of loss arising out of wrongful refusal to work will be applied to contracts of employment generally. This application could be significant in that it will normally be easier for an employer deprived of services in breach of contract to show wasted expenditure (for instance, on selection of the employee) than specific loss of profit.

---

[1] *Anglia Television Ltd.* v. *Reed* [1972] 1 **QB** 60.

Chapter Five

TERMINATION BY NOTICE
AND AGREEMENT

INTRODUCTION

The subject-matter of the present chapter is the termination of the contract of employment by the agreement of the parties, or at least that which the law is prepared to regard as their agreement. That agreement may be expressed in various different ways. It may form part of the original contract of employment. In that case it may consist of an agreement that the contract shall be of a certain fixed duration or that it shall be terminable by notice. An agreement for termination by notice may by prior or subsequent agreement be transformed into payment in lieu of notice. The termination of the contract may also be effected by agreement made separately from the original contract.

All these forms of termination of the contract of employment have in recent years become more important because of their relation to the concept of 'dismissal', which is central to the statutory provisions concerning redundancy payments and remedies for unfair dismissal. Moreover, the law concerning the duration and terminability of the contract of employment serves to define the extent of contractual security of employment in a more general sense. Hence this chapter considers in detail the conditions upon which various kinds of termination by agreement may be effected.

SECTION 1: DURATION AND NOTICE—TERMS IMPLIED BY COMMON LAW

For contracts in general, the typical method of lawful termination is by full performance. In the case of a contract where obligations are expressed in terms of periods of time, due performance takes the form of expiry of a fixed term. Contracts of employment are untypical in that they are usually contracts of indefinite duration, of which the standard method of lawful termination is the giving of notice.

In deciding the duration of the contract of employment, or its terminability by notice (or by payment in lieu of notice), the courts are engaged upon a process of construction of the intentions of the parties themselves. Those intentions have, however, been sufficiently unclear, in a sufficient number of cases, for the courts to have evolved patterns which they have then imposed upon particular contracts of employment. This section examines the different forms of contract of employment which have been recognized at common law.

A. The Implied Fixed Term of a Year

If the common law concerning the duration and terminability of contracts of employment appeared for many years remote both from contemporary employment practice and from the general principles of the law of contract, the reason was to be found in the persistence of the presumption of the year's duration. The persistence of the rule has recently been attributed to a judicial nostalgia for the rustic way of life.[1] That is perhaps an exaggeration; but it may be said that this presumption did at one stage spread beyond those types of employment in which it represented existing custom. The implied fixed term of a year antedated the industrial revolution and represented a custom of agricultural employment. We proceed to examine its impact in the area of industrial and commercial employment, where the contract of employment has been gradually forged into its present shape.

The presumption of employment for the fixed term of a year was very widely applied in the early years of the nineteenth century, and could include industrial employees in its scope.[2] It is clear that during this period certain types of industrial employees were employed for substantial fixed terms, indeed that they were bound to their employers in the manner of apprentices.[3] The Report of the

[1] Drake, 'The Deserted Village' (a note on *Richardson* v. *Koefod* [1969] 1 WLR 1812) at (1970) 33 MLR 325.
[2] e.g. *Turner* v. *Robinson* (1833) 5 B & Ad. 789 (foreman to silk manufacturers; apparently a manual rather than a managerial employee).
[3] e.g. *R.* v. *St. John Devizes (Inhabitants)* (1829) 9 B & C 896 (mill-worker; four-year term); *Pilkington* v. *Scott* (1846) 15 M & W 657 and *Hartley* v. *Cummings* (1847) 5 CB 247 (glass-blowers; seven-year terms); *Williamson* v. *Taylor* (1843) 5 QB 175 (coal-miner; year's term—type of contracts known as 'pit-bond'). See Meyers, *Ownership of Jobs* (UCLA 1964) p. 18 and texts there cited; Page Arnot, *The Scottish Miners* (London 1955) Chapter 1; Hammond and Hammond, *The Skilled Labourer* (London 1919) Chapter 2 (miners of the Tyne and Wear).

Select Committee on the Law of Master and Servant (1866) shows evidence of a custom in the pottery trade whereby the employee was bound for a fixed term of a year from Martinmas to Martinmas, though the employer was entitled to terminate by a month's notice.[1]

However, this practice gradually gave way to a practice of employment for an indefinite period terminable by notice, most typically by fourteen days' notice.[2] It would seem that this process was so far advanced by 1862 that the courts would no longer presume a yearly hiring in cases of industrial employment.[3] Moreover, the same Report of the Select Committee on the Law of Master and Servant provides evidence of the spread in industrial employment of contracts terminable upon very short notice or at will, including the 'minute contract'—so called because it was regarded as terminable upon a nominal minute's notice.[4] It appears, however, that the 'minute contract' itself never gained the same currency in England as it had in Scotland. The customary terms in industrial employment in England would tend to provide for short notice rather than termination at will.[5]

The tendency to abandon the practice of long fixed-term contracts in favour of contracts terminable by short notice would be encouraged by employers of industrial labour, as enabling them to expand or contract their labour force more quickly and easily in response to the state of trade.[6] It was on the other hand acceptable to employees and their unions because it reduced their exposure to imprisonment for absence in breach of contract under the Master and Servant Acts

[1] Parly. Papers 1866 Vol. 13 pp. 1 ff.; evidence of Newton, ibid. at p. 15 qu. 77. See Meyers, op. cit. at p. 21.

[2] e.g. *Re Bailey, Re Collier* (1854) 3 E & B 607 (coal-miner—month's notice); *Mary Taylor* v. *Carr & Porter* (1861) 30 LJ (NS) MC 201 (mill-worker—two weeks' notice); *Whittle* v. *Frankland* (1862) 2 B & S 49 (coal-miner—month's notice); *Rideout* v. *Jenkinson* (1874) 38 JP 424 (journeyman in paper factory—two weeks' notice); *Carus* v. *Eastwood* (1875) 32 LT 855 (mill-worker—two weeks' notice).

[3] *Alice Taylor* v. *Carr & Porter* (1862) 2 B & S 335 (mill-worker).

[4] P.P. 1866 Vol. 13 pp. 1 ff. (above); Evidence of Newton, p. 15, qu. 79–82 (carpenters and joiners of Glasgow); Campbell, p. 30, qu. 383–92 (engineering, shipbuilding, and building trades in Glasgow); Dickinson, p. 106, qu. 2113–28 (miners in Lancashire).

[5] Ibid; Evidence of Lancaster p. 64, qu. 1457–65 (miners in England generally); Forster, p. 78, qu. 1546–55, 1577–80 (miners in North of England); Mathews, p. 131, qu. 2496–8; p. 132, qu. 2514–18 (coal and iron industry in south Staffordshire).

[6] See Hobsbawn, *Labouring Men* (London, 1964) Chapter 17—'Custom, Wages & Workload in Nineteenth Century Industry', p. 356 and note 43.

in force before 1867. Meyers notes that the passing of the statutes of 1867 and 1875 halted the movement for contracts of employment terminable at will and without notice, but that the excessively long notice periods, and the contracts for a fixed term for very long periods, seem gradually to have disappeared.[1] Hence, during the nineteenth century the presumption of a yearly hiring became progressively less applicable in the context of industrial employment.

So far did this tendency progress towards a reduced security of employment for manual workers, that we find the courts regarding the contract of employment terminable at will as an established pattern of employment for munitions workers of the First World War.[2] Tillyard records, indeed, that the custom of 'no notice on either side' was positively favoured by the Amalgamated Society of Engineers (as it then was) on the grounds that it enabled employees to move immediately to jobs offering increased wages.[3] In any event it is clear that even in the absence of this custom, a manual industrial employee would by that time normally be entitled only to one day's, or at best one week's, notice, and that the presumption of a fixed term of a year could not reasonably be applied in this context.

The presumption of a yearly hiring was taken still further out of its original context in the case of managerial employees.[4] Moreover, in the sphere of managerial, technical, and executive employment, the presumption continued to be applied long after the time at which it had any counterpart in employment practice.[5] The cases in which this was done may be explained on the grounds that a provision for termination upon reasonable notice would not be implied where that was regarded as inconsistent with the nature of the employment. Hence, for example, Du Parcq L.J. in *Jackson* v. *Hayes Candy & Co.*

---

[1] Op. cit. at p. 21.
[2] *Hulme* v. *Ferranti Ltd.* [1918] 2 KB 426. *Contra—Payzu Ltd.* v. *Hannaford* [1918] 2 KB 348 (see below, p. 153). But Tillyard says that case conflicted with a widespread belief in practice that the contracts of manual workers were terminable at will—*The Worker & The State* (London 1923) at pp. 10–11.
[3] Op. cit. at pp. 9–10.
[4] e.g. *Fawcett* v. *Cash* (1834) 5 B & Ad. 904—warehouseman (in the sense of manager of a warehouse); *Baxter* v. *Nurse* (1844) 6 M & G 935 (editor of a periodical) where, however, the presumption was regarded as a flexible one and was in fact held to be rebutted.
[5] *Buckingham* v. *Surrey & Hants Canal Co.* (1882) 46 LT 885 (consulting engineer at a salary of £500 p.a.); *Vernon* v. *Findlay* [1938] 4 All ER 31 (reversed by CA on a different ground [1939] 2 All ER 716) (sales manager at £350 p.a. plus commission).

Ltd.[1] was not prepared to treat the contract of employment as terminable by notice in the middle of a year, because the employee was paid partly by a commission calculated upon complete years and expressed to be payable only upon complete years.

However, the presumption of a yearly hiring was an archaic and inappropriate solution to this type of problem; and after several decisions in which it was held that the presumption of terminability upon reasonable notice should be preferred,[2] it has finally been ruled by the Court of Appeal, in the context of managerial employment, that the presumption of a yearly hiring no longer applies, and has been replaced by the presumption of terminability upon reasonable notice.[3] Edmund Davies L.J. commented that 'It may well be that, after this lapse of time, and in the light of so complete a transformation in our economic and industrial structure, there is little (if any) room for such a general presumption as anciently prevailed in this country.'[4] It is therefore now confirmed that the presumption of a fixed term of a year has outlived its usefulness in all the main types of employment to which it was once applied. It was ousted by other patterns of contracting which are examined in the course of this section.

B. *The Periodic Contract of Employment*

There is some suggestion in early cases that the courts were inclined to regard certain types of contract of employment as conforming to the pattern of periodic tenancies. The characteristics of periodic tenancies are:

(1) that the tenancy renews itself automatically at the end of each period unless terminated by prior notice, and
(2) that the notice required to terminate the tenancy must
    (a) in the case of yearly tenancies, be a notice terminating with

---

[1] [1938] 4 All ER 587. The case concerned an assistant buyer in a clothing store. Presumption regarded as still existing, though not applicable on the facts, in *Mulholland* v. *Bexwell Estates Co. Ltd.* (1950) 66 TLR pt. 2 p. 764 Parker J.

[2] *De Stempel* v. *Dunkels* [1938] 1 All ER 238 (aff'd by HL (1939) 55 TLR 655 on a different issue) (clerk with special responsibilities); *Fisher* v. *Dick & Co. Ltd.* [1938] 4 All ER 467 (engineering salesman); *Adams* v. *Union Cinemas Ltd.* [1939] All ER 136 (cinema manager).

[3] *Richardson* v. *Koefod* [1969] 1 WLR 1812 (manageress of a café); see Lord Denning M.R. at 1816 D–E; Fenton Atkinson L.J. at 1818 B.

[4] Ibid. at 1817 G.

the end of a period, whatever the required length of the
notice;
(b) in the case of periodic tenancies for shorter periods, such
as monthly tenancies, be a notice as long as the period and
terminating with the end of the period.[1]

It seems to have been thought at one time that similar rules applied
to contracts of employment for a fixed period in the first instance
which continued beyond the original fixed period.[2]

However, the influence of the pattern of the periodic tenancy upon
the contract of employment was not very extensive or very long-lived.
In *Ryan* v. *Jenkinson*,[3] it was held that where a schoolmaster was
employed at an annual salary upon terms of three months' notice
to terminate on either side, it was not essential to the validity of the
notice that it should expire at the end of a year; and Coleridge J.
expressly distinguished this case from that of the periodic tenancy
on policy grounds:

'In the case of land there would be great inconvenience arising from the
nature of the property and the course of husbandry to allow the relation
of landlord and tenant to be terminated at any time; but with regard to a
school it might be of great importance that a master who had done some
act not sufficient to justify immediate expulsion should not be allowed to
continue in his office until the expiration of the current year.'[4]

As the schoolmaster of a charity school, the plaintiff was the holder
of an office rather than an ordinary employee,[5] but it would
seem that this reasoning would *a fortiori* be applicable to ordinary
employees, because the law normally accords a greater security of
tenure to the holders of office. The analogy with yearly tenancies
was again rejected, this time in the case of the contract of a foreign
correspondent of a newspaper in 1892[6]; and by 1925 the view was
taken that tenancy agreements and service agreements were in quite

---

[1] See Megarry and Wade, *Law of Real Property* (4th edn. 1975) pp. 633–7
(yearly tenancies) and 637–8 (other periodic tenancies).
[2] Cf. Best C.J. in *Beeston* v. *Collyer* (1827) 4 Bing. 309, 311–12; Littledale J.
in *Williams* v. *Byrne* (1837) 7 A & E 177, 182–3.
[3] (1855) 25 LJ(NS) QB 11.
[4] Ibid. (i.e. Coleridge J. was saying that the school required the protection of a
right to give notice at any time).
[5] See below, pp. 285–7.
[6] Lord Coleridge C.J. in *Lowe* v. *Walter* (1892) 8 TLR 358 at 359 *arguendo*.

distinct classes, and that tenancy agreements depended on different considerations by reason of the rule about holding over.[1]

The influence of the pattern of the periodic tenancy may, however, have been responsible for the view which was once held that the reasonable period of notice required to terminate contracts of employment was a period as long as the period of the calculation of wages (so that if an employee was paid weekly wages, his contract would be terminable upon a week's notice).[2] This view would not now seem to be tenable, and it may in general be said that contracts of employment will not now be treated as analogous to periodic tenancies. Instead they will be treated either as contracts for fixed terms (whether or not terminable by notice) or as contracts for indefinite periods terminable by notice.[3]

C. The Purpose Contract

The contract of employment whose duration is that of a specific task or purpose (such as the completion of a given building) is recognized at common law. Thus it may be held for the purpose of vicarious liability in the law of tort that a person employed for the duration of a specific task is a servant employed under a contract of service. It was so held in *Sadler* v. *Henlock* (1855),[4] which concerned a contract whereby a labourer undertook to clean out a drain, for which he was paid the lump sum of 5 shillings. Crompton J. commented: 'No distinction can be drawn from the circumstances of the man being employed at so much a day or by the job.'[5]

However, although the contract of employment for the duration of a particular purpose is one known to the law, it will not be of very frequent occurrence because the duration for the particular purpose tends to characterize the contract as a contract for services and the person employed as an independent contractor. This is

---

[1] Per Sir Ernest Pollock M.R. in *Costigan* v. *Gray Bovier Engines Ltd.* (1925) 41 TLR 372 at 373; see Megarry and Wade, op. cit. pp. 634–6. A holding-over may, instead of resulting in a periodic tenancy, create a tenancy at will (ibid. p. 638) or a tenancy at sufferance (ibid. p. 640).

[2] See below, pp. 153–4.

[3] A periodic contract of employment would probably be treated as a fixed-term contract for the purpose of s. 1(4) of the 1972 Act. S. 3(1)(b) of the 1965 Act and s. 23(2)(b) of the 1971 Act would probably apply to the termination of a periodic contract of employment, even if that were not a dismissal on other grounds.

[4] 4 E & B 570.   [5] Ibid. at 578.

apparent in the context of vicarious liability in the law of tort.[1] It was upon this ground, moreover, that in certain early cases piece-workers were held to lie outside the scope of the Master and Servant Act 1823 which applied only to persons serving under certain contracts *of service*.[2]

Where a contract of employment has the duration of a specific task or purpose, there is some doubt whether it counts as a 'fixed-term contract' or a 'contract for a term certain', for the purposes of the 1965, 1971, and 1972 Acts. In *Whiles* v. *Harold Wesley Ltd.*,[3] following the reorganization of a company, a book-keeper employed by the company was placed on a short-term basis, the agreement being that she should work either to the end of a given month or until her work had been completed. (The evidence did not distinguish clearly between the two.) It was held that the termination of this contract probably fell within Section 3(1)(b) of the 1965 Act (expiry of fixed-term contracts), but, if not, was an ordinary dismissal within Section 3(1)(a). The question remains undecided.

D. *The Customary Notice*

The recognition of customary terms for the termination of contracts of employment by notice has played an important part in the development of the presumption that contracts of employment are terminable by either side upon reasonable notice. The best-known custom of termination of contracts of employment by notice is that whereby the contracts of employment of domestic servants are terminable by a month's notice given by the employee and by a month's notice or payment in lieu of notice given or made by the employer.[4] This custom was one of which judicial notice was taken, so that it need not be proved afresh on each particular occasion. After an initial

[1] See Atiyah, *Vicarious Liability in the Law of Torts* (London 1967) p. 67.
[2] 4 Geo. IV c. 34. The cases were: *Hardy* v. *Ryle* (1829) B & C 603 (silk-weaver); *Lancaster* v. *Greaves* (1829) 9 B & C 628 (contract by a wall-builder to make a stretch of road); *Ex p. Johnson* (1839) 7 Dowl. 702 (calico printer). Note the social change which was recognized in *Ex p. Gordon* (1855) 25 LJ (NS) MC 12—journeyman tailor treated as within the 1823 Act because, although paid by the price under a contract terminable on the completion of any piece of work, he worked wholly on the premises under the control of a single employer. See Tillyard, *The Worker and the State* (London 1923) pp. 8–9, 10.
[3] (1966) 1 ITR 342.
[4] See for example: *Robinson* v. *Hindman* (1800) 3 Esp. 235 per Lord Kenyon at 235; *Beeston* v. *Collyer* (1827) 4 Bing. 309 per Gaselee J. at 313; *Turner* v. *Mason* (1845) 14 M & W 112 per Parke B. at 116; *Brittain* v. *London & N.W. Ry. Co.* (1857) 28 LT (OS) 253 *per curiam* at p. 253.

refusal[1] the courts were persuaded to take general notice in the same way of a custom whereby a domestic servant might, after the first two weeks of his employment, give notice to terminate at the end of the first month—i.e. he might at that point terminate by two weeks' notice.[2] It would seem that this custom conferred a corresponding right upon the employer. So well was it established that this custom applied to all domestic servants that it gave rise to litigation upon the question whether particular employees were counted as domestic.[3] Hence the custom became in effect a legal norm of general application to a whole class of employees.[4]

Where the incorporation of a custom into a contract of employment has to be proved in a particular case, it must then satisfy the tests of certainty, reasonableness, and notoriety or universality.[5] It would seem that antiquity need not be proved as a separate requirement, because these are trade customs or usages rather than customs in the general sense.[6] These restrictions did not prevent the successful proof of customary provisions for termination by notice in the cases especially of commercial and clerical employments in the middle years of the nineteenth century,[7] to the point where a right to terminate by notice became the widespread rule in cases other than that of domestic service.

The rôle of trade customs in providing for notice has been to a considerable extent superseded by provisions for minimum periods of notice in collective agreements, and by the statutory provisions for the same purpose. Moreover, arguments about the incorporation of customary terms providing for notice will have been to a great extent eliminated by the requirement of Section 4 of the Contracts of

---

[1] *Moult* v. *Halliday* [1898] 1 QB 125.

[2] *George* v. *Davies* [1911] 2 KB 445.

[3] e.g. *Todd* v. *Kerrich* (1852) 8 Ex. 151—governess not a domestic servant; *Nicoll* v. *Greaves* (1864) 17 CB (NS) 27—huntsman was a domestic servant; *Wilson* v. *Ucelli* (1929) 45 TLR 395—private tutor not a domestic servant.

[4] Which might, however, in a given case be overridden by the minimum-notice provisions of the 1972 Act.

[5] *Devonald* v. *Rosser & Sons* [1906] 2 KB 728 per Farwell L.J. at 743; *Sagar* v. *Ridehalgh & Son Ltd.* [1931] 1 Ch. 310 per Lawrence L.J. at 338.

[6] See Allen, *Law in the Making* (7th edn. 1964) p. 135. Byles J., in *Foxall* v. *International Land Credit Co.* (1867) 16 LT 637 at 639, required a custom for termination by notice to be 'of some reasonable antiquity and standing'—but not to date from time immemorial.

[7] *Metzner* v. *Bolton* (1854) 9 Ex. 518 (commercial traveller—three months' notice); *Fairman* v. *Oakford* (1860) 5 H & N 635 (clerk—three months' notice); *Foxall* v. *International Land Credit Co.* (1867) 16 LT 637 (above).

Employment Act 1972 that written particulars of terms of employment, including terms as to notice,[1] be issued by the employer within thirteen weeks of the commencement of an employment. The customary terms concerning notice were, however, essential to the growth of the implied provision for termination upon reasonable notice.

E The Implied Provision for Termination by Reasonable Notice

In the latter part of the nineteenth century the courts came to recognize that a provision for termination by employer or employee upon reasonable notice was generally to be implied into contracts of employment in the absence of contrary evidence. This development gave a new shape to the contract of employment as interpreted by the courts. It gradually ousted the implied fixed term of a year, and replaced it by an implied indefinite duration limited by the right of either party to terminate upon reasonable notice. This was essentially a judicial adaptation to a changing practice of employment.

The idea of a contract of employment terminable upon 'reasonable' notice occurs sporadically in the early and middle years of the nineteenth century. We find various instances of contracts of employment being pleaded as contracts terminable upon reasonable notice.[2] In a case decided in 1837 concerning the employment of a newspaper reporter, the right to terminate by reasonable notice was pleaded on behalf of the employer, and it was sought to justify that plea by alleging a term generally implied into contracts of employment for termination in that way.[3] This was, however, premature, for the court held that such a term required positive proof.[4] In 1857 a court could still reject the finding of a jury that the contract of employment of a clerk was terminable upon reasonable notice where no special evidence was offered of such a right to terminate.[5] It was held that there was no general rule of law conferring such a right.[6]

It has, however, been shown that the middle years of the nineteenth

---

[1] Section 4(1)(e).

[2] *Wilkinson* v. *Gaston* (1846) 9 QB 137 (employment as a secretary); *Lilley* v. *Elwin* (1848) 11 QB 742 (farm labourer, held to be a yearly hiring); *Nicoll* v. *Greaves* (1864) 17 CB 27 (huntsman, held to be a domestic service terminable at a month's notice).

[3] *Williams* v. *Byrne* 7 A & E 177 at p. 181 (counsel for defendant, *arguendo*).

[4] Ibid. at p. 183 (Littledale J.).

[5] *Brittain* v. *London & N.W. Ry. Co.* (1857) 28 LT 253.

[6] Ibid. at p. 253.

century saw an increasingly widespread legal recognition of customs for the termination of employment by notice, especially in domestic and clerical employment.[1] The step from the frequent recognition of customs for notice, which must comply with a requirement of reasonableness, to an implied term for termination by reasonable notice, is but a short one. We may observe that step being taken, for example, in a direction to a jury given by Byles J. in 1867.[2] And to Hawkins J. in 1879, the case 'of a servant hired generally whose service may be determined by reasonable notice at any time' was a familiar one.[3]

This development crystallized in the latter years of the nineteenth century. Thus in *Vibert* v. *Eastern Telegraph Co.*[4] in 1883, Stephen J. was prepared, in the case of an action by a clerk employed at a yearly salary, simply to leave it to the jury to say what was a reasonable notice in the plaintiff's situation. By 1886, in *MacDowall's Case*,[5] the customary notice of three months in the case of higher-grade clerks had become, for Chitty J., 'the notice which the law in an ordinary case allows and requires for a person in the position of [this employee]'. This indicates the change from custom to term implied by law. In *Lowe* v. *Walter*,[6] where the issue was the period of notice to which a foreign correspondent of *The Times* was entitled, Lord Coleridge C.J. directed the jury that if nothing was said as to notice, then, in the absence of custom, the question was, what was reasonable notice.

This development of the implied provision for termination by reasonable notice was reinforced by cases decided during the same period, where employers alleged that certain contracts of employment were terminable at will. The courts, finding the idea of contracts of employment terminable at will an unacceptable one, held that the contract was terminable only upon reasonable notice. It was so held in *Creen* v. *Wright*[7] which was the case of a ship's master whose employers alleged that his contract of employment was terminable at will between voyages. Lord Coleridge C.J. commented that 'As the master could not, except under very unusual circumstances, be dismissed during the continuance of a voyage and while the vessel

---

[1] See above, pp. 149–50.   [2] *Hiscox* v. *Batchellor* (1867) 15 LT 543 at 544.
[3] *Davey* v. *Shannon* (1879) 4 Ex. D 81, 86.
[4] (1885) Cab. & El. 17.   [5] (1886) 32 Ch. D. 366, 371.
[6] (1892) 8 TLR 358, 367. A closely similar direction was given to the jury by Lord Russell C.J. in *Fox-Bourne* v. *Vernon & Co. Ltd.* (1894) 10 TLR 647.
[7] (1876) 1 CPD 591.

was at sea, so he was entitled to some notice, and that is to reasonable notice, before dismissal in this country.'[1]

That this principle applies equally against the employee was shown by the decision in *Payzu Ltd* v. *Hannaford*,[2] where a machinist employed at wages paid weekly terminated her employment without notice at the end of a week. She was successfully sued for damages by the employer under the Employers and Workmen Act of 1875 on the ground that 'To terminate the service during the week is manifestly a breach of this contract; the utmost the law can imply in order to give some elasticity to it is a right to determine upon giving a reasonable notice.'[3] It is shown by a number of later dicta that the pattern of contract now generally accepted and applied by the courts in the absence of evidence to the contrary is one of employment for an indefinite period terminable by either party upon reasonable notice, but only upon reasonable notice.[4]

Certain principles, or at least tendencies, of the common law exist to determine what is the length of reasonable notice in a given case. Firstly, the pattern of the periodic contract has been influential upon this issue.[5] The result was a tendency to hold, for example, that contracts of employment for wages calculated and paid weekly are terminable by one week's notice. This explains why Pollock C.B. could rule in 1861 that 'No doubt the general rule is, that notice need not be more extensive than the period of payment.'[6] So in *Evans* v. *Roe*[7] in 1872, it could be ruled that a works foreman could be dismissed upon a mere week's notice because his written contract of employment provided for the payment of a weekly 'salary'; this resulted in the finding of a weekly hiring. Since that time, the influence of the periodic pattern upon the ascertainment of 'reasonable notice'

---

[1] Ibid. at 595.   [2] [1918] 2 KB 348.

[3] Ibid. at pp. 350–1 (A. T. Lawrence J.). *Contra*, however, *Hulme* v. *Ferranti Ltd.* [1918] 2 KB 426 (which may more accurately have reflected contemporary practice—see above, p. 145).

[4] *De Stempel* v. *Dunkels* [1938] 1 All ER 238, Greer L.J. at 247 F–H; Slesser L.J. at 252 H–253 A; Scott L.J. at 261 H (aff'd by HL on a different ground—55 TLR 655); *Fisher* v. *W. B. Dick & Co. Ltd.* [1938] 4 All ER 467, Bramson J. at 469 B–F; *Adams* v. *Union Cinemas Ltd.* [1939] 3 All ER 136, Du Parcq L.J. at 140 F–G, Atkinson J. at 143 E (cf. *Mulholland* v. *Bexwell Estates Co. Ltd.* (1950) 66 TLR pt. 2 p. 764, Parker J. at 767); *James* v. *Thomas H. Kent & Co. Ltd.* [1951] 1 KB 551, Somervell L.J. at 555, Denning L.J. at 556; *Richardson* v. *Koefod* [1969] 1 WLR 1812, per Lord Denning M.R. at 1816 E, Fenton Atkinson J. at 1818 B–C.

[5] See above, p. 148.   [6] *Davis* v. *Marshall* (1861) 4 LT 216, 217.

[7] (1872) LR 7 CP 138.

has declined, but has none the less been perceptible at times. Thus we find in the judgment of Lord Goddard C.J. in *Marshall* v. *English Electric Co. Ltd.*[1] the suggestion that an hourly-paid worker could be regarded as employed under a periodic contract which renews itself from hour to hour and is therefore terminable at an hour's notice. He regarded this as the position of very many industrial employees at that time.[2] However, it is very unlikely that any court would analyse contracts of employment in that way at the present day, quite apart from the impact of statutory reform.[3]

The other principle or tendency underlying the ascertainment of 'reasonable' notice is that the courts, in deciding that question in relation to a particular contract of employment, will take into account the nature of that employment, extending the period of notice as the degree of responsibility and the intellectual content of the job become greater. Thus a compilation which has been made[4] of the decided cases suggests as an approximate scale of length of reasonable notice (in descending order): managers and directors, editors and journalists, commercial travellers and salesmen, clerks, superior employees in manual occupations, and subordinate employees generally. A sampling of the cases of this kind is to be viewed with caution because of the very long period over which they range and the changes in employment practice during that period. However, the general conclusion may be drawn that the common law, in applying the concept of reasonable notice, recognizes that a greater degree of security of employment is associated with the higher social standing of one type of occupation over another.

F. Contracts for Permanent Employment

In order to complete this examination of the duration of the contract of employment, it will be considered whether the law recognizes a contract which is for permanent employment in the sense of being neither for a fixed term nor terminable by notice. The matter may be regarded as a problem of general contract principle, but this approach provides no clear answer. In the area of contracts of employment in particular, it seems to be accepted that a contract for permanent employment will not be treated as contrary to public policy, but an

---

[1] [1945] 1 All ER 653 at 655 A–E. [2] Ibid. at p. 655 A.
[3] See below, pp. 159–61.
[4] *Chitty on Contracts* (23rd edn. 1968) Vol. II Para 712.

examination of the authority for this proposition casts some doubt upon that rule.

1. *General Contract Principle.* A comprehensive study was made by Carnegie of the question whether there is a general principle of contract law dealing with the terminability of contracts of unspecified duration.[1] It was there shown that there was authority in the later nineteenth century[2] for a presumption that such contracts were generally intended to be of a perpetual duration. There are also, however, instances of specific types of contract which the courts have presumed to be terminable. Thus, there may be a presumption that contractual licences to occupy are terminable at will.[3] There would seem to be a presumption that the contract between principal and agent is terminable,[4] either at will or by notice according to the construction of the particular contract. In the case of contracts of partnership, the common-law presumption of terminability has been codified in Section 26 of the Partnership Act 1890. Carnegie concludes that there is probably a similar presumption of terminability in the case of retainers for professional service; and that there may be a more general principle that contracts are presumed to be terminable where they are of such a nature as to require trust and confidence between the parties.[5] If there is a general principle of that kind, then the presumption that contracts of employment are terminable by reasonable notice may be seen as an application of it. However, the cases dealing with this question in relation to contracts of employment have not proceeded upon general contract principles but rather upon reasoning limited to the context of the employment relationship.

2. *Public Policy and Restraint of Trade.* There would in principle

---

[1] 'Terminability of Contracts of Unspecified Duration' (1969) 85 LQR 392.

[2] *Llanelly Railway & Dock Co.* v. *London & North Western Ry. Co.* (1875) per James L.J. in CA (1873) LR 8 Ch. App. 942 at 949–50, per Lord Selborne in HL (1875) LR 7 HL 550 at 567.

[3] Per Lord Porter in *Winter Garden Theatre (London) Ltd.* v. *Millenium Productions Ltd.* [1948] AC 173 at 194–5; doubted by Buckley J. in *Re Spenborough U.D.C.'s Agreement* [1968] Ch. 139 at 149 D–150 B (no presumption either way); Carnegie, op. cit. pp. 398–9; cf. *Beverley Corporation* v. *Richard Hodgson & Sons Ltd.* (1973) 225 EG 799 (Templeman J.).

[4] Per McNair J. in *Martin Baker Aircraft Ltd.* v. *Murison* [1955] 2 QB 556 at 567; *Bowstead on Agency* (13th edn. 1968) at p. 200; Carnegie, op. cit. p. 400. Contrast *Re Berker Sportcraft Ltd.'s Agreements* (1947) 177 LT 420, Jenkins J. at pp. 427–8.

[5] Op. cit., pp. 401, 403, referring to Fenton Atkinson J. in *J. H. Milner & Son* v. *Percy Bilton Ltd.* [1966] 1 WLR 1582.

be a strong argument for regarding it as both contrary to public policy and as an unreasonable restraint of trade for an employer to contract to employ for a perpetual duration, and perhaps even more so for an employee to contract to serve one employer throughout his working life. (The precise duration of a contract for permanent employment is considered below.[1]) The cases suggest that the contrary view has been taken by the courts, and that the objections of public policy and restraint of trade have not been taken; but it is the view of this writer that the issue ought not, on the state of the authorities, to be regarded as finally settled.

The decision in *Wallis* v. *Day* (1837)[2] is generally accepted as authority for the proposition that it is neither contrary to public policy nor in restraint of trade for an employee to contract to serve for life. It was indeed expressly so ruled by Lord Abinger C.B.[3] However, the case may well be seen as turning upon its own special facts. These were that the plaintiff, having for many years carried on the business of a carrier, sold his business to the defendants on the terms that they should employ him at a weekly wage for the rest of his life. It may well be that what was apparently a contract of service for life was really an agreement whereby the vendor of a business secured a pension for himself, and at the same time under-took to safeguard the goodwill of the business sold. Thus Lord Abinger C.B. asked rhetorically, 'Suppose a man engaged in trade is desirous, when old age approaches, of selling the goodwill of his business—why may he not bind himself to enter into the service of another, and to trade no more on his own account?'[4] Moreover, it was the purchasers of the business who contested the validity of the undertaking to serve for life, and it may well have been felt that it did not lie in their mouths to do so.

That case was followed and applied in a decision of the Divisional Court in 1899,[5] but it is to be hoped that the extreme harshness of that later decision towards the employee would render it unacceptable at the present day. The employee had contracted to serve the plaintiffs without provision for the termination of his service, as a glass engraver at a daily wage for days actually worked. The employer was obliged to find the employee the same share of work as the other men engaged on the same class of work, but was otherwise

---

[1] See below, pp. 158–9.   [2] (1837) 2 M & W 273.   [3] Ibid. at p. 281.
[4] Ibid.   [5] *Phillips* v. *Stevens* (1899) 15 TLR 325.

free to lay him off or put him on short-time.[1] The employee, having given a fortnight's notice to quit, was successfully sued for damages under the Employers and Workmen Act 1875. It was held that the employers had done no more than was necessary to protect a secret involved in their glass engraving; and that the employee could not complain even if he was left with less than a subsistence wage for the rest of his days. Channell J. commented that 'Whether it was a good or bad bargain for the man himself did not matter.'[2]

In 1927, Eve J. decided that a contract whereby a clerical employee contracted to serve a firm of merchants for life was contrary to public policy and unenforceable as being in restraint of trade.[3] *Wallis* v. *Day* was distinguished on the ground that, whereas that contract had contained provision for referring disputes concerning the employees' conduct to arbitration, the agreement in the present case was wholly one-sided.[4] This was itself a special case in that the contract entitled the employer to terminate the contract of employment upon three months' notice (as well as summarily for misconduct) with no provision at all for termination by the employee. The *ratio* of that case ought, however, to be regarded as capable of extension.

In the later case of *Salt* v. *Power Plant Co. Ltd.*,[5] no objection in terms of restraint of trade was taken against a contract whereby a company was held to have conferred a life-long security of tenure upon their secretary, following an initial three years' probation, subject only to a right in the directors to terminate the contract if the employee ceased to perform his duties to their satisfaction. It may, however, still be that the courts would take a different view if the employer's right to terminate the contract was more narrowly defined; and it is even more strongly arguable that it would be open to the courts to object to a contract whereby the *employee* undertook a permanent obligation, on the ground that the employee was subjected to a bondage of a servile character. Thus, although the decision in *McClelland* v. *Northern Ireland General Health Services Board*[6] is authority for the view that it is not contrary to public policy for a public authority to contract to give permanent employment, that was, however, a case in which the employee, on her side, was entitled to terminate her contract upon a month's notice.

---

[1] Compare above, pp. 86–91 (suspension for economic reasons).

[2] 15 TLR 325 at 326.

[3] *W. H. Milstead & Son Ltd.* v. *Hamp and Ross & Glendinning Ltd.* [1927] WN 233.

[4] Ibid. at p. 234.   [5] [1936] 3 All ER 322.   [6] [1957] 1 WLR 594.

3. *Construction of Contracts of Employment which lack Provision for Termination.* The House of Lords held in *McClelland* v. *Northern Ireland General Health Services Board* by a bare majority that where the contract of employment of a senior clerk was based upon an advertisement for 'permanent and pensionable' employment, and where it contained express provision for termination by the employing authority by notice in the event of gross misconduct, then it was not terminable by notice, by the employer, in any other event. This construction may, however, be contrasted both with earlier decisions and with current employment practice. Thus, for example, in the earlier case of *Savage* v. *British India Steam Navigation Company Ltd.*,[1] Wright J. tended towards a presumption that a provision for termination by the employer upon reasonable notice could be implied into a contract of employment which would otherwise last until the retirement of the employee.

McClelland's case may be distinguishable from the decision of Wright J. on the ground that the express provision in Mrs McClelland's contract of employment for termination in certain events excluded a construction in favour of termination in other events. There are nevertheless other decisions and dicta which make it clear that an employment may be terminable despite the mere description of it as 'permanent'. Thus for instance in *Ward* v. *Barclay Perkins & Co. Ltd.*,[2] Oliver J. held that the employer's right to terminate a contract of employment upon 'ordinary notice, such as would suffice for an ordinary employee',[3] was not excluded by the admission of the employee into a contributory pensions scheme for 'permanent staff'. This seems to represent a correct interpretation of the practice of employers, for whereas they would at that time habitually confer upon certain types of employee a greater security of employment and social status by distinguishing them as 'permanent staff', they would not thereby intend to exclude all right to terminate the employment before retirement date.

An employment which is interpreted as not being terminable either by the expiry of a fixed term or by notice must surely be regarded as an employment until the standard age of retirement—at present generally 65 for men and 60 for women; it cannot be

---

[1] (1930) 46 TLR 294 (captain of an ocean passenger steamer).
[2] [1939] 1 All ER 287; also *Great Western Railway Co.* v. *Bater* [1922] 2 AC 1, 25 (Lord Sumner).
[3] [1939] 1 All ER 287, 288 D (in this case, three months' notice).

treated as an employment for the *life* of the employee. In so far as *Wallis* v. *Day*[1] suggests the contrary it should be seen as based on the express covenants in issue. In *Salt* v. *Power Plant Co. Ltd.*[2] the Court of Appeal implied an employment for the *life* of the employee, but the decision seems questionable to that extent.

A contract for permanent employment at common law is not rendered terminable by notice by the provisions of Section 1 of the Contracts of Employment Act 1972. That section provides that 'the notice required to be given by an employer to terminate the contract of employment . . . shall be not less than [a certain minimum]' and makes a similar formulation in the case of the notice required to be given by the employee. It would probably be held that these provisions can operate only upon an existing term (express or implied) for termination by notice, and that they therefore cannot operate upon a permanent employment to transform it into a terminable one. This section may therefore be concluded by the finding that there is now a general common-law presumption of terminability of contracts of employment upon reasonable notice. In exceptional cases, however, the courts may accept the possibility of a permanent tenure, and will not in such cases imply a right of termination upon reasonable notice.

SECTION 2: THE IMPACT OF STATUTE LAW

Recent statutes have made several crucial changes to the common-law patterns of duration and notice of contracts of employment. Firstly, minimum periods of entitlement to notice have been introduced. Secondly, remuneration has been guaranteed during certain periods of notice. Thirdly, the expiry of fixed-term contracts has been assimilated to dismissal in its effects. This section examines these various statutory improvements in the law protecting the employee upon the termination of his employment.

A. *Statutory Minimum Notice*

The rights of the employee and the employer to minimum periods of notice, which are now conferred by Section 1 of the 1972 Act[3] represent in certain significant respects a new pattern recognized by the law for the termination of contracts of employment. They also

---

[1] (1837) 2 M & W 273 (above).   [2] [1936] 3 All ER 322 (above).
[3] Originally by 1963 Act s. 1.

mark a substantial advance in the legal protection of the security of employment.

The statutory right of the employee to a minimum period of notice is a seniority right. It applies after a qualifying period of thirteen weeks and rises from one week at that stage to two weeks after two years, four weeks after five years, and, since the 1971 Act, six weeks after ten years and eight weeks after fifteen years.[1] Hence the Act not only increases the legal protection of security of employment, but also recognizes that it is an interest which increases in value as the working life of an employee progresses in one employment.

The seniority provisions of the Act apply, however, only to the entitlement of the *employee* to minimum periods of notice, for the employer is entitled only to a minimum period of one week's notice from the employee, whatever the duration of employment (provided in any event that the employee has been employed for thirteen weeks or more)[2]. The Act in this respect departs from the pattern of reciprocity which seems to run throughout the common law concerning notice; that is to say, the presumption that each party is bound to give notice of the same length as that which he is entitled to receive. The Contracts of Employment Bill as at first proposed would have caused the employer's right to notice to increase together with that of the employee.[3] This represented indeed a substantial *quid pro quo* for the additional obligations to be imposed upon employers. This element of mutuality was, however, removed at the committee stage on the ground that it might operate as an undue restriction upon the mobility of the employee who wished to take up a vacancy requiring him to start work very soon after being appointed.[4]

Although not providing for very long minimum periods of notice, the 1963 Act made a very substantial difference to the contractual terms and conditions in practice enjoyed by employees in general, and industrial employees in particular. For although the statutory minimum period of notice was shorter than the reasonable period at common law in the case of the more senior and responsible grades of employee, and shorter also than the rights to notice expressly conferred upon many such employees, it represented a real improve-

---

[1] Now 1972 Act s. 1(1). See Appendix, para. 6.   [2] Ibid. s. 1(2).

[3] The history of the Act is described by Meyers, *Ownership of Jobs* (UCLA 1964) pp. 41–2.

[4] *Parly. Debates* (*H.C.*) Official Report of Standing Committees. Session 1962–3, Vol. II. Cols. 85–93; on Report—*Parly. Debates* (*H.C.*) Vol. 676, cols. 1092–115.

ment in the rights enjoyed by employees with jobs of lesser standing. The 1971 amendment, by creating an eight-week period of notice,[1] extends considerably the number of employments whose terms as to notice are substantially altered by the legislation; though there is not a great awareness in practice of this further change because so long a period of continuous employment is necessary before it applies.

B. Guaranteed Wages during Notice

The Contracts of Employment Act 1972 guarantees to the employee during the minimum period of notice the wage which he would ordinarily receive during a full basic working week, protecting him against loss of wages as the result of suspension of work.[2] It provides that his pay is secured during that period if he does not work during some or all of his normal working hours because his employer provides no work for him although he is ready and willing to work; or because he is incapable of work because of sickness or injury; or because he is on holiday.[3] An employee who has no normal working hours is to be paid for each week of notice at a rate not less than his average weekly rate of pay in the last twelve weeks before notice was given.[4]

The employer is protected from major breach of contract by the employee during the guarantee period by the provision that if, during notice, the employee commits a serious breach of contract which results in his employer being entitled to dismiss him summarily, and the employer does so, then the guarantee applies only up to the time of the termination of the contract.[5] Moreover, the employer is given an added security in cases where the employee has given notice, by means of a provision that the guarantee does not apply if, on or before the termination of the contract, the employee takes part in a strike.[6]

This guarantee of full wages during the minimum period of notice has greatly enhanced the rights of the employee during notice, by comparison with the position at common law, because it is quite possible that the employee might apart from the statute be entitled

---

[1] 1971 Act s. 19, now re-enacted in 1972 Act s. 1(1)(d) and (e). See Appendix, para. 8.
[2] Section 2(1) (notice given by employer); Section 2(2) (notice given by employee).
[3] Schedule 2 para. 2.   [4] Ibid. para. 3.   [5] Ibid. para. 6(2).
[6] Ibid. para. 5. This seems to cover the case where the notice to terminate is itself the strike notice.

to no wages at all during a period of notice. This would be the case, for example, where an employee is absent as the result of sickness for a period exceeding the time during which the employer is liable under the contract for sick-pay. If notice is given outside the sick-pay period it will not, at common law, involve a revival of the right to remuneration during the period of notice.

There is, however, this major limitation upon the application of the statutory guarantee, that where the employee has a right to a period of notice from the employer which exceeds the statutory minimum by a week or more, the guarantee does not apply to any notice given by either party, whatever its length.[1] It would be more satisfactory if the guarantee were still to apply for the statutory minimum period, though not beyond it.

C. The Statutory Treatment of Fixed-term Contracts

Contracts of employment for a fixed term create in respect of the period after their expiry only an expectation of renewal (and that not in every case); they create no right to a continuance of employment beyond the stipulated term. However, in the recent legislation concerning the rights of individual employees, that expectation has been treated as if it were indeed a right to the continuance of employment, so that the new statutory rights attach to it as if to the termination of a contract of employment for an indefinite period. This is a radical extension of the employee's rights upon the termination of the employment relationship.

There are two types of provision of this kind. First, Section 1(4) of the 1963 Act provided that: 'Any contract of employment of a person who has been continuously employed for twenty-six weeks or more which is a contract for a term certain of four weeks or less shall have effect as if it were for an indefinite period and, accordingly, the statutory rights of employer and employee to a minimum period of notice shall apply to the contract.' This provision was not limited to the purposes of the 1963 Act; it is interesting to consider whether the draftsman intended it to have any consequences at common law. The reason for the limitation to contracts of four weeks or less was presumably the view that if the contract was for a longer fixed term, the employee would in any event have at least the maximum security of tenure originally provided by the 1963 Act, namely four weeks. This four-week upper limit has remained in force,[2] although the

[1] Section 2(3).   [2] 1972 Act s. 1(4).

period of notice which the legislation now requires may be as long as eight weeks (after fifteen years' service).[1] It follows that the original explanation for the four-week restriction no longer holds good, and the present provision simply achieves the limited effect of preventing the Act from being blatantly avoided by the making of a series of very short fixed-term contracts.

The second provision of this kind is that of Section 3(1)(b) of the 1965 Act and Section 23(2)(b) of the 1971 Act whereby it is provided that an employee shall, for the purposes of that part of that Act, be taken to be dismissed by his employer if he is employed under a contract for a fixed term and that term expires without being renewed under the same contract. The force of these provisions is weakened by the qualifying provisions of Section 15 of the 1965 Act and Section 30 of the 1971 Act which are that the above provisions do not apply to the termination of fixed-term contracts for two years or more if the contract was made before the appointed days (which were 6 December 1965 and 28 February 1972 respectively); and that in the case of fixed-term contracts for two years or more made after the appointed day, the right to redundancy payment or to remedies for unfair dismissal which might so arise may be waived by the employee by an agreement in writing made before the expiry of the term. The effect of that seems to be that this particular type of waiver will be treated as valid even if it takes place after the formation of the original contract and the employer gives no consideration for it, provided only that it is expressed in writing. Since the minimum qualifying period of service for the statutory rights is itself two years,[2] the effect of these qualifications is to ensure that the Acts shall not apply to the expiry of fixed-term contracts made before they came into force, and to enable employers to obtain an express surrender of the statutory rights of their employees in the case of the expiry of other fixed-term contracts exceeding two years' duration. However, despite these qualifications, the recent legislation has brought about a very significant change in thus reducing the contrast between employment for a fixed term and employment for an indefinite period terminable by notice.

There may none the less be some difficulty in applying the statutory concept of the fixed-term contract to certain arrangements which combine an element of fixed-term contracting with some other

[1] Ibid. s. 1(1)(e).
[2] 1965 Act s. 1(1) and 8(1); 1971 Act s. 28(1). See Appendix, para. 2.

kind of terminability. The cases of the periodic contract of employ-ment and the contract for the duration of a particular task have already been considered.[1] It appears that the courts will tend where possible to treat other variants as fixed-term contracts. Thus in *B.B.C.* v. *Ioannu*[2] a contract 'for a period of one year unless previously determined by either party giving to the other not less than three months' prior notice in writing' was treated simply as a fixed-term contract. It does seem to have been the intention of the legislation both of 1965 and also 1971 that the concept of dismissal should include any case of termination of contractual employment by an employer, including any omission or refusal on his part to extend the period of employment. In view of that, it is appropriate for the courts to interpret the Acts as covering any contracts which are hybrids between the fixed term and the indefinite term subject to notice.

SECTION 3: THE REQUIREMENTS FOR A VALID NOTICE

A. Requirement of Writing

It seems that a contract of employment may effectively impose formal requirements upon the exercise of a right to terminate by notice. Comparison may be made with the decision in *Latchford Premier Cinemas Ltd.* v. *Ennion & Paterson*.[3] The resignation of a director was required by the Articles of association to be in writing. Oral resignations were tendered by two directors and accepted by the annual general meeting. The two directors later claimed, by reason of the informality of their resignations, never to have vacated their offices. It was held that they had validly resigned, but as the result of mutual agreement rather than as the result of proper notice.

It would seem to follow that a notice not complying with the required formalities constitutes a mere offer to terminate, which, if accepted, results in a termination by agreement. Alternatively, it would seem that the party receiving the informal notice could regard it as a wrongful repudiation, treat the contract as wrongfully termina-ted, and claim damages. These might well, however, be only nominal damages, for the party receiving the notice may be regarded as having suffered no loss by reason merely of the informality of the notice.

---

[1] See above, pp. 148 note 3, 149.
[2] [1974] IRLR 77 (NIRC)—but see CA—[1975] IRLR 185 and *Note*, below, p. 193.
[3] [1931] 2 Ch. 409.

As a further alternative, the party receiving the informal notice may disregard it. If it is then followed by a dismissal or departure by the party giving the notice, that would constitute a wrongful termination giving rise to damages. Again, these might well be nominal damages only.

It may therefore be thought that, whereas the informality of a notice alters the legal method of termination, that informality has no great practical consequence. There is, however, at least one context in which the distinction may be one of substance, because if the termination is regarded as being by mutual agreement,[1] it could be held not to be a dismissal *by the employer* for the purposes of the 1965 Act and the unfair dismissal provisions of the 1971 Act. The result is that an employee who accedes to an informal notice given by an employer might find himself deprived of a redundancy payment by virtue of a technicality.

B. Time must be Ascertained or Ascertainable

The courts have in recent years imposed this requirement upon notice to terminate, and have attached a new and significant effect to the absence of it. In *Morton Sundour Fabrics Ltd.* v. *Shaw*[2] the Divisional Court held that if an employer notifies an employee of his intention to terminate the employment at some future date, but neither states the date nor renders it ascertainable, then no valid notice to terminate has been given. In the words of Widgery J.,

'It is the law, as I understand it, that just as a tenancy determined by notice to quit requires a certain amount of particularity in the notice, so there are certain formalities about the type of notice necessary to determine a contract of employment. The notice may be a peremptory notice, sometimes referred to as a dismissal without notice, but if it is to operate on a future day, the notice must specify that date or at least contain facts from which that date is ascertainable.'[3]

The effect of an informality of this kind is that the notification by the employer is not a legally significant act at all. The result is that if the employee disregards this mere warning, his employment

---

[1] Compare, however, *Lees* v. *Arthur Greaves Ltd.* [1974] ICR 501 where the Court of Appeal showed a general scepticism towards 'mutually agreed termination'.

[2] (1967) 2 ITR 84. Cf. the earlier Tribunal decision in *Reynolds* v. *Groom* (1966) 1 ITR 74.

[3] (1967) 2 ITR 84, 87.

continues unimpaired until an act of termination by the employer. But if the employee heeds the warning and finds another job elsewhere, then the ensuing termination of employment is treated as the act of the employee alone, and therefore cannot entitle him to a redundancy payment.[1] To the criticism that this would drive a coach and horses through the 1965 Act by penalizing employees who acted in mitigation of their impending loss, the sanguine reply was offered that 'The effect of the employer's warning is not in any way to derogate from [the employee's] statutory rights, but to give him an alternative, which if he is so minded, he can accept.'[2]

It may be said that there is in such a case more than a mere absence of formality in the employer's notification; there is the absence of an intention to terminate the contract. That may be true in a narrow sense; but there is very likely to be a hope and expectation that the employment will be terminated; and even if the formal act of termination is that of the employee, the employer ought not to be heard to deny that it was of his volition. Comparison may be made with the distinction which is taken in the law of tort between procurement of breach of contract and mere information or advice,[3] and also with that which is drawn between an intimidatory threat and a mere warning.[4] It has been observed[5] that the courts have recently tended more readily than before to find the persuasive element necessary to transform information into procurement of breach; and they are similarly willing to discern the coercive element necessary to convert a warning into a threat.[6] If that is a proper approach to the communications of union officials in the contemplation of industrial action, then it would seem equally applicable to the actions of an employer in contemplation of impending redundancies.

---

[1] Otherwise, however, if the employer has repudiated the contract, e.g. by warning the employee that he is about to impose a change of location not within the scope of the contract—*Maher* v. *Fram Gerrard Ltd.* [1974] ICR 31.

[2] (1967) 2 ITR 84 at 87.

[3] The authorities are collected by Wedderburn in *Clerk and Lindsell on Torts* (13th edn. 1969) at Para. 795, pp. 389–90.

[4] Ibid. Para. 799, p. 398.

[5] Ibid. Para. 795, p. 389, citing *Stratford* v. *Lindley* [1965] AC 269, *Torquay Hotel Co. Ltd.* v. *Cousins* [1969] 2 Ch. 106, and *Square Grip Reinforcement Ltd.* v. *MacDonald* [1968] SLTR 65.

[6] *Rookes* v. *Barnard* [1964] AC 1129 and *Morgan* v. *Fry* [1968] 2 QB 710 may be contrasted with the older authorities cited by Wedderburn, op. cit. at p. 398, note 41.

C. Collective Notice

The question whether the law makes it a formal requirement of a valid notice to terminate a contract of employment that it shall emanate from an individual and be addressed to an individual, is of particular consequence in the sphere of industrial action. There is some scope for discussion as to the validity of collective notice on behalf of many individuals. In *Rider* v. *Wood* (1859)[1] a collective notice, to terminate employment unless former piece-rate prices were restored, was expressed to be given by 'the Anchor-Smiths of Saltney', and was delivered by one of their number. The court expressly left open[2] the question of the validity of the notice with regard both to its conditional character and its collective nature, and decided the question whether the employees had committed offences under one of the Master and Servant statutes, upon other grounds.

On the other hand, it would seem that there are cases in which strike action has been regarded as taking the form of lawful notice to terminate contracts of employment, and that in those cases no objection has been taken on the ground of the collective nature of the notice given.[3] In one of the leading authorities on trade-union law it is unequivocally asserted that the legal effectiveness of notice to terminate employment does not depend upon its being an individual act; so that 'As a prelude to strike action, management or employer are not legally justified in demanding that each prospective striker hand in his, or her, own notice. It is sufficient if their authorised agent, the union official or unofficial strike leader, hands in a collective "strike notice".'[4] That passage was written upon the assumption that the courts have in the past very often interpreted strike notice as notice to terminate contracts of employment. The courts have recently departed from that view;[5] but this does not affect the question of the validity of collective notice to terminate. It would seem that, in spite of the uncertainty shown at the time of *Rider* v. *Wood*, it is now the preferable view that a collective notice

---

[1] (1859) 2 El. & El. 338.   [2] Ibid. at 343.

[3] e.g. *Santen* v. *Busnach* (1913) 29 TLR 214—see per Vaughan Williams L.J. at p. 215; *White* v. *Riley* [1921] 1 Ch. 1, see per Younger L.J. at pp. 29–30. The terms of notice are described at p. 4 of the report. (The strike notices discussed in the second *Osborne* case, *Osborne* v. *Amalgamated Society of Railway Servants* [1911] 1 Ch. 540, were rather different, for they were in effect collections of individual notices signed by each employee. See Buckley L.J., ibid. at 571).

[4] Grunfeld, *Modern Trade Union Law* (1966) at pp. 319–20.

[5] See below, pp. 170–1.

to terminate given on behalf of a group of employees will be a valid notice.[1]

D. Notice Given or Received by an Agent

The question of the validity of collective notice raises the further issue of the extent to which notice can validly be given or received by an agent. It would seem that there is no objection in principle to the giving or receiving of notice through an agent; these appear to be delegable functions. However, the courts will not lightly assume that a valid agency has been established for this purpose, and will scrutinize the particular transaction concerned to satisfy themselves of this. In *Riordan* v. *War Office*[2], Diplock J. held that a notice of resignation given by a civilian employee of the War Office to his superior officer was received by that superior officer as an agent for the commanding officer of the establishment, and that as a result the notice was effectively lodged and became irrevocable immediately upon being handed in by the employee. He also recognized the possibility of a converse situation in which a notice of resignation might be given to the immediate superior of the employee as agent of the employee for its transmission to higher authority, though he did not regard that analysis as applicable to the facts before him.[3]

In *Morris* v. *C. H. Bailey Ltd.*[4] the Court of Appeal, whilst not objecting in principle to the suggestion that a notice to terminate given by the employer could be received by a district union official as the agent of his members employed by that employer, were in no doubt that this was not the proper analysis of a communication to a union official from an employers' association that 'if at the date of expiry of this notice no agreement has been arrived at, then as and from [a certain date] employment will only be available to your members at the establishments of our member firms on the basis of the new working rules'. Their main reason for holding that this was not a notice of termination of individual contracts of employment was its conditional character, which is considered below; but even

---

[1] 'The first objection . . . was that this [strike] notice does not specify the names of persons on whose behalf it is given. In our judgment it need not do so. . . . That view is reinforced when it is remembered that under the general law of contract it is open to an agent to contract on behalf of an unnamed principal.' Sir John Donaldson in *Horizon Holidays Ltd.* v. *ASTMS* [1973] IRLR 22 at p. 23 Para. 7. See Appendix, para. 8.

[2] [1959] 1 WLR 1046 (affirmed on other grounds [1961] 1 WLR 210).

[3] [1959] 1 WLR 1046, 1054–55.   [4] [1969] 2 Lloyd's Rep. 215.

apart from that, the judges in the Court of Appeal were far from convinced that they could have regarded the notice as addressed to the union official in the capacity of agent for his members, though their language makes it plain that this is in principle possible.[1] This approach of recognizing the theoretical possibility of an agency to give or to receive notice to terminate, whilst displaying caution in its practical application, seems the most appropriate method of giving effect to the intentions of the parties, and yet protecting them from excessive informality of notices to terminate.[2]

E. Conditional Notice

It would seem that the law does not impose a requirement that a notice to terminate must, in order to be valid, be unconditional in character. The cases in which it was accepted that notice to terminate by way of strike action could validly be given on behalf of a group of men collectively[3] seem also to show that notice may be valid though conditional. Thus in *Santen* v. *Busnach*[4] it appears from the report that the notice to the employer was probably conditional upon his retaining the non-union employee, and yet the notice was held a valid one. In *White* v. *Riley*[5] that is made quite clear, as the report quotes the wording of the notice, which was: 'Sirs, we hereby give you notice that we shall cease work on Friday next unless E. White either joins our Society or leaves your employment.'[6]

However, although a notice may be valid despite its conditional character, it appears that the imposition of multiple conditions may have the result that the communication in question cannot be regarded as a notice to terminate at all. This is the effect of the decision in *Morris* v. *C. H. Bailey Ltd.*[7] that there was no valid notice to terminate individual contracts of employment where an employers' association in effect told a union official that *unless* a new collective agreement was reached within a certain time, the

---

[1] Ibid. at 220 (Salmon L.J.); 221 (Winn L.J.).

[2] In *Ideal Casements Ltd.* v. *Shamsi* [1972] ICR 408 it was held that a shop steward's power to give valid strike notice on behalf of the workers he represented depended upon his acting in his capacity as a union official. In *Horizon Holidays Ltd.* v. *ASTMS* [1973] IRLR 22 the Industrial Court held that a divisional officer of ASTMS could validly give strike notice on behalf of the members of ASTMS employed by Horizon, the members being unnamed principals. See Appendix, para. 8.

[3] See above, p. 167.   [4] (1913) 29 TLR 214.

[5] [1921] 1 Ch. 1.   [6] Ibid. p. 4.

[7] [1969] 2 Lloyd's Rep. 215 (above).

employment of his members would be terminated *unless* they accepted changed terms and conditions of employment. It may well be thought that in deciding the requirements of a valid notice, especially in the context of collective action, the courts are really examining and evaluating the *intentions* of the parties. It is therefore appropriate to consider, as a distinct issue, what is the intention which is required by law for the giving of proper notice to terminate contracts of employment.

F. The Element of Intention in Notice

1. *Intention to Terminate a Contract Distinguished from Intention to Break a Contract.* One of the major upheavals which have occurred in the last decade in the law concerning industrial action has been the suggestion that notice to strike cannot be regarded as notice to terminate because the persons giving the notice have no intention of severing the contractual relationship. This was the suggestion contained in the celebrated dicta of Lords Donovan, Devlin, and Denning.[1] In the cases in which these dicta occurred, it was thought that the necessary result of this view was that a strike must constitute a breach of the individual contract of employment. Lord Denning M.R. was later to hold that 'There must be something wrong with that argument; for if [it] were correct, it would do away with the right to strike in this country.'[2] But his escape from this difficulty consisted in the discovery that there was a right to suspend the contract of employment by way of strike action,[3] and he did not disturb the earlier view that a strike notice was not intended to be a notice to terminate the contract, whatever else its legal consequences might be. Section 147 of the 1971 Act specifically provided that due notice of a strike should not be treated as notice to terminate the contract.[4] But the proposition that strike notice does not constitute notice to terminate probably still remains a rule of common law[5] as well as

---

[1] Per Donovan L.J. (as he then was) in the Court of Appeal in *Rookes* v. *Barnard* [1963] 1 QB 623, 682–3; per Lord Devlin in the House of Lords in the same case: [1964] AC 1129 at 1204; per Lord Denning M.R. in the Court of Appeal in *Stratford* v. *Lindley* [1965] AC 269 at 285 (decision reversed by H.L. on other grounds [1965] AC 307).

[2] *Morgan* v. *Fry* [1968] 2 QB 710 at 725 D–E.

[3] See above, pp. 102–3.   [4] See Appendix, para. 8.

[5] Unless s. 147(1) of the 1971 Act is treated as having abolished the corresponding part of the common law. This is unlikely because, for instance, s. 147 was confined to disputes falling within the *statutory* definition of strike and does not extend to all strike notices.

of statute law, and as far as the common law is concerned, it is a rule grounded in the intention of the parties.

Powerful arguments have been advanced against this view of the intention underlying strike notice. It has been urged that even if the motive underlying the notice is to secure a desired result by economic pressure while preserving the continuity of employment, yet the immediate intention is to act in accordance with the contracts of employment by means of a proper termination of them: 'Termination of the *legal* relationship may be regarded as no more than observance of the formal procedural steps required to remain within the permissive scope of the common law.'[1]

It is possible to take the argument one stage further, and to question as a matter of general contract principle the correctness of this inquiry into the intention of the party giving notice. It is true that in the context of a hire-purchase agreement the House of Lords was prepared to examine the intention of the hirer in returning the motor vehicle concerned to the dealer and in refusing to continue the payments.[2] They concluded from his apologetic tone that he regarded himself as breaking his contract rather than as exercising the option to terminate the hiring which was conferred by the contract; and they held that his action was in an objective sense a breach of contract because that was his subjective view of it.[3]

However, it may be noted that Lord Denning there thought that: '[The hirer's] conduct should be interpreted on the assumption that he would do that which is the least burdensome to him, rather than that which is the most profitable to the hire-purchase company . . .'[4] There is further authority also in analogous types of case for the view that a party to a contract is entitled to present his actions according to the most favourable analysis of his contractual rights, irrespective of his actual intentions at the time. The most obvious example is the right to justify the summary repudiation of a contract by reference to a right of repudiation even though that right was not a motivating factor at the time of repudiation.[5] A particular

---

[1] Grunfeld, op. cit. at 333. Cf. O'Higgins (1972) 2 ILJ 152 for discussion of the relation between legal categories and the actual practice of strike notices.

[2] *Bridge* v. *Campbell Discount Co. Ltd.* [1962] AC 600 (see Treitel, *Law of Contract* (4th edn. 1975) at pp. 575–6. (Breach Distinguished from Lawful Termination)).

[3] Per Lord Morton, ibid. at 615; per Lord Radcliffe at 621; per Lord Devlin at 632.   [4] Ibid. at 631–2.

[5] Cf. *Universal Cargo Carriers Corporation* v. *Citati* [1957] 2 QB 401; Devlin J. at 443 (affirmed on a different issue [1957] 1 WLR 979).

instance is the right of the employer to justify a summary dismissal by reference to misconduct upon which he was not acting, or even of which he did not know, when carrying out the dismissal.[1] It may well be thought that this provides a counter-argument to the dicta of the three Law Lords who favoured the imposition of a requirement of intention upon the giving of valid notice to terminate.

2. *Intention to Terminate and Intention to Vary.* It seems that where one party to the contract of employment, usually in practice the employer, gives notice that after a certain date the employment will continue only upon changed terms and conditions, and where the other party treats the contract as terminated, the notice may be treated by the courts as valid notice to terminate the contract, provided that it is of the requisite length for a proper termination of the contract. It may be so treated even although the intention of the party giving the notice was to vary the terms of the contract rather than to terminate it. This is in accordance with the rule, described in earlier pages,[2] that a notice will be treated as valid to terminate a contract although it is conditional in character. But it stands in sharp contrast to the other common-law rule that the courts will not regard a strike notice as valid notice to terminate where the intention is to continue the contractual relationship, and it casts further doubt upon the latter, somewhat questionable, rule.

That the courts may, where necessary, regard a notice to vary the terms of employment as a valid notice to terminate is suggested by a dictum in *Marriott* v. *Oxford & District Co-operative Society Ltd.*[3] In that case the employer gave notice, shorter than the four weeks' notice requisite for the proper termination of the contract, of his intention to offer employment only on inferior terms and conditions compared with those hitherto enjoyed by the employee. In the Divisional Court, Lord Parker C.J. indicated that, if the notice had been of four weeks' length, it would have constituted a valid and lawful termination of the contract, whatever the true intention of the employer.[4] The clear implication is that the notice was deficient only as regards length, and not as regards intention. It is the view of this

---

[1] See below, pp. 221–2.   [2] See above, pp. 169–70.

[3] (1968) 3 ITR 121 (later proceedings: *Marriott* v. *Oxford & District Co-operative Society Ltd.* (No. 2)—[1970] 1 QB 186 reversing [1969] 1 WLR 254).

[4] (1968) 3 ITR 121, 124. Cf. also *Miller* v. *Nettle Accessories Ltd.* (1966) 1 ITR 328 where an Industrial Tribunal held that an offer of alternative work, accompanied by notice of the proper length, was in effect a notice of dismissal if the alternative employment was not accepted.

writer that a notice to vary should be treated as a valid notice to terminate only if it is made quite clear by the notice that there will be a termination if the changed terms are not accepted by the party receiving the notice. In any event, a clarification is required as to the element of intention to terminate which is required to constitute a proper notice of termination.

SECTION 4: CURTAILMENT OF NOTICE

By curtailment of notice, we refer to the situation where employment is cut short before a period of notice has run its full course. Recent case-law has shown that curtailment of notice may create confusion about the legal mechanism by which the contract is terminated. For this reason it is worth attempting a systematic analysis of the situations in which this problem may arise.

Two problems arise in relation to curtailment of notice:
(a) Is the party who curtails the period of notice acting in breach of contract?
(b) At what point is the contract of employment terminated?

These problems have to be resolved in different terms according to whether the curtailment is the employer's act, the employee's act, or an act of mutual agreement. We proceed to deal with those different situations, taking the case where the original notice was given by the employer.

A. Notice Curtailed by Employer

The first situation is that where the curtailment of the notice is regarded as the act of the employer. There are two main variations of that situation: the one is where the curtailment is accompanied by payment in lieu of the remainder of the notice, and the other is where there is no such payment.

Where payment in lieu is *not* given, the employer's curtailment of notice would seem to constitute a breach of contract by him unless the employee has by misconduct entitled the employer to dismiss him summarily.[1] The employer's action cannot be regarded as a

---

[1] Note the provision of s. 10(3) of the 1965 Act leaving it to an Industrial Tribunal to decide what proportion of the redundancy payment it is 'just and equitable' for the employee to receive in such a case of misconduct during notice.

mere waiver by the employer of his right to the full period of notice, because he is at the same time depriving the employee of the corresponding opportunity to work and to earn remuneration.

The law concerning the date of termination of the contract where the employer curtails a period of notice without any payment in lieu is in a controversial state. In *H. W. Smith (Cabinets) Ltd.* v. *Brindle*[1] the Court of Appeal were concerned to avoid the injustice of allowing employers to complete a dismissal by curtailing a period of notice just before the Act came into force. That undesirable result was avoided by a unanimous decision that dismissal in the relevant statutory sense did not take place until the contract of employment was terminated, and that termination occurred only when the due date for the expiry of the notice arrived, even if the notice had in fact been curtailed before then.

The difficulty about that solution is that it conflicts with the general rule that a contract of employment can be effectively terminated by dismissal even though the dismissal is wrongful.[2] The general rule seems to apply to termination by payment in lieu of notice—treated as wrongful because viewed as the payment of *damages*, yet immediately effective.[3] The same seems true of outright wrongful dismissal.

We can find a distinction in principle between those situations and the situation of wrongful curtailment only by saying that once a notice has actually been given its date of expiry is the date of termination of the contract whatever wrongful curtailment may occur in the interim. If on the other hand due notice is never actually given, the courts will not extend the date of termination to the notional date when a hypothetical notice would have expired. It remains to be seen whether that will prove to be a viable distinction.

The problems which ultimately arise from the ruling in *H. W. Smith (Cabinets) Ltd.* v. *Brindle* can be appreciated when we take the case of curtailment by the employer *with* payment in lieu of remainder of notice. As to the legality of such an action by the employer, it would seem that such action will normally be contractually wrongful (though that is a matter of little enough practical significance). For if, as now seems likely, payment in lieu of the whole period of notice is in principle breach plus liquidated damages,[4] then payment in lieu of an unexpired part of the notice is *a fortiori* wrongful. As to the date of termination of the contract, the rule in *Smith (Cabinets)*

---

[1] [1973] ICR 12.   [2] See below, pp. 292 ff.   [3] See below, pp. 188–9.
[4] See below, p. 189.

v. *Brindle* as explained above should result in an extension of the contract to the date the due notice would have expired.[1] But if that is correct, there is an unsatisfactory contrast between the effect of curtailment by payment in lieu and the effect of payment in lieu from the outset, which, as is explained in later pages,[2] seems to produce an immediate termination of the contract.

B. *Notice Curtailed by Employee*

There is little case-law on the situation where it is the employee who cuts short the period of notice. But it is a situation which is specially treated in certain statutory provisions, and whose effects at common law can largely be deduced from the decisions in cases where the employer cut short the notice.

Curtailment by the employee may take the form either of immediate termination of work at some point during the currency of the notice, or of giving a counter-notice to expire before the employer's notice. Where the employer wishes the notice to be worked out, but the employee terminates the employment by an immediate cessation of working, the effect will usually be that of a termination in breach of contract by the employee. However, he may be entitled so to terminate either by reason of an expressly agreed right of summary termination (an unusual situation)[3] or by reason of the employer's repudiatory conduct. In the latter case the employee's action constitutes an acceptance of repudiation as a termination of the contract. Whether in breach of contract or not, the employee's action should result in an immediate termination of the contract at the date of cessation of working.[4] Even a wrongful cessation of actual employment is effective to terminate the contract,[5] and there is no special reason, by virtue merely of the employer's previously served

---

[1] It was so held by a majority of the Court of Appeal in *Lees* v. *Arthur Greaves Ltd.* [1974] ICR 501; see per Lord Denning M.R. at 505 F–G, Scarman L.J. at 509 C–F. But contrast *Leigh* v. *James Arnold Ltd.* (1973) 8 ITR 364 per Sir Hugh Griffiths at 366 B–C, rejecting a submission to the same effect.

[2] See below, pp. 188–9.

[3] A right of summary termination, although rare in practice, is probably not rendered impossible by 1972 Act s. 1 because that section operates only where *some* notice is required—cf. the wording of s. 1(1).

[4] This is in a sense a doctrine of constructive termination by the employee. In *Jones* v. *Liverpool Corporation* [1974] IRLR 55, Sir John Donaldson doubted the existence of such a doctrine at p. 56 Para 5; but the factual context was very different from that under consideration in this section.

[5] See below, pp. 222–300.

notice, to hold there to be a notional period of employment beyond the actual period of working.

If the employee curtails the employment by counter-notice, the legality of his action will depend upon whether he has given the notice required for a proper termination of the contract by him in the ordinary way.[1] If the employee's counter-notice is not long enough to constitute due notice to terminate, then it must almost necessarily constitute anticipatory breach of contract by the employee when it is given, and actual breach when it expires. For even if the employer has by his repudiatory conduct entitled the employee to terminate summarily, it is doubtful whether the employee's exercise of that right can take the form of the giving of notice.[2] It would seem likely that his right to accept the repudiation is only a right to leave immediately and not a right to give notice of his own.[3] As far as the date of termination is concerned, curtailment by the employee by notice should result in a termination of the contract of employment at the date of cessation of working. That is for the same reasons as those which obtain in the situation, discussed above, where the employee curtails a period of notice by leaving without notice.

To this analysis of the effect of curtailment by the employee must be added reference to two statutory provisions dealing with this problem, designed to prevent the employee from losing his statutory rights by failing to serve his full period of notice. Section 4 of the 1965 Act provides that where an employee under notice from his employer himself gives proper notice in writing to terminate his employment, his entitlement to redundancy pay is preserved provided that his employer does not object to his early departure. The employer is entitled, however, to request the employee to withdraw the notice, and if the employee does not comply with that request, he is entitled to the redundancy payment only when and to the extent that an Industrial Tribunal thinks it just and equitable. That rather elabor-

---

[1] This will normally depend upon the employee being bound to a shorter period of notice than the employer. But that is perfectly possible and is indeed brought about by the application of the 1972 Act s. 1(1) and s. 1(2) (see above, p. 160, where this disparity is discussed).

[2] Cf. *Jones* v. *Liverpool Corporation* [1974] IRLR 55—employers who had given payment in lieu of notice could not claim that they were accepting the employee's wrongful repudiation.

[3] Thus the employee forfeits, by giving notice, his right to treat the employer's conduct as constructive wrongful dismissal. This trap assumed statutory form in s. 3(1)(c) of the 1965 Act—Sir John Donaldson in *GKN (Cwmbran) Ltd.* v. *Lloyd* [1972] ICR 214 at 221 D–F.

ately qualified provision may well be regarded as an inadequate recognition of the employee's need to be free to take up another job straight away once he has come under notice of redundancy.

Section 23 of the 1971 Act goes further than that towards preserving the character of a curtailed notice as an employer's dismissal.[1] It provides that the employer's notice will still give rise to a dismissal by the employer even if curtailed by the employee's counter-notice, provided that the counter-notice falls within the period of notice which the employer was obliged to give, working backwards from the date on which the employer's notice was to expire. The employee's counter-notice is not on the face of the statute required to be full notice; if that interpretation is correct, it is open for decision what is the minimum counter-notice the employee must give in order to claim the benefit of the subsection concerned.

C. Notice Curtailed by Mutual Agreement

A system of individual employment law which bases extensive consequences upon a unilateral act of the employer—dismissal—is liable to be stultified where termination of employment is viewed as the result of a consensus between employer and employee. This observation has been borne out by recent case-law concerning curtailment of notice. We are considering the fact situation in which notice is curtailed by the request or suggestion of one party with the assent or acquiescence of the other. We assume for the purposes of discussion that the original notice was given by the employer.

The cases indicate the following possible alternative views of that fact situation. In *McAlwane* v. *Boughton Estates Ltd.*[2] the Industrial Court recognized two possibilities:

(1) the employer agrees to vary his notice of dismissal by causing it to take effect on an earlier date—there is a dismissal on that earlier date; or

(2) the termination results from an agreement which supersedes the earlier notice and terminates the contract without there being a dismissal by the employer at all.[3]

In the case of *Lees* v. *Arthur Greaves Ltd.*[4] the Industrial Court had recognized these two possibilities, plus a third:

(3) the employer agrees to waive his right to services during the

---

[1] 1971 Act s. 23(3)–(4). [2] [1973] ICR 470.
[3] Ibid. at 472 G–473 A (Sir John Donaldson).
[4] [1973] ICR 90 (overruled by CA [1974] ICR 501).

remainder of the notice, so that there is a dismissal taking effect at the due date of expiry of the notice.[1]

Within those possibilities, the cases suggest the following principles for selecting the appropriate possibility. In *McAlwane* v. *Boughton Estates Ltd.* the Court approached the possibility of consensual termination cautiously and preferred the view that the employer had varied his own earlier notice, advancing its date of operation but not altering its character as a dismissal. The Court suggested that 'it would be a very rare case indeed in which it could properly be found that the employer and the employee had got together and, notwithstanding that there was a current notice of termination of the employment, agreed mutually to terminate the contract'.[2] In *Lees* v. *Arthur Greaves Ltd.*, all three members of the Court of Appeal endorsed the doctrine of the *McAlwane* case and expressed in strong terms their distrust of the consensual termination view, reversing the first-instance decision in the case before them.[3] The Court of Appeal then divided about the further consequences of the view they had unanimously taken. The majority held that the contract continued in force till the original expiry date of the notice, the employer having waived his right to the services of the employee in the meantime. Stamp L.J., dissenting, held the contract to have been summarily terminated by the employer when the notice was cut short. The view of the majority is in this respect in line with the decision in *H. W. Smith (Cabinets) Ltd.* v. *Brindle.*[4]

We may now consider which of the three possibilities under discussion is in principle the most appropriate one. Possibility (2) as set out above, i.e. consensual termination negativing dismissal, was rightly viewed with scepticism in the *McAlwane* and *Lees* cases. The agreement occurs in the context of a notice to quit already presented by the employer, and there is little reason in fact or law to let the agreement override the notice retroactively, unless there is some specific indication the parties so intended—e.g. to avoid the odium of notice to quit. Possibility (3) as set out above, i.e. waiver of services by employer not advancing the date of dismissal, is more appropriate but is subject to the criticism that it treats the curtail-

[1] [1973] ICR 90 at 94 A (Sir Samuel Cooke).
[2] [1973] ICR 470, 473 E–F (Sir John Donaldson).
[3] [1974] ICR 501 at 505 B–E (Lord Denning M.R.); 506 C-G (Stamp L.J.); 507 H–508 G (Scarman L.J.).
[4] [1973] ICR 12 (above).

ment of employment, on payment in lieu, as something entirely within the employer's gift; in fact it may in certain circumstances involve a corresponding concession by the employee of his opportunity to work. It is therefore suggested that there should be a presumption in favour of possibility (1), i.e. consensual variation of the date on which the notice terminates; but that this presumption should be rebuttable in favour of (3) if the facts specially suggest that the employer is conceding leave of absence without advancing the date of termination.

SECTION 5: REVOCATION OF NOTICE

The Redundancy Payments Act 1965 gave rise to decisions concerning the problem of whether notice, once given, is revocable. It had previously been ruled by Diplock J.[1] that notice of resignation by an employee became irrevocable as soon as given, so that in the case before him an unestablished civil servant (for this purpose in the same position as an ordinary employee) could not revoke his notice within 55 minutes of delivering it to his immediate superior (who was held to have received it as the agent of the head of the establishment), with the result that the refusal of the War Office to employ him beyond the expiry date of the notice could not be regarded as a wrongful dismissal, but was rather an acceptance of the original notice. Diplock J. commented that 'The giving of a notice terminating a contractual employment, whether by employer or employee, is . . . a unilateral act requiring no acceptance by the other party and, like a notice to quit a tenancy, once given it cannot . . . be withdrawn save by mutual consent.'[2]

A different view was taken by various Industrial Tribunals, when they first began to apply the Redundancy Payments Act. In *Miller* v. *Nettle Accessories Ltd.*[3] they held that a notice of four weeks given by an employer had been effectively rescinded by him on the day on which it had been made, and replaced by an offer of employment on different terms and conditions. That latter offer was itself held to amount to a dismissal when rejected by the employee; but the revocability of the original notice was recognized in principle. In

---

[1] In *Riordan* v. *War Office* [1959] 1 WLR 1046 (affirmed on other grounds [1961] 1 WLR 210).

[2] [1959] 1 WLR 1046 at 1054.   [3] (1966) 1 ITR 328.

Edwards v. *Arbuthnot & Sons*[1] a Scottish tribunal took this new departure further, holding that a notice of four weeks could validly be revoked after a week (during which the employers had obtained new orders). The result was that when the employee, having in the meantime obtained other employment and put up his house for sale, left his employment on the expiry date of the notice, it was held that he had not been dismissed at all. The Tribunal thought that there was no dismissal until the expiry of the notice, and that the notice could be withdrawn at any time before then. Furthermore, a Scottish tribunal decided in *McHardy* v. *The Caledon Shipbuilding Company Ltd.*[2] that a week's notice to terminate given to a ship's plater could validly be commuted to a notice of suspension after two days, so that the later action of the employee in treating his employment as at an end constituted a voluntary leaving on his part.

However, more recent decisions of the Tribunals and a decision of the NIRC reversed that trend and treated notice as irrevocable; as in *Bryan* v. *George Wimpey & Co. Ltd.*,[3] where the view was taken that a purported revocation of notice could be regarded only as an offer to renew the contract, which the employee was not unreasonable in refusing because he felt bound by a new engagement elsewhere which he had obtained in the interim period. So also in *Gallagher* v. *Union Transit Company Ltd.*[4] it was held that an employer who had given a month's notice could not, after three weeks, unilaterally postpone the operation of the notice, and that accordingly when the employee left shortly after the original expiry date of the notice, he had been dismissed by the employer, for the purposes of the Redundancy Payments Act.

An employee's notice has since been held to be irrevocable in the decision of the NIRC in *Harris & Russell Ltd.* v. *Slingsby*[5] where the irrevocability of notice was declared to be a principle generally applicable to notices given by either party to the contract of employment.

It is the view of this writer that notice to terminate should in general be regarded as irrevocable. In *Riordan* v. *War Office*, Diplock J. canvassed the possibility that the notice of resignation given by the employee might be effective only when it reached the head of the establishment at which the plaintiff was employed, and that the notice would therefore be revocable before that time. He held that the notice

[1] (1967) 2 ITR 282.   [2] (1967) 2 ITR 337.   [3] (1968) 3 ITR 28.
[4] (1969) 4 ITR 214.   [5] [1973] ICR 454.

was effective in this particular case immediately upon being handed to the plaintiff's immediate superior, on the ground that the immediate superior received it as an agent for the head of the establishment.[1] It might, however, in a given case be possible to hold that the immediate superior of the employee received the notice as the employee's agent, and that his authority to transmit it to a higher quarter could be revoked by the employee before it was executed. This analysis might make sound sense where, for example, the employee gave notice to the foreman in a fit of temper and repented of the matter before the notice was passed on to the management. It may well be thought that there should be some such scope for an evaluation of whether an effective irrevocable notice has been given.

SECTION 6: PAYMENT IN LIEU OF NOTICE

A. *The Scope of the Right to Terminate by Payment in Lieu of Notice*

1. *At Common Law.* By the middle years of the nineteenth century it was accepted by the courts that the custom for termination of the contracts of employment of domestic servants was by 'a month's wages or warning';[2] and there is some evidence of the occurrence of express provisions in contracts of employment for termination by payment of the wages for a certain period as an alternative to notice of that duration.[3] The courts did not, however, decide at that time whether it was a general principle that the right to terminate by payment in lieu of notice was always a valid alternative to an existing right to terminate by notice.

There was, indeed, good reason why there was no need to decide that further point, because in cases where the employer had a right to terminate the contract by notice, and he in fact terminated it summarily without justification, the damages recoverable by the employer would, in any event, be regarded as limited to the wages

---

[1] [1959] 1 WLR 1046 at 1054.

[2] Parke B. in *Fewings* v. *Tisdale* (1847) 1 Ex. 295 at 299; Channell J. in *Moult* v. *Halliday* [1898] 1 QB 125 at 130.

[3] e.g. *East Anglian Railway Co.* v. *Lythgoe* (1851) 10 CB 726 (clerk whose employment was determinable upon three months' notice or the payment of three months' salary); *Pilkington* v. *Scott* (1846) 15 M & W 657 (skilled glassmaker whose employment was terminable by the employer on giving him a month's wages or a month's notice).

for the period of notice.[1] A provision for payment of wages on termination was regarded, by at least some of the judges, as a 'liquidated damages' clause.[2] Hence, on that view of the measure of damages for wrongful dismissal, and of the effect of a provision for payment in lieu of notice, it made no difference at all whether the contract provided for payment in lieu of notice or not. In either event, the summary dismissal would be regarded as a dismissal in breach of contract, with damages being fixed at the wages for the period of notice.[3]

We find evidence also of a different view, namely that where the contract provided for termination by payment in lieu of notice, a summary termination would have the result that the payment in lieu of notice would be due to the employee, not as damages, but as a money-debt.[4] It would follow from this view of the nature of the payment that the dismissal would not be a wrongful dismissal, but a lawful dismissal wanting only in the payment of a debt. There would, on this view, be a true right to terminate by payment of wages in lieu of notice, as opposed to a power to terminate coupled with a limitation of liability for so terminating. But this was, understandably, not a distinction with which the judges concerned themselves.

Hence the question, whether a right to terminate by notice included a further right to terminate by payment in lieu of notice, was one of theoretical interest only, unless it could be claimed that the damages for wrongful dismissal were not limited to wages for the period of notice, or unless it was, for some other purpose, important to decide whether the dismissal was in principle wrongful or lawful. The issue was raised in *Austwick* v. *Midland Railway Co.*,[5] where a locomotive fireman, whose contract provided for termination upon a fortnight's notice, was dismissed on the grounds of certain union activity but was paid in lieu of a fortnight's notice. In order to establish the wrongfulness of the dismissal, the employee sued for damages and it was argued on his behalf by Sir Edward Carson that a provision for fourteen days' notice was not satisfied by payment of wages in lieu of notice. Grantham J., however, avoided the issue by holding that the dismissal was justified by the misconduct of the plaintiff.

---

[1] See below, pp. 250–2.
[2] e.g. per Patteson J. in *Goodman* v. *Pocock* (1850) 15 QB 576, 581.
[3] Cf. per Alderson B. in *Fewings* v. *Tisdale* (1847) 1 Ex. 295, 299.
[4] In *East Anglian Railway Co.* v. *Lythgoe* (1851) 10 CB 726; Maule J. at 736; Williams J. at 737; Talfourd J. at 738.
[5] (1909) 25 TLR 728.

The report suggests that it was, in any event, his view that damages would have been limited to fourteen days' wages.[1] But the case does not, as has been said of it by certain writers,[2] establish that a right to terminate by payment in lieu of notice automatically follows upon a right to terminate by notice.

Two decisions of the same period[3] suggest that an employee, whose contract provides for his dismissal upon notice, is properly dismissed if he is given a payment in lieu of notice, unless he can show some special obligation on the part of the employer to provide him with work as well as to pay him. These were cases where employers who had dismissed their employees with payments in lieu of notice sought to enforce restrictive covenants against them, and where the employees argued that the covenants were unenforceable against them because they had been wrongfully dismissed.[4] It was held in both cases that as the employer was under no obligation to the employee to allow him to work as well as to pay him, it followed that there was no breach of contract in paying him a week's wages and dispensing with his services for a week. This reasoning may be criticized, for even if the employee has no interest in being allowed to work as such,[5] he has a general interest in remaining an employee in accordance with his contract of employment, and that wider interest suffers if he is summarily dismissed with payment in lieu of notice. In the earlier of the two cases, Swinfen-Eady J. said that the dismissal with payment in lieu of notice was tantamount to the employer's saying, 'I give you a week's notice now, and I will pay you your one week's salary now; so you need not come up next week; I will pay it now instead.'[6] But this is to allow the employer to benefit from a fiction. His basic promise under the contract of employment is to maintain the employment relationship for a certain length of time, and these cases cannot be regarded as satisfactory

---

[1] Ibid. at 729.

[2] Fridman, *The Modern Law of Employment* (London, 1963) p. 471; Knight Dix, *Contracts of Employment* (3rd edn. 1968) at p. 28; cf. 4th edn. 1972 at p. 71.

[3] *Dennis & Sons Ltd.* v. *Tunnard Bros. & Moore* (1911) 56 Sol. Jo. 162; *Konski* v. *Peet* [1915] 1 Ch. 530.

[4] Cf. *General Billposting Co. Ltd.* v. *Atkinson* [1909] AC 118 (HL) (wrongful repudiation entitling the injured party to treat the contract as terminated and to disregard restrictive covenants).

[5] The cases in which the employee does have such an interest, such as where he gains publicity or valuable experience from actual work, are considered above at pp. 25–7.

[6] 56 Sol. Jo. at 162.

in so far as they allow the employer to curtail that obligation by making a payment in lieu of notice.

The view that it depends upon a construction of the particular contract whether provision is made for termination by payment in lieu of notice was expressed in *White* v. *Riley*,[1] where employees procured the dismissal of a non-union employee by the threat of a strike, and the employee concerned was dismissed with a week's wages in lieu of notice. It was important for the purposes of tortious liability to consider whether the dismissal had been in breach of contract or not (though it was ultimately unnecessary to decide the question, for reasons which are not material here). Of this question Lord Sterndale M.R. commented:

'It may be that he was employed on such terms that he was not entitled to any notice at all. It may be that he was employed on such terms that he should receive a week's notice, and that paying a week's wages would only be compensation for a breach of the contract to give him a week's notice. It might be that he was employed on the terms that his employment might be terminated either by a week's notice, or by payment of a week's wages, and the evidence, so far as it goes, seems to me to show that the third of these methods of employment was the one which was assumed to exist by all parties concerned with the matter.'[2]

It is the view of this writer that this is the most satisfactory approach to the problem of whether the employer has a right to terminate by payment in lieu of notice; and that in interpreting a contract which does not deal expressly with this question, the courts should consider, not merely the special interest of some employees in being allowed to do actual work, but the general interest, which may be important to a far wider class of employees, in continuing to be employed for the time stipulated in the contract.

The problem of the true analysis of payment in lieu of notice has been considered by the Industrial Court, with fairly inconclusive results. In *Dixon* v. *Stenor Ltd.*[3] Sir John Donaldson said of payment in lieu of notice that it was, as a matter of law, damages for breach of contract.[4] This suggests that the employer has no right to impose payment in lieu of notice but that he has an unqualified power to terminate the contract and pay liquidated damages on the spot. But elsewhere in the same judgment the Court recognized another 'situation'—where the employee does not work after he has been

[1] [1921] 1 Ch. 1.   [2] Ibid. at 6.
[3] [1973] ICR 157.   [4] Ibid. at 158 G.

given notice but is in fact on paid leave.[1] This is not really a different situation—but merely a different analysis of the same situation. We are left with the difficulty of deciding which analysis to apply to any given case.

The right to terminate the contract of employment by payment in lieu of notice is normally a right of the employer alone, and the employee does not normally have that right. It is certainly the case that the measure of damages against the employee for summary departure should not be taken to be his wages for the period of notice required of him to terminate his contract. In the case where that was established,[2] it was indicated in an *obiter dictum* that the employee has no right to terminate his contract by making a payment in lieu of notice; and it would seem inappropriate that he should have, because the payment equal to wages for the period of notice is not related to the loss caused by the summary departure of the employee. The employee who does in fact depart summarily offering a payment in lieu of notice cannot, of course, be compelled by law to work out his period of notice, any more than the employer can be compelled to employ during the period of notice. And if the offer of payment in lieu of notice is accepted, there will have been a termination by agreement, which will not constitute a breach of contract by the employee. But if the offer is rejected, the employee cannot, in the absence of express provision, be said to have a right to terminate the contract in this way.

2. *The Effect of the Contracts of Employment Act 1972 upon the Employer's Right to Terminate the Contract of Employment by Payment in Lieu of Notice.* The Contracts of Employment Act 1972 seems to have the effect that the employer is not normally regarded as having the right to terminate the contract of employment by a payment in lieu of notice, and that everything depends upon whether the employee has voluntarily accepted such a payment. This result has been produced by Section 1(3) of that Act, which provides that Section 1(1) and (2), which confer rights upon the employer and the employee to minimum periods of notice, 'shall not be taken to prevent either party from waiving his right to notice on any occasion, or from accepting a payment in lieu of notice'. It was presumably

---

[1] Ibid. at 159 E–F. Cf. the view of the majority of CA in *Lees* v. *Arthur Greaves Ltd.* [1974] ICR 501.
[2] *Cherry* v. *Wergles Ltd.* (1954) *The Times*, 13 Jan.—so also *Trotter* v. *Luxton* (1929) 73 Sol. Jo. pt. 1, p. 56 (*Cty. Ct.*).

the intention of this provision to preserve existing rights to terminate by payment in lieu of notice, and to make it possible to provide for termination in that way in future contracts of employment. It appears, however, to have had the effect that termination by payment in lieu of notice has since been regarded as proper termination only where there has been an acceptance of such payment by the employee at the time of termination.

The issue arose in a number of decisions of Industrial Tribunals in the early days after the coming into effect of the Redundancy Payments Act 1965, because a number of employers, anxious to avoid the application of that Act, had dismissed employees shortly before the day appointed for the coming into effect of the Act[1] with payments in lieu of notice, at such times that a termination by proper notice would have taken effect after the appointed day. The employees concerned argued that they must be regarded as having been dismissed on the later date, so that they would be entitled to a redundancy payment. In cases where the employee was regarded as having accepted the payment in lieu of notice, that argument was unsuccessful;[2] but where it could be shown that there had been no such acceptance, the dismissal was indeed regarded as falling within the time of operation of the Act. It was so held in *Chapman, Blair & Atchinson* v. *Executors of W. G. Leadley*,[3] where the payment in lieu of notice was simply included in the pay packet for the week gone by. Sir Diarmaid Conroy Q.C.[4] stated that 'This specific provision [section 1(3)] alters the Common Law position. Unless an employee waives his right to notice, or accepts a payment in lieu of notice, he is entitled to notice of prescribed length.'[5] To like effect was the decision in *Johnson* v. *John Thompson Ltd.*,[6] where the employee was first given four weeks' notice, and then a week later was given payment in lieu of notice, and where it was held that it was merely a convenient method of making the payments which the employers were obliged to make, they knowing that they would have no further work for him during notice. The Tribunal was there motivated, it

---

[1] 6 December 1965.

[2] *Ryan* v. *Liverpool Warehousing Co. Ltd.* (1966) 1 ITR 69; *Taylor's Cater Inns Ltd.* v. *Minister of Labour* (1966) 1 ITR 242 (the Ministry challenging the employer's right to rebate on the ground that there was no liability for redundancy payment).

[3] (1966) 1 ITR 84.

[4] The (then) President of the Industrial Tribunals for England and Wales.

[5] (1966) 1 ITR 84, 85.   [6] (1966) 1 ITR 261.

would seem, by an anxiety to prevent avoidance of the Act.[1] But in any event this approach seems an appropriate one in view of what was said earlier concerning the interest of the employee in the continuance of his employment for the time promised.

B. The Effect of Termination by Payment in Lieu of Notice

1. *The Quantum of Payment in Lieu of Notice.* The phrase 'termination by payment *of wages* in lieu of notice' has been avoided in the preceding pages, because it begs the question of the character of these payments. It is, none the less, the case that the payment in lieu of notice is normally quantified as the wages for the period of notice required to terminate the contract. It is suggested that such a payment may differ in certain respects from the remuneration which the employee would have received during a period of actual notice. It was ruled in *Gordon* v. *Potter*[2] that payment in lieu of notice need not take into account the benefits in kind which the employee would have received during the period of notice, here 'board-wages', which were free board and lodging during employment. If the employee is entitled to payment only in respect of cash earnings during the period of notice, it would seem also that he is entitled only to those sums which the employer was bound to enable him to earn during the period of notice, and not, for example, to anticipated overtime earnings where the overtime was not compulsory upon the employer. The payment should probably be seen as having to include anticipated earnings from third parties such as tips, by analogy with the principles governing damages for wrongful dismissal.[3] But in so far as the payments fall short of anticipated earnings during the period of notice, that is an argument for holding that the right to terminate by payment in lieu of notice should not be seen as following automatically from the existence of a right to terminate by notice. It is true that the employee who has received a payment in lieu of notice has the opportunity to earn money elsewhere during the period of notice. But that opportunity may be of no value in an adverse labour market; this is a matter which should perhaps be taken into account in deciding whether a right to terminate by payment in lieu of notice exists.

[1] The correctness of this method of preventing avoidance of the statute was, however, later doubted by Sir Diarmaid Conroy Q.C. himself in *Nightingale* v. *Biddle Bros. Ltd.* (1967) 2 ITR 624; see below, p. 296 note 5.

[2] (1859) 1 F & F 644—see below, pp. 256–7.

[3] Cf. *Manubens* v. *Leon* [1919] 1 KB 208—see below, p. 259.

2. *The Time of Termination.* It would seem that a lawful termination by payment in lieu of notice normally results in an immediate termination of the contract of employment. The termination will not be projected to the end of the notional period of notice. The payment should be regarded as a lump-sum payment, equal to the amount of wages during the period of notice, rather than as payment of actual wages for a period of notice during which the services of the employee are not required. This view is implicit in those Industrial Tribunal decisions discussed earlier[1] in which it was considered whether or not there had been an immediate termination by payment in lieu of notice. It is also borne out by those decisions concerning income tax which indicate that such a payment will not be regarded as remuneration for services during a notional period of notice,[2] unless the person employed can be called upon to render any services during that period.[3] It would seem also that termination with payment in lieu of notice will, in practice, be regarded as resulting in an immediate termination of employment for the purposes of liabilities of employer and employee to social security contributions. It would in general seem correct to hold that such payments in lieu of notice result in an immediate termination of the contract of employment because the payment is related to wages only in that these quantify the payment. In the words of Stamp J., the essential elements of a contract of employment are absent during the period following the payment because the former employee cannot be required to perform any duties and has no right to perform them.[4]

An apparent exception to this analysis is constituted by the provision of the National Insurance (Unemployment and Sickness Benefit) Regulations 1967 that unemployment benefit is not payable in respect of a period 'in respect of which a person receives a payment in lieu of . . . notice'.[5] But this can be regarded as a provision against double compensation for loss of employment, rather than the result of a theoretical view that the employment continues during that period.

However, the Industrial Court and the Court of Appeal also

---

[1] See above, pp. 186–7. See also below, pp. 296–7.

[2] *Du Cros* v. *Ryall* (1935) 19 TC 444; *Clayton* v. *Lavender* [1965] TR 461. Distinguishable are *Dale* v. *De Soissons* (1950) 32 TC 118; *Henry* v. *Foster* (1931) 16 TC 605.

[3] Cf. per Stamp J. in *Clayton* v. *Lavender* [1965] TR 461 at 463.

[4] *Ibid.* at p. 463.

[5] 1967 S.I. No. 440, Reg 7(1)(e).

recently cast some slight doubt upon the view that the contract of employment terminates immediately upon the giving of payment in lieu of notice. For although the NIRC has taken the view that payment in lieu is normally to be viewed as the payment of liquidated damages for an already complete termination of the contract, they have also indicated that payment in lieu may on occasion constitute a mere waiver by the employer of his right to require services, the contract continuing despite such waiver of services. The matter was so stated in *Dixon* v. *Stenor Ltd.*[1] and it was so decided on the facts in *Lees* v. *Arthur Greaves Ltd.*[2] However, this should probably still be viewed as the untypical analysis of payment in lieu, leaving immediate termination as the ordinary and presumed effect of such payments.[3]

SECTION 7: TERMINATION BY AGREEMENT

The effectiveness in law of an agreement between employer and employee to terminate their contract of employment, reached subsequently to the making of the contract, is not in doubt. The consideration is provided by the release of mutual future obligations.[4] Nor is there any requirement of formality for such an agreement, even when the contract of employment is itself in writing, or requires written notice of unilateral termination.

Furthermore, where there is a change in the terms and conditions of an employment, and that change is of a sufficiently basic kind, it will be regarded, in law, as the consensual termination of the existing contract of employment, coupled with its replacement by a new and different contract, with the consequences which flow from the fact of a division of a period of employment into separate contracts of employment.[5]

This method of termination of the contract of employment—

---

[1] [1973] ICR 157, 158 G, 159 D–F (Sir John Donaldson).
[2] [1974] ICR 501 (Stamp L.J. dissenting).
[3] e.g. *Dedman* v. *British Building Appliances Ltd.* [1974] ICR 53.
[4] Hence the agreement is an example of 'accord and satisfaction'; see per Stamp L.J. in *Lees* v. *Arthur Greaves Ltd.* [1974] ICR 501 at 506 D.
[5] Cf. *B.B.C.* v. *Ioannu* [1974] IRLR 77 at para. 17 (Sir John Donaldson): 'Any renewal of a fixed term contract must involve an amendment of its provisions to take account of the extension of the term and we see no reason why other provisions should not be added, amended or deleted *provided that the changes are not so extensive as to create a new contract*' (emphasis added); and see above, pp. 72 ff. (Decision affirmed [1975] IRLR 185.)

termination by mutual agreement—has assumed some importance with the growth of statutory rights associated with dismissal. The importance is of a negative character: consensual termination is inconsistent with dismissal and hence a finding of termination by agreement negatives the statutory rights of the employee. The extent to which termination by agreement has encroached upon the areas of termination by employer and by employee can be realized by considering three types of factual situation:

(a) genuinely bilateral agreement to terminate;
(b) termination agreed between the parties but initiated by employer;
(c) termination agreed between the parties but initiated by employee.

A. Termination Genuinely Bilateral

Where this situation is found on the facts to exist, there will necessarily be held to be a mutual agreement to terminate rather than a dismissal by the employer or for that matter a quitting by the employee; but the courts and tribunals will be cautious about accepting this analysis, and will require conclusive support from the facts. Thus in *Hempel* v. *Parrish*[1] it was held that there had been a termination by mutual agreement, rather than a dismissal, where an employee who had been employed as a mate to a painter agreed with him that they should both go into the employment of a larger firm. And in *Scott* v. *The Executors of A. E. Marchant*[2] it was again so held where an employee who had been employed by his father-in-law as the manager of the business of a wholesale fish merchant was given the business for which he worked. The former owner of the business was quite willing that his son-in-law should make this claim, for the rebate from the redundancy fund would then accrue to the advantage of the business; but the Tribunal would not regard this collusive transaction as a dismissal.

There are, however, clear suggestions that courts and tribunals will not, outside these special situations, lightly hold that there has been a termination by agreement, rather than a dismissal, in cases where the prime mover in the termination was the employer. There were strong comments to that effect in *Scott* v. *The Executors of A. E. Marchant*.[3] Moreover, comparison may now be made with the decision of the Court of Appeal in *Marriott* v. *Oxford & District*

---

[1] (1968) 3 ITR 240.   [2] (1969) 4 ITR 319.   [3] Ibid. at 324–5.

Co-operative Society Ltd. (No. 2)[1] that where an employer success-fully imposed changed terms and conditions of employment upon an employee for a short period, that was not to be regarded as other than a dismissal of the employee from his original employment. It did not constitute either a consensual variation or a consensual rescission and replacement of the contract of employment, because the requisite element of consent was lacking. Lord Denning M.R. put the matter thus: '[The employee] never agreed to the dictated terms. He protested against them. He submitted to them because he did not want to be out of employment. By insisting on new terms to which he never agreed, the employer did, I think, terminate the old contract of employment.'[2] Both there and in later decisions, the indications are that the courts will examine critically any claims that there has been a termination by mutual agreement rather than a termination by the employer.[3]

B. *Termination Agreed but Initiated by Employer*

The clearest and most significant case of agreed termination initiated by the employer is that where the employee offers his resignation because he knows that the employer wishes the employment to terminate, and because he wishes to avoid the odium of dismissal. The Industrial Court gave a firm ruling in *East Sussex C.C.* v. *Walker*[4] that where the employer has invited the employee to resign, the resignation is to be treated as amounting to a dismissal by the employer, rather than a termination by agreement or by the act of the employee.

Although that rule is in principle just and correct, it is, as the result of an anomaly, capable of working to the grave disadvantage of employees in the application of pension schemes. Thus in *Stephenson* v. *London Joint Stock Bank Ltd.*[5] a bank clerk was entitled to a pension from his employers in the event of his 'retirement with their consent' but not in the event of his being dismissed. His resignation and the company's acceptance thereof, following their

---

[1] [1970] 1 QB 186 (distinguished in *Lowe* v. *East Lancs. Paper Mill Ltd.* (1970) 5 ITR 132). See above, pp. 60–1.
[2] [1970] 1 QB 186, 191.
[3] *Shields Furniture Ltd.* v. *Goff* [1973] ICR 187 esp. at 189 H–190 F (Sir John Brightman); *Sheet Metal Components Ltd.* v. *Plumridge* [1974] ICR 373. Cf. *Lees* v. *Arthur Greaves Ltd.* [1974] ICR 501.
[4] (1972) 7 ITR 280.   [5] (1903) 52 WR 183.

request that he resign on account of his misconduct, were held to be tantamount to a dismissal. The possibility of anomaly is further demonstrated in *Young* v. *Associated Newspapers Ltd.*[1] where Brightman J. ruled that journalists dismissed by reason of redundancy upon the absorption of the *Daily Sketch* by the *Daily Mail* were not persons 'retiring with the consent of the company' so as to entitle them to deferred pensions under an early retirement clause in the rules of a non-contributory pension scheme. Brightman J. indicated that it was not surprising to find that a dismissed employee was excluded from benefiting under the early retirement clause, and that the company had power to relieve in cases of hardship by inviting employees, in appropriate cases, to resign and indicating that its consent to the retirements would be forthcoming.[2] However, such a device is liable to be defeated by the construction of the transaction as being in substance a dismissal, and therefore the relief of hardship depends both upon the whim of the employer and upon the operation of an uncertain construction of law. This seems to be a matter requiring regulation on grounds of public policy.[3]

C. Termination Agreed but Initiated by Employee

The most significant example of termination which is an agreed termination although initiated by the employee is that where the employee prefers, rather than to leave outright or give notice, to offer his resignation and have it accepted by the employer. There are no rules established by case-law concerning the effect of an offer of resignation by an employee—if only because there has been no practical importance attached to the distinction between consensual termination and termination by the employee. Some guidance can however be drawn from the case where the employer initiates an ostensibly bilateral termination. By parity of reasoning, the termination should be seen as the act of the employee if, but only if, his offer to resign is accompanied by an intention to leave in any event, if necessary without the consent of the employer.

These comments upon termination of the contract of employment by agreement subsequent to the making of the contract may be concluded by the observation that, although the analysis of this kind of termination is still in a rudimentary state as far as the case-law is concerned, the topic is one of growing importance. The

[1] (1971) 11 KIR 413.   [2] Ibid. at 423.   [3] See Note below, p. 383.

element of speculation which at the moment necessarily pervades the construction of principles about termination by agreement may well be reduced by judicial pronouncements in future. This is particularly likely because of the crucial effect of termination by agreement as negativing the statutory rights based upon dismissal by the employer.

Note:—Fixed-term and Probationary Contracts (see pp. 162–4)

The definition of fixed-term contracts has recently come under scrutiny because of the possibility of excluding liability for redundancy payments and unfair dismissal in the case of fixed-term contracts of two years or more (see now Trade Union and Labour Relations Act 1974 Sched. I Para. 12). The Court of Appeal in *B.B.C.* v. *Ioannu* [1975] IRLR 185 (see above, p. 164) considerably limited this method of contracting out of the legislation by holding that a contract did not count as being "for a fixed-term" where it contained provision for termination by notice during its term. It was indicated that a provision for termination *for the employee's misconduct* was not inconsistent with the statutory concept of the fixed-term contract. It is possible that notice for termination by the employee alone might also be within the definition.

One variant on the fixed-term contract, namely the probationary appointment, is becoming a source of difficulty with the reduction of the unfair dismissal qualifying period to six months (Trade Union and Labour Relations Act 1974 Sched. I Para. 10). The legislation is so framed that the refusal to confirm a fixed-term probationary appointment will almost inevitably count as a dismissal for statutory purposes, and the probationary nature of the appointment will be relevant only to the question of fairness, and not to that of whether the employee has been dismissed. An Industrial Tribunal has held that a probationary three-year appointment did not even count as a fixed-term contract where the terms of appointment quoted an incremental salary scale continuing well beyond three years (*Weston* v. *University College Swansea* (1975) 10 ITR 60).

Chapter Six

SUMMARY DISMISSAL

INTRODUCTION

By summary dismissal we mean dismissal without notice which is justifiable at common law by reference to the conduct or capabilities of the employee. The common law of summary dismissal is today important chiefly for the comparison and contrast between it and the law concerning unfair dismissal. The present work confines itself to a statement of the common law, but that statement is made with the still not fully formulated case-law of unfair dismissal in mind as a standard of reference. It is still too early in the history of the unfair dismissal jurisdiction for a point-by-point comparison of thet wo systems to be useful.[1] The object of this chapter is to describe as fully as possible the common law part of this dual system.

The common law of summary dismissal provides a particularly clear instance of interaction between general contractual principles and rules peculiar to the contract of employment. The rules special to the contract of employment consist of an only partially up-dated code of offences justifying the dismissal of employees, having its origin in nineteenth-century decisions and nineteenth-century social attitudes. It will be shown that the severity of these rules has been somewhat tempered by superimposing general contractual principles, requiring breach of condition or repudiation to justify rescission of contracts. Hence this chapter begins by considering dismissal for the specific offences of misconduct, disobedience, and incompetence, and continues by examining the application of general contractual principles.

The common law of summary dismissal gave such wide freedom to the employer that it has not been very frequently invoked by employees. It was this failure to provide socially adequate or acceptable protection for employees which led ultimately to the introduction of the law of unfair dismissal. This inadequacy of the common law manifests itself as much in the failure to control dismissal procedure

---

[1] Certain important comparisons and contrasts with the law on unfair dismissal are, however, made in the notes to this chapter. See Appendix, para. 2.

as in the laxity of the substantive rules. Especially now that one has the law of unfair dismissal in mind as a basis of comparison, it is appropriate for the discussion of summary dismissal in the present chapter to include a consideration of the procedural standards envisaged by the common law in connection with dismissal.

In addition to these substantive and procedural aspects of the law of summary dismissal, there is an important remedial question. This concerns the extent to which the common law (combined with the rules of equity) will on the one hand impose, or on the other hand allow employers to impose, forfeitures of remuneration and incidental benefits upon summarily dismissed employees. Thus there are suggestions in the case-law of a doctrine of forfeiture of accrued remuneration. Even if there is in fact no positive doctrine of forfeiture at common law, it is possible that the law looks leniently upon certain conditions in contracts of employment and in pension schemes which do in fact amount to forfeitures in the event of summary dismissal. It may well be that existing rules of law could be deployed against these instances of forfeiture, thereby preventing a particular kind of unjust enrichment.

SECTION 1: DISMISSAL FOR MISCONDUCT, DISOBEDIENCE, AND INCOMPETENCE

The rights of the employer to dismiss for misconduct, disobedience, or incompetence were recognized in the early and middle years of the nineteenth century. Certain principles and tendencies have emerged in the application of these concepts, which are of substantial importance in considering the reasons why the law has become remote from the realities of the employment relationship in this context.

A. Dismissal for Misconduct

By recognizing the general heading of 'misconduct', the courts reserved a wide discretion to decide whether any dismissal was justified on its facts. The width of this discretion has been asserted in a number of decisions in which the courts have held that justification of the particular dismissal was a question of fact alone,[1] governed

---

[1] Williams J. in *Amor* v. *Fearon* (1839) 9 A & E 548, 553; Coleridge J. in *Read* v. *Dunsmore* (1840) 9 C & P 588, 594 (*arguendo*); Maule J. in *East Anglian Railway Co.* v. *Lythgoe* (1851) 10 CB 726, 736; Cockburn L.J. in *Churchward* v. *Chambers*

by no rigid standards of any kind.[1] Thus Lord James in *Clouston & Co. Ltd.* v. *Corry* laid it down that 'there is no fixed rule of law defining the degree of misconduct which will justify dismissal'.[2] A small number of general principles have, however, been established concerning the meaning of misconduct.

Thus, for example, misconduct justifying dismissal can be constituted by a single isolated act of sufficient gravity; it need not consist in a course of conduct. It was so held by Bowen L.J. on the ground that questions of misconduct were issues of fact rather than law: 'I think the view that if it is an isolated case, it does not amount to such misconduct as would entitle the master to determine the service, is a mistake. It seems to me to be a confusion between the duty of the judge to draw inferences of fact and the duty of the judge to pronounce a decision of law.'[3] It has also been established that misconduct justifying dismissal may be constituted by conduct outside the course of employment provided that it affects the employment relationship.[4] Drunkenness outside working hours may thus justify dismissal in an appropriate case. But the courts have, on the whole, refrained from laying down rules as to what may constitute 'misconduct' and what may not.[5]

This compares with the treatment of 'misconduct' by the National Insurance Commissioners for the purposes of unemployment benefit.

(1860) 2 F & F 229, 230 (*contra*, Grantham J. in *Austwick* v. *Midland Railway Co.* (1909) 25 TLR 728—but an unclear report of the case).

[1] Bramwell B. in *Horton* v. *McMurtry* (1860) 5 H & N 667, 676; cf. Parke B. in *Lomax* v. *Arding* (1855) 10 Ex. 734, 736.

[2] [1906] AC 122, 129; cf. Channell J. in *Baster* v. *London & County Printing Works* [1899] 1 QB 901, 904: 'The question [what misconduct justified summary dismissal] is one of fact and degree in all cases.'

[3] In *Boston Deep Sea Fishing Co.* v. *Ansell* (1888) 39 Ch. D. 339, 363; cf. Darling J. in *Baster* v. *London and County Printing Works* [1899] 1 QB 901, 903, where he really transformed the 'habitual neglect' of earlier cases into simple 'neglect'.

[4] *Clouston & Co. Ltd.* v. *Corry* [1906] AC 122. It had been found by the Court of Appeal of New Zealand—(1904) 7 Gaz. LR 213—that misconduct had occurred outside working hours.

[5] The NIRC has shown a similar reluctance to impose limitations upon those reasons relating to the conduct of the employee which may prevent a dismissal from being unfair (1971 Act s. 24(1), 24(2)(b)), e.g. *Turner* v. *Wadham Stringer Commercials Ltd.* [1974] ICR 277; cf. also *Dalton* v. *Burton's Gold Medal Biscuits Ltd.* [1974] IRLR 45—no legal definition of gross misconduct for the purposes of para. 133 of the *I.R. Code of Practice;* and it was equally slow to interfere with Tribunal assessments of blameworthy conduct on the part of the employee leading to reduction of compensation, e.g. *Munif* v. *Cole & Kirby Ltd.* [1973] ICR 486.

Section 22(2) (a) of the National Insurance Act 1965 provides that 'a person shall be disqualified for receiving unemployment benefit for a period not exceeding six weeks . . . if . . . he has lost his employment through misconduct'. The Commissioners have refused to fetter this discretion. Thus, they have held that the fact that a claimant was not in the course of his employment at the time of the alleged misconduct would not in itself enable him to escape disqualification.[1] They have refused to hold that any and every breach of an employer's formal rules will constitute misconduct justifying disqualification.[2] And they have refused to hold that criminal misconduct must have been prosecuted to conviction in a court of law.[3] Hence there is here a refusal to determine 'misconduct' according to a system of rules and precedent, similar to that of the courts on the common-law issue.

B. Dismissal for Disobedience

In recognizing the right of the employer to dismiss for wilful disobedience to lawful orders,[4] the courts were, as in the case of dismissal for misconduct, treating the employer's right to dismiss as a wide one. Lord Evershed M.R. insisted that 'wilful' disobedience necessitated 'a deliberate flouting of the essential contractual conditions'.[5] Comparison may be made with the judgment of Isaacs C.J. in the leading Australian case of *Adami* v. *Maison de Luxe Ltd.*[6] where he held that a dismissal could not be justified on the ground merely of the 'wilfulness' of an act of disobedience (if 'wilful' meant only 'intentional' or 'deliberate')—the disobedience must in addition amount to repudiation of the contract. But these are relatively recent developments. It would appear that 'wilfulness' was not a stringent requirement in the nineteenth century.

In so far as the term 'lawful' has been defined at all in this context, it was defined by the suggestion of Rolfe B. in *Turner* v. *Mason*[7]

---

[1] R(U) 7/57 (lorry driver drunk in charge of motor-car outside course of employment), R(U) 14/57 (drunkenness outside hours—customer complained).

[2] R(U) 25/56 (breach of rule forbidding Post Office servants from betting by post. This particular misconduct held to justify disqualification).

[3] R(U) 10/54.

[4] *Spain* v. *Arnott* (1817) 2 Stark 256; *Callo* v. *Brouncker* (1831) 4 C & P 518; *Amor* v. *Fearon* (1839) I. Perry & Davison 398–401 (the authorised report, 9 Ad. & El. 548, omits this point); *Turner* v. *Mason* (1845) 14 M & W 112, 116–17.

[5] *Laws* v. *London Chronicle Ltd.* [1959] 1 WLR 698, 701.

[6] (1924) 35 CLR 143, 148–53 (High Court of Aust.).

[7] (1845) 14 M & W 112, 118.

that 'It is an unlawful order to direct a servant to continue where she is in danger of violence to her person, or of infectious disease'. The examples of unlawful orders given by Rolfe B. were used to decide the extent to which the employer was entitled to subject the employee to danger, in two opinions of the Judicial Committee of the Privy Council.[1]

In the former of these cases it was decided that an order to an Armenian employee to go to the bank's branch in Messina was not unlawful because the employee did not allege personal danger in going—hence his refusal to go was held to be a good ground for dismissal. But it was held in the latter case that an order to remain in Constantinople was unlawful because the employee did show that this involved personal danger, so that his refusal to stay there did not justify his dismissal.

The dividing line between the two cases falls in such a place as to show that an order will be treated as 'unlawful' only in a narrow range of circumstances.

There are suggestions that the orders must be 'reasonable' in order for disobedience to them to justify dismissal.[2] In the early Poor Law settlement case of *R.* v. *Islip (Inhabitants)* (1721)[3] the facts had been closely parallel to those in *Turner* v. *Mason*, and the opposite result had been reached by applying a test of reasonableness. But no such suggestion appears in the leading case of *Turner* v. *Mason*, nor has it affected the the subsequent development of the law.

In *Beale* v. *Great Western Railway Co.*[4] a test of reasonableness was applied to an order given to a railway employee to attend his work at a distant place, with the effect of increasing his travelling time; but more because the rules of the Great Western Railway, which formed part of the contract of employment, provided that 'all persons employed by the Company must attend at such hours as may reasonably be required', rather than because common law required the order to be reasonable. It cannot today be said that a

---

[1] *Bouzourou* v. *Ottoman Bank* [1930] AC 271; *Ottoman Bank* v. *Chakarian* [1930] AC 277. Comparison may be made with other cases and dicta in different contexts on the extent to which the employee is entitled to refuse to submit himself to hazards, e.g. Lord Abinger C.B. in *Priestley* v. *Fowler* (1837) 3 M & W 1, 6; Alderson B. in *Wiggett* v. *Fox* (1856) 11 Ex. 832, 839; Cockburn C.J. in *Woodley* v. *Metropolitan District Railway Co.* (1877) 2 Ex. D. 384, 388; *Palace Shipping Co. Ltd.* v. *Caine* [1907] AC 386; *Robson* v. *Sykes* [1938] 2 All ER 612 (cf. below, p. 239).

[2] *Jacquot* v. *Bourra* (1839) 7 Dowling 348, 352 *per curiam; Price* v. *Mouat* (1862) CB (NS) 508 per Williams J. at 511.

[3] 1 Stra. 423.   [4] (1901) 17 TLR 450.

requirement of reasonableness qualifies the orders whose breach may justify summary dismissal.

The rule that an employee may be dismissed for wilful disobedience to any lawful order has the effect of allowing the employer a prerogative to issue any work-directions he may please to the employee, subject only to the limitations that the order does not expose the employee to immediate danger to life or limb or require him to engage in unlawful conduct.[1] This result was in accordance with the views taken in the early part of the nineteenth century about the rights of the employer under the contract of employment. This is well illustrated by the decision in *R. v. St. John Devizes*[2] (1829):

The issue was whether a settlement had been acquired under a particular contract of employment.[3] The rule was that a settlement could not be gained under any contract of service which limited the hours of work; the employee must be at beck and call of the employer at all times. This was a contract of employment of a weaver, whereby she agreed expressly to obey all the rules and regulations made by the master. The evidence was that the rules had not been put into writing; they 'existed only in the breast of the master, but were known to and acted on by the work people'.[4] It was held that the express agreement to obey the rules did not constitute a limitation on the contract; in the words of Parke J., 'That imports no more than a contract to obey the orders of her master, which is a term implied in every contract of hiring.'[5]

Thus there was at that time a legal presumption that servants were obliged by their contracts of employment to obey any and every lawful order of their masters.

It was necessary for a white-collar employee to challenge his employer's right to order him to perform manual tasks, before the courts would modify this view of the nature of the contract of employment. For in the later case of *Price* v. *Mouat* (1862)[6] it was recognized that disobedience of an order will justify dismissal only where the order is within the scope of the employment.

---

[1] This latter limitation appears from *Morrish* v. *Henlys* (*Folkestone*) *Ltd.* [1973] ICR 482 at 484 H–485 A (Sir Hugh Griffiths) (employee entitled to refuse an order to connive at falsification of records).

[2] 9 B & C 896.

[3] The point is that under the then operative Poor Laws, service under the appropriate type of contract of employment was one way of establishing residence in a particular parish, which accordingly became liable for the support of the employee concerned.

[4] Ibid. at 897.   [5] Ibid. at 901; cf. per Bayley J. at 900.

[6] 11 CB (NS) 508.

In that case an employer, seeking a pretext to dismiss his employee, who was employed as a lace-buyer—a supervisory and executive occupation—ordered him to undertake the manual work of carding lace. The employee refused, regarding the order as incompatible with his employment. The employer dismissed him and relied upon the defence of wilful disobedience to lawful orders. It was held that it was a proper direction to the jury to ask them whether the orders were such as a person in that position was bound to obey.

There has been no further definition for the purposes of summary dismissal of what orders the employees are bound to obey, except for the suggestion made by Lord Denning M.R. and Roskill L.J. that the legal status of a works rule book is that it contains rules which are not terms of the contract of employment itself but are contractual instructions to a man as to how he is to do his work.[1] There is apart from this extremely little guidance as to the managerial prerogative which is (in theory) enforceable by summary dismissal.[2]

C. Dismissal for Incompetence

The right to dismiss for misconduct was extended by the decision in *Harmer* v. *Cornelius* (1858)[3] to include a right to dismiss for incompetence.

The defendant advertised in a newspaper for 'two first-rate scene painters'. The plaintiff replied enclosing a picture of his work. He was engaged,

---

[1] *Secretary of State for Employment* v. *ASLEF* (No. 2) [1972] ICR 19 at 54 B (Lord Denning M.R.) and 71 B (Roskill L.J.).

[2] The law of unfair dismissal is in a state of uncertainty in relation to managerial prerogative; but there are some indications that an employer may be able to justify a dismissal on the ground of the employee's refusal to obey an instruction even if the employer was not contractually entitled to give that instruction. See *Mawson* v. *Leadgate* [1972] IRLR 105, *Morrison* v. *Marquess of Exeter* [1973] IRLR 74, *Knighton* v. *Henry Rhodes Ltd.* [1974] IRLR 71, and cf. *R.S. Components Ltd.* v. *Irwin* [1973] ICR 535 (refusal to enter into a covenant against competition). But *contra*, *Wallace* v. *Biggs Wall Ltd.* [1972] IRLR 17, *Kemp* v. *Robin Knitwear Ltd.* [1974] IRLR 69. On the other hand, even when acting within his contractual prerogative, an employer *was* held to an obligation to engage in customary negotiations as a precondition to fair dismissal—*Wallace* v. *Guy Ltd.* [1973] ICR 117; and has also been required to observe procedural safeguards, particularly that of giving a warning where insistence on his contractual rights would take the employee by surprise—see Anderman, *Unfair Dismissals and the Law* (I.P.M., London, 1973) pp. 54–5—and see also below, pp. 219 note 2, 221 note 2.

[3] 5 CB (NS) 236 followed in *Searle* v. *Ridley* (1873) 28 LT 411 (general superintendent of building works); contrast *Van Weyenbergh* v. *British Acetate Ltd.* (1930) 74 Sol. Jo. Pt. 1, p. 90 (chemist and works manager). Held competent on the evidence.

but was found to be so incompetent that he was dismissed within two days of starting work. His action for wrongful dismissal failed on the ground that his incompetence justified the dismissal.

The incompetence was held to justify dismissal on the ground that the plaintiff had impliedly warranted his competence, and that failure to fulfil the warranty constituted misconduct justifying dismissal: 'Misconduct in a servant is, according to every day's experience, a justification of a discharge. The failure to afford the requisite skill which had been expressly or impliedly promised is a breach of a legal duty, and therefore misconduct.'[1]

It was essential to this decision that the employment concerned was of a skilled nature. In *Lister* v. *Romford Ice and Cold Storage Co. Ltd.*,[2] Viscount Simonds held that the duty of possessing skill, recognized in *Harmer* v. *Cornelius*, included a duty of exercising care, even in the case of the unskilled worker:

'I see no ground for excluding from, and every ground for including in, this category [i.e. the persons included in the dictum of Willes J. above] a servant who is employed to drive a lorry which, driven without care, may become an engine of destruction. . . . Nor can I see any valid reason for saying that a distinction is to be made between possessing skill and exercising it. . . . I have spoken of using skill rather than using care, for "skill" is the word used in the cited case [i.e. *Harmer* v. *Cornelius*], but this embraces care. For even in so-called unskilled operations, an exercise of care is necessary to the proper performance of duty.'[3]

This represents a major extension of the rule in *Harmer* v. *Cornelius*, because that earlier case turns upon the representation or warranty of specialist skill.

It has been pointed out that in *Harmer* v. *Cornelius* the formation of the contract of employment rather than the performance of it constituted the culpability of the employee:

'Where an employee puts forth his best efforts, and yet is unable to perform a job, either at all or with the requisite efficiency, he may justly claim that he is not at fault in so far as any present breach of duty is concerned. Since misconduct and disciplinary punishment pre-suppose fault, some other breach of duty must be found. The law finds it in the initial hiring itself. It casts a duty on the prospective employee to ascertain the requirements of a job for which he applies, and to either apply [*sic*] only for

---

[1] 5 CB (NS) 236, 247 (Willes J.).   [2] [1957] AC 555.
[3] Ibid. at 573.

jobs he can do, or, if he has any doubts about his ability to do them, to reveal such doubts to the employer.'[1]

There are serious objections to finding such culpability in all cases except those where the employee has obtained his job dishonestly; for if there is no element of fraud on the part of the employee, then the appointment may well reflect upon the employer's methods of selection and training. The employer will moreover generally be in a better position to assess the requirements of the particular job than the employee, and where that is so, the employee should not be liable to summary dismissal because an error of judgment has been made in selection.

Moreover, allegations of incompetence or of inefficiency may in present-day conditions point to an inability on the part of the employee to adapt to technological change, rather than an inability to do the work for which he was originally employed.[2] Furthermore, an employee may be found too expensive when his work is of so high a standard that he cannot attain the necessary speed of output profitable to the employer.[3] Such an employee may well be the victim of a generally prevailing decline in the standards of workmanship, and ought not to be liable to summary dismissal. For these reasons, the language of implied representation or implied warranty is generally more appropriate to the contract made by the expert independent contractor than to the contract of employment.[4]

---

[1] Avins, *Employee's Misconduct as a Cause for Discipline and Dismissal in India and the Commonwealth* (Allahabad 1968) s. 51, pp. 87–8.

[2] Compare the redundancy payments case of *North Riding Garages Ltd.* v. *Butterwick* [1967] 2 QB 56 (Div. Ct.).

[3] Compare the redundancy payments case of *Hindle* v. *Percival Boats Ltd.* [1969] 1 WLR 174.

[4] A group of Industrial Tribunal decisions reported in [1973] IRLR perhaps indicate a stringent approach, in the law of unfair dismissal, towards dismissal for incompetence. These decisions perhaps show a willingness to see such dismissals as the result of defects in management for which the employee must not bear the whole responsibility. Thus *Cockroft* v. *Trendsetter Furniture Ltd.* [1973] IRLR 6 (inadequate investigation by employer; inadequate clerical assistance); *Woodward* v. *Beeston Boilers Ltd.* [1973] IRLR 7 (lack of trained subordinates); *Fox* v. *Findus Ltd.* [1973] IRLR 8 (insufficient instruction or guidance given by employer). The Industrial Tribunal decisions also show a scepticism towards claims of incompetence at an evidentiary level, e.g. *Rayner* v. *Remploy Ltd.* [1973] IRLR 3, *Price* v. *Gourley Bros. Ltd.* [1973] IRLR 11; and Anderman, op. cit. at 46–8, argues that a test of factual adequacy (i.e. an objective criterion) is applied in such cases. Cf. also the procedural safeguards applied in such cases— below, pp. 221 note 2, 224 note 1.

SECTION 2: THE APPLICATION OF GENERAL PRINCIPLES
OF CONTRACT LAW

The grounds for dismissal described in the preceding section are by their very nature concerned with the contract of employment and not with other types of contract. However, those grounds of dismissal represent a part only of the common-law rules concerning the dismissal of employees for good cause, and the other part consists in an application of general principles of contract law.

Two principles of the general law of contract have exerted a special influence upon the law concerning the contract of employment: the right (i) to rescind a contract for breach of condition and (ii) to rescind in response to wrongful repudiation.

A. The Meaning of Rescission

In some contexts, notably that of rescission for misrepresentation, the term connotes a complete retroactive cancellation of the contract and a restoration of the *status quo ante*,[1] by means of an indemnity if necessary.[2] In the different context where rescission is part of the process of claiming a restitutionary remedy, there is controversy about the extent of complete cancellation and restoration of the *status quo ante*,[3] but the rescission is still in principle retroactive.[4] However, the term 'rescission' may be used to describe the termination of a contract in response to breach of condition or wrongful repudiation, where the rescinding party refuses further contractual performance and perhaps in addition claims damages for breach of contract. Here the term 'rescission' is used to mean prospective rather than retroactive termination of the contract. This is well illustrated by the decision in *Heyman* v. *Darwins Ltd.*[5], which concerned the rescission of an agreement making the appellants the sole selling agents, in an extensive area of the world, of steel manufactured by the respondents, and where Lord Wright commented that '. . . if the repudiation is wrongful and the rescission is rightful, the contract is ended by the rescission, but only as far as concerns

---

[1] As in *Redgrave* v. *Hurd* (1881) 20 Ch. D. 1 (sale of land).

[2] As in *Whittington* v. *Seale-Hayne* (1900) 82 LT 49 (lease).

[3] Contrast *Hunt* v. *Silk* (1804) 5 East 449 (agreement for lease) with *Fibrosa Spolka Akcyjna* v. *Fairbairn, Lawson Ltd.* [1943] AC 32 (sale of goods—frustration). See Goff and Jones, *The Law of Restitution* (London, 1966) pp. 24–5, 341–2.

[4] See below, p. 209.   [5] [1942] AC 356.

future performance, It remains alive for the awarding of damages either for previous breaches or for the breach which constitutes the repudiation.'[1]

That the term 'rescission' bears this meaning, when it is used to describe a dismissal by an employer, is shown by the judgment of Bowen L.J. in *Boston Deep Sea Fishing Co.* v. *Ansell*[2] where he said:

'It [i.e. a dismissal] is not a rescission of the contract in the sense in which the term ordinarily is used, viz. that you relegate the parties to the original position they were in before the contract was made. That cannot be, because half the contract has been performed. It is really only a rescission in this sense, that an act occurs which determines the relation of master and servant for the future. . . . '

That the dismissal of an employee does operate as a prospective termination and not a retroactive cancellation of the contract of employment is well illustrated by the decision in *Renshaw* v. *Queen Anne Mansions Co.*[3]:

A contract for the employment of the plaintiff by the defendants as the manager of a private power station for five years made provision for the dismissal of the plaintiff in the event of gross misconduct, and also for the referral to arbitration of any dispute between the parties concerning their rights and liabilities under the contract. The defendants dismissed the plaintiff, alleging misconduct. To the plaintiff's claim for damages for wrongful dismissal, the defendants claimed the right to an arbitration.

If that contract had been retroactively cancelled, either by the justified dismissal by the defendants, or by the wrongful dismissal and the acceptance of wrongful dismissal as a termination by the plaintiff, then the arbitration clause would be cancelled too, and there would be no right to an arbitration under the contract. But it was held that the defendants were entitled to an arbitration; and Lord Esher, M.R commented:

'I cannot see any ground for the contention that by the dismissal of the plaintiff the whole contract was put an end to so as to be no longer existing. The question was whether the dismissal of the plaintiff was a breach of the contract by the defendants, and, by virtue of the provision for reference of any dispute to arbitration contained in the contract, I think the judge had power to make the order which he made [for a referral to arbitration].'[4]

---

[1] Ibid. at 379. But cf. below p. 293, notes 4 & 5.　　[2] (1889) 39 Ch. D. 339, 365.
[3] [1897] 1 QB 662; followed in *Parry* v. *Liverpool Malt Co.* [1900] 1 QB 339.
[4] [1897] 1 QB 662, 665.

The term 'rescission' is accordingly used in this work, unless the context otherwise indicates (as where rescission is associated with a restitutionary claim), to mean the prospective termination of a contract in the exercise of a right result:ng from the fault of the other party.[1]

B. The Right to Rescind for Breach of Condition

The right to rescind for breach of condition originated in cases decided before the beginning of the nineteenth century, which distinguished between dependent covenants and independent covenants, and held that the failure to perform a covenant released the other party from covenants dependent upon it, but not from covenants independent of it.[2] If the covenants were dependent upon each other, the performance of one was a condition precedent to liability under the other. By a distortion of usage the promise itself, rather than the performance of it, became known as the 'condition'. Strictly speaking it is incorrect to refer to a breach of condition—there is the breach of a contractual obligation, the performance of which is a condition of the liability of the other party.[3]

A body of case-law of extreme technicality developed to decide whether covenants were dependent or independent,[4] until in *Boone* v. *Eyre* (1777) Lord Mansfield ruled that, 'where mutual covenants go to the whole of the consideration on both sides, they are mutual

---

[1] The view of rescission here stated represents an orthodox approach to the common law as it was established from *Heyman* v. *Darwins Ltd.* onwards if not before. But recent decisions concerning demurrage clauses—*Suisse Atlantique case* [1967] 1 AC 361—and exception clauses—the *Harbutt's 'Plasticine' case* [1970] 1 QB 447—have tended towards a view of rescission for breach as retroactive, as far as the effect upon such clauses is concerned. See Coote 'The Effect of Discharge by Breach on Exception Clauses' [1970] CLJ 221 at 226–7. For the purposes of an account of the contract of employment, where exception clauses do not occur in practice, the traditional view of rescission for breach as prospective still seems preferable.

[2] See Holdsworth HEL VIII pp. 72–5; Smith, *Leading Cases* (13th edn., ed. Chitty, Denning & Harvey, 1929), notes to *Cutter* v. *Powell* (Vol. II, pp. 9 ff.) esp. at pp. 9–16; Street, *Foundations of Legal Liability* (New York 1906), Vol. II, Chapter XIV—Dependence of Mutual Promises—pp. 132–40. Cf. *Pordage* v. *Cole* (1669) 1 Wms. Saund. 319; *Campbell* v. *Jones* (1796) 6 TR 570; *Morton* v. *Lamb* (1797) 7 TR 125.

[3] Cf. Reynolds, 'Warranty, Condition and Fundamental Term' (1963) 79 LQR 534 at 535.

[4] Williams' Saunders Reports—Notes to *Pordage* v. *Cole*, pp. 320 ff. (in the 1871 edn. (ed. Vaughan Williams) Vol. I, pp. 548 ff.); Glanville Williams, 'Partial Performance of Entire Contracts' (1941) 57 LQR 373, 490 at 490–1.

conditions, the one precedent to the other. But where they go only
to a part, where a breach may be paid for in damages, there the defendant has a remedy on his covenant, and shall not plead it as a
condition precedent.'[1] As originally stated by Lord Mansfield,
the rule was that the right to rescind depended entirely upon the
importance of the promise which had been broken. This could lead
to hardship where one party was guilty of a minor breach of a covenant going to the whole of the consideration; for then his minor
breach entitled the other party to rescind the contract *in toto*.[2]
But in *Campbell* v. *Jones*[3] the court, in holding that the defendant
was not entitled to rescind the contract, took into account the fact
that the plaintiff had rendered part performance of his obligations,
as well as the fact that the covenant broken by the plaintiff did not
go to the whole of the consideration. These cases were later treated
as authority for a rule that where one party has performed a substantial part of his obligations, then the other party cannot rescind
the contract for breach, even though the term broken was at the
outset a term going to the whole consideration. Thus the judgment,
for instance, of Pollock C.B. in *Ellen* v. *Topp* (1851) shows how the
right of rescission could be seen as depending upon the importance
of the breach of contract as well as of the term broken.[4]

The distinction between terms the breach of which gave a right
to rescind, and terms the breach of which did not give such a right,
came to be described as the distinction between 'conditions' and
'warranties'.[5] The existence of the distinction between 'conditions'

---

[1] 1 H.Bl. 273 n.—a similar wording at 6 TR 373.

[2] A problem discussed in *Duke of St. Albans* v. *Shore* (1789) 1 H.Bl. 270.
In so far as these cases deal with the particular problem of shortage on a sale of
land, they have been made obsolete by developments in equity dealing with this
particular type of contract.

[3] (1796) 6 TR 570.

[4] 6 Ex. 424, 441–2. So also: Lord Ellenborough C.J. in *Davidson* v. *Gwynne*
(1810) 12 East 381, 389; Littledale J. in *Franklin* v. *Miller* (1836) 4 A & El.
599, 605; Tindal C.J. in *Glaholm* v. *Hays* (1841) 2 M & G 257, 268; Pollock C.B.
in *Tarrabochia* v. *Hickie* (1856) 1 H & N 183, 187; Martin B. in *Seeger* v. *Duthie*
(1860) 8 CB(NS) 45, 75–6.

[5] Probably largely as the result of the codificatory influence of Chalmers.
The distinction appears in its present form in Chalmers, *Sale of Goods Act*
(London, 1894) p. 168. Chalmers seems to have been imposing a new terminology
arrived at by adaptation of the existing law. Cf. Stoljar, 'Conditions and
Warranties on Sale' (1952) 15 MLR 425 at 436–8, and (1953) 16 MLR 174 at
188–90. Cf. also his discussion of the twentieth-century case taking up the
distinction, *Harrison* v. *Knowles and Foster* [1917] 2 KB 606 (affd. [1918] 1 KB
608)—(1953) 16 MLR 184–8.

and 'warranties' reinforces the idea that the right to rescind for breach of condition should be tested according to the importance of the term broken rather than the importance of the breach.[1] This aspect of the right to rescind for breach of condition has not been applied in the context of contracts of employment, where the emphasis is generally on the importance of the breach rather than of the term broken.[2] Rule books and company handbooks issued to employees frequently state it to be a 'condition' of employment that the employee shall contribute to the employer's pension scheme. That is in order to make it compulsory upon employees to join the pension scheme when commencing their employment. But apart from that, written contractual documents stating the terms of contracts of employment rarely distinguish expressly between 'conditions' and other terms.

However, even in cases other than those of contracts of employment, there has in recent years been a tendency to emphasize that the nature of the term broken is but one aspect of the right to rescind for breach of condition. This tendency is associated with the judgment of Diplock L.J. in the *Hongkong* case, where it was laid down that the nature of the term is not decisive of the right to rescind, but that this right generally depends on the nature of the event resulting from the breach—whether it was an event frustrating the contract.[3] The other two judges in the Court of Appeal were prepared, if not to go so far, at least to treat the nature of the breach as predominating in this case over the nature of the term broken.[4] The effect of this development is to emphasize the analogy between summary dismissal and the general right to rescind a contract for breach of condition.

The right to rescind a contract by reason of serious breach of contract has come to be described by a number of different metaphors, such as a right to rescind for a breach 'going to the root of the

---

[1] Cf. *The Mihalis Angelos* [1971] 1 QB 164 (charter-party); *Wickman Machine Tool Sales Ltd.* v. *L. Schuler A.G.* [1974] AC 235 (agency contract).

[2] Though cf. *Gould* v. *Webb* (1855) 4 E & B 933—dismissal not justified because certain particular terms broken were not 'conditions'—an exceptional case—see below, p. 212.

[3] *Hongkong Fir Shipping Co. Ltd.* v. *Kawasaki Ltd.* [1962] 2 QB 26, 69; cf. the same judge in *Hardwick Game Farm Ltd.* v. *Suffolk Agricultural Poultry Producers' Assn.* [1966] 1 WLR 287 at 341 (affd. [1969] 2 AC 31). See Devlin, op. cit. [1966] CLJ 192 at 192–202.

[4] Upjohn L.J. [1962] 2 QB 26, 64; Sellers L.J. at 57.

contract'[1] or a breach 'substantially depriving the injured party of what he bargained for'[2] or even a 'fundamental breach' (unless that term has a further and separate meaning).[3] It is outside the scope of this work to relate to each other all the different modes of describing the right to rescind. They express minor historical developments of their own, and it cannot be regarded as settled that they all give rise to the same result when applied to a particular case. But they are sufficiently closely related to each other for it to be possible to regard them all as coming within the broad category of the right to rescind for breach of condition.[4] The really important contrast is between the right to rescind for breach of condition and the right to rescind in response to wrongful repudiation.

C. The Right to Rescind in Response to Wrongful Repudiation

The right to rescind a contract for breach of condition arises by reason of a failure of performance which has occurred in the past, provided that the failure is of sufficient gravity or relates to a sufficiently major term of the contract. The right to rescind a contract in response to repudiation arises, not so much by reason of a failure of performance in the past, as by reason of the manifesting of an intention not to perform contractual obligations in the future. Where one party to a contract repudiates his still outstanding obligations under a contract, the other party is thereby entitled to repudiate. This is especially important in the case of contracts involving continuing reciprocal obligations spread over a period of time, such as contracts for the sale of goods by instalments. It is for this reason that the right to rescind in response to repudiation is important in relation to the contract of employment.

The right to rescind a contract in response to repudiation was recognized in several different contexts. It was recognized, for example, that where a contract for services was repudiated by the employer, the injured party may rescind the contract and recover, on a restitutionary basis, the value of work so far done, at a *quantum*

---

[1] Per Lord Blackburn in *Mersey Iron & Steel Co.* v. *Naylor Benzon & Co.* (1884) LR 9 App. Cas. 434, 443.

[2] e.g. per Diplock L.J. in the *Hongkong* case [1962] 2 QB 26 at 70.

[3] See Coote, loc. cit. [1970] CLJ 221 at 223 for discussion of these various terminologies.

[4] Cf. Devlin, loc. cit. [1966] CLJ 192 at 214; Treitel, 'Some Problems of Breach of Contract' (1967) 30 MLR 139 at 214.

meruit rate. The leading authority for that rule is *Planché* v. *Colburn* (1831).[1]

The defendant engaged the plaintiff to write a treatise on armour for a periodical called the Juvenile Library, for £100. Before completion of the contract, the defendants repudiated the contract by refusing to publish the treatise in the Juvenile Library, because that periodical had failed. Their offer to publish the treatise in a work for adults was not an acceptable alternative because the work had been prepared for children. It was held that the plaintiff could recover on a *quantum meruit* basis, and the jury awarded £50.

Tindal C.J. ruled that 'where a special contract is in existence and open the plaintiff cannot sue on a *quantum meruit*. Part of the question here, therefore, was whether the contract did exist or not. It distinctly appeared that the work was finally abandoned and the jury found that no new contract had been entered into.'[2]

The rule was followed and applied in later cases.[3] In this particular context, rescission involves more than prospective termination.[4] It involves a retroactive cancellation of the contract; probably not in the fullest sense of a restoration of the *status quo ante* by means of the restoration of property and the giving of indemnity, but in the sense of treating the relations between the parties as if they had never been governed by the contract in question.[5] There has to be a retroactive cancellation in this kind of case, because there is a rule that restitutionary recovery on a *quantum meruit* basis is not possible where the relations giving rise to the *quantum meruit* claim are still governed by a contract.[6]

A second context, in which it was recognized that repudiation entitled the injured party to rescind the contract, was that of anticipatory repudiation. The case in which that principle was established was *Hochster* v. *De la Tour* (1853),[7] which was discussed earlier in this work.[8] In that case the right of the employee to terminate the performance of his own contractual obligations in response to the

---

[1] 8 Bing. 14.   [2] Ibid. at 16.

[3] *Prickett* v. *Badger* (1856) 1 CB(NS) 296 (commission agency for sale of land); *De Bernardy* v. *Harding* (1853) 8 Ex. 822 (commission agency for sale of tickets). The difficulties attending the decision in *Prickett* v. *Badger* are fully explained in a learned treatise—Ash, *Willing to Purchase* (London, 1963), which deals with the law of contracts with estate agents and auctioneers.

[4] See above, p. 203.

[5] See Goff and Jones, *The Law of Restitution* (1966) pp. 341-2.

[6] *Goodman* v. *Pocock* (1850) 15 QB 576 (rule applied to wrongfully dismissed employee).

[7] (1853) 2 E & B 678.   [8] See above, pp. 118-21.

anticipatory repudiation was not directly in issue, for the employee was not being sued for failure to perform his own contractual obligations. The employer, having dispensed with the services of the employee, had no further interest in holding the employee liable for not performing those services, and did not attempt to do so. However, the right of the injured party to refuse further performance was referred to in an *obiter dictum*, when Lord Campbell C.J. said 'after the renunciation of the agreement by the defendant, the plaintiff *should be at liberty to consider himself absolved from any further performance of it*, retaining his right to sue for any damage he has suffered from the breach of it'[1] (emphasis added).

The next step occurred when, in *Danube & Black Sea Railway Co.* v. *Xenos* (1863),[2] it was the *ratio* of the decision that an anticipatory repudiation entitled the injured party, not only to sue for breach of contract, but also to treat the contract as at an end in the sense of refusing any further performance of it. Some years after the decision in *Hochster* v. *De la Tour*, the view could still be expressed that the principle of that case applied only to the relationship of master and servant;[3] but in *Frost* v. *Knight* it was accepted as a general principle applicable to the case of a promise to marry that 'the promisee may, if he thinks proper, treat the repudiation of the other party as a wrongful putting an end to the contract, and may at once bring his action as on a breach of it'.[4] Dicta in a case concerning a lease suggest that an anticipatory repudiation entitles the other party to repudiate the contract only when it relates to the major obligations of the contract.[5] However, the right to rescind a contract in response to anticipatory repudiation could, with that qualification, be regarded as an established general contractual principle.

If anticipatory repudiation entitled the injured party to rescind the contract, then it would seem that *immediate* repudiation should, *a fortiori*, have the same effect. There was authority to this effect from the early part of the nineteenth century.

Thus in *Withers* v. *Reynolds* (1831),[6] the defendant contracted to sell to

[1] 2 E & B 678, 690.   [2] 11 CB(NS) 152; 13 CB(NS) 825.
[3] Per Bramwell B. in *Hall* v. *Wright* (1858) EB & E 765 at 783.
[4] (1872) LR 7 Ex. 111 at 113 (Cockburn C.J.).
[5] *Johnstone* v. *Milling* (1886) 16 QBD 460 at 468 (Lord Esher M.R.); cf. Cotton L.J. at 471, Bowen L.J. at 474.
[6] 2 B & Ad. 882; and compare also *Robson & Sharpe* v. *Drummond* (1831) 2 B & Ad. 303, and *Franklin* v. *Miller* (1836) 4 A & E 599.

the plaintiff straw at the rate of three loads per fortnight for a period of about eight months. After a few months the plaintiff fell into arrears with payment, and refused to pay for the latest load, saying that he intended to keep in hand the payment for one load. The defendant refused to supply any further hay and was sued for damages. It was held that the plaintiff could not recover because he was guilty of wrongful repudiation, and that the defendant had been entitled to rescind the contract.

Patteson J., in particular, made it clear[1] that it was the refusal to continue to pay on delivery, rather than the failure to pay for one particular instalment, which justified rescission. The decisive factor was the indication that the buyer was seeking to make a fundamental variation in the terms of the contract. His attempts unilaterally to alter the contract in this way constituted a repudiation of it.

It was then established in cases decided in the later years of the nineteenth century that rescission was justified where 'the acts or conduct of the one . . . amount to an intimation of an intention to abandon and altogether to refuse performance of the contract',[2] or where, in other words, they 'evince an intention no longer to be bound by that contract'.[3] This statement of the law was approved and followed by the House of Lords in later cases.[4] It provided a useful basis upon which to rationalize and reconcile a group of earlier cases concerning instalment contracts for the sale of goods,[5] which had left the law concerning the right to rescind in a very confused state. The law concerning anticipatory repudiation and that concerning immediate repudiation have developed along somewhat separate lines and in separate cases, because they tend to arise in the context of different problems. The law concerning anticipatory repudiation generally deals with the question whether the injured party can sue immediately upon a repudiation to take effect in the future. The law concerning immediate repudiation usually deals with the question whether the injured party can rescind the contract in the sense of refusing further performance.

There is judicial authority, however, to the effect that the criterion for repudiation is the same in both cases. It has been stated in a

[1] 2 B & Ad. 882 at 885.
[2] Per Lord Coleridge C.J. in *Freeth* v. *Burr* (1874) LR 9 CP 208 at 213.
[3] Ibid. at 213.
[4] *Mersey Iron & Steel Co.* v. *Naylor Benzon & Co.* (1884) LR 9 App. Cas. 434 per Lord Selborne L.C. at 438–9, Lord Blackburn at 442–4; *General Billposting Co.* v. *Atkinson* [1909] AC 118 per Lord Collins M.R. at 122.
[5] *Hoare* v. *Rennie* (1859) 5 H & N 19; *Simpson* v. *Crippin* (1872) LR 8 QB 14; *Honck* v. *Muller* (1881) 7 QBD 92.

court of first instance that 'there is neither any good reason for a distinction, nor, in my view, does there exist any distinction between the nature of the repudiation which is required to constitute an anticipatory breach, and that which is required where the alleged breach occurs after the time for performance has arisen'.[1]

That this applies equally to the contract of employment is indicated by a dictum of McCardie J. that ' "Wrongful dismissal" is, I think, a mere illustration of the general legal rule that an action will lie for unjustifiable repudiation of a contract. The doctrine of repudiation equally applies when the master wrongfully refuses, before the period of employment has commenced, to take the servant into his service.'[2] This dictum provides an introduction to the problem of relating the general contract principles to the rules governing contracts of employment.

D. Application to the Contract of Employment

During the nineteenth century these general contract principles were not normally invoked for the purpose of deciding whether summary dismissal of an employee was justified. Exceptions can be found, but not a pattern of exceptions. An example is *Gould v. Webb* (1855),[3] in which a dismissal was judged according to whether or not the term of the contract, which had been broken by the employee, was a condition of the contract.[4]

The direct application of general contract principles may again be seen in the decisions in *Bettini v. Gye*[5] and *Poussard v. Spiers.*[6]

In the former case, the plaintiff was engaged as a singer in Grand Opera, for three and a half months as from 30th March 1875, the plaintiff agreeing to be in London for rehearsals six days before commencement of the engagement. The plaintiff having been prevented by illness from being in London before the 28th March, the defendant dismissed him, and relied upon the term requiring the plaintiff to be in London six days before the engagement as justifying the dismissal. It was held that the dismissal was not justified, and that the plaintiff was entitled to damages on the ground

---

[1] *Thorpe* v. *Fasey* [1949] Ch. 649 at 661 per Wynn-Parry J., quoted with approval by Devlin J. in *Universal Cargo Carriers Corporation* v. *Citati* [1957] 2 QB 401 at 438.

[2] *Re Rubel Bronze & Metal Co. & Vos* [1918] 1 KB 315 at 321.

[3] 4 E & B 933.

[4] Per Lord Campbell C.J. at 942 and Crompton J. at 944.

[5] (1876) 1 QBD 183.

[6] (1876) 1 QBD 410. This case is considered from the point of view of the law of frustration below at pp. 304, 321–2.

that the stipulation as to rehearsals was not a stipulation 'going to the root of the matter, so that a failure to perform it would render the performance of the rest of the contract by the plaintiff a thing different in substance from what the defendant has stipulated for'.[1]

In the latter case, the question of whether rescission was justified was again answered in terms of general contract principles; but in this case the attention of the court was concentrated upon the effect of the breach rather than the importance of the term broken.

The plaintiff's wife was engaged to sing in a vaudeville opera for three months, provided the opera ran for that time, commencing on or about November 14th. The first performance being announced for 28th November, the plaintiff's wife attended several rehearsals, but was then prevented by illness from attending final rehearsals and the first four days of the performances. The defendants engaged an understudy for one month if the opera ran for that time, and dismissed the plaintiff's wife.[2] It was held on appeal that the dismissal was justified, because there had been a sufficient failure of consideration to justify rescission.[3]

A number of grounds may be suggested for distinguishing between the facts of the two cases—such as that Bettini was not engaged for a specific part, while Mme. Poussard was; or that Bettini's absence was shorter than that of Mme. Poussard, and did not extend to actual performance; or that there was continuing uncertainty when Mme. Poussard would be available and no such uncertainty about Bettini. It may be questioned whether there can properly be said to have been a breach of contract in either case, as opposed to a non-culpable failure of performance; but that distinction was treated as not material for the purpose of deciding whether or not the rescission of the contract was justified.[4]

Whatever the distinction between the two cases, both were treated in terms of general contract principles, rather than in terms of the accepted grounds for the dismissal of employees. It would be a

---

[1] Per Blackburn J. (1876) 1 QBD 183 at 188.

[2] Husband suing by reason of the incapacity of married woman.

[3] Per Blackburn J. (1876) 1 QBD 410 at 416. The test of 'failure of consideration' was here used interchangeably with the test of 'failure going to the root of the matter'—cf. per Blackburn J. at 414, 415.

[4] Cf. per Diplock L.J. in *Hongkong Fir Shipping Co.* v. *Kawasaki* [1962] 2 QB 26, 65–6, 69 where he holds that the test for rescission for breach of condition is the same as the test for termination under the doctrine of frustration. Also *per curiam* in *Harbutts 'Plasticine' Ltd.* v. *Wayne Tank & Pump Co. Ltd.* [1970] 1 QB 447 at pp. 465 B–E; see below, pp. 323–4.

difficult question to decide whether the artistes in those cases were employed under contracts of service or for services. Even if they would, by present-day criteria, be regarded as employed under a contract of service, it is less likely that they would have been so regarded at the time those cases were decided, because 'so long as the control test in its traditional form was virtually the sole criterion applied by the courts, difficulty was not surprisingly felt in treating actors and artistes as servants.'[1] Even if the singers in those cases could have been regarded as employees, they were employees of a kind quite different from those manual employees, labourers, and artificers, to whom the Master and Servant Acts applied.[2] Hence these cases would not be seen as falling within the area in which issues of justification for dismissal were resolved by reference to those standards such as 'misconduct' or 'neglect' which closely resembled the statutory criteria for the criminal jurisdiction of the magistrates in master and servant cases.[3]

In cases where the persons employed were more recognizable as servants employed under contracts of service, the direct application of the general contract principles to issues of dismissal was very much the exception rather than the rule in the nineteenth century. But on the other hand, in the case of white-collar workers, the courts would not on the whole tend to apply the special tests of 'misconduct, disobedience or neglect'[4] in the way that they applied those tests in the case of manual workers. White-collar workers occupied a different social stratum from that of the manual workers who were subject to the Master and Servant Acts, and who were

---

[1] Atiyah, *Vicarious Liability in the Law of Torts* (London, 1967) p. 85. Contrast *Fraser-Wallas* v. *Elsie and Doris Waters* [1939] 4 All ER 609 and *Gould* v. *Min. Nat. Ins.* [1951] 1 KB 731, with *Performing Rights Society Ltd.* v. *Mitchell & Booker Ltd.* [1924] 1 KB 762, *Stagecraft Ltd.* v. *Min. Nat. Ins.* [1952] SC 288 and *Whittaker* v. *M.P.N.I.* [1967] 1 QB 156.

[2] Master and Servant Act 1823 (5 Geo. IV c. 34): Master and Servant Act 1867: Employers and Workmen Act 1875 (repealed in so far as still in force by Statute Law (Repeals) Act 1973).

[3] See Daphne Simon, 'Master & Servant', Chapter 6 of *Democracy and the Labour Movement* (ed. Saville) (London 1954), an account of the Master and Servant laws and the movement for their reform.

[4] See for instance Parke B. in *Callo* v. *Brouncker* (1831) 4 C & P 518, 519; cf. *Jacquot* v. *Bourra* (1839) 7 Dow. 348, 351 ('immoral conduct, wilful disobedience or habitual neglect'); *Hicks* v. *Thompson* (1857) 28 LT 255 ('wrongful and improper neglect to perform duties, absence without reasonable cause, insolent and improper conduct'); Darling J. in *Baster* v. *London & County Printing Works* [1899] 1 QB 901, 903 ('neglect').

somewhat differently treated in this respect. There are many cases in which the dismissal of white-collar workers was tested according to whether the conduct of the employee was incompatible with the continuance of the relationship of master and servant.[1]

The test of incompatibility with the continuance of the employment was applied particularly in cases where white-collar employees, entrusted with the property or confidential information of their employer, were dismissed for fraud, dishonesty, corruption, or other lack of fidelity towards the employer. It is still occasionally invoked in that type of case, as in *Sinclair* v. *Neighbour*.[2]

The manager of a betting shop was dismissed for borrowing money from the till for the purpose of gambling; a loan which his employer would not have allowed had his permission been asked. The employee contended that he had not been guilty of dishonesty, in that he had no intention of misappropriating the money without repaying it. But it was held that the dismissal was nonetheless justified, on the ground that his conduct was incompatible with the continuance of employment, in view of the confidential nature of the relationship.

Thus, in the words of Sellers L.J.: 'The whole question is whether that conduct was of such a type that it was inconsistent, in a grave way— incompatible with the employment in which he had been engaged as a manager.'[3]

And in those of Sachs L.J.: 'It is well established law that a servant can be instantly dismissed when his conduct is such that it not only amounts to a wrongful act inconsistent with his duty towards his master, but is also inconsistent with the continuance of confidence between them.'[4]

This test enabled the courts to consider the importance of the breach of contract in the context of the relationship as a whole. It

---

[1] *Ridgway* v. *Hungerford Market Co.* (1835) 3 A & E 171, 180 per Coleridge J. ('inconsistent with his service') (company clerk); *Edwards* v. *Levy* (1860) 2 F & F 94, 97 per Hill J. ('conduct incompatible with the continuance of the relationship') (music critic of a newspaper); *Smith* v. *Allen* (1862) 3 F & F 157, 162 per Cockburn C.J. ('Misconduct in any essential particular—such for instance as that a master could not fairly or reasonably be expected to submit to, or to continue that person in his employment thereafter') (superintendent of chemical factory); *Procter* v. *Bacon* (1886) 2 TLR 845 per Lord Esher M.R. at 845 ('misconduct so serious as to be inconsistent with the continuance of the relationship of master and servant') (governess); *Pearce* v. *Foster* (1886) 17 QBD 536, 542 per Lopes L.J. ('misconduct inconsistent with the faithful discharge of duty') (clerk in charge of foreign correspondence); *Boston Deep Sea Fishing Co.* v. *Ansell* (1888) 39 Ch. D 339, 363, per Bowen L.J. ('inconsistent with his duty towards his master and the continuance of confidence between them') (managing director) (cf. per Cotton L.J. at 358).
[2] [1967] 2 QB 279. [3] Ibid. at 287. [4] Ibid. at 289.

was thus less harsh towards the employee than the rules concerned with 'misconduct, disobedience or neglect'; and it was closer to the general contract principles concerning rescission for breach of condition or in response to repudiation—so much closer indeed that Lord James in *Clouston & Co. Ltd.* v. *Corry* was able to combine the test of 'incompatibility' with that of breach of condition and to state that 'misconduct inconsistent with the fulfilment of the express or implied conditions of service will justify dismissal.'[1]

Dicta occurring in decisions in the earlier years of this century indicate that the judges were at that time uncertain whether the law concerning dismissal was dictated by *sui generis* rules relating to the contract of employment, or by a general principle of contract law; and if a general principle, whether that of rescission for breach of condition, or that of rescission in response to repudiation. Thus Lush J. in *Hanley* v. *Pease & Partners Ltd.*:

'Whether the right of a master to dismiss a servant for misconduct or breach of duty or anything else of the kind is treated as a right arising out of the ordinary right of the contracting party to put an end to the contract where there has been a repudiation by the other party, or whether it is treated as a right which the master has on the ground that obedience to lawful orders must be treated as a condition of the contract, is wholly immaterial. I do not think it is necessary to say which is the proper way to regard it, because in either view the right of the master is merely an option.'[2]

A similar uncertainty was shown by McCardie J. in *Re Rubel Bronze & Metal Co. & Vos* where he says in an *obiter dictum*,

'Today it is well settled that a master may dismiss his servant for many reasons such as misconduct, substantial negligence, dishonesty and the like. Such matters may, I think, be said to constitute such a breach of duty by the servant as to preclude the further satisfactory continuance of the relationship and to justify the master in electing to treat the contract as repudiated by the servant. But the point is one of doubt, as the light of formulated *ratio* illuminates but few of the decisions. Perhaps the modern view has been that continued good conduct by the servant is a condition, either express or implied, of the contract of service, the breach of which entitles the master to end the employment.'[3]

But despite the traces of doubt, it was becoming clear that the

---

[1] [1906] AC 122, 129. [2] [1915] 1 KB 698, 705.
[3] [1918] 1 KB 315, at 321.

special employment rules referring to misconduct, neglect, or dishonesty could be regarded as falling under the general heading of conduct inconsistent with the continuance of the employment relationship. This could in turn be regarded as an application of the right to rescind a contract in response to repudiation.

In recent cases, it has been firmly established that the special rules as to misconduct, wilful disobedience, etc., are to be regarded as an application of the general contract principles, so that the justification for dismissal is tested according to the general contract principles. In *Laws* v. *London Chronicle Ltd.*,[1] the effect was to prevent the employers' right to summary dismissal from being an unduly wide one.

A secretary followed her immediate superior out of a meeting at which there had been a quarrel. She did so in defiance of an order given by the chairman and managing director, and was summarily dismissed. It was held that the dismissal was wrongful in spite of the fact that there had been disobedience of a lawful order.

Lord Evershed M.R. said that it could not be held that every act of disobedience of a lawful order must entitle the employer to dismiss, and that 'since a contract of service is but an example of contracts in general, so that the general law of contract will be applicable, it follows that the question must be—if summary dismissal is claimed to be justifiable—whether the conduct complained of is such as to show the servant to have disregarded the essential conditions of the contract of service'.[2] And later he says, 'One act of disobedience or misconduct can justify dismissal only if it is of a nature which goes to show (in effect) that the servant is repudiating the contract, or one of its essential conditions.'[3]

Hence in that case the Court of Appeal committed itself to the view that general contract principles were applicable, but did not decide between applying the right to rescind in response to repudiation, and the right to rescind for breach of condition. In the recent decision in *Pepper* v. *Webb*[4], the Court of Appeal favoured the language of repudiation, rather than the language of breach of condition.

[1] [1959] 1 WLR 698; cf. *R. J. Hewitt Ltd.* v. *Russell* (1969) 4 ITR 260 (employee walked out after a quarrel with manager 20 minutes before time. Next day her employer told her she was dismissed. It was held that she had not intended to repudiate her contract by walking out and that her dismissal had been by reason of redundancy).
[2] [1959] 1 WLR 698, 700.   [3] Ibid. at 701.
[4] [1969] 1 WLR 514 (annotated—Grime (1969) 32 MLR 575, Baker (1969) 85 LQR 326).

The plaintiff was employed as a head gardener. Having failed to give satisfaction over a period of time, he then refused to follow instructions given by the wife of the employer, and, after a quarrel with the employer, walked off, saying 'I couldn't care less about your bloody greenhouse and your sodding garden.' The Court of Appeal, reversing the judgment of the County Court, held that this was conduct repudiatory of the contract which justified dismissal.

Of the three judges in the Court of Appeal, Harman L.J. seems to have attached undue significance to the particular words used by the employee:

'Now what will justify an instant dismissal?—something done by the employee which impliedly or expressly is a repudiation of the fundamental terms of the contract; and in my judgment if ever there was such a repudiation this is it. What is the gardener to do? He is to look after the garden, and he is to look after the greenhouse. If he does not care a hoot about either, then he is repudiating the contract.'[1]

And Karminski L.J. seems to have accepted that the old harsh rule, that any wilful disobedience of a lawful order justifies dismissal, still applies in the form of the general principle of the right to re-scind in response to repudiation: 'It has been part of our law that a servant repudiates the contract of service if he wilfully disobeys the lawful and reasonable orders of his master.'[2] It was Russell L.J. who emphasized the most defensible ground for the decision of the Court of Appeal when he said that: 'against the background of . . . quite a number of disobediences and a certain amount of insolence, it must be taken as conduct repudiatory of the contract, justifying summary dismissal.'[3]

Cases concerning the employer's right to dismiss for misconduct do not frequently come before the higher courts at the present day; and that makes it unwise to generalize from the very small number of decisions. But the reasoning in these latest cases suggests that, even though the application of general contract principles has tended to modify the severity of the nineteenth-century decisions towards

---

[1] Ibid. at 517 G–H; cf. Baker, op. cit. 328: 'The Major [the employer] during his service in the army must have heard from time to time a soldier say that he did not care a hoot about the bloody army but this did not mean that he intended to desert.'

[2] [1969] 1 WLR 514, 518 E–F.

[3] Ibid. at 518 C–B. A contrasting result was reached in *Wilson* v. *Racher* [1974] ICR 428, where the facts were similar except that the Court thought the employer's provocative conduct was decisive.

the employee, there is still evidence of reasoning which is remote from the problems of industrial relations which are raised by dismissal situations. It would be retrograde if dismissals were to be held justified on the grounds of words spoken which constituted a 'repudiation' in a purely formal sense, and if the common law were to place no pressure upon the employer to give the employee an opportunity to improve his performance before dismissing him.[1]

SECTION 3: DISCIPLINARY PROCEDURE AND THE COMMON LAW OF DISMISSAL

The historical development of the law concerning the employer's right of dismissal makes the common law rather irrelevant to the disputes about dismissal which occur in practice. This same historical development has resulted in an absence of procedural requirements for valid dismissal at common law. This absence of procedural requirements further emphasizes the remoteness of the common law from the problems concerning dismissal which arise in practice.[2] The procedural standards at common law, or the lack of them, may be considered under these specific heads:—

(a) the requirement of warning before dismissal;

---

[1] The opportunity to improve performance has been one of the most important aspects of the law of Unfair Dismissal and is further considered below in the context of disciplinary procedure. See below, p. 221 note 2.

[2] One of the most significant differences between the common law of summary dismissal and the law of unfair dismissal consists in the concern of the latter with procedural standards. This results from the view taken by the NIRC that observance of the provisions of the *I.R. Code of Practice* (see now Trade Union and Labour Relations Act 1974 s. 1(1)(a) and Schedule I Part I), and of the intentions underlying them, is essential to a fair dismissal:*Earl* v.*Slater & Wheeler (Airlyne) Ltd.* [1972] ICR 508; *Clarkson International Tools Ltd.* v. *Short* [1973] ICR 191. But this doctrine has been offset by three further case-law developments:

(a) It has been recognized that the procedural standards of the code may be inapplicable in particular cases: *Dunning & Sons Ltd.* v. *Jacomb* [1973] ICR 448; *Lewis Shops Group* v. *Wiggins* [1973] ICR 335; *James* v. *Waltham Holy Cross U.D.C.* [1973] ICR 398.

(b) Some cases have held that no financial loss results from the procedural defect, so that no compensation is payable: *Earl* v. *Slater & Wheeler (Airlyne) Ltd.* (above).

(c) Some cases have held that the employee's blameworthiness may be a ground for reduction of compensation despite its lack of relevance to the procedural unfairness of the dismissal: *Scottish Co-op Ltd.* v. *Lloyd* [1973] ICR 137; *Springbank Sand & Gravel Co. Ltd.* v. *Craig* [1974] ICR 7; *Maris* v. *Rotherham Corporation* [1974] ICR 435.

(b) the obligation to give reasons for dismissal;
(c) the obligation to provide a hearing or appeal before dismissal;
(d) the time limit within which disciplinary action must be taken;
(e) the obligation to impose the appropriate punishment.

A. The Requirement of Warning before Dismissal

The common-law rules concerning the employer's right of dismissal impose no requirement upon an employer that he should issue a warning before treating a given type of conduct as justifying dismissal; nor that he should give the employee any opportunity to improve his performance before dismissal. If a warning is given, there is no requirement that it should precede the dismissal by a reasonable interval. This is well illustrated by the decision in *Chell* v. *Hall and Boardman* (1896).[1]

A miner was employed under a contract of employment whereby he was paid according to the weight of minerals gotten. The manager of the mine threatened the employees with dismissal if the tubs sent up continued to contain slack or dust; and shortly afterwards, dismissed them. It was held that the dismissal was justified by the disobedience to orders, irrespective of the seriousness of the particular breach of contract; the court did not consider the adequacy of the warning.

The term implied by law, subject to evidence of a different term, that dismissal is justified on the ground of wilful disobedience to lawful orders, thus enables the employer to make a dismissal issue out of any dispute of right which he has with the employee. In failing to impose upon the employer any requirement of reasonable warning before dismissal, the common law falls short of the standards of good industrial relations practice. The National Joint Advisory Council recommended[2] to the Department of Employment that an opportunity to improve performance was among the features which should be included in all internal dismissal procedures: 'After probation, a worker whose performance becomes unsatisfactory should not be dismissed without having been given fair warning and full opportunity to improve, including guidance on where his failings lie, and a trial on other work if appropriate.' In making no requirement of a warning before dismissal, the common law concerning the contract

---

[1] 12 TLR 408. The prohibition on deduction from wages in Section 12 of the Coal Mines Regulation Act 1887 was held not to protect the employee from dismissal for doing that for which deduction from wages was illegal.
[2] *Report on Dismissal Procedures* (H.M.S.O. 1967) at Para. 124.

of employment follows the general principles of contract law, for there is no requirement that the rescission of other types of contract for good cause should be preceded by warning or an opportunity to put matters right. There is a rule that if a warning is given, the injured party cannot go back on the forbearance which he has offered, without giving reasonable notice[1]—but there is no rule requiring such forbearance in the first place. But whereas the commercial morality attending the practice of business contracts may require no warning before rescission, it does not follow that the same principle should be applied to the contract of employment.[2]

B. The Requirement that Reasons be given for Dismissal

It is a well-established rule of the common law that the employer is under no obligation to give reasons for dismissal at the time of dismissal.[3] Indeed the common law goes further and holds that the dismissal may be justified by facts not known at the time, or not acted upon at the time.

Thus in *Ridgway* v. *Hungerford Market Company* (1835)[4] the plaintiff was employed as clerk to a company. After a decision had been taken to dismiss him he entered a protest against his impending dismissal on the minute book of the company. He was then dismissed without notice. It was held that the summary dismissal could be justified on the ground of this misconduct, in spite of the fact that it was clear that this was not the predominant reason for the dismissal.

Lord Denman C.J. ruled 'Now it is not necessary that a master, having a good ground of dismissal, should either state it to the servant, or act

---

[1] *Charles Rickards Ltd.* v. *Oppenhaim* [1950] 1 KB 616.

[2] The *I.R. Code of Practice* by *Para. 133* requires that disciplinary procedure should normally operate so that the first step is a warning and so that no employee is dismissed for a first breach of discipline except in cases of gross misconduct.
  The case-law has treated the giving of a warning and opportunity to improve performance as a crucial aspect of procedural fairness, where the complaint is of inefficiency or incompetence as well as of misconduct: *McKinney* v. *Bieganek* [1973] IRLR 311; *O'Hara* v. *Fram Gerrard Ltd.* [1973] IRLR 94; *Winterhalter Gastronom Ltd.* v. *Webb.* [1973] ICR 245. But there has been recognition of the lack of necessity to give such warning where it would be obviously futile to do so: *Dunning & Sons Ltd.* v. *Jacomb* [1973] ICR 448; *James* v. *Waltham Holy Cross UDC* [1973] ICR 398.

[3] Certain dicta in the decision in *Beeston* v. *Collyer* (1827) 4 Bing. 309 suggest that reasons must be given for summary dismissal; but they mean that a justification must be produced before the court rather than at the time of dismissal. See Best C.J. at 311, Park J. at 312, Burrough J. at 312; cf. Lord Reid in *Ridge* v. *Baldwin* [1964] AC 40, 65.

[4] 3 A & E 171.

upon it. It is enough if it exist, and if there be improper conduct in fact.'[1]

Patteson J. added, 'if we were to hold that it was necessary to trace the dismissal to the act which is to justify it, it would follow that a master, who had made up his mind to dismiss a servant, would give the servant, if he discovered his master's intention, licence to act just as he pleased afterwards.'[2]

In a later case, Lord Denman C.J. said of this decision 'That case is right because if good ground of dismissal existed, the plaintiff suffered no wrong from the dismissal from not having been accused of it.'[3]

At one stage, it was ruled that the employer could not rely upon a ground of dismissal of which he did not know at the time of dismissal.[4] But that view was not followed in later cases,[5] and does not now seem to be part of the law.[6] The present-day rule that the employer need not have known of the ground in question, at the time of dismissal, is easier to justify in the case of concealed frauds than in the case of misconduct which does no lasting damage to the employer. This rule of the law of the contract of employment reproduces a rule to be found in relation to other types of contracts, that a rescission which was carried out for an invalid reason may be justified by a valid reason which in fact existed.[7] But in the cases in which it has been so held in relation to other types of contracts, the context has been one in which there could be an adjustment of mutual rights and liabilities on an entirely objective basis as between men of business. The context of the employment relationship is a very different one, in which it may be thought that requirements of good procedure should become an integral condition of the employer's right to rescind the contract. The National Joint Advisory Council Report recommended[8] that any internal dismissal procedure should involve telling the employee the reason for his dismissal.[9]

---

[1] Ibid. at 177.

[2] Ibid. at 179; cf. also *Willets* v. *Green* (1850) 3 C & K 59 per Alderson B. at 60; *Baillie* v. *Kell* (1838) 4 Bing. NC 638 per Tindal C.J. at 650.

[3] *Mercer* v. *Whall* (1845) 5 QB 447 at 466.

[4] Parke B. in *Cussons* v. *Skinner* (1843) 11 M & W 161, 172–3.

[5] *Spotswood* v. *Barrow* (1850) 5 Ex. 110; *Boston Deep Sea Fishing & Ice Co.* v. *Ansell* (1888) 39 Ch. D. 339.

[6] Cf. *Cyril Leonard & Co.* v. *Simo Securities Trust Ltd.* [1973] 1 WLR 80. Annotated by the present author—(1972) 1 ILJ 100.

[7] Lord Sumner in *British & Beningtons Ltd.* v. *N.W. Cachar Tea Co.* [1923] AC 48, 71–2 (sale of goods); Devlin J. in *Universal Cargo Carriers Corporation* v. *Citati* [1957] 2 QB 401–43 (charter-party).

[8] At Para. 124 of their Report.

[9] The *I.R. Code of Practice* does not make a specific requirement that reasons

C. *The Requirement of a Hearing*

It follows from what has been said above concerning the absence of an obligation upon the employer to give reasons for dismissal, that the employer can be under no obligation to allow the employee a hearing before dismissal; in the words of Lord Reid in *Ridge* v. *Baldwin*, 'The question in a pure case of master and servant does not at all depend on whether the master has heard the servant in his own defence, it depends on whether the facts emerging at the trial prove breach of contract.'[1] That the steady advance of requirements of procedural fairness has stopped short of the contract of employment was recently confirmed by the Privy Council in *Vasudevan Pillai* v. *City Council of Singapore*, where it was ruled that 'the relationship of master and servant or employer and employee gives rise to no application of the principle of *audi alteram partem* on dismissal.'[2] The recommendation of the National Joint Advisory Council Report on Dismissal Procedures was that 'Before any decision to dismiss is taken, the worker should have the opportunity to state his side of the case personally (and to make written representations if he wishes), assisted, if he wishes, by his trade union representative or by a "friend" (e.g. a fellow worker).'[3] A model procedure in which provision is made for a hearing before dismissal is to be found in the Police (Discipline) Regulations 1965,[4] whereby the member of the police force who is subject to the procedure is entitled to a preliminary opportunity for personal explanation, to a precise statement of the charges against him, and an examination of relevant documents. The procedure at the hearing itself is regulated, and provision is made for the representation of the accused by another police officer. The police officer is suspended on two-thirds of his usual pay between the complaint against him and the completion of the procedure; and if he

---

be given for dismissal. But it does in Para. 132 make provisions concerning a fair hearing and a right of appeal, and it has been held by an Industrial Tribunal that these requirements imply an obligation upon the employer to notify the employee before dismissal of the allegations against him: *Greenhalgh* v. *Exors. of James Mills Ltd.* [1973] IRLR 78.

[1] [1964] AC 40, 65; see also his remarks to the same effect in *Malloch* v. *Aberdeen Corporation* [1971] 1 WLR 1578, 1581 G.

[2] [1968] 1 WLR 1278, 1284 H (Lord Upjohn). This rule was reaffirmed in *Malloch* v. *Aberdeen Corporation* [1971] 1 WLR 1578, though statutory provisions relating to the employment were there held to take this case out of the ordinary employer/employee rule—see below, pp. 283–4.

[3] At Para. 124 of their Report.

[4] S.I. 1965 No. 543 (as amended by S.I. 1967 No. 185 and S.I. 1971 No. 133).

is not ultimately dismissed, then his pay during suspension is made up to the full rate.[1]

D. A Time Limit upon the Right to Dismiss without Notice

It has been ruled that the right to dismiss an employee without notice must be exercised within a reasonable time of the cause coming to the notice of the employer, for otherwise he will be held to have waived his right to dismiss by condoning the misconduct.[2] It was, however, affirmed by the Privy Council in *Federal Supply Co.* v. *Angehrn*[3] that there is no such waiver unless and until the employer has full knowledge of the misconduct; so that a master would not be held to have condoned the misconduct of his servant where he believed the servant's denial of the misconduct imputed to him and continued him in his employment without making further inquiries which would have disclosed the truth; in such a case, he is justified in dismissing him at a later date when the true facts have come to his knowledge[4]. The rule that the employer, by delaying, waives his right to dismiss, has its counterpart in the general principles of contract law. It may be regarded as an application of the principle that a party faced with a wrongful repudiation has an election whether to rescind the contract.[5] If he elects to affirm the contract, he takes the risk that the bargain may turn out adversely for him.[6] Alternatively,

---

[1] The *I.R. Code of Practice* requires as a characteristic of a disciplinary procedure that it should give the employee the opportunity to state his case and the right to be accompanied by his employee representative—Para. 132(ii).

The Industrial Court recognized the right to a hearing as integral to fair dismissal in the case in which they first developed the procedural dimension of unfair dismissal: *Earl* v. *Slater & Wheeler (Airlyne) Ltd.* [1972] ICR 508. But this right has been held to be inapplicable where, in effect, the Industrial Tribunal is satisfied that a hearing could not have revealed any grounds against the dismissal: *James* v. *Waltham Holy Cross UDC* [1973] ICR 398. Furthermore, in the original decision in *Earl* v. *Slater & Wheeler (Airlyne) Ltd.* the NIRC deprived their doctrine of practical significance by denying compensation on the ground that no financial loss could be attributed to the procedural defect in the dismissal. See the annotation to that case by Anderman and the present author, (1973) 2 ILJ 43.

[2] *Horton* v. *McMurtry* (1860) 5 H & N 667 per Bramwell B. at 675; *Phillips* v. *Foxall* (1872) LR 7 QB 666 per Blackburn J. at 680; *Boston Deep Sea Fishing & Ice Co.* v. *Ansell* (1888) 39 Ch. D 339 per Cotton L.J. at 348; *Beattie* v. *Parmenter* (1889) 5 TLR 396 per Lord Esher M.R. at 397.

[3] (1910) 103 LT 150.   [4] Lord Atkinson, ibid. at 152.

[5] Cf. per Lord Reid in *Suisse Atlantique* v. *Kolen Centrale* [1967] 1 AC 361 at 397 B–C, 398 D–F.

[6] *Avery* v. *Bowden* (1856) 6 E & B 953 (contract ultimately frustrated).

it may be regarded as comparable to those cases arising out of the Statute of Frauds, in which a waiver has been held to be binding[1]; cases which may now be seen as giving rise to a principle analogous to an equitable quasi-estoppel.[2] However, it should be noted that the employer does not necessarily, by waiving his right to dismiss, also waive his right to damages for breach of contract. It was so held in *Wynnstay Collieries* v. *Edwards*,[3] where the employers obtained damages against a miner, apparently for striking. In the view of the court, the employers would have been entitled to dismiss the employee; but the fact that they had not done so did not constitute a waiver of the right to damages. The rule concerning waiver of the right to dismiss provides one instance in which the law does intervene to secure a minimum procedural standard in matters of dismissal.[4]

E. Appeals against Dismissal

Just as the common law provides no general right to a hearing before dismissal, so also there is no general legal right to an appeal from a dismissal. The provision of a right of appeal is treated by the National Joint Advisory Council Report as one of the essentials of a good internal dismissal procedure, the recommendation being that:

Any worker should have the opportunity to appeal against dismissal. Where the appeal is to a higher level of management, it is vitally important that the person hearing the appeal should be impartial and be seen to be impartial. . . . A worker appealing against dismissal should, of course, be given proper facilities for stating his case personally, with assistance if he wishes, to the person hearing the appeal.[5]

An example of a statutory appeal procedure is provided by the

---

[1] *Ogle* v. *Earl Vane* (1868) LR 3 QB 272; *Hickman* v. *Haynes* (1875) LR 10 CP 598.

[2] Cf. *Charles Rickards Ltd.* v. *Oppenhaim* [1950] 1 KB 616.

[3] (1898) 79 LT 378.

[4] The *I.R. Code of Practice* makes no special requirement as to the time limit within which the employer must act upon the grounds for dismissal which exist. But Anderman nevertheless shows that a doctrine of waiver of dismissal by lapse of time does arise in the case-law of unfair dismissal to the extent that the fact of long service without complaint by the employer will cast doubt, at least at an evidentiary level, upon a dismissal for inadequate performance—citing *Price* v. *Gourley Bros. Ltd.* [1973] IRLR 11 (*Unfair Dismissals and the Law*) (London, 1973) at p. 63).   [5] At Para. 124 of their Report.

Dock Workers Employment Scheme 1967,[1] whereby any person aggrieved by suspension, summary dismissal, or termination of his employment by the local Dock Labour Board has five working days in which to appeal to an appeal tribunal, which may reinstate the employee and may order that he be paid in full for the period between the suspension or dismissal and the hearing of his appeal.[2]

F. The Choice of the Appropriate Penalty

A disciplinary procedure which conforms to high standards of industrial relations practice will normally provide for a number of alternative penalties of differing severity, such as reprimand and warning, down-grading, suspension without pay, dismissal with notice, and dismissal without notice. The National Joint Advisory Council Report recommended that: 'Dismissal is not, and should not be, the only disciplinary action available to management. There is a wide range of other measures which may be appropriate according to the circumstances, among them warnings (including the formal warning, that unless there is improvement, further action will have to be considered) and financial penalties.'[3] However, the common-law rule is one of dismissal or nothing, because at common law a right to suspend or to demote will not be implied; for suspension or demoting will, in the absence of special provision for them,[4] be treated as wrongful repudiation of the contract by the employer. These rules in themselves provide a valuable protection against the imposition of disciplinary measures upon the employee without his prior agreement to the availability of such measures against him. But when they are combined with the rules which confer upon the

[1] Dock Workers (Regulation of Employment) (Amendment) Order 1967 (S.I. 1967 No. 1252).

[2] The *I.R. Code of Practice* requires of a disciplinary procedure that it shall provide for a right of appeal, wherever practicable, to a level of management not previously involved. In the law of Unfair Dismissal it has been recognized that the right of appeal to a higher level of management is not practicable in small family companies where the decision to dismiss is likely to be taken by the senior director—*Tiptools Ltd.* v. *Curtis* [1973] IRLR 276. And generally the right of appeal has not been the aspect of procedure with which the law of unfair dismissal has been most concerned. But it has been held that where an appeals procedure does operate, the employee should be told of its findings on request and the Industrial Tribunal ought to have evidence of those findings: *James* v. *Waltham Holy Cross UDC* [1973] ICR 398.

[3] At Para. 125 of their Report.

[4] *Hanley* v. *Pease & Partners Ltd.* [1915] 1 KB 698 (suspension); *Marriott* v. *Oxford Co-operative Society Ltd.* (No. 2) [1970] 1 QB 186 (demoting).

employer a rather wide right of summary dismissal, the resulting pattern is one of rough justice rather than good procedure.[1]

It will thus be evident that in various respects the common law of the contract of employment fails to impose procedural standards upon the disciplinary process. That omission is a predictable result of the historical development of the law concerning the employer's right of dismissal. The main period of growth of that body of law occurred at a time long before social attitudes to the contract of employment would have recognized an obligation upon the employer to provide a good procedure. Moreover, the application of the general principles of contract law to the employer's right to dismiss, while on the whole restricting the employer's right of dismissal, none the less caused the dismissal to be seen as the assertion of an absolutely objective right analogous to the right of a merchant to reject unsatisfactory goods, or to load his cargo into a different ship. Hence the analogy with other contracts, whilst it may be beneficial to the employee as far as his substantive rights are concerned, perhaps militates somewhat against the protection by the law of the interests in good personal and industrial relations which are involved in the employment relationship.

SECTION 4: SUMMARY DISMISSAL AND THE LAW CONCERNING FORFEITURE

In certain cases, decided in the earlier part of the nineteenth century, employees who departed in breach of contract or who were justifiably dismissed were held not to be entitled to recover any arrears of wages.[2] In these cases, it was not made clear whether the reason was that the contracts were entire contracts which had not been fully

---

[1] The *I.R. Code of Practice* requires management to make known to each employee the type of circumstances which can lead to suspension or dismissal (Para. 131(ii)) and to specify who has the authority to take various forms of disciplinary action and ensure that supervisors do not have the power to dismiss without reference to more senior management.

In the law of Unfair Dismissal, the reasonableness of the dismissal in the particular circumstances is a specific issue to be considered (1971 Act s. 24(6)) and Industrial Tribunals have on occasion considered under that heading the question of whether a less drastic penalty should have been chosen: *Ross* v. *Aquascutum Ltd.* [1973] IRLR 107; contrast *Ryder* v. *Scot Bowyers Ltd.* [1973] IRLR 109.

[2] Especially *Turner* v. *Robinson* (1853) 5 B & Ad. 789; *Ridgway* v. *Hungerford Market Co.* (1835) 3 Ad. & E. 171.

performed, or, on the other hand, that they were divisible contracts, but that the employee, upon justified dismissal or wrongful departure, *forfeited* all wages due but not yet paid. That this uncertainty results from the early cases is borne out by the decision in *Boston Deep Sea Fishing & Ice Co.* v. *Ansell* (1888), where two judges in the Court of Appeal expressly left open the question whether there might be a rule of forfeiture of arrears of wages in the case of a managing director who was dismissed for making a secret profit.[1] They did not have to decide the question because they held that the agreement with the director was entire and indivisible, so that there was no salary due to which a forfeiture might apply.

Furthermore, in *Moriarty* v. *Regents Garage Co. Ltd.*, Lush J. and McCardie J. commented in *obiter dicta* that it might not be possible to apply the Apportionment Act 1870 in favour of a salaried employee where the employee had been dismissed for misconduct.[2] There is Canadian authority to the effect that a landlord who wrongfully evicts his tenant cannot take advantage of an apportionment provision in a statute to recover rent, though that case might be distinguished on the ground of the tortious nature of the eviction.[3]

There is a third sense in which the law of summary dismissal shows traces of a doctrine of forfeiture. The summarily dismissed employee will not be allowed any *restitutionary* remedy in respect of remuneration for an incomplete period of service. If the summary dismissal occurs in the middle of an entire and indivisible period of work, the employee forfeits the restitutionary remedy he would have in the event of frustration of the contract or wrongful dismissal. Thus Bowen L.J. in the *Boston Deep Sea* case: 'The servant who is dismissed for wrongful behaviour cannot recover his current salary. He cannot recover . . . on the special contract [by reason of the doctrine of entire contracts] nor can he recover on a *quantum meruit*, because he cannot take advantage of his own wrongful act to insist that the contract is rescinded.'[4] This rule is one from which the American common law of contract had departed at an early date,[5] and it is

---

[1] (1888) 39 Ch. D. 339, Cotton L.J. at 360; Bowen L.J. at 365.

[2] [1921] 1 KB 423 (reversed on other grounds [1921] 2 KB 766), Lush J. [1921] 1 KB 423 at 434; McCardie J., ibid. at 449.

[3] *Murphy* v. *Wood* [1941] 4 DLR 454. See Dore, article on Partial Performance (1967) 17 University of New Brunswick Law Journal 30.

[4] (1888) 39 Ch. D. 339, 364–5.

[5] *Britton* v. *Turner* (1834) 6 New Hampshire Reports 481. See *Corbin on Contracts* (1963, Minnesota) S. 1127 'Restitution in Favour of a Defaulting Employee'.

arguably a source of unjust enrichment to the employer unless the employee has been guilty of concealed fraud or other misconduct over a period of time.

However, despite these various dicta it is thought by this writer that there is no general rule of forfeiture at common law at the present day in the case of justified dismissal or wrongful departure of an employee, except possibly in the event of continuing dishonesty on the part of the employee during the employment. There are several decided cases in which employees have recovered accrued wages in spite of having been justifiably dismissed.[1] And it was expressly decided that there was no rule of forfeiture in a case where a domestic employee terminated her employment in breach of contract.[2] The expression of opinion on this point was *obiter* to the decision in the case, but was emphasized in the judgment of Lord Coleridge J.

The plaintiff was a domestic servant employed at wages calculated yearly and paid monthly, there being no express agreement as to notice. After a fortnight of employment she gave a fortnight's notice. At the end of the month the defendant refused to pay her wages for the month. The employee relied upon a custom in domestic service entitling her to terminate by a fortnight's notice after a fortnight's service.

It was held that she was entitled to recover the arrears of wages because the County Court judge had been correct in taking judicial notice of the custom; but that in any event the month's wages had accrued due and were not forfeited by her departure even if it were wrongful. Lord Coleridge J. said:

'The defence set up is that she broke her contract by leaving the service without giving one month's notice, and that therefore she is not entitled to recover any wages for the month she has served. In my opinion that would not deprive her of the right to recover the month's wages which had already accrued due to her, though it might give rise to a cause of action in the master for damages for breach of contract.'[3]

There are important examples in practice of express clauses in contracts of employment which provide for forfeiture of accrued remuneration upon wrongful departure or justified dismissal. It is

---

[1] *Button* v. *Thompson* (1869) LR 4 CP 330; *Parkin* v. *South Hetton Coal Co.* (1907) 97 LT 98, 98 LT 162; *Healey* v. *Societé Anonyme Française Rubastic* [1917] 1 KB 946.
[2] *George* v. *Davies* [1911] 2 KB 445.   [3] Ibid. at 449.

suggested in *Batt on the Law of Master and Servant* that 'Frequently the contract of service contains a term that the master may retain any wages due to the workman wrongfully leaving him without notice as liquidated damages for the loss he sustains through such breach of contract.'[1] This term is no longer so widespread a practice as once it was; but it has been replaced by other types of express provisions for forfeiture whose significance should not be overlooked. Thus there is frequently found in works rules a provision that the employee is not entitled to accrued holiday pay if he is dismissed for dishonesty or misconduct. A provision for the forfeiture of a week's holiday credits in the event of wrongful termination by the employee was made by collective agreement in the building industry, in order to impose a small sanction upon employees who leave their employment without due notice.[2]

Moreover, the rules of occupational pension schemes generally provide for automatic or discretionary forfeiture of accrued pension rights in the event of certain types of termination of employment. The rules of pension schemes generally distinguish between:

(a) employees dismissed through no fault of their own, e.g. by reason of redundancy;

(b) employees whose employment is terminated by reason of their fraud or misconduct (this need not be summary termination, and it may include resignation by the employee by reason of fraud or misconduct);

(c) employees leaving service of their own free will (this need not necessarily be termination in breach of contract).[3]

Different treatment is generally accorded by the rules of the scheme to each of these cases, i.e.:

(a) the employee dismissed through no fault of his own is generally accorded the full benefit of his accrued pension rights, either by means of the immediate purchase of a pension for him or by purchase of equivalent rights in the pensions scheme of his new employer;

---

[1] (5th edn. London, 1967, ed. Webber) p. 258.
[2] *Rule 1(B)* of the *National Working Rule Agreement* for the Building Industry.
[3] Cf. Hosking, *Pension Schemes* (2nd edn. 1960) pp. 42 ff. A typical example of pension fund rules of the kind here discussed is to be found in *Re Leek* [1969] 1 Ch. 563. See Note, below, p. 383.

(b) the employee whose employment is terminated by reason of his fraud or misconduct generally forfeits all his accrued pension rights as far as the law allows[1] and is entitled only to the return in cash of his own contributions—sometimes without interest;

(c) in the case of the employee leaving voluntarily, a discretion is generally reserved to the employer whether or not to grant pension rights.

The rules for automatic forfeiture in the event of termination by reason of fraud or misconduct impose a concealed penalty upon the employee which may amount to an unreasonable punishment. They give rise to disputes in practice upon the question of whether and when an employee dismissed for *inefficiency* forfeits his pension rights. The rules for discretionary forfeiture enable the employer at his option to place a very substantial fetter upon the ability of the employee to change his job. It would seem to be arguable that such a provision may be contrary to public policy as being in restraint of trade.[2] But it might well not be possible to sever the discretion from the basic provision for the payment of benefit. In that case it would not be possible for the employee to challenge the exercise of the discretion against him.

Arguments based upon public policy have been invoked unsuccessfully against forfeiture clauses in contracts of employment. Thus in *London Tramways Co. Ltd. v. Bailey*,[3]

the contract of employment of a tram-conductor provided for the deposit by the employee of £5 and for the forfeiture of that sum and his wages for the current week upon breach of contract by him, the manager of the company to be the sole judge as between the company and the conductor of the amount to be forfeited. It was argued for the employee that this provision was contrary to public policy as an ouster of the jurisdiction of the courts, but the argument was rejected, Lush J. commenting 'It has been said that this clause is harsh and unjust, but it was a matter for his consideration before he gave his consent.'[4]

However, this particular type of provision for forfeiture of wages at

---

[1] That is to say, hitherto, subject to the obligation under Sections 57–9 of the National Insurance Act 1965 upon an employer who has contracted out of the graduated part of the state pensions scheme to provide benefits equivalent to those which the employee would have enjoyed if he had been a participating employee—see Note, below, p. 384.

[2] Cf. *Wyatt* v. *Kregginger and Fernau* [1933] 1 KB 793; *Bull* v. *Pitney Bowes Ltd.* [1967] 1 WLR 273—see Note, below, p. 383.

[3] (1877) 3 QBD 217.   [4] Ibid. at 222.

the discretion of the manager of the company—apparently a common custom among tramway companies in the late nineteenth century[1]— was later held to be subject to the very important qualification that the employee must be heard in his own defence, it being held that the employee could not be said to have 'submitted to the arbitration' of the manager by virtue only of the forfeiture provision in the contract itself.[2] Lord Esher M.R. commented that 'If the agreement is not a submission, is there not a natural implication that, in accordance with the natural rules of justice [sic], a man's wages already earned cannot be forfeited without his having an opportunity of being heard on the question whether they should be forfeited or not?'[3] Nevertheless, in *Joyce* v. *Lord Ebury*[4] the argument based upon public policy was raised and rejected against a provision very comparable to the provisions found in present-day pensions schemes for the forfeiture of pension rights upon the termination of employment:

An employee had been a contributor to an employer's provident fund, one of the rules of which provided that 'no person dismissed from the [employer's] employment or leaving it of his or her own accord, or ceasing to be a member of the fund at his or her own request shall have any claim upon the fund; but the trustees shall have absolute discretion to return to him the whole or any part of the sum which he or she has subscribed'. It was held that there was a voluntary leaving within this rule when the employee volunteered for military service with the leave of his employer;[5] and that there was nothing in the rule which was contrary to public policy.

The decision is questionable upon both grounds, and it is possible that the rules of public policy would be allowed a wider sphere of operation against such clauses by present-day judges.

It might be arguable that express provisions for forfeiture of accrued remuneration could be struck down by way of equitable relief—by analogy with the distinction which is drawn between contractual provisions which form a genuine pre-estimate of

---

[1] Cf. *Wilson* v. *Glasgow Tramway Co. Ltd.* (1878) 5 Rettie 981.
[2] *Armstrong* v. *The South London Tramways Co. Ltd.* (1891) 64 LT 96.
[3] Ibid. at 97.   [4] [1917] WN 51.
[5] A similar result was reached in *Stretch* v. *Scout Motors Ltd.* (1918) 87 LJ (NS)KB 1006.

damages and those constituting a penalty *in terrorem*.[1] Comparison may be made with the discussion of the effect of 'minimum payment' provisions in contracts of hire-purchase in the House of Lords in *Bridge* v. *Campbell Discount Co. Ltd.*,[2] in which one particular provision for minimum payment in the event of cancellation by the hirer was treated as a penalty clause, and in which Lord Denning expressed the view that the courts had jurisdiction to grant relief against a penal sum contained in a minimum-payments clause, no matter for what reason the hiring was terminated.[3] It may well be that compensation for unfair dismissal will now be available in particular cases to offset any forfeitures brought about by the law or practice of summary dismissal. But where a dismissal is held both lawful in a contractual sense and not unfair for statutory purposes, the capacity of the common law and of the rules of equity to prevent unconscionable forfeitures may still prove significant.

---

[1] Compare the relief against forfeiture given in *Stockloser* v. *Johnson* [1954] 1 QB 476 (instalment payments under contract of sale).

[2] [1962] AC 600. See Guest, *The Law of Hire Purchase* (London, 1966) at Paras 633–8.

[3] [1962] AC 600 at 631. Contrast *Associated Distributors Ltd.* v. *Hall* [1938] 2 KB 83.

Chapter Seven

WRONGFUL DISMISSAL

INTRODUCTION

The legal concept of wrongful dismissal forms in many ways the focal point of the law concerning the termination of the individual contract of employment.

This chapter begins by considering the meaning of the term 'wrongful dismissal' and relates it to the concept of wrongful repudiation. Whilst the simplest concept of wrongful dismissal is that of the wrongful outright termination of the employment relationship, that concept cannot be considered in isolation from those actions on the part of the employer which constitute a wrongful repudiation of his contractual obligations without amounting to wrongful dismissal. The essence of the distinction between wrongful dismissal and wrongful repudiation of contractual obligations by the employer is that the former consists in an outright termination of the employment relationship, and for that reason probably effects a termination of the contract of employment; while the latter does not itself terminate the relationship and normally does no more than entitle the employee to terminate the contract. But the existence of the employee's right to terminate in response to wrongful repudiation extends in an important direction the protection which is conferred by the action for wrongful dismissal itself. For it means that the employee is entitled to the protection, not merely of the continuity of his employment, but also of his interest in the preservation of his terms and conditions of employment. The concept of wrongful repudiation combines with the concept of wrongful dismissal to create a situation in which the employer's obligation to employ is enforced in content as well as in duration. It is shown also how wrongful repudiation has in some cases come to be treated as 'constructive dismissal' for statutory purposes.

Having considered the meaning of wrongful dismissal, this chapter goes on to examine the remedies to which it may give rise. The main remedy available against a wrongful dismissal is the claim in damages, and the principles governing the award of such damages are of far-reaching importance. They delimit the extent to which the law will uphold and enforce the employer's obligation to employ, most notably by virtue of the rule that damages shall be quantified with reference to the period of notice required for a proper termination of the contract. They also dictate the scope of the legal recognition of the various interests of the employee which are affected by wrongful dismissal, other than the primary interest in prospective employment with the employer concerned. For example, it will be seen that the law accords only limited recognition to the interest of the employee in his future employability, and affords somewhat limited protection to incidental rights and expectations such as pension rights, in so far as they are liable to be prejudiced by wrongful dismissal.

Various other remedies which are sometimes available against breach of contract are not available to the wrongfully dismissed employee. The law will not normally enforce the contract of employment directly against employer or employee. It is particularly by virtue of this rule that a wrongful dismissal is usually regarded as effective in law to terminate the contract of employment; and the question whether this is an appropriate rule depends upon attitudes towards the employment relationship. The other of the remedies for breach of contract which is generally unavailable as a remedy against wrongful dismissal is that of a declaration of the invalidity of a dismissal. The refusal to declare wrongful dismissal to be invalid in the generality of employment cases is based upon the fact that the courts will not enforce the contract of employment *in specie*: hence the refusal of the declaration is a practical application of the theory that wrongful dismissal is effective in law to terminate the contract. The exceptions which have been made to the rule against declarations constitute a legal vindication of the status conferred by certain types of employment relationship; and the question arises whether such exceptions should be extended to cover a wider range of employment relationships.

Having examined the nature of wrongful dismissal and wrongful repudiation and the remedies available in relation to them, this chapter concludes by a consideration of the effect of wrongful dismissal and wrongful repudiation as a matter of contractual theory. This relates to the problem of whether the contract of employment is effectively terminated by wrongful dismissal.

SECTION 1: WRONGFUL DISMISSAL AND
WRONGFUL REPUDIATION

A. Wrongful Repudiation distinguished from Wrongful Dismissal

Wrongful dismissal means dismissal of an employee in breach of his contract of employment. There are thus two elements in the definition of wrongful dismissal, on the one hand that of breach of contract; on the other, that of the meaning of 'dismissal' itself. The element of breach of contract has been considered in an earlier chapter, where it was shown that wrongful dismissal is the breach of a contractual duty placed upon the employer to maintain the employment relationship.[1] The meaning of 'dismissal' is a matter of some difficulty and obscurity, largely because of a confusion between dismissal and other forms of repudiation of the contract of employment by the employer.

The concept of 'dismissal' can best be defined as the exclusion of the employee from further employment, with the intention of severing the relationship of employer and employee. Dismissal thus contains the objective element of the discontinuance of the exchange of work for wages; and the subjective element of the intention to end the employment relationship. Neither element is sufficient by itself. The discontinuance of work and wages without the intention of terminating the relationship creates a situation of suspension of employment, rather than one of dismissal.[2] If, on the other hand, the employee is allowed to continue to perform his contractual obligations under the contract of employment, then the mere intention on the part of the employer to end the relationship would not by itself constitute a dismissal. Hence it is a necessary condition of dismissal that both the subjective and the objective elements be present.

Wrongful dismissal as here defined does not cover certain actions of the employer in which there is no outright exclusion from employment, and no intention to end the relationship, but which the employee may treat as wrongful repudiation of the contract of employment. For where the conduct of the employer falls short of outright dismissal, but none the less constitutes a fundamental breach of contract or evinces an intention no longer to be bound by the contract, the employee may treat the employment as terminated and sue for damages as upon wrongful dismissal.[3]

[1] See above, pp. 21–3.   [2] See above, pp. 77–8.   [3] Cf. above, pp. 205–12.

The main importance of wrongful repudiation of the contract of employment has been as an extension of the statutory concept of dismissal under the 1965 and 1971 legislation. We proceed to consider how wrongful repudiation has come to be considered as 'constructive wrongful dismissal' for the purpose of these statutes.

B. Wrongful Repudiation as Constructive Dismissal[1]

The rights conferred upon employees by the 1965 Act and the unfair dismissal provisions of the 1971 Act depend upon the statutory concept of dismissal. The basic definition of dismissal in that legislation is as a termination of the contract of employment by the employer.[2] It has always been assumed that wrongful dismissal is to be treated as statutory dismissal in this sense. The theoretical difficulties about this view are considered at the conclusion of this chapter.[3] The problem for immediate consideration is how wrongful repudiation is brought within the statutory concept of dismissal. Wrongful repudiation has come to be regarded for statutory purposes as 'constructive dismissal'.

The 1965 Act expressly distinguished between outright dismissal, dealt with by Section 3(1)(a), and constructive dismissal, dealt with by Section 3(1)(c) which provides that 'for the purposes of the Act there shall be taken to be a dismissal by the employer where the employee terminates his employment without notice in circumstances such that the conduct of the employer has entitled him to do so.' The nature of the entitling conduct was almost certainly to be determined by applying the common-law concepts of wrongful repudiation or fundamental breach.[4]

However, the distinction between wrongful dismissal and wrongful repudiation was eliminated in the case-law applying the 1965 Act. In the *Marriott* case,[5] the employer imposed a reduction of wages upon the employee and demoted him. The employee remained at work for a few weeks, then gave notice himself and left because he was dissatisfied with the new terms. The employer's conduct was

---

[1] See Appendix, para 3.

[2] 1965 Act s. 3(1)(a); 1971 Act s. 23(2)(a). The most important extension of this basic definition relates to the expiry of fixed-term contracts without renewal. See above, pp. 163–4.

[3] See above, pp. 295 ff.

[4] Cf. *GKN (Cwmbran) Ltd.* v. *Lloyd* [1972] ICR 214 at 221 D–G (Sir John Donaldson).

[5] *Marriott* v. *Oxford Co-operative Society Ltd.* (No. 2) [1970] 1 QB 186.

treated as a dismissal under Section 3(1)(a) of the 1965 Act. Thus Section 3(1)(a) was interpreted to include this type of wrongful repudiation as well as wrongful dismissal. Thus there was a considerable overlap between Section 3(1)(a) and Section 3(1)(c) as far as wrongful repudiation was concerned.[1]

Marriott's case had established that 'termination of the contract by the employer' in Section 3(1)(a) included constructive termination in the sense of wrongful repudiation acted upon by the aggrieved employee; so much so that the draftsmen of the 1971 legislation felt safe in defining dismissal in the same terms as Section 3(1)(a) of the 1965 Act, omitting any counterpart of Section 3(1)(c) and leaving the single statutory formula of 'termination of contract by employer' to do duty for constructive dismissal as well.[2] The case-law applying Section 23(2)(a) of the 1971 Act, in which that definition of dismissal appears, has duly treated the single concept as having the constructive as well as the literal aspect.[3] Hence wrongful repudiation as defined in the succeeding pages of the present section is significant under both the 1965 and the 1971 legislation as part of the statutory concept of dismissal.

C. *The Scope of the Concept of Wrongful Repudiation by the Employer*

1. *Increased Danger as Wrongful Repudiation.* In defining the circumstances in which the employee may treat wrongful repudiation by the employer as terminating the contract, comparison may be made with the case of *Burton* v. *Pinkerton* (1867)[4] where it was held that a seaman could treat the action of his captain, in turning an ordinary voyage into a gun-running voyage involving greater danger,

---

[1] But in order to invoke s. 3(1)(c) the employee has to leave without notice. This meant s. 3(1)(c) was a potential trap for employees—though this is less of a danger now that s. 3(1)(a) has been widely interpreted. Cf. Sir John Donaldson in *GKN (Cwmbran) Ltd.* v. *Lloyd* [1972] ICR 214, 221 D–G.

[2] This, at least, was the view taken of the draftsmen's reasons by Sir John Donaldson in *Sutcliffe* v. *Hawker Siddeley Aviation Ltd.* [1973] ICR 560 at 564 G. *Contra*, O'Higgins (1973) 2 ILJ 238, citing evidence from the Parliamentary debates of a deliberate intention to exclude constructive dismissal.

[3] See the passage from the judgment of Sir John Donaldson in *Sutcliffe* v. *Hawker Siddeley Aviation Ltd.* cited in the footnote above.

[4] LR 2 Ex. 340. By Sections 22 and 23 of the Merchant Shipping Act 1970 a procedure is established whereby a seaman may make a complaint to the master of the ship about his conditions of employment and whereby the master is obliged to permit him to complain to an external authority if he remains dissatisfied.

as entitling him to quit the service and to claim damages for loss of wages. But in later cases concerning the effect upon seamen of increased risk becoming apparent during a voyage, the seamen generally sued to recover their wages for the rest of the voyage rather than damages for breach of contract.[1] By so doing they were treating the contract of employment as continuing in force rather than as having been wrongfully repudiated.

Certain dicta in cases other than those of the seamen show that an employee who is subjected to a great increase in the danger of his employment is entitled to leave.[2] These dicta deal, however, with the right of the employee to protect himself against the danger by leaving his employment, rather than with his right to recover damages as if he had been wrongfully dismissed. As such they emphasize only one aspect of the right of the employee to treat his contract of employment as terminated, namely his right to protect his own safety by physical departure. Moreover they deal with a type of case in which there is not necessarily a wrongful repudiation. The increase in danger may lie outside the area of responsibility of the employer, as with the visitation of infectious illness upon a domestic establishment,[3] in which case the employee would be entitled to leave his employment, but not to claim damages; for that would then be a case of frustration rather than of repudiation.[4] The issue of whether the employee was entitled to terminate his employment by reason of wrongful repudiation by the employer has arisen also in cases where the employer has dismissed the employee for disobedience to orders and the employee has claimed that the orders subjected him to such increased danger as to amount to wrongful repudiation.[5] These claims have met with varying success, and quite a high degree of unanticipated danger seems necessary to substantiate a claim of repudiation.

[1] *O'Neil* v. *Armstrong, Mitchell & Co.* [1895] 2 QB 418; *Austin Friars SS. Co.* v. *Strack* [1905] 2 KB 315; *Palace Shipping Co. Ltd.* v. *Caine* [1907] AC 386; cf. *Edward* v. *Trevillick* (1854) 4 E & B 59 (unreasonable flogging).

[2] Lord Abinger C.B. in *Priestley* v. *Fowler* (1837) 3 M & W 1, 6; Alderson B. in *Turner* v. *Mason* (1845) 14 M & W 112, 117, 118; Alderson B. in *Wiggett* v. *Fox* (1856) 11 Ex. 832, 839; Cockburn C.J. in *Woodley* v. *Metropolitan Railway Co.* (1877) 2 Ex. D 384, 388. Cf. *Robson* v. *Sykes* [1938] 2 All ER 612 (no offence of desertion where danger was increased).

[3] Cf. Alderson B. in *Turner* v. *Mason* [1845] 14 M & W 112, 117. (Cf. above, p. 198.)

[4] Cf. pp. 320–3, below (Frustration and Lack of Fault).

[5] *Bouzourou* v. *Ottoman Bank* [1930] AC 271; *Ottoman Bank* v. *Chakarian* [1930] AC 277.

It is perhaps no accident that these few early cases and dicta deal only with this one particular aspect of wrongful repudiation. The claim of wrongful repudiation made by the employee is a claim that he has not been employed according to the terms and conditions of employment to which he is entitled. These early authorities deal only with the most basic of terms and conditions of employment, i.e. those concerned with the safeguarding of the employee from danger to life and limb. Other authorities, and decisions in particular under the Redundancy Payments Act 1965, show that wider issues, as of the non-observance of important terms and conditions of employment by the employer, may be raised by way of the question whether there has been a wrongful repudiation by the employer.

2. *Wrongful Suspension as Wrongful Repudiation.* The relationship between wrongful dismissal and wrongful repudiation was analysed as regards wrongful *suspension* of employment by McCardie J. in *Re Rubel Bronze & Metal Co. & Vos*.[1] The effect of the decision is that wrongful suspension by the employer of work and wages constitutes a wrongful repudiation which entitles the employee to terminate his employment and to claim damages as upon wrongful dismissal.

The Rubel Bronze Company suspended their manager without work and without pay in breach of their contract with him. They did so in a manner casting obvious doubt upon his competence or his honesty. The employee took the view that he had been wrongfully dismissed; accordingly he refused to comply with a request, made a week later by the board of the company, to appear before them. They dismissed him for the refusal to appear before them, and he claimed damages for wrongful dismissal.

McCardie J. held that the wrongful suspension was a wrongful repudiation and that the wrongful repudiation could properly be described as a wrongful dismissal. Thus he says that:

'If the conduct of the employer amounts to a basic refusal to continue the servant on the agreed terms of the employment, then there is at once a wrongful dismissal and a repudiation of the contract. I can see no distinction in such a case as the present between repudiation by the defendants of their contractual obligations, and a 'wrongful dismissal' in the ordinary sense of that phrase.'[2]

It should be noted that McCardie J. did not say that wrongful

---

[1] [1918] 1 KB 315.
[2] Ibid. at 323. This dictum foreshadows the doctrine of constructive dismissal.

dismissal and wrongful repudiation were identical concepts *for all purposes*; and that would be a false conclusion, because wrongful dismissal probably has the special effect of resulting in *ipso facto* termination of the contract of employment relationship.

Where the employer wrongfully suspends work and wages, e.g. where he lays the employee off work in breach of contract because of the unavailability of work, the employee is also entitled to treat that as a dismissal by the employer for the purposes of claiming a redundancy payment. Thus in *Jones* v. *Harry Sherman Ltd.*[1], the facts of which were considered above,[2] an Industrial Tribunal held that a wrongful suspension constituted a dismissal within Section 3(1)(a) of the Redundancy Payments Act 1965. Comparison may be made with *Sneddon* v. *Ivorcrete (Builders) Ltd.*[3] where the employer attempted to lay an employee off for three weeks. Advised by his union, the employee said that the employer had no right to lay him off. The employer then purported to dismiss him for three weeks only. It was held that this amounted to a complete dismissal within Section 3(1)(a) of the 1965 Act. This is an example of wrongful repudiation being treated as constructive dismissal for statutory purposes.

3. *The Wrongful Withholding of Work as Wrongful Repudiation.* It was shown in an earlier chapter that the employer is in certain cases obliged to provide his employee with actual work in order to enable him to gain publicity or experience which was for him an essential part of the consideration for the contract, or in order to avoid injury to his business or professional reputation.[4] It was suggested that there is also a duty in a rather wider range of situations to enable an employee to fill and maintain the particular office or post to which he was appointed.[5] Where such a duty is imposed upon the employer, the withholding of work constitutes not merely a breach of contract, but also a wrongful repudiation entitling the employee to terminate the contract and to claim damages as upon wrongful dismissal. This was the remedy successfully claimed in *Collier* v. *Sunday Referee Publishing Co. Ltd.*[6] by the sub-editor whose employers, having sold their newspaper, did not dismiss him but expected him to attend at their offices and to do entirely nominal work as the condition for the continuance of his salary. In this way the employee is given an effective remedy against the withholding of

---

[1] (1969) 4 ITR 63.   [2] See above, pp. 89–90.   [3] (1966) 1 ITR 538.
[4] See above, p. 25.   [5] See above, pp. 25–7.   [6] [1940] 2 KB 647.

work. This is an entirely correct development in that it should not be necessary for the employee faced with the withholding of work to make out a special right to publicity or experience. Even if he has no such special interest in the work for its incidental benefits to him, his security of employment is none the less fundamentally threatened by the withholding of it, and he ought not to lack a remedy.

4. *Imposed Variation of the Terms and Conditions of Employment as Wrongful Repudiation.* In recent years it has been recognized in an increasingly wide range of cases that attempts by the employer to impose a variation of terms and conditions of employment may constitute a wrongful repudiation. This is especially important in the context of the Redundancy Payments Act 1965, because very often the attempt to impose a major variation of terms and conditions of employment upon the employee is, in reality, an attempt to transfer him to a different job; and if the employee can show this to amount to a dismissal within the meaning of the Act, he may then be entitled to a redundancy payment. In order that the attempt by the employer to impose a variation of terms and conditions of employment upon the employee may be treated as amounting to a dismissal within the meaning of Section 3 of the Redundancy Payments Act 1965, it is necessary first to establish that it is not a variation within the prerogative of the employer under the original contract.[1]

If it can once be shown that the attempt to impose a variation of working conditions upon the employee goes outside the scope of the contractual right of the employer to alter the work directions, then the right of the employee to treat attempts to impose variations as wrongful repudiation is a wide one. Thus the attempt to impose quite a minor change in the geographical location of employment has been held to entitle employees to terminate their employment, and to claim a dismissal within Section 3(1)(c) of the 1965 Act.[2] The attempt to reduce an employee in status from a branch manager to that of an ordinary showroom employee by appointing a manager in charge over him was held by an Industrial Tribunal to be a repudiation by the employer, so that when the employee terminated

---

[1] See above, pp. 40–41.
[2] *Charles* v. *Spiralynx* (*1933*) *Ltd.* (1970) 5 ITR 82 (move from Hanbury Street to Canning Town in London); cf. *Shields Furniture Ltd.* v. *Goff* [1973] ICR 187 (move from Chelsea to Fulham; but also new premises less satisfactory than old).

his employment there was a dismissal within Section 3(1)(c).[1] Again, the attempt to transform the basis of employment of a building worker from that of an employed person to that of an independent labour-only sub-contractor has also been held to amount to a dismissal within Section 3 when employment terminates upon the refusal of the employee to change to labour-only sub-contracting.[2] An attempt to transfer an employee into the employment of another employer without his consent, by first loaning him to that other employer for a few days with his consent, and by then transferring his cards and purporting to transfer all liability for him, was held by the Court of Appeal to constitute a repudiation by the original employer, so that a termination of employment by the employee counted as a dismissal by the original employer within Section 3(1)(c).[3]

It has not yet been decided how great must be the variation which the employer attempts to impose for the attempt to be able to be treated by the employee as a wrongful repudiation. Two approaches are possible. On the one hand, it may be argued that the variation must be a fundamental one, i.e. the variation of a fundamental term, before it can amount to repudiation.[4] On the other hand, it may be argued that the deliberateness of the attempt to impose a variation turns it into a repudiation irrespective of its magnitude.[5] The traditional test of whether the employer 'has evinced an intention no longer to be bound by the contract' is not very helpful, because it still requires a judgment to be made as to how great a variation is required as evidence of such an intention. The recent case-law seems to indicate that if an imposed variation is found to be outside the latitude allowed by the contract, that very fact demonstrates the repudiatory character of the conduct concerned.[6] Not every breach

---

[1] *Skillen* v. *Eastwoods Froy Ltd.* (1967) 2 ITR 112; cf. *Trevillion* v. *The Hospital of St. John and St. Elizabeth* [1973] IRLR 176; cf. also *Goode & Cooper Ltd.* v. *Thompson* [1974] IRLR 111.

[2] *Kemp* v. *Milton Estates Ltd.* (1967) 2 ITR 64.

[3] *Duckworth* v. *Farnish Ltd.* (1970) 5 ITR 17.

[4] Cf. McCardie J. in *Re Rubel Bronze & Metal Co.* [1918] 1 KB 315, 322.

[5] Cf. per Salmon L.J. in *Morris* v. *C. H. Bailey Ltd.* [1969] 2 Lloyd's 215 at 219.

[6] Cf. *GKN (Cwmbran) Ltd.* v. *Lloyd* [1972] ICR 214 (change from skilled to unskilled work—implied power to vary was rejected); *Davis Transport Ltd.* v. *Chattaway* [1972] ICR 267 (discontinuance of all bonuses against 10% increase in basic pay—imposition of this change regarded as a lock-out and a repudiation); *Chapman* v. *Goonvean & Rostowrack China Clay Co. Ltd.* [1973] ICR 310 (withdrawal of transport service to and from work). In all these cases the breach could be regarded as a major one; the point is that the attempt to vary the contract was treated as decisive *per se*.

of contract constitutes an attempt to vary the terms of the contract; those breaches which do amount to unilateral variation are coming to be regarded as comparable with outright dismissal.

SECTION 2: DAMAGES FOR WRONGFUL DISMISSAL

The remedy of damages for wrongful dismissal is the most important remedy given by the common law, or by the rules of equity, for the protection of the job-security of the employee. Indeed, in the case of an ordinary contract of employment, it is the only remedy given for that purpose, because specific performance or declaration of invalidity of dismissal will not normally be allowed; and the employee will not be allowed to claim wages in respect of the period following wrongful dismissal.

It follows that the measure of damages obtainable for wrongful dismissal is of great consequence, because it is the measure of the protection of security of employment at common law.[1] The general principle underlying the assessment of damages in contract is that of *restitutio in integrum*. This principle has been applied in a restrictive manner to the case of wrongful dismissal, both as to the heads of damage which may be considered, and as to the assessment of damages under those heads. An outstanding example of the restrictive approach is the rule in *Addis* v. *Gramophone Co. Ltd.*[2] that injury to feelings and reputation cannot be taken into account in assessing damages for wrongful dismissal. Another example is the rule that damages in respect of loss of earnings are limited to earnings during the period of notice required to terminate the contract. These are not the only examples of a restrictive approach; it may be observed also in the failure to compensate adequately for the loss of fringe benefits and seniority rights. The recovery of damages for wrongful dismissal is qualified by the rules concerning the mitigation of loss, whose application results in the formulation of norms about the extent to which the employee may be expected to be occupationally or geographically mobile as to his employment. A further type of qualification upon the right to damages, which involves a different type of policy consideration, is the reduction of damages by reason of the incidence of taxation or by reason of other types of collateral

---

[1] In the course of this section, comparisons with the rules governing compensation for unfair dismissal are made in footnotes.

[2] [1909] AC 488.

benefit. Another factor controlling the quantum of damages for wrongful dismissal, and a factor whose operation is somewhat uncertain, is the accounting for contingencies which may intervene during the reckonable period of loss of employment. It is finally to be considered what remedies are available to the employee to recover wages for past services upon wrongful dismissal. Where wages have not accrued due, the employee has remedies both in damages and of a restitutionary kind.

A. The General Principle of Restitutio in Integrum

The basic principle underlying the assessment of compensatory damages both in contract and in tort is that of *restitutio in integrum*—meaning the putting of the plaintiff in the position in which he would have been if he had not sustained the wrong.[1] The object is to compensate the plaintiff for damage or loss suffered. But that is an ambiguous concept where damages for breach of contract are concerned. The ambiguity moreover cannot be resolved merely by reference to the rule in *Hadley* v. *Baxendale*.[2] That rule requires the plaintiff to prove either that the damage arose naturally from the breach or that it arose from special circumstances contemplated by the parties. This is a rule about remoteness of damage; it is not an explanation of the way in which the general concept of *restitutio in integrum* is to be applied to contracts.[3]

The basic ambiguity of the concept of *restitutio in integrum* in the context of contract is as between the two meanings of: (1) putting the plaintiff in the position he would have been in if he had never made the contract, i.e. *status quo ante*; or (2) putting the plaintiff in the position he would have been in if the contract had been duly

---

[1] Lord Blackburn in *Livingstone* v. *Rawyards Coal Co.* (1880) LR 5 App. Cas. 25, 39. See Street, *Principles of the Law of Damages* (London, 1962) p. 3; Blain J. in *Yetton* v. *Eastwoods Froy Ltd.* [1967] 1 WLR 104, 115 A–C (contracts of employment); Ogus, *The Law of Damages* (London, 1973) pp. 17–21, 282–8.

[2] (1854) 9 Ex. 341 at 354 (Alderson B.).

[3] Compare Street at pp. 236–7: 'The rule [in *Hadley* v. *Baxendale*] has attained an unnecessarily dominant place in judicial thinking on the law of damages in the law of contract. One might get the impression that all problems of damages in contract were capable of being answered by the rule. . . . An important consequence is that little attention has been paid to the development of principles in respect of other aspects of the law of damages in contract.' The rule in *Hadley* v. *Baxendale* has now been interpreted and explained in *Koufos* v. *C. Czarnikow Ltd.* (*Heron II*) [1969] 1 AC 350, but in an aspect which does not affect the present discussion.

performed.[1] In the terminology of Fuller and Perdue[2] it is possible to protect three kinds of interest:

(i) *the restitution interest*—the interest in compelling the defendant to disgorge value received when the defendant's promise was unfulfilled, i.e. the prevention of unjust enrichment;

(ii) *the reliance interest*—the interest in obtaining compensation from the defendant in respect of benefit lost, or of detriment incurred, in reliance on his promise;

(iii) *the expectation interest*—the interest in obtaining compensation from the defendant in respect of the benefit lost, or detriment incurred, as the result of non-fulfilment of the promises made by him.

In this scheme, the reliance interest is the interest in the restoration of the *status quo ante*, whilst the expectation interest is the interest in reaching the position which would have arisen if the contract had been performed.

The interpretation of *restitutio in integrum* adopted in the context of contract is that of protecting the expectation interest, and perhaps to a slight extent the reliance interest.[3] This might appear surprisingly generous to the plaintiff, but the measure of generosity is then restricted by the rule in *Hadley* v. *Baxendale*. The protection of the restitution interest is almost entirely relegated by English law to the sphere of quasi-contract. In awarding damages for wrongful dismissal, the courts are almost entirely concerned with the protection of the expectation interest. The wrongfully dismissed employee is entitled to recover the expenses of the journey home, at least where there was an express agreement to pay the expenses of the journey to the place of employment.[4] In such a case, as where allowance is made in damages for any expenses incurred by an employee in course of employment, it is the reliance interest which is being protected.

---

[1] See Street, op. cit. pp. 240–7 (expectation and reliance interests).

[2] Fuller and Perdue (1936) 46 YLJ 52, 373—'The Reliance Interest in Contract Damages'.

[3] See, in the context of breach of contract by the employee, the statement to that effect by Roche L.J. in *Ebbw Vale Steel Iron & Coal Co.* v. *Tew* (1935) 1 LJNCCA 284 at 285–6. 'The plaintiffs must be placed, so far as men can do it, in as good a situation as if the contract had been performed.'

[4] *Gordon* v. *Potter* (1859) 1 F & F 644; contrast *French* v. *Brookes* (1830) 6 Bing. 354, where it was held that the plaintiff was not entitled to the expense of returning his family home from South America. (These cases might be regarded as depending upon expenses provisions in the particular contract. In *Gordon* v. *Potter* there was an express agreement to pay for the employee's journey *to take up* his employment.)

However, the reliance interest is not normally protected when the employee sues for damages for wrongful dismissal, and any apparent departures from the rule probably depend upon the express provisions of particular contracts of employment.

The main *restitution* interest which may arise in the context of wrongful dismissal is the claim of the employee to the return of his contributions to the pension fund. This would normally have to be claimed as money had and received (i.e. in a restitutionary claim rather than as contract damages.[1] In one case it was indicated *obiter* that an employee, if he had been wrongfully dismissed, could have recovered contract damages in respect of money which he had paid to the employer for the purchase of collecting books to enable him to carry on the work of collector of weekly premiums of members of a friendly society.[2] But restitutionary claims are very exceptional.[3]

B. Loss of Reputation and Injury to Feelings

The decision of the House of Lords in *Addis* v. *Gramophone Company Ltd.*[4] is the origin of a restrictive approach to the measure of damages for wrongful dismissal. This makes it important to state precisely the *ratio* of the case:

[1] The rules of the pension fund may, however, give the employee a contractual right to the return of his contributions upon the termination of employment, in which case he can claim that sum as a contract debt. Moreover, the employee may claim for loss of expected pension *benefits* rather than in respect of past contributions, in which case damages are available in respect of the expectation interest—see below, p. 252–6 and Note, pp. 382, 383.

[2] Stephen J. in *Ellwood* v. *Liverpool Victoria Legal Friendly Society* (1880) 42 LT 694, at 697 col. 2.

[3] The measure of compensation for Unfair Dismissal has proceeded upon the same basic principles of *restitutio in integrum* as the common law of damages for wrongful dismissal. But within that basic similarity, the following very significant contrasts with the common law may be observed:

(a) Compensation for unfair dismissal is not limited to comparison with the situation if the contract had been properly performed. Thus compensation for loss of employment is not restricted to loss of employment during the period of contractual notice (see below, p. 252 note 6).

(b) The law concerning loss of expected benefits has been much more fully developed in the context of unfair dismissal, e.g. in relation to loss of protection against redundancy (see below, p. 261 note 3).

(c) Compensation for unfair dismissal has been considerably limited by reference to the fault or contributory conduct of the employee, statutory provision for reduction of this kind being made by s. 116(3) of the 1971 Act.

For the effect of the repeal of the 1971 Act upon the remedies for unfair dismissal, see Appendix, para. 2.

[4] [1909] AC 488.

The manager of the Calcutta branch of the business of the defendants, who was paid a weekly salary of £15 plus commission, was given six months' notice of termination in accordance with his contract. During the currency of that notice, the employers sent out his successor to take over from him and informed the local bank that the employee was no longer to act for them. The employee left and sued for damages for wrongful dismissal. It was held by the House of Lords that the employee was entitled to damages in respect of—

(1) salary for the unexpired part of the six months;
(2) commission actually earned by the new manager for the unexpired period;
(3) an allowance of £340, which the jury estimated as the additional commission which the plaintiff himself would have earned had he been managing the business himself (i.e. assuming that he would have done better business than his successor).

The award of the jury was, however, disallowed in so far as it went outside those heads. The particular claim which was rejected was expressed by four of the Law Lords composing the majority of five to one, as a claim representing the injury to the feelings of the plaintiff, and the increased difficulty in obtaining other employment resulting from the defamatory manner of dismissal from employment.[1] The decision shows that in actions for wrongful dismissal, one is unlikely to recover exemplary damages, aggravated damages, damages for non-economic loss consisting in injury to feelings, or damages in respect of loss of reputation caused by the manner of dismissal.[2]

The difficulty surrounding the decision is that of deciding whether it went to the further lengths of holding that damages could not be recovered for loss of prospects of other employment resulting from the *fact* of the dismissal as opposed to the damaging *manner* of dismissal. Only one of the five Law Lords composing the majority committed himself to such a proposition, ruling that, 'If there be a dismissal without notice, the employer must pay an indemnity, but that indemnity cannot include compensation either for the injured feelings of the servant, or for the loss he may sustain from the *fact that his having been dismissed of itself* makes it more difficult to

---

[1] Lord James, ibid. at 492; Lord Atkinson at 493; Lord Gorell at 501; Lord Shaw at 504.

[2] In *British Guiana Credit Corporation* v. *Da Silva* [1965] 1 WLR 248, the Privy Council refused, in an action for wrongful dismissal, to allow damages under the head of 'humiliation, embarrassment and loss of reputation'. See Lord Donovan at 259 D–E.

obtain fresh employment'.[1] If the decision does give rise to that further rule, the result is that an employee cannot recover damages attributable to the fact that dismissal prevents him from obtaining a qualification or a fund of experience which he would have gained from the employment had he not been dismissed, and which would have increased his ability to obtain, or his earnings in, subsequent employment.

It would seem that, although only one of the judgments in the House of Lords provides direct support for such a view, it is widely thought that the majority of the Law Lords were supporting such a rule. That was, for example, the view taken of the decision by the Court of Appeal in *Dunk* v. *George Waller & Son Ltd.*[2] In that case, the damages awarded to an apprentice for wrongful dismissal included an allowance for the fact that if the plaintiff had been permitted to serve out his apprenticeship, he would have been able to start work at wages of £1–£2 per week more than he could earn without a completed period of apprenticeship.[3] But in order to award such damages, it was regarded as necessary to distinguish the contract of apprenticeship from the contract of employment, because it was the view of the court that the rule in *Addis* v. *Gramophone Co. Ltd.* precluded the award of such damages as between employer and employee. Lord Denning M.R. quoted, as the *ratio* of the decision of the House of Lords, the dictum of Lord Loreburn that an employee cannot get compensation for the loss he may sustain from the fact that his having been dismissed of itself makes it more difficult to obtain fresh employment.[4] It is, however, suggested that this dictum represents a minority view point in *Addis* v. *Gramophone Co. Ltd.*; and that the decision does not preclude the award of damages to an employee for the loss of a status, qualification, or other enhancement of earning capacity which would have been obtained by him had it not been for the dismissal.[5]

---

[1] Lord Loreburn L.C. [1909] AC 488 at 491 (emphasis added).
[2] [1970] 2 QB 163.
[3] A period of approximately two years was taken into account in estimating this loss, and the sum of £180 was awarded under this head.
[4] [1970] 2 QB 163 at 168 C.
[5] In the law of Unfair Dismissal, injuries to feelings and reputation will not be treated as totally irrelevant, but they will influence compensation only where financial loss (typically in the form of loss of employment prospects) can be shown to follow from them. See *Norton Tool Co. Ltd.* v. *Tewson* [1972] ICR 501 at 504 G & 506 E (Sir John Donaldson); *Vaughan* v. *Weighpack Ltd.* [1974]

C. Loss of Earnings and the Period of Notice

The basic head of damages recoverable for wrongful dismissal is that of the loss of the amount the employee would have earned if the contract had been performed.[1] The recovery in respect of loss of earnings is, however, fundamentally limited by the rule that where the contract of employment is terminable by the employer by notice, or by payment in lieu of notice, the only period which may be taken into account in assessing loss of earnings is the period of notice.[2] The early cases upon this point proceed upon particular views of the effect of a contractual right to terminate by notice or by payment in lieu of notice.[3] Thus it was thought at one time that if the contract provided for termination by notice and the employee was dismissed without notice, then the breach of contract consisted only in the failure to give proper notice or to pay wages in lieu, rather than in the denial of a promised period of employment. This point emerges clearly from the framing of the claim for damages for wrongful dismissal in *Turner* v. *Mason*,[4] in which the breach claimed was not wrongful dismissal at large, but rather the failure to give the one month's notice.

The limitation of damages in respect of loss of earnings to the period of notice was also justified in one of the leading early authorities on this point, on the ground that the provision for termination by one month's notice constituted a provision fixing liquidated damages for the breach.[5] A clause fixing damages in the event of breach will not be implemented where it is in the nature of a penalty fixed *in*

ICR261 at 265 G–266A (Sir Hugh Griffiths); cf. *John Millar & Sons* v. *Quinn* [1974] IRLR 107 at 108 Para. 5 (Lord Thomson).

[1] Cf. Erle J. in *Beckham* v. *Drake* (1849) 2 HLC 579, 608.

[2] Tindal C.J. in *French* v. *Brookes* (1830) 6 Bing. 354 at 360; Lord Denman C.J. in *Hartley* v. *Harman* (1840) 11 A & E 798 at 801; Hill J. in *Gordon* v. *Potter* (1859) 1 F & F 644 at 645; Mr. Commissioner Winslow in *Ex parte Allpas* (1867) 17 LT 179 at 179; Blackburn J. in *Shaw* v. *Alderson* (1875) 44 LJ(NS)MC 160; Grantham J. in *Baker* v. *Denkara Ashanti Mining Corporation Ltd.* (1903) 20 TLR 37 at 38; Bray J. in *Lindsay* v. *Queen's Hotel Co. Ltd.* [1919] 1 KB 212 at 213; Wright J. in *Savage* v. *British India Steam Navigation Co. Ltd.* (1930) 46 TLR 294 at 296: Lord Donovan in *British Guiana Credit Corporation* v. *Da Silva* [1965] 1 WLR 248 at 259 H–260 B (below).

[3] See above, p. 181–2.

[4] (1845) 14 M & W 112; so also Patterson J. in *Goodman* v. *Pocock* (1850) 15 QB 576, 581, commenting upon *Hartley* v. *Harman* (1840) 11 A & E 798.

[5] Lord Denman C.J. in *Hartley* v. *Harman* (above) at 801.

terrorem of the party in breach.[1] But on the other hand, if such a provision is not a penalty in that sense, it will be implemented even though it prevents the injured party from receiving adequate compensation for his loss.[2] In such a case, the provision stipulating damages will be treated, not as a penalty imposed upon the injured party, but as an effective limitation of liability by the party in breach.[3] But it may well be argued that a provision for the termination of a contract by notice or even by payment in lieu of notice ought not to be regarded as concerned with the assessment of damages in the event of wrongful dismissal.

The limitation of damages in respect of loss of earnings to the period of notice required for the proper termination of the contract can be based also upon a general principle that damages are to be assessed on the assumption that the defendant would have performed the contract in the manner least disadvantageous to himself. This was originally stated as a rule that 'where there are several ways in which the contract may be performed, that mode is adopted which is the least profitable to the plaintiff, and the least burthensome to the defendant'.[4] And it later appeared in the form that 'a defendant is not liable in damages for not doing that which he is not bound to do'.[5] The principle of performance in the manner least disadvantageous to the defendant has now been recognized as applying to the employer's right to give notice.[6]

Where damages in respect of loss of earnings are limited by reference to the period of notice, then it is likely, especially in the case of manual employees, that the damages will be based upon earnings in respect of a short period—weeks rather than months or years. This raises a problem of what account is to be taken of short-term fluctuation of earnings in ascertaining the week's wages upon which the damages are to be based. In *Devonald* v. *Rosser & Sons*

---

[1] Per Lord Dunedin in *Dunlop Pneumatic Tyre Co. Ltd.* v. *New Motor & Garage Co. Ltd.* [1915] AC 79 at 86.

[2] *Diestal* v. *Stevenson* [1906] 2 KB 345 (sale of goods).

[3] *Cellulose Acetate Silk Co. Ltd.* v. *Widnes Foundry Ltd.* [1933] AC 20 (contract for the installation of industrial plant). The rule in this case is subject to the effect of the doctrine of fundamental breach—cf. *Harbutt's Plasticine Ltd.* v. *Wayne Tank & Pump Co. Ltd.* [1970] 1 QB 447.

[4] Maule J. in *Cockburn* v. *Alexander* (1848) 6 CB 791, 814 (charter-party).

[5] Scrutton L.J. in *Abrahams* v. *Herbert Reiach Ltd.* [1922] 1 KB 477 at 482 (contract with an author for the publication of a series of articles).

[6] *British Guiana Credit Corporation* v. *Da Silva* [1956] 1 WLR 248 per Lord Donovan at 259 H–260 B.

(1906)[1] damages for the loss of six weeks' earnings were assessed on the basis of 'the average wages earned by the plaintiffs for some time preceding the stoppage'.[2] This was agreed between the parties to give rise to a claim for £14 for the six weeks, and so the case throws no further light upon the period of time to be taken into account in arriving at the normal rate of earnings.[3]

The limitation of damages for loss of earnings to the period of notice will not apply in the case of every wrongful dismissal, for not every contract of employment is terminable by notice. In particular, a contract of employment for a fixed term is not subject to an implied term allowing it to be terminated by notice. Where a contract of employment is made for a fixed term, the courts have in many cases awarded damages for wrongful dismissal in respect of loss of employment for the remainder of the fixed term, subject only to the rules concerning the mitigation of loss.[4] However, the courts will also recognize and implement a contract of employment of indefinite duration which is not terminable by notice.[5] In the case of such a contract, there is no natural *terminus ad quem* short of the retirement date of the employee by reference to which to limit the damages for wrongful dismissal; and it is uncertain how damages are to be assessed in that situation.[6]

D. Loss of Pension Rights and other Incidental Benefits

The law concerning damages for wrongful dismissal is not well

---

[1] [1906] 2 KB 728.   [2] Ibid. at 735 per Jelf J.

[3] Schedule 2 of the 1972 Act provides a method of assessing the week's pay for the purposes of the 1965 and 1972 Acts. If the employee has no normal working hours, the week's pay is averaged over the twelve weeks preceding termination of employment (Schedule 2 Para. 3).

[4] e.g. *Davis* v. *Marshall* (1861) 4 LT 216; *Smith* v. *Thompson* (1849) 8 CB 44; *Re Golomb & William Porter & Co. Ltd.'s Arbitration* (1931) 144 LT 583. See *Slingsby* v. *News of the World Organisation Ltd.*, The Times, 2 May 1970, p. 2— advertising director recovered for wrongful dismissal £27,976 for loss of salary and £3,600 for loss of pension rights—apparently employed for a substantial fixed term.

[5] Cf. *McClelland* v. *Northern Ireland General Health Services Board* [1957] 1 WLR 594. See above, pp. 154–9.

[6] Loss of earnings during the period of notice has a radically different rôle in the law of unfair dismissal. Whereas at common law the loss of employment of which account will be taken is limited to the period of notice, in the law of compensation for unfair dismissal the period of notice constitutes a measure of the *minimum* compensation attributable to loss of employment: *Norton Tool Co. Ltd.* v. *Tewson* [1972] ICR 501 at 505 G (Sir John Donaldson); *Vaughan* v. *Weighpack Ltd.* [1974] ICR 261 at 263 C–E (Sir Hugh Griffiths).

developed in the direction of protecting the employee against pecuniary loss other than the loss of basic earnings. The general principle governing the recovery of damages under this head would seem to be that the plaintiff should recover for the deprivation of his contractual rights, but should not recover on account of mere factual expectations in excess of legal rights.

1. *Pension Rights.* The most important of the fringe benefits which may be considered in calculating damages for wrongful dismissal is that of pension rights. Loss of pension rights forms a recognized head of damages in calculating damages for wrongful dismissal.[1] The general principle applicable to assessing the damages for loss of pension rights would seem to be that the employee ought to be put in as good a position as he would have been in if the employer had performed the contract, assuming that the employer had performed the contract in the manner least disadvantageous to himself. The claim for damages for loss of pension rights resulting from wrongful dismissal is a claim in respect of the loss of the increase in the value of pension rights which would have been enjoyed had it not been for the dismissal. If the employee had remained in his employment, his pension would have become more valuable. He is compensated for the fact that this increase in value has not occurred. If, however, the continuation of pension contributions, or the ultimate payment of benefit, is a matter within the discretion of the employer and not a legal obligation upon him, then the rule of least disadvantageous performance applies, and no damages are payable under this head.[2]

In general, in order to evaluate the pension rights for the loss of which the employee is to be compensated in damages, it is necessary to compare the pension rights to which the employee is entitled upon being wrongfully dismissed, and secondly, the pension rights to which he would have become entitled had he not been dismissed.[3]

---

[1] *Bold* v. *Brough, Nicholson & Hall Ltd.* [1964] 1 WLR 201; cf. *Judd* v. *Hammersmith Hospital Board of Governors* [1960] 1 WLR 328 (personal injuries). See *White* v. *Bloomfield Ltd.*, *The Guardian*, 8 Dec. 1966 (Wedderburn, *Cases and Materials on Labour Law* (Cambridge, 1967) p. 179 n.).

[2] *Beach* v. *Reed Corrugated Cases Ltd.* [1956] 1 WLR 807. But the rule of least disadvantageous performance does not apply to the employer's right (if any) to discontinue his entire pensions scheme in relation to his employees at large—Phillimore J. in *Bold* v. *Brough, Nicholson Ltd.* [1964] 1 WLR 201 at 211–12; Diplock L.J. in *Lavarack* v. *Woods of Colchester Ltd.* [1967] 1 QB 278 at 295 F– 297 B: see below, Note, pp. 382, 383.

[3] The discussion which follows (in the text) derives much of its importance

The case will be considered of a pensions scheme to which the employee as well as the employer contributes, as that is the more complex case than that where the employee does not contribute, and also because that is the more common case. The employee who is dismissed is normally entitled to the benefit of his own contributions, whatever the reason for the dismissal. He may take that benefit either in the form of a cash refund or in the form of a pension purchased with those contributions. The employee whose employment is terminated before retirement, for reasons other than those of fraud or misconduct, is generally entitled in addition to a pension representing the employer's contributions. Therefore, upon wrongful dismissal, the employer normally becomes liable for a contractual debt, equal to the sum required for the purchase of a pension representing his contributions and those of his employee to date. In order to evaluate the additional pension rights which should be taken into account it is necessary to consider what the employee's pension rights would have been if he had not been dismissed. There are various possibilities; one possibility is that the employee would have remained in his employment till retirement date. Another is that he would have made an early retirement at some date between the dismissal and the expected retirement date. Thirdly, he might have remained in employment until the expiry of a fixed-term contract of employment, or until termination by due notice as the case may be.

Each of these situations is generally treated in a different way under the rules of pensions schemes.[1] Upon retirement at the *normal retirement* date the employee becomes entitled to a full pension. Upon *early retirement*, the employee normally becomes entitled to an immediate pension representing the value of his expected pension rights on normal retirement, reduced by the value of contributions which would have been expected to be made between early retirement and normal retirement, and reduced also by an 'early retirement

---

from the freedom of an occupational pension scheme to differentiate its benefits according to the circumstances of termination of employment, and indeed to provide for forfeiture of benefits in the event of dismissal. That freedom has been substantially curtailed since the provisions of the Social Security Act 1973 relating to the occupational pension schemes came into force. These provisions have taken effect and pension rights now receive greater statutory protection in the event of wrongful dismissal. See Note, below, p. 382).

[1] See Pilch and Wood, *New Trends in Pensions* (London 1964) pp. 39–42; and their *Pension Scheme Practice* (London 1967) p. 72.

factor' representing the fact that earlier contributions remain in the fund for less time than they would have done upon normal retirement with corresponding loss of interest upon them. Upon termination of employment at the expiry of a fixed term contract, or upon due notice, the employee will become entitled to a pension representing only contributions to date; but those contributions would be greater than those made by the time of a wrongful dismissal, because the contributions would have continued for the additional period of the currency of notice or the effluxion of the fixed term.

It will be apparent that in each of these situations, i.e. normal retirement, early retirement, or dismissal at the proper time, the pension rights of the employee are greater than his pension rights at the time of the wrongful dismissal. But the degree by which they are greater is different in each situation. It is therefore important to see which situation the courts will take as the basis for comparison.

In *Bold* v. *Brough, Nicholson Ltd.*[1], all three of these situations were put forward as alternatives. In each case the employee claimed the present actuarial value of a pension representing the difference between his present pension rights and the pension rights he would enjoy in the situation concerned.[2] The hypothesis of normal retirement was rejected on the ground that the employer was under no contractual obligation to continue the employment until normal retirement. The hypothesis of early retirement was rejected on the ground that the early retirement rules in the pension scheme referred only to the possibility that the employee might of his own volition wish to conclude his working life early; and that this had no relevance to the situation where the employer dismissed the employee.

The hypothesis adopted was that of the termination of the employment by the employer at the first opportunity allowed by the contract, so that the employee recovered only relatively small damages for loss of pension rights. In effect, the principle of least disadvantageous performance was applied, and the entitlement of the employer, either to refrain from renewing a fixed-term contract, or to terminate a contract of employment by notice, was taken into account. So not only is the employee's right to damages in respect of loss of earnings limited by the right of the employer to terminate the

---

[1] [1964] 1 WLR 201.

[2] The claims were £4,296 on the basis of retirement at 65; £3,751 on the basis of early retirement with employer's consent; £729 on the basis of termination by the employer at the earliest date lawful.

contract of employment by notice; but also the right to damages in respect of the loss of pension rights is limited in the same way.

Having established the basis of comparison, we require further rules to assess damages in respect of the loss of pension rights. The common law offers little guidance in this respect. For instance, in the *Bold* v. *Brough, Nicholson* case the court left unresolved the problem where the employee, if he had not been dismissed, would have had to go on making contributions to his pension.[1] It is arguable that in these cases the courts should either require the employee to give credit for the contributions he would have made, or should consider only the pension rights which would have derived from the employer's contributions alone. However, the common law, by taking into account what is usually only a short period of loss of employment, has in practice barred the way to very large claims for damages for loss of pension rights and has accordingly not needed to refine the assessment of these damages. Another unresolved problem is how the loss of various kinds of contingent and future pension benefits is to be translated into a present money value. A further issue is how far the employee should give credit for possible pension benefits derived from employment elsewhere, following the dismissal. There is thus still scope for considerable argument about how these damages should be calculated.[2]

2. *Earnings in Kind.* There are significant limitations upon the rights of the employee to recover other heads of damage in an action for damages for wrongful dismissal. He is entitled to damages representing loss of earnings in kind,[3] particularly rent-free residence or board and lodging,[4] during the period which is taken into account in calculating his loss of money earnings. But that is subject to the

---

[1] This point may have been neglected *per incuriam* or may have been allowed for in the size of the claims made.

[2] The law of unfair dismissal requires compensation to be assessed for loss of pension rights and is not restricted, as the common law is, in the matter of how much loss of employment can be taken into account. Hence the problems of quantification left unresolved at common law appear in a magnified form, and the case-law shows how wide a variety of methods of assessment is available— e.g. *Scottish Co-op. Ltd.* v. *Lloyd* [1973] ICR 137; *Cawthorn & Sinclair Ltd.* v. *Hedger* [1974] ICR 146; *John Millar & Sons* v. *Quinn* [1974] 107; *Gill* v. *Harold Andrews Sheepbridge Ltd.* [1974] ICR 294. See Jackson, (1975) 4 ILJ 24.

[3] The problem of whether and when to treat earnings in kind as equivalent to money earnings arises in the context of income tax: *Owen* v. *Pook* [1969] 2 WLR 775; *Heaton* v. *Bell* [1970] AC 728; and in the calculation of redundancy payments: *S. & U. Stores Ltd* v. *Wilkes* [1974] ICR 645.

[4] *Re English Joint Stock Bank*, (*Yelland's Case*) (1867) LR 4 Eq. 350.

anomalous rule in *Gordon* v. *Potter* (1859)[1] which was qualified, but not abrogated, by the decision in *Lindsay* v. *Queens Hotel Ltd.* (1919).[2]

In *Gordon* v. *Potter* (1859) it was held that a domestic servant who had been wrongfully dismissed could recover only damages equivalent to one month's wages, and could not recover 'board wages'. That meant that she could not recover damages representing the value of the free board and lodging which she would have received if her employment had continued.

In *Lindsay* v. *Queens Hotel Ltd.* (1919) Bray J. held that the employee could recover board wages, i.e. damages under the head of loss of benefits in kind, even though the employer had a right to terminate by payment of a month's wages in lieu of notice, where the employer had dismissed summarily during the currency of a notice given by the employee.

The earlier case proceeds on the basis that the employer who dismisses summarily is merely to be held liable for payment in lieu of notice, which, it is accepted, does not include board wages.[3] The later case accepts that this is the general rule but says that in the special case of dismissal during the employee's notice, the employer cannot be treated as if he had merely failed to make a payment in lieu of notice and must pay damages representing actual pecuniary loss. But the earlier case is open to criticism on the ground that the employer should not be treated as if he had dismissed the employee lawfully when he has not, and should pay damages representing actual pecuniary loss in every case, loss of benefits in kind being included therein.

A similar result was reached by a different method of reasoning in a County Court decision in *McGrath* v. *de Soissons*.[4]

An assistant architect was dismissed with one month's salary in lieu of notice. He claimed damages in respect of:
(a) loss of earnings, in that he should have been given three months' salary in lieu of notice, and
(b) loss of the value of luncheon vouchers at 15s. per week in respect of the period represented by the payment in lieu of notice.

It was held that one month's salary was a sufficient payment in lieu of notice, and that the employee could not claim the loss of the value of luncheon vouchers in respect of that one month, because he was entitled to vouchers in respect only of days of actual work

[1] (1859) 1 F & F 644.
[3] See above, p. 187.
[2] [1919] 1 KB 212.
[4] (1962) 112 LJ 60.

(and not, for example, for weekend days, holidays, and days of absence). The defendants were not obliged to find him work during the period for which he was entitled to notice, and so need not pay him in respect of loss of luncheon vouchers. The reasoning is suspect, because damages for wrongful dismissal in respect of loss of earnings are assessed on the assumption that the plaintiff had been allowed to earn remuneration by working for the proper period of notice. It is illogical to depart from that assumption in respect of benefits in kind. The judge may well have had in mind the tax concession which is made in respect of luncheon vouchers on the basis that they assist employees in the actual performance of their duties.

3. *Bonus Payments.* The question whether the wrongfully dismissed employee can recover damages in respect of loss of bonus payments which he would have received during the reckonable period of loss of employment depends upon the basic issue of whether, and how far, factual expectations can be taken into account in damages when those expectations exceed the legal rights of the plaintiff.

The term 'bonus payment' is used here to refer to payments over and above the contractually agreed remuneration, which are not, however, related to any particular extra work done by the employee, unlike overtime payments or incentive payments in general. The bonus payment is therefore an additional reward for the basic work which the employee has contracted to do. That which is nominally a bonus payment may be treated by the courts as having become a contractual obligation upon the employer; and as having therefore become merely a part of the contractual remuneration.[1]

It is clear that the loss of prospective bonus payments of that kind will be recoverable in damages for wrongful dismissal.[2] The case of the bonus payment which is *not* a contractual obligation upon the employer was considered in the important case of *Lavarack* v. *Woods of Colchester Ltd.*,[3] in which the principle of performance least disadvantageous to the defendant was applied to this problem.

The plaintiff was employed under a contract for a fixed term of five years at a certain salary plus 'such bonus (if any) as the directors . . . shall from

---

[1] *Powell* v. *Braun* [1954] 1 WLR 401. Contrast *Grieve* v. *Imperial Tobacco Ltd.*, *The Guardian*, 30 April 1963. Wedderburn, *Cases and Materials*, p. 118.

[2] *Lake* v. *Campbell* (1862) 5 LT 582.

[3] [1967] 1 QB 278 at 298 E–F (Russell L.J.); 287 F–288 C (Lord Denning M.R.); 297 C–E (Diplock L.J.).

time to time determine'. He was wrongfully dismissed after two years. The position was complicated by the fact that the bonus was, after a further year, discontinued in relation to the remaining employees, and commuted for an increase in salary. The plaintiff claimed as part of his damages for wrongful dismissal an allowance representing either the bonuses which he would have received if he had remained in his employment and if the bonus scheme had continued, or representing the salary increase which he would have received as its equivalent if he had remained in his employment and had accepted the changed arrangements which were in fact made.

It was held by a majority of the Court of Appeal that he could not recover damages under this head.

Russell L.J. applied strictly the principle that damages are to be assessed on the basis that the defendant would have performed the contract in the manner least disadvantageous to himself, and would not have done anything for the plaintiff beyond that which he was legally obliged to do. Diplock L.J. based his refusal to award damages in respect of the loss of bonus on the different ground that the bonus had in fact been discontinued.

Lord Denning M.R., dissenting, took the view that the plaintiff was entitled to be compensated for the loss of expected benefits which would have accrued to him, even if they would not have been legal rights. Strongly in favour of that view is the decision in *Manubens* v. *Leon*[1] where Lush J. brought the anticipated receipt of tips into the area of recoverable damages by holding that 'the contract was that the defendant would not prevent the plaintiff from receiving the remuneration which he would have received in the ordinary course of events if he fulfilled the duty for which he was engaged'.[2]

It was also the view of Lord Denning that this right to compensation was not defeated by the discontinuance of the bonus scheme, because the salary increase was its true equivalent. Lord Denning's dissenting view represents a far more realistic approach to the contract of employment than does the approach of the majority of the Court of Appeal. In formulating structures of remuneration, employers are very likely to emphasize the discretionary and *ex gratia* character of a part of the total remuneration. Their purpose in so doing is to enhance the incentive character of those payments. There is no overriding reason why the employee, who has been wrongfully dismissed, should be deprived of compensation for the loss of that expectation.

[1] [1919] 1 KB 208.   [2] Ibid. at 211.

The fact that a bonus scheme is continued in force after the wrongful dismissal, in relation to remaining employees, should entitle the dismissed employee to compensation under this head; and the fact that it is commuted into an increase of salary should not detract from that entitlement.[1]

4. *Incentive Payments and Commission.* In the case where the remuneration of the employee consists wholly of payment based on the actual work done, as where a commercial employee is remunerated wholly by commission, or an industrial employee wholly upon piece-rates, it is clear that the employer is obliged to provide enough work to enable remuneration to be earned at a reasonable level.[2]

Where the employee is remunerated partly by a fixed wage and partly by incentive payment for extra work, there is conflict in the cases upon the question whether the employer is obliged to provide that extra work.[3] It is the view of this writer that the courts will, after the decision in *Bauman* v. *Hulton Press Ltd.*,[4] be likely to hold that there is, in these cases also, an obligation to enable the total remuneration to reach a reasonable level. But it might none the less be held that, on given facts, an employer was under no obligation to provide opportunities for overtime working.

Where the employee can show that it was a contractual obligation upon the employer to allow him to earn incentive payments, then he is entitled, in an action for wrongful dismissal, to damages representing the loss of those earnings during the reckonable period of loss of employment.[5] Where, however, the employee has only a factual expectation of such earnings and not a contractual right to the opportunity to earn them, then it would seem from the state of the law concerning bonus payments[6] that he will not recover damages in respect of that expectation. The principle of performance in the least disadvantageous manner will apply again here.

---

[1] In assessing compensation for unfair dismissal the NIRC has treated itself as free from this restriction upon contractual damages and has allowed an award representing anticipated salary increase, expressly departing from the *Lavarack* doctrine: *York Trailer Co. Ltd.* v. *Sparkes* [1973] ICR 518, 522 E-F (Sir Hugh Griffiths).

[2] See above, pp. 23-4. [3] See above, p. 24 notes 5-6.

[4] [1952] 2 All ER 1121.

[5] *Hartland* v. *General Exchange Bank Ltd.* (1866) 14 LT 863; *Re Patent Floor Cloth Co. Ltd.* (1872) LJ(NS)Ch. 476; *Addis* v. *Gramophone Co.* [1909] AC 488; *Bauman* v. *Hulton Press Ltd* [1952] 2 All ER 1121 (above).

[6] See above, pp. 258-60.

5. *Rights based on Continuity of Employment.* No recognition has yet been accorded to the importance of seniority rights in awarding damages for wrongful dismissal. Mention may, however, be made of the decision in the early case of *Richardson* v. *Mellish* (1824)[1] where a sea captain who had been wrongfully dismissed was compensated for the loss of the expectation that his contract would be renewed for a second voyage subject to a veto by the charterers. The case is difficult to reconcile with the later applications of the rule as to least disadvantageous performance, except on the ground that the 'contingency' was a virtual certainty. The awarding of damages for loss of seniority rights is difficult, because they are generally rights which operate only in contingency situations such as sickness or redundancy; and because it would be difficult to quantify their value in those situations. But here the principle of *Chaplin* v. *Hicks*[2] can be applied, that once given a contractual obligation, the element of chance inherent in the quantification of that obligation does not prevent an award of damages. It is arguable that there should be recognition in damages of the loss of statutory seniority rights—for example, the loss of accrued service for the purpose of entitlement to a minimum period of notice under Section 1 of the 1972 Act or to remedies for unfair dismissal under the 1971 Act or for the purpose of entitlement to a redundancy payment under the 1965 Act.[3]

E. The Mitigation of Loss

It has long been recognized that the right to damages for wrongful dismissal is qualified by the rules as to mitigation of loss. This appears in the best-known early statement of the principle governing the

---

[1] (1824) 2 Bing. 229.   [2] [1911] 2 KB 786.

[3] The case-law concerning compensation for unfair dismissal establishes a well-recognized head of compensation consisting in loss of statutory protections based upon continuity of employment. Loss of protection in respect of unfair dismissal or dismissal by reason of redundancy was recognized in *Norton Tool Co. Ltd.* v. *Tewson* [1972] ICR 501, 506 H–507 A. Loss of statutory entitlement to notice was recognized in *Hilti (GB) Ltd.* v. *Windridge* [1974] ICR 352. Loss of protection against redundancy has been much the most significant of these three heads of compensation; the other two give rise only to small awards if any. Loss of protection from redundancy has tended to be valued at 50% of the amount of redundancy payment which the employee would receive (or does receive) at the time of dismissal, e.g.: *Norton Tool Co. Ltd.* v. *Tewson* (above); *Garratt* v. *Platt International Ltd.* [1974] ICR 142; *Bateman* v. *British Leyland (UK) Ltd.* [1974] ICR 403.

measure of damages for wrongful dismissal, where Erle J. said, in *Beckham* v. *Drake*,[1]

'The measure of damages for the breach of contract now in question is obtained by considering what is the usual rate of wages for the employment here contracted for, and what time would be lost before a similar employment could be obtained. The law considers that employment can be obtained by a person competent for the place, and that the usual rate of wages for such employment can be proved and that . . . it is the duty of the servant to use diligence to find another employment.'

There are two rules of mitigation which are relevant in an action for damages for wrongful dismissal. These have been distinguished and characterized as:

(a) the rule as to avoidable loss—no recovery for loss which the the plaintiff ought to have avoided; and

(b) the rule as to avoided loss—no recovery for loss which the plaintiff has avoided, unless the matter is collateral.[2]

The element of value judgment enters into the rule as to avoidable loss rather than the rule as to avoided loss. If the plaintiff actually avoids his loss by obtaining other employment, then his earnings in that other employment go to reduce his damages, even though the non-acceptance of that other employment would not have constituted a failure to mitigate.[3] But if he does not actually avoid his loss, then a value judgment is involved in deciding what steps he ought to have taken to avoid the loss. The question of what steps the plaintiff must take to avoid his loss has two main aspects. The one aspect is the question of how far the plaintiff must be prepared to be mobile in the choice of new work, either occupationally or geographically. The other is the question of how far the plaintiff is entitled to insist upon congenial personal relations in his further employment.

Where the opportunity for mitigation arises from an offer made by the employer himself, the major consideration is that of how far the employee may invoke his unwillingness to work for an employer who has wrongfully dismissed him and with whom personal relations

---

[1] (1849) 2 HLC 579, 606–7; cf. Blackburn J. in *Sowdon* v. *Mills* (1861) 30 LJ (NS) QB 175 at 176–7.

[2] See *McGregor on Damages* (13th edn. 1972) Para. 205. The second of the three rules there quoted is not relevant to actions for wrongful dismissal.

[3] Cf. *Collier* v. *Sunday Referee Publishing Co. Ltd.* [1940] 2 KB 647—a case of (partly) *avoided* loss which would probably not have been treated as *avoidable* loss.

have become strained. It has been established that the employee need not mitigate by accepting another offer of employment from his present employer when the dismissal has taken place in such a manner as to prejudice good personal relations between the parties.[1] And it would seem that an employee may properly be sceptical of the genuineness of an offer made by the employer at a time when the relations between them have been placed into the hands of their lawyers, especially when the offer is made on the terms that the employee should not act on such legal rights as he has for damages for breach of contract against the employer.[2] It has been recognized that there is a contrast here between the impersonal considerations which arise when an opportunity for mitigating results from an offer made by a party to a contract for the sale of goods and the personal considerations operating in the context of the contract of employment.[3]

The decision in *Brace* v. *Calder*[4] suggests, however, that where the wrongful dismissal is a technical one constituted by a change in the composition of an employing partnership, then an offer of continued employment by the continuing partners will be treated as enabling the employee to avoid his loss in full, with the result that his damages are nominal.

Where the issue is the possibility that the dismissed employee might have reduced his loss by obtaining employment with another employer, then the question is what standard of occupational mobility and geographical mobility is required of the employee. The decided cases do not afford detailed guidance upon this point. They show that the employee is required to minimize his loss by a reasonable course of conduct (though the onus is upon the defaulting defendant to show that it could be, or could have been, done, and is not being, or has not been, done).[5] This clearly means that the employee is not bound to accept any other possible employment regardless of change in location, occupation, or remuneration. Thus,

[1] Bankes L.J. in *Payzu Ltd.* v. *Saunders* [1919] 2 KB 581, 588–9; *Yetton* v. *Eastwoods Froy Ltd.* [1967] 1 WLR 104; *Shindler* v. *Northern Raincoat Co. Ltd.* [1960] 1 WLR 1038 (Diplock J.).

[2] *Shindler* v. *Northern Raincoat Co. Ltd.* [1960] 1 WLR 1038 (above).

[3] Bankes L.J. in *Payzu Ltd.* v. *Saunders* [1919] 2 KB 581, 588–9: also Scrutton L.J. at 589; Blain J. in *Yetton* v. *Eastwoods Froy Ltd.* [1967] 1 W; LR 104 at 118 C–D.

[4] [1895] 2 QB 253. See below, p. 346.

[5] Blain J. in *Yetton* v. *Eastwoods Froy Ltd.* [1967] 1 WLR 104 at 115 B–C.

in *Jackson* v. *Hayes, Candy & Co. Ltd.*,[1] the refusal of an offer of re-engagement at a lower salary was held to be reasonable for the purposes of the rule as to mitigation of loss. Again, in *Yetton* v. *Eastwoods Froy Ltd.*,[2] it was held that it had been reasonable for the plaintiff to refuse:

(a) an offer of alternative employment made by his existing employer, because it involved a demotion from joint managing director to assistant managing director, and also because the defendants had placed him in an invidious position by their treatment of him (in a take-over situation); and[3]

(b) opportunities of employment elsewhere at decreased salaries.[4]

It has been found also that the pressure upon the employee to mitigate his loss may bring him into conflict with his trade union; and it was recognized in an important decision on common-law damages for wrongful dismissal that loss of employment will not be treated as avoidable loss where acceptance of employment would have brought the employee into breach of his contract of membership with his trade union, or would have rendered him liable to expulsion from his union, in a closed-shop trade.[5] Salmon L.J. commented that

'It might have been thought that whether, or not, the [employers] dismissed the [employee] in breach of contract, he had suffered no damage because his duty was to mitigate the damage by taking all reasonable steps that he could to do so. But that point has not been argued, and very rightly has not been argued, for the obvious reason that if the [employee] had agreed to an alteration in terms of service in defiance of his union, he would have been committing an offence under the union rules and would be subject to an expulsion from the union.'[6]

Comparison may be made with the provision of Section 22(5)(a) of the National Insurance Act 1965, designed to preserve the neutrality of the National Insurance Fund in trade disputes, that 'employment

---

[1] [1938] 4 All ER 587.   [2] [1967] 1 WLR 104 (above).

[3] A further example of the rule that the employee need not accept an offer made by his existing employer with whom personal relations have deteriorated.

[4] Cf. *Edwards* v. *SOGAT* [1971] Ch. 354 where it was held that damages awarded to a union member against the union for loss of employment resulting from wrongful deprivation of membership would not be reduced on account of the possibility that the plaintiff, a skilled printer, could have obtained employment as a labourer in the trade.

[5] *Morris* v. *C. H. Bailey Ltd.* [1969] 2 Lloyd's Rep. 215.

[6] Ibid. at 219.

shall not be deemed to be employment suitable in the case of any person if it is . . . employment in a situation vacant in consequence of a stoppage of work due to a trade dispute'.[1]

F. Collateral Benefits

Wrongful dismissal may place the employee in a position where he receives benefits which he would not have received had it not been for the wrongful dismissal. Thus it may result in his receiving unemployment benefit and Supplementary Benefit (formerly National Assistance), or private unemployment benefit from his union. Equally, it may result in his being free of financial liabilities which he would otherwise have incurred, such as income tax upon his earnings or the payment of National Insurance contributions during his employment. The question whether damages should be reduced with regard to these factors raises fundamental problems of principle. The problem is really a single one, in that a collateral liability from which the plaintiff is spared by reason of the wrongful dismissal, is comparable with a collateral benefit which he receives by reason thereof.[2]

The conflict of principle concerning collateral benefits is between the view that damages ought not to be reduced by reason of such benefits which the defendant has not provided; and on the other hand, that damages are intended to be compensatory rather than punitive, and therefore should not exceed the plaintiff's loss.[3] In awarding damages for wrongful dismissal this conflict has to be resolved in relation to:

(a) income tax liability saved;

(b) National Insurance contributions saved;

---

[1] The assessment of compensation for unfair dismissal is required by s. 116(2) of the 1971 Act to follow the common-law rule concerning mitigation of loss. In applying this rule, the NIRC has established a standard of reasonableness. The working-out of this concept has produced a series of different rulings. Those imposing a relatively severe duty to mitigate have been: *McKinney* v. *Bieganek* [1973] IRLR 311; *Bessenden Properties Ltd.* v. *Corness* [1973] IRLR 365 (affirmed [1974] IRLR 338); *Archbold Freightage Ltd.* v. *Wilson* [1974] IRLR 10. Earlier rulings imposing a less severe duty to mitigate had been: *Bracey* v. *Iles* [1973] IRLR 210; *Tiptools Ltd.* v. *Curtis* [1973] IRLR 277.

[2] Cf. Atiyah, 'Collateral Benefits Again' (1969) 32 MLR 397, 398.

[3] See McGregor, 'Compensation versus Reinstatement in Damages Awards' (1965) 28 MLR 629; Atiyah, loc. cit. (1969) 32 MLR 397. Both these writers, and more especially Atiyah, are exponents of the view that damages should be compensatory only, and that deduction should therefore be made in respect of collateral benefits.

(c) unemployment benefit received;

(d) Supplementary Benefit received;

(e) unemployment assistance received from private sources such as a trade union;

(f) redundancy payment received.

1. *Income Tax Liability Saved.* It was established by the decision of the House of Lords in *British Transport Commission* v. *Gourley*[1] that, where two conditions are fulfilled, damages for personal injuries in respect of loss of earnings should be reduced to take account of notional tax liability from which the plaintiff is freed. The two conditions are that the amount, in respect of the loss of which the damages awarded constitute compensation, would have been subject to tax, and that the damages awarded would not themselves be subject to tax in the hands of the plaintiff. The rule in *British Transport Commission* v. *Gourley* has been applied to cases of wrongful dismissal; damages have been reduced in respect of notional tax liability which was avoided by the wrongful dismissal.[2] The propriety of applying the principle of *Gourley* to cases of wrongful dismissal was questioned, by Sellers L.J. in *Parsons* v. *B.N.M. Laboratories Ltd.*,[3] on the ground that this would confer an unjustified gain upon the employer. He asked counsel for the defendants 'Why should you wrongfully dismiss this man and put the tax into your pocket?'[4] However, the opposite view has clearly now prevailed.[5]

2. *National Insurance Contributions Saved.* In *Cooper* v. *Firth Brown Ltd.*,[6] where the claim was for damages for personal injuries, one head being loss of earnings, it was held that damages were to be reduced in respect of the contributions to National Insurance which would have been deducted from the employee's wages if he had been at work during the relevant period of loss of earnings. It was argued

---

[1] [1956] AC 185.

[2] *Beach* v. *Reed Corrugated Cases Ltd.* [1956] 1 WLR 807; *Phipps* v. *Orthodox Unit Trusts Ltd.* [1958] 1 QB 314; *Shindler* v. *Northern Raincoat Co. Ltd.* [1960] 1 WLR 1038 (Diplock J.): *Barber* v. *Manchester Regional Hospital Board* [1958] 1 WLR 181; *Bold* v. *Brough, Nicholson & Hall Ltd.* [1964] 1 WLR 201.

[3] [1964] 1 QB 95 at 107–16 (in a dissenting judgment).

[4] Ibid. at 99 (*arguendo*).

[5] The details of how the *Gourley* rule is applied in view of the tax payable upon damages for wrongful dismissal in excess of £5,000 (ss. 187 and 188 of the Income & Corporation Taxes Act 1970) are examined in *McGregor on Damages* (13th edn. 1972) at Para. 889.

[6] [1963] 1 WLR 418 (Lawton J.).

on his behalf that, as the provisions of Section 2 of the Law Reform (Personal Injuries) Act 1948 would oblige the court to take into account one half of the National Insurance industrial injury and sickness benefits received by the plaintiff over a period of five years, the defendants should not at the same time have the benefits of the contributions to National Insurance out of which those benefits arose. That argument was, however, rejected by Lawton J.[1] If that deduction is to be made in spite of that argument, then it will *a fortiori* be made in a wrongful dismissal case where the argument does not apply.

3. *National Insurance Unemployment Benefit Received.* In relation to collateral benefits, in the sense of gains which the plaintiff makes following the wrongful dismissal (as opposed to liabilities from which he is spared), two principles seem to apply. If a benefit received from a third party is discretionary or gratuitous, then the benefit should not be taken into account, the argument being that the defendant should not get the advantage of the third party's generosity, which was directed towards, and intended for, the plaintiff.

The other principle is that, whereas deduction may be made in respect of payments in the nature of wages, deduction should not be made in respect of payments in the nature of contingency insurance to which the plaintiff had contributed the whole or part of the premiums, the argument being that the latter represent the fruits of the thrift and foresight of the plaintiff, of which he should not be deprived.

In the context of wrongful dismissal it has been held that un-employment benefit received after wrongful dismissal is to be deducted from damages.[2] The reasons advanced for making this deduction were that, in so far as these benefits represented insurance moneys, it was an insurance to which the employee was bound to contribute and to which the employer also contributed, so that it did not especially represent the thrift and foresight of the plaintiff;[3] or on the less precise ground that the benefit was not 'too remote from', or 'too collateral to', the wrongful dismissal.[4]

---

[1] Ibid. at 419–20.

[2] *Parsons* v. *B.N.M. Laboratories Ltd.* [1964] 1 QB 95 (Sellers L.J. agreeing on this point) following *Lindstedt* v. *Wimborne Steamship Co. Ltd.* (1949) 83 Ll. LR 19; *Dunk* v. *George Waller & Son Ltd.* [1970] 2 QB 163 (prospective unemployment benefit deducted from damages for wrongful dismissal of an apprentice).

[3] Sellers L.J. [1964] 1 QB 95 at 120–1; Harman L.J., ibid. at 130–1.

[4] Pearson L.J., ibid. at 143–4.

4. *Supplementary Benefit Received.* On the other hand, it has been held in the context of an action for damages for personal injuries[1] that, in assessing loss of earnings, National Assistance payments (now Supplementary Benefit) should not be taken into account, because of the discretionary nature of this 'modern successor of poor law relief'. Stephenson J. there clearly took the view that cases on personal injury and cases on wrongful dismissal could be applied interchangeably in this area. It would seem that the same argument would apply in wrongful dismissal cases.

5. *Private Unemployment Assistance Received.* A difficult problem might arise if it were to be argued that unemployment benefit paid by a union to a member should be deducted from the damages which that member claimed from his employer for wrongful dismissal.[2] It would seem that they should not be deducted, either on the ground that they constitute a gratuitous or discretionary payment from a third party to the employee, or on the ground that they constitute the benefits of an insurance which the employee has provided for himself.

6. *Redundancy Payment Received.* The most important decision of recent years concerning collateral benefits in damages for wrongful dismissal was given in *Stocks* v. *Magna Merchants Ltd.*[3] Here it was held that a statutory redundancy payment made in respect of the dismissal was deductible from damages. Arnold J. held that the deductibility was to be judged according to a principle of remoteness, whereby the payment was deductible if it was a direct consequence of the particular termination of employment which occurred rather than a necessary consequence of any termination of the employment concerned.[4] In this respect he regarded the redundancy payment as a proximate consequence of the particular dismissal and the particular motivation for the dismissal.[5] He regarded the redundancy payment as more analogous to (deductible) unemployment benefit than to a (non-deductible) retirement pension.[6] This judgment is subject

---

[1] *Foxley* v. *Olton* [1965] 2 QB 306.

[2] In Grunfeld, *Modern Trade Union Law* (1966) it seems unemployment benefit provided by a union may fall under the category of 'trade benefit', i.e. benefit issued in pursuance of industrial dispute activities, like strike pay, or under the category of 'provident benefit', like sick pay. He says the former at p. 139, but the latter at p. 9.

[3] [1973] ICR 530.

[4] Ibid. at 534 C (rejecting a test based upon whether the plaintiff alone paid the premiums or contributions).

[5] Ibid. at 534 D–E.   [6] Ibid. at 534 F–G.

to the criticism that it ignores the plaintiff's loss for the future of his accumulated rights in respect of redundancy payment, as has since been recognized.[1]

G. Accounting for Contingencies in Damages for Wrongful Dismissal

The methods which are used for accounting for contingencies in damages for wrongful dismissal are ill defined, and follow no formulated principles. They may well produce results which would be highly unsatisfactory by the standards of actuarial calculations. The main requirement of an accounting for contingencies in quantifying damages for wrongful dismissal occurs in estimating the period of prospective loss of employment. This has been treated as requiring an allowance for the possibility that the contract of employment might have been frustrated by the incapacity of the employee during that relevant period, or terminated by reason of his misconduct, or voluntarily by him. For example, in *Re English Joint Stock Bank* (*Yelland's Case*)[2] the compensation payable to a bank manager for loss of employment resulting from the compulsory winding-up of the employing company[3] was reduced on account of 'the risk to health and life'.[4]

In *Salt* v. *Power Plant Co. Ltd.*[5] the damages for wrongful dismissal awarded to a company secretary, whose employment was terminable upon his ceasing to perform his duties 'to the satisfaction of the directors', were held to be subject to a reduction on account of the possibility that the directors might at a future date have thought they had good reasons, connected with the conduct of the employee,

---

[1] The principle of deduction of collateral benefits has been rigorously applied in awarding compensation for unfair dismissal, in so far as the NIRC has repeatedly ruled that all losses of earnings must be considered net of tax: *Norton Tool Co. Ltd.* v. *Tewson* [1972] ICR 501, 506 B–C (Sir John Donaldson); *Scottish Co-op. Ltd.* v. *Lloyd* [1973] ICR 137; *Springbank Sand & Gravel Co. Ltd.* v. *Craig* [1974] ICR 7. Furthermore, it was held in *Hilti (GB) Ltd.* v. *Windridge* [1974] ICR 352 that notional income tax must be deducted from compensation for loss of statutory protection of the right to minimum notice, and that deduction must be made in respect of unemployment benefit received. The notable exception to deductibility occurs in the ruling that redundancy payment was not deductible in *Yorkshire Engineering Ltd.* v. *Burnham* [1974] ICR 77 (not following *Stocks* v. *Magna Merchants Ltd.*). Section 150 of the 1971 Act made provision for regulations to be made concerning the relationship between unfair dismissal compensation and redundancy payments, but no regulations were made under this provision. See *Millington* v. *Goodwin & Sons Ltd.* [1975] ICR 104.

[2] (1867) LR 4 Eq. 350. [3] See below, pp. 332–4.
[4] Vice-Chancellor Wood, LR 4 Eq. 350 at 352. [5] [1936] 3 All ER 322.

for terminating the employment.[1] And in *Bold* v. *Brough, Nicholson Ltd.*,[2] the damages for wrongful dismissal of a managing director were reduced on account of the possibility of serious illness extending beyond six months and thus giving the employers the right to terminate the contract according to its terms.[3]

The estimation of the period of prospective loss of employment also involves a calculation of the probabilities of the plaintiff's being able to obtain suitable alternative employment. The process of accounting for contingencies in damages is at this point closely linked with the rules concerning mitigation of loss which were considered above. The process of accounting for the contingency of the plaintiff's mitigating his prospective loss of employment by obtaining employment elsewhere has been carried out in various different ways. Thus in *Yetton* v. *Eastwoods Froy Ltd.*,[4] Blain J. made a downward adjustment in the size of the salary which he assumed that the plaintiff would be able to obtain elsewhere, in order to take account of the contingency of his not being able to obtain suitable employment at all.

By contrast, in *Edwards* v. *Society of Graphical & Allied Trades*[5] the damages for loss of employment awarded against a union which had wrongfully expelled the plaintiff from membership were reduced to take account of the possibility of suitable alternative employment by adjusting the length of the notional period of prospective loss of employment. Assessing damages as if for personal injuries, Buckley J. applied a multiplier of ten years to the annual loss of earning capacity, calculating the multiplier according to the probability of other employment as a skilled craftsman.[6] Yet a further different method of accounting for this contingency was employed in *Slingsby* v. *News of the World Organisation Ltd.*[7] where a percentage reduction of 1 per cent was made on account of the possibility of the dismissed editor obtaining an executive position elsewhere.

There is a serious possibility of inconsistency when all these different methods are used to account for the contingency of alternative employment. There is, moreover, a danger that the courts may thereby encroach upon the rule that account is to be taken of the

---

[1] Greer L.J. [1936] 3 ALL ER 322, 325.   [2] [1964] 1 WLR 201.
[3] Phillimore J., ibid. at 206.   [4] [1967] 1 WLR 104 (above).
[5] [1970] 1 WLR 379. The damages were later reduced by the Court of Appeal—[1971] Ch. 354—where the method of assessment was much less specific.
[6] [1970] 1 WLR 379 at 387 H–388 A.   [7] *The Times*, 2 May 1970.

possibility only of *suitable* alternative employment. (That rule was discussed in the context of the mitigation of damages.[1]) There is an even more serious absence of general principle in those cases in which account is taken of the possibility that the employee might not have completed his period of employment under his original contract had it not been for the dismissal complained of.[2]

H. *Damages and Restitutionary Claims in respect of Past Services*

The courts have recognized a head of damages for wrongful dismissal consisting in damages for loss of wages in respect of a broken period of service actually rendered. If an employee is remunerated by salary which is calculated and paid by the month, and if the obligation to work is entire by the month, so that no remuneration is due in respect of an incomplete month, an employee who is wrongfully dismissed in the middle of the month will have no claim for *wages due* in respect of service rendered from the beginning of the month down to the date of wrongful dismissal. The wrongfully dismissed employee, however, has a claim in damages representing the loss of wages in respect of services actually rendered.[3]

The wrongfully dismissed employee can also recover that loss of wages in a totally different way, by making a *quantum meruit* claim of a restitutionary nature. This right of action was established in the case of a contract to write a series of articles for an encyclopedia in *Planché* v. *Colburn*;[4] and it was later regarded as applicable in cases of wrongful dismissal.[5] The remedy is available for recovery of the value of services for which payment had not accrued due under the contract at the time of the wrongful dismissal. The restitutionary

---

[1] See above, pp. 262–5.

[2] The law of compensation for unfair dismissal, being freed from some of the major restrictions upon common-law damages, has been required to contemplate longer periods of and wider varieties of loss than the common law was normally called upon to do. This has emphasized the complexity of the task concerned, and we can see the growth of new forms of accounting for contingencies in compensating for dismissal, as well as the reappearance of old forms. See, e.g., *Scottish Co-op. Ltd.* v. *Lloyd* [1973] ICR 137, 141C; *Vaughan* v. *Weighpack Ltd.* [1974] ICR 261; *Winterhalter Gastronom Ltd.* v. *Webb* [1973] ICR 245; *Vokes Ltd.* v. *Bear* [1974] ICR I.

[3] *Goodman* v. *Pocock* (1850) 15 QB 576, 580, per Lord Campbell C.J.; cf. the illuminating judgment of Latham C.J. in the Australian case of *Automatic Fire Sprinklers Proprietary Ltd.* v. *Watson* (1946) 72 CLR 435 at 451.

[4] (1831) 8 Bing. 14. See Goff and Jones, *The Law of Restitution* (1966) pp. 340–6 (rescission).

[5] *Goodman* v. *Pocock* (1850) 15 QB 576 per Lord Campbell C.J. at 580.

remedy has in recent times been relied upon only in the special case where the original contract is unenforceable against the employer for want of compliance with requirements of form.[1] With the reduction in scope of Section 4 of the Statute of Frauds 1677 by the Law Reform (Enforcement of Contracts) Act 1954, the remedy has lost its importance in that aspect too. The restitutionary claim is of small importance in the context of wrongful dismissal at the present day, and is mentioned for the sake of completeness.

SECTION 3: SPECIFIC PERFORMANCE AND INJUNCTIONS

The view that the contract of employment is effectively terminated by wrongful dismissal depends to a considerable extent upon the fact that the courts will not grant equitable remedies which would result in compulsory reinstatement of the employee. The reasoning is that the dismissal is effective in so far as no remedy is available to undo its effect. If the only remedy available is that of damages, it would seem to follow that the law treats the dismissal as a *fait accompli*.[2] The refusal of equitable remedies to compel the performance of the contract of employment[3] has two applications. The one is a refusal of orders of reinstatement directed against the employer, and the other is a refusal of orders to work directed against the employee. This section is devoted to an examination of the development of, and reasons for, this dual role. The early cases show that the objections to such orders were not operative before the nineteenth century; and that when they were recognized, it was in procedural rather than substantive terms. It was recognized in the course of the nineteenth century that there were substantive policy objections to the enforcement of the contract of employment. It is noticeable that the objections to reinstatement were more strongly felt than the objections to orders to work. There has, however, more recently been some judicial recognition of the arguments in favour of reinstatement. We proceed to examine these developments.

[1] *Scott v. Pattison* [1923] 2 KB 723, where the remedy was used to recover remuneration during sickness. For a criticism of the decision, see Goff and Jones, op. cit. p. 284.

[2] See below, pp. 294 ff.

[3] See *Chitty on Contracts*, (23rd edn. 1968) Vol. I, Ch. 27, Paras. 1529 ff.,1557 ff. *Fry on Specific Performance* (6th edn. 1921) pp. 51 ff.; *Kerr on Injunctions* (6th edn. 1927) pp. 412 ff.; Hanbury, *Modern Equity* (9th edn. 1969) (ed. Maudsley) Chapter 2, s. 7; Clark, 'Unfair Dismissal and Reinstatement' (1969) 32 MLR 532 at 534–8.

A. The Early Development of the Rule against Specific Performance

Certain early cases suggest that specific performance would at one time be awarded against an employer. *Ball* v. *Coggs* (1710)[1] was apparently such a case; it concerned a plaintiff employed as general manager of a brass-wire works for his life and remunerated at a yearly wage plus a commission in respect of every hundredweight of brass wire manufactured. Following his wrongful dismissal, he obtained an order requiring the employers to pay him his salary and requiring him to work for them, should they request him to do so. This was really an order upon the employer to continue to pay the employee rather than an order to reinstate him (though obviously it would have acted as a substantial inducement towards reinstatement). That much is made clear by a later judicial comment that 'In *Ball* v. *Coggs* specific performance was decreed in the House of Lords of a contract to pay the plaintiff a certain annual sum for his life and also a certain other sum for every hundredweight of brass wire manufactured . . .'[2] As such, the decision in *Ball* v. *Coggs* is an early exception to the rule that remuneration cannot be claimed after wrongful dismissal, rather than to the rule that reinstatement cannot be obtained after wrongful dismissal. If that case may be seen as not involving actual reinstatement, it is otherwise in the later case of *East India Co.* v. *Vincent* (1740)[3] where Lord Hardwicke L.C. made an order which involved actual reinstatement. This is, however, an isolated case which must be regarded as entirely overruled or disregarded by the many later authorities refusing remedies in the nature of reinstatement.

The cases in which it was established that specific performance would not be ordered of an obligation to perform personal services[4] proceed on the ground that equity will not make an order whose performance it cannot effectively supervise or whose performance would require constant supervision.[5] Thus Lord Eldon L.C.

[1] 1 Bro. Parl. Cas. 140.

[2] Sir John Leach V.C. in *Adderly* v. *Dixon* (1824) 1 Simons & Stuart 607 at 611.

[3] 2 Atkyns 83.

[4] *Clarke* v. *Price* (1819) 2 Wils. Ch. 157; *Baldwin* v. *Society for Diffusion of Useful Knowledge* (1838) 9 Simons 393 (obligation to act as a draughtsman of maps). Cf. *Kemble* v. *Kean* (1829) 6 Simons 333—refusal to enforce by injunction an obligation not to act except in a certain theatre, because that would be indirectly enforcing a positive obligation which the court could not enforce directly.

[5] Cf. *Ryan* v. *Mutual Tontine Association* [1893] 1 Ch. 116; see Megarry J. in *C.H. Giles & Co. Ltd.* v. *Morris* [1972] 1 All ER 960, 969 f–970 c, where the doctrine of impossibility of supervision is examined with scepticism; but Megarry J.

commented in *Clarke* v. *Price*,[1] a case concerning a law reporter who refused to perform his contract, 'If I cannot compel Mr. Price to remain in the Court of Exchequer for the purpose of taking notes, I can do nothing.' It was not until a rather later date that the refusal to make an order which would directly or indirectly compel persons to perform personal services was stated in terms of a humanitarian objection to involuntary servitude.[2]

It is not surprising that the humanitarian objection to orders to work was not strongly felt at an earlier date, for the law was not lacking in processes whereby pressure was put upon employees or upon other employers tending to ensure that obligations to render personal services were performed *in specie*. There were in force until 1867[3] a series of Master and Servant Acts which enabled manual employees to be imprisoned for absence in breach of their contracts of employment. The Master and Servant Act 1867 provided for the making of orders of specific performance against employees.[4] And the Employers and Workmen Act 1875 which repealed and replaced that Act conferred upon the County Courts[5] and magistrates[6] a power to take security for the performance of the contract of service by either party, in place of damages, and then to order performance of the contract (though that applied only where the defendant was willing to give security instead of paying damages). A power was also conferred to order the specific performance of his contract against an apprentice.[7]

B. *The Reasons for the Refusal of Orders of Specific Performance*

The policy objections to granting an order of reinstatement against the employer were recognized and acted upon much earlier than were the policy objections to ordering the employee to perform his

---

advances an alternative rationale which is really no more than a sophisticated variation upon the same theme.

[1] (1819) 2 Wils. Ch. 157 (above) at 165.

[2] e.g. by Fry L.J. in *De Francesco* v. *Barnum* (1890) 45 Ch.D. 430, 438; Lindley M.R. in *Robinson & Co.* v. *Heuer* [1898] 2 Ch. 451, 456.

[3] The Master and Servant Act 1867. The criminal jurisdiction survived in attenuated form until the Conspiracy & Protection of Property Act 1875 s. 17 and remained only in the special cases dealt with by Sections 4 and 5 of that Act: s. 4 was repealed by s. 133 of the 1971 Act.

[4] By Section 3 of the 1867 Act.   [5] Section 3 of the 1875 Act.

[6] Section 4 of the 1875 Act.

[7] The Employers and Workmen Act 1875 was repealed in its entirety, for obsoleteness, by the Statute Law (Repeals) Act 1973.

obligations.[1] The force which was accorded to the policy considerations against reinstatement of individual employees may be seen from *Johnson* v. *Shrewsbury & Birmingham Railway Co.*[2] where Knight-Bruce L.J. justified his decision in terms of the policy objections to compelling an individual employer to tolerate an individual employee whom he found incompatible.[3]

The refusal to allow reinstatement to an employee is elsewhere justified on the ground that the employee has no property interest in his job at all.[4] Thus Jessel M.R. stated in *Rigby* v. *Connol*[5] that:

'The Courts as such have never dreamt of enforcing agreements strictly personal in their nature, whether they are agreements of hiring and service, being the common relation of master and servant, or whether they are agreements for the purposes of pleasure . . . or scientific pursuits . . . or charity or philanthropy—in such cases no Court of Justice can properly interfere so long as there is no property the right to which is taken away from the person complaining.'[6]

That view was expressed in the context of a judgment about the jurisdiction of the courts in respect of members' rights against unincorporated associations and against trade unions in particular.[7] It was later applied to justify refusing an injunction to restrain the wrongful suspension or dismissal of a person employed as a surgeon by a charity hospital.[8] The complete denial of any property right in

---

[1] *Pickering* v. *Bishop of Ely* (1843) 2 Y & C Ch. Cas. 249 (office of receiver of profits for a bishop); *Stocker* v. *Wedderburn* (1857) 3 K & J 393 (employment as a company-promoter); *Brett* v. *East India Shipping Co. Ltd.* (1869) 2 Hem. & M 404 (employment as a broker); *Bainbridge* v. *Smith* (1889) 41 Ch. D 462 (employment as managing director).

[2] (1853) 3 De G, M & G 914.

[3] Ibid. at 926. Cf. Lord Abinger's use of analogies drawn from domestic service in *Priestley* v. *Fowler* (1837) 3 M & W 1 of which Lord Wright later commented that they expressed 'personal apprehensions rather than any principle': *Radcliffe* v. *Ribble Motor Services Ltd.* [1939] AC 215, 239.

[4] Compare the stages of the process of recognition of a proprietary interest in the job in the USA described by Meyers, *Ownership of Jobs* (UCLA, 1964) p. 3.

[5] (1881) 14 Ch. D. 482, 488.

[6] The dictum is ambiguous—it could refer either to relationships which are not the subject of any legal obligations, or to obligations which are not *specifically* enforceable. It seems to mean the latter in relation to master and servant.

[7] In relation to contracts of trade-union membership, and in applying the now repealed Section 4 of the Trade Union Act 1871, the courts moved away from this position. This case was practically overruled in *Amalgamated Society of Carpenters* v. *Braithwaite* [1922] 2 AC 440. See Grunfeld, *Modern Trade Union Law*, pp. 78–82.

[8] *Millican* v. *Sullivan* (1888) 4 TLR 203.

the job is significant; and may be contrasted with the recognition of a proprietary interest of the employer in the services of the employee, which was inherent in the torts protecting the employer against interference with the services of the employee.[1]

The refusal of an order of specific performance against the employer is sometimes justified on the ground that there would be a lack of mutuality in the granting of such a remedy. In the context of contracts involving obligations to perform personal services, the rule of mutuality has been applied to the effect that an order of reinstatement cannot be obtained against an employer, because specific performance will not lie to compel the rendering of personal services.[2] It is a rule which can be applied against either the employer or the employee. In *Page One Records Ltd.* v. *Britton*,[3] the argument of mutuality was applied in refusing to grant an injunction to restrain a pop-group from employing anybody other than the plaintiff as their manager, the argument being that the manager could not have been compelled to work for them by an order of specific performance, so that the grant of an injunction to him would lack mutuality.[4] The refusal of the injunction was also justified on the alternative ground that the grant of it would effectively compel the pop-group to work under the management of the plaintiff;[5] that is to say, it would have been a 'perform or starve' order. The argument as to mutuality should be approached with caution in the context of the contract of employment, because the merits of granting specific performance against the employee may well be very different from the merits of granting reinstatement to the employee. To treat the two arguments

---

[1] See, in relation to the tort of harbouring a servant, the remarks of Lord Goddard C.J. in *Jones Bros. (Hunstanton) Ltd.* v. *Stevens* [1955] 1 QB 275, 282. In *Attorney-General for New South Wales* v. *Perpetual Trustee Co. Ltd.* [1955] AC 457, the *actio per quod servitium amisit* was seen as having a similar historical basis—see Viscount Simonds at 482–3. Cf. *Inland Revenue Commissioners* v. *Hambrook* [1956] 2 QB 641 at 651–2 (Lord Goddard C.J.).

[2] *Pickering* v. *Bishop of Ely* (1843) 2 Y & C Ch. Cas. 249 (above); *Johnson* v. *Shrewsbury & Birmingham Railway Co.* (1853) 3 De G, M & G 914 (above); *Ogden* v. *Fossdick* (1862) 4 De G F & J 426; *Blackett* v. *Bates* (1865) LR 1 Ch. App. 117. The rule against specific enforcement of the employee's obligation to work or attend for work was given statutory force by section 128(1) of the 1971 Act. See Appendix, para. 9.

[3] [1968] 1 WLR 157.   [4] Stamp J., ibid. at 165 A–H.

[5] Ibid. at 166 F–167 B. A negative injunction which indirectly has the effect of specifically enforcing a positive obligation to work under a contract of employment may fall within the prohibition imposed by section 128(1) of the 1971 Act upon injunctions compelling the performance of service obligations. See above, note 2, and Appendix, para. 9.

as if they stood or fell together is to impose a purely formal equality between the parties which has little to do with the realities of the employment relationship.

C. Recent Developments in the Equitable Doctrine

The hopes which were entertained in some quarters that unfair dismissal legislation might provide the occasion for a discarding of earlier misgivings about compulsory reinstatement were not realized.[1] The Report of the Royal Commission expressed a rather traditionally formulated caution in the matter,[2] and the Industrial Relations Act ultimately did no more than empower Industrial Tribunals to recommend re-engagement on pain of an increase in the employee's compensation by reason of non-compliance with the recommendation—but still within the over-all upper limits upon compensation of £4,160 or 104 weeks' pay, whichever is the less.[3] At the time of writing, the unfair dismissal provisions are rapidly assuming the role of provisions concerned almost exclusively with compensation rather than reinstatement.[4]

It is therefore slightly ironical that when the Court of Appeal in *Hill* v. *C. A. Parsons & Co. Ltd.*[5] disregarded the long-standing rule of equity against compulsory reinstatement, they did so in order to safeguard the position of the employee concerned until the date of coming into force of the unfair dismissal provisions of the Industrial Relations Act. The plaintiff in that case was a chartered engineer aged 63 and a member of a union of professional engineers called UKAPE. He was dismissed by his employers reluctantly and solely

---

[1] The case in favour of reinstatement was powerfully argued by Clark, 'Unfair Dismissal and Reinstatement' (1969) 32 MLR 532 and in *Remedies for Unfair Dismissal*—PEP Broadsheet No. 518 June 1970. See also Wedderburn's *Evidence to the Royal Commission*—Minutes of Evidence, Day 31, p. 1261; The White Paper '*In Place of Strife*' (Cmnd. 3888) Para. 104.

[2] *Report of the Royal Commission* Chapter IX Paras. 551–2.

[3] 1971 Act ss. 106(4), 116(4), 118(1). See Appendix, Para. 2.

[4] Recommendations of re-engagement were made or upheld by the NIRC in *Curtis* v. *Paterson (Darlington) Ltd.* [1973] ICR 496 (damages awarded for non-compliance); *Shipside (Ruthin) Ltd.* v. *T.G.W.U.* [1973] ICR 503. In *Williams* v. *Loyds Ltd.* (1973) 8 ITR 502 Sir Diarmaid Conroy Q.C. set out the arguments for exemplary damages for non-compliance with such a recommendation. But the generally cautious approach to re-engagements is indicated by the relative rarity of recommendations for it, and also by the NIRC itself in *Morris* v. *Gestetner Ltd.* [1973] ICR 587, 592 B–F (Sir John Donaldson); *Coleman* v. *Magnet Joinery Ltd.* [1974] ICR 25, 30 G–31 B (Sir Hugh Griffiths); *Bateman* v. *British Leyland (UK) Ltd.* [1974] ICR 403, 407 D–H (Sir Hugh Griffiths).

[5] [1972] 1 Ch. 305.

by reason of pressure placed upon them by the trade union DATA.[1] The dismissal was upon one month's notice, which the Court of Appeal was satisfied was substantially shorter than the notice to which he was entitled under the common-law implied term as to reasonable notice.[2] In these circumstances, the Court of Appeal granted an injunction restraining the employers from treating their notice as having determined the employment concerned.

The limits of this decision are narrower than might at first be assumed. On the one hand the majority in the Court of Appeal was required to, and did, deny the absolute standing of the rule of equity against injunctions of this kind. In the words of Lord Denning M.R., 'It may be said that by granting an injunction in such a case, the court is indirectly enforcing specifically a contract for personal services. So be it.'[3] Sachs L.J. denied that the practice of refusing such injunctions in the case of the contract of service had become 'an inflexible rule of law which brooked no exceptions'.[4]

On the other hand, both members of the majority in the Court of Appeal were very clear in asserting that such injunctions were wholly exceptional.[5] The justification for departing from the general rule was to be found in the cumulative effect of, firstly, the impending application of the 1971 Act; secondly, the inadequacy of damages resulting from that fact; and thirdly, the reluctance of the employer to dismiss and the subsistence of mutual confidence between employer and employee.[6] These factors take the case a very substantial distance away from an ordinary issue of compulsory reinstatement. This decision has the character of a holding of the ring in an industrial dispute concerning union recognition. It has probably impinged only very slightly upon the previously existing attitude of the courts towards compulsory reinstatement.

SECTION 4: DECLARATIONS OF INVALIDITY OF WRONGFUL DISMISSAL

The unavailability of orders for the specific enforcement of the

---

[1] The inter-union recognition dispute which formed the background to this case is examined in *Commission on Industrial Relations Report No. 32 (1971)—C. A. Parsons & Co. Ltd. & associated companies.*
[2] See above, pp. 153–4.   [3] [1972] 1 Ch. 305, 315 A.
[4] Ibid. at 320 C–D.
[5] Lord Denning M.R., ibid. at 334 B, E; Sachs L.J. at 320 E.
[6] Cf. Sachs L.J., ibid. at 320 H.

contract of employment has led wrongfully dismissed employees to seek declarations that their dismissal was null and void, in order to establish that they are still in the position of persons employed under contracts of employment. The general rule has been that no such declaration will be made, because the wrongful dismissal is effective to terminate the contract of employment. There is, however, an important, and apparently widening, group of exceptions to that general rule. This group of exceptions represents, in fact, the encroachment of the principles of public and administrative law upon the private law of the contract of employment. Thus the courts have recognized that certain types of employee have the benefit of a specially protected status which justifies a declaration of invalidity of wrongful dismissal, and that in certain types of employment wrongful dismissal may be treated as *ultra vires* the employing body and void upon that ground. The width of these categories of employment is ill defined. In other cases, it has been recognized that a declaration may be available on the basis that the person employed is the holder of an office rather than an employee. It would also seem that a declaration may be available where a dismissal is prohibited by statute or regulation.

A. The General Principle

In the case of an ordinary contract of employment, the court will not grant a declaration that the wrongful dismissal was null and void.[1] A declaration will lie to declare a breach of contract,[2] and it would seem that there could be no objection to a declaration that a dismissal was *wrongful*. Thus Barry J. in *Barber* v. *Manchester Regional Hospitals Board*[3] commented that:

'The second claim is for a declaration that his employment with the board has never been validly determined. The significant word is the word *validly*. If the declaration asked for was one which merely declared that the plaintiff's employment had never been *lawfully* or *rightly* determined, that is a declaration which, if necessary at all, would follow from the findings which I have already made.'

The refusal to declare invalidity of wrongful dismissal in the

---

[1] *Vine* v. *National Dock Labour Board* [1957] AC 488; Viscount Kilmuir L.C. at 500; Lord Keith at 507.
[2] See Zamir, *The Declaratory Judgment* (London 1962) pp. 129–37, for an account of the scope of the declaration in contract cases.
[3] [1958] 1 WLR 181 at 194–5.

ordinary case of employer and employee has sometimes been seen as a consequence of the unavailability of specific performance.[1] Elsewhere it has been seen as resulting from the fact that the contract of employment is in principle terminated by wrongful dismissal. However, this principle is itself largely the result of the unavailability of a claim for continuing wages or a claim for specific performance, as is indicated in this dictum of Lord Keith: 'Normally, and apart from the intervention of statute, there would never be a nullity in terminating an ordinary contract of master and servant. Dismissal might be in breach of contract and so unlawful, but could only sound in damages.'[2] This reasoning may be questioned on the ground that one remedy is being refused on the ground of the unavailability of another. That reasoning does not apply throughout the law concerning declarations. Thus Zamir has shown how declaratory relief may be available in some cases where statutes expressly disallow actions for the enforcement of a contract.[3]

B. The Exceptions—Protected Status and Ultra Vires

There are certain types of employment, or of relationships akin to contracts of employment, in which the principle examined in the preceding subsection will not apply, and wrongful dismissal will be declared null and void. The first considered departure from the rule against declarations of invalidity of dismissal occurred in Vine v. National Dock Labour Board.[4] Declarations of invalidity of dismissal had earlier been made in favour of teachers,[5] but without consideration of the objection in principle to such a declaration.[6]

---

[1] e.g. Lord Morris, delivering the advice of the Privy Council in Francis v. Kuala Lumpur Councillors [1962] 1 WLR 1411, 1417–18.

[2] Lord Keith in Vine v. N.D.L.B. [1957] AC 488, 507. So also, Barry J. in Barber v. Manchester Regional Hospital Board [1958] 1 WLR 181 at 195. See below, pp. 294 ff.

[3] Op. cit. pp. 135–7, citing, inter alia, the grant of declarations in relation to contracts between unions and their members, the direct enforcement of which was prevented by s. 4 of the Trade Union Act 1871.

[4] [1957] AC 488 applying Barnard v. N.D.L.B. [1953] 2 QB 18—in which a declaration of invalidity of suspension had been made on the ground of improper delegation.

[5] Martin v. Eccles Corporation [1919] 1 Ch. 387; Hanson v. Radcliffe R.D.C. [1922] 2 Ch. 490; Sadler v. Sheffield Corporation [1924] 1 Ch. 483.

[6] Except that Lawrence J. commented in Fennell v. East Ham Corporation [1926] 1 Ch. 641, 642 that Short v. Poole Corporation [1926] 1 Ch. 66 had 'disposed of the objection that the action was in substance for the specific performance of a contract of service'. No ground for this view is stated.

This case concerned the dismissal of the plaintiff by the National Dock Labour Board from the reserve pool of dockers. The reserve pool was part of the Scheme constituted by the Dock Workers (Regulation of Employment) Order 1947[1] whereby the National Dock Labour Board was required to keep a register of dock workers and to pay stand-by wages to casual dock workers during the time when they were not employed. The plaintiff's dismissal from the reserve pool, and his deregistration from the Scheme, were procedurally incorrect in that the local Dock Labour Board had improperly delegated its disciplinary function to a disciplinary committee.

This departure from the general rule may be regarded as having been based upon one or both of two grounds:—

(a) The purported dismissal was *ultra vires* a statutory body.[2]
(b) The Docks Work Scheme conferred upon the registered dock worker a special status, that is to say it gave him an interest of a proprietary nature distinct from the ordinary contractual interest under a contract of employment.[3] The Scheme may be regarded as having conferred a 'status' in various senses:—
    (i) It guaranteed a fall-back wage irrespective of availability of actual work.
    (ii) It conferred an exclusive opportunity for employment as a dock worker; deregistration would have the consequence that the person concerned would not be allowed to obtain employment as a dock worker.
    (iii) It conferred a particular security of tenure in that dismissal by the local Dock Labour Boards was limited by the Scheme to cases where the employee failed to comply with the provisions of the Scheme.[4]

It is a matter of some importance as to which one or more of these factors must be present in order to justify the departure from the rule against declarations of invalidity of dismissal. The cases in which declarations have been given to declare dismissal of school-

---

[1] S.I. 1947 No. 1189, now greatly amended by the Dock Workers (Regulation of Employment) (Amendment) Order 1967 (S.I. No. 1252) which implements the decasualization of employment in the docks.

[2] Viscount Kilmuir [1957] AC 488 at 500; Lord Cohen, ibid. at 505–6.

[3] Lord Keith, ibid. at 508; Lord Morton at 503–4 and Lord Somervell at 512–13, adopting the views of Jenkins L.J. (diss.) in CA [1956] 1 QB 658 at 674–7.

[4] Lord Morris delivering the advice of the Privy Council in *Francis v. Kuala Lumpur Councillors* [1962] 1 WLR 1411 (above) treats this as the feature distinguishing the Dock Work Scheme from an ordinary contract of employment (at p. 1418).

teachers invalid seem to proceed primarily upon the ground that the dismissal was *ultra vires* a body whose powers were defined by statute.[1] That reasoning is explicit in the judgment of Barry J. in *Price v. Sunderland Corporation*,[2] where he says,

'. . . A local authority or any statutory body cannot . . . either employ or dismiss servants except under statutory authority; their powers are derived from the statute or statutes under which they are created, and it is a well-known principle of law that statutory powers can only be exercised for the purposes for which they are granted.'[3]

This represents a very wide view of the power of the courts to review dismissals of employees of public authorities on the grounds of *ultra vires*.

It should be noted, however, that a number of the cases concerning the dismissal of teachers have been cases where the local authority has not been the employer of the teachers but has been intervening to exercise special powers of dismissal conferred as against teachers in non-provided schools.[4] The cases where the local authority intervened to insist upon dismissal, not as the employer, but as the third party, were often cases in which the managers or governors of the school themselves opposed the dismissal; the cases were in one sense disputes concerning the extent of local authority control over independent schools rather than ordinary disputes between employer and employee.[5] The argument against reinstatement is much weaker

---

[1] *Martin* v. *Eccles Corporation* [1919] 1 Ch. 387; *Hanson* v. *Radcliffe R.D.C.* [1922] 2 Ch. 490; *Sadler* v. *Sheffield Corporation* [1924] 1 Ch. 483; cf. Lord Reid in *Malloch* v. *Aberdeen Corporation* [1971] 1 WLR 1578, 1584 E–F: 'if an employer [sc. a public authority] fails to take the preliminary steps which the law regards as essential, he has no *power* to dismiss and any purported dismissal is a nullity' (emphasis added).

[2] [1956] 1 WLR 1253.   [3] Ibid. at 1268–9.

[4] *Martin* v. *Eccles Corporation* [1919] 1 Ch. 387; *Hanson* v. *Radcliffe R.D.C.* [1922] 2 Ch. 490; *Sadler* v. *Sheffield Corp.* [1924] 1 Ch. 483. By contrast, *Price* v. *Rhondda U.D.C.* [1923] 2 Ch. 372, *Short* v. *Poole Corp.* [1926] 1 Ch. 66 and *Fennell* v. *East Ham Corp.* [1926] 1 Ch. 641 were cases where the teachers were in the employment of the local authority, but where it was held that the dismissals had been *intra vires*.

[5] The dichotomy between the employer and the local education authority in such cases is a source of potential injustice to the teacher, which the 1971 Act recognized and largely removed by enacting that a teacher in an aided school, dismissed on the requirements of the local education authority, should have rights in respect of unfair dismissal directly against the authority as if they had been his employer and had dismissed him (s. 148).

in those cases, in that there was no question of forcing an employee upon an unwilling employer.

The uncertainty concerning the grounds upon which a court may declare a wrongful dismissal null and void is increased by two contrasting decisions concerning personnel employed by regional hospital boards. Both cases concerned contracts of employment whose terms were controlled by ministerial directives which provided for an appeal against dismissal. In *Barber* v. *Manchester Regional Hospital Board*,[1] Barry J. held that a dismissal which had taken place without implementation of the appeal procedure could not be declared null and void, because the contract was in essence nothing more than an ordinary contract between master and servant despite the strong statutory flavour attaching to it.[2] However, in the Scottish case of *Palmer* v. *Inverness Hospitals Board of Management*,[3] a person similarly employed was held to be entitled to an order for reduction of the dismissal (which is the remedy in Scots law corresponding to a declaration of invalidity of dismissal),[4] where the principles of natural justice had not been observed in the course of the appeal procedure. The cases can be distinguished on the ground that *Barber's* case concerned an external appeal to the Minister while *Palmer's* case concerned an internal appeal to an appellate committee; but it is the view of this writer that this distinction is an unduly narrow one which conceals a more general uncertainty about the ambit of the principle of *ultra vires* in dismissal cases.

It may be that a declaration of invalidity of dismissal will be made on the basis that the contract of employment concerned was for permanent employment and was not terminable except on specified grounds. This may confer upon the employee that protected status which comes within the principle of *Vine* v. *National Dock Labour Board*. This may be inferred from the grant of a declaration of invalidity of dismissal in *McClelland* v. *North Ireland General Health Services Board*.[5] The point, however, was not there discussed, and against that must be set the reaffirmation by the Privy Council, more recently expressed,[6] of the principle that wrongful dismissals

---

[1] [1958] 1 WLR 181.   [2] Ibid. at 196.   [3] [1963] SLTR 124.
[4] Lord Guest's assertion in *Malloch* v. *Aberdeen Corporation* [1971] 1 WLR 1578, 1594 E, that the remedy of declaration bears no resemblance to the Scottish action of reduction seems hard to support in this context.
[5] [1957] 1 WLR 594.
[6] In *Francis* v. *Kuala Lumpur Councillors* [1962] 1 WLR 1411 at 1418.

will be declared invalid only in special circumstances and at the entire discretion of the court.

The general conclusion may be drawn that the grounds upon which a declaration of invalidity of dismissal was granted in *Vine* v. *National Dock Labour Board* are of a very wide potential application; so wide that there is a marked need for further rules to establish its limits. The House of Lords showed recently in *Malloch* v. *Aberdeen Corporation*[1] how fine the dividing line may be between an ordinary contract of employment and a specially protected status. This case concerned a Scottish teacher employed by a local education authority subject to statutory provisions for prior discussion by the authority of any motion to dismiss a teacher, with three weeks' notice to the teacher of the meeting at which the dismissal was to be considered. It was held by a bare majority[2] that these statutory safeguards impliedly conferred upon the teacher the right to a hearing before dismissal, which right in turn conferred a protected status upon the employee such that a dismissal not complying with that condition was to be invalidated by the remedy of reduction. This case bears out the view that the development of protected employment status is very closely bound up with the gradual and uncertain extension of the principles of natural justice into the employment relationship.[3]

The principles which have been discussed in this subsection are not necessarily limited entirely to public employment in their application. The doctrine of *ultra vires* as it applies to companies has been invoked to challenge the capacity of the company as to the type of activity which it may undertake, rather than in order to challenge the exercise of existing powers,[4] and to that extent is unlikely to operate to invalidate dismissals of employees of the company.[5] However, the idea of a specially protected status may very well have some application in private employment. Comparison may be made with the decision of the Court of Appeal in *Dunk* v. *George Waller Ltd.*,[6] in which it was held that an apprentice in

---

[1] [1971] 1 WLR 1578.

[2] Lords Reid, Wilberforce and Simon; Lords Morris and Guest dissenting.

[3] Compare Ganz, 'Public Law Principles Applicable to Dismissal from Employment' (1967) 30 MLR 288 esp. at 291–2.

[4] See Gower, *Modern Company Law* (3rd edn. 1969) Ch. 3, esp. p. 83.

[5] The *ultra vires* doctrine is probably now precluded from any theoretical possibility of use in this contest by Section 9(1) of the European Communities Act 1972.

[6] [1970] 2 QB 163—see above, p. 249.

effect had such a status by reason of the qualification which he would obtain by the completion of his apprenticeship.

C. Nullity of Wrongful Dismissal in the case of Office-holders

There is some suggestion in the cases that the availability of a declaration to declare a wrongful dismissal invalid may depend upon whether the claimant can be regarded as the holder of an office or as an officer.[1] The consequences of tenure of office, where it is not an office terminable at pleasure,[2] are twofold. Firstly, the office-holder is entitled to the benefit of the principles of natural justice in deciding whether or not he is liable to dismissal.[3] Secondly, if those principles have not been observed, then he is entitled to an order of *certiorari* to quash the dismissal or a declaration to render it invalid.[4]

There is, however, a lack of any satisfactory criterion for distinguishing between the holder of an office and an ordinary employee. We consider first certain employments whose holders are recognized to be the holders of office, and examine what are the distinguishing features of those employments. The case of the police officer is a clear one, for he has been held not to be an ordinary employee of either the local authority[5] or any other body or person.[6] The older

---

[1] Cf. *Vidyodaya University Council* v. *Silva* [1965] 1 WLR 77 at 88–9 (Lord Morris).

[2] See per Lord Reid in *Ridge* v. *Baldwin* [1964] AC 40, 65–6 for the distinction between 'dismissal from an office held during pleasure and dismissal from office where there must be something against a man to warrant his dismissal'. And see *Tucker* v. *Trustees of British Museum, The Times* 8 December 1967, (1968) 112 Sol. Jo. 70 where it was held that a scientific officer held an office terminable at the pleasure of the Trustees. It is now suggested by dicta in *Malloch* v. *Aberdeen Corp.* [1971] 1 WLR 1578 that an office held during pleasure is held subject to removal upon reasonable notice, but for which the reasons need not be stated, i.e. it is like an ordinary contract of employment: see Lord Reid at [1971] 1 WLR 1581 H, Lord Guest at 1592 D–G citing *Morrison* v. *Abernethy School Board* (1876) 3 Rettie 945.

[3] *R.* v. *Smith* (1844) 5 QB 614, Lord Denman C.J.; *Osgood* v. *Nelson* (1872) LR 5 HL. 636; *Fisher* v. *Jackson* [1891] 2 Ch. 84; *Cooper* v. *Wilson* [1937] 2 KB 309; *Hogg* v. *Scott* [1947] KB 759; *Ridge* v. *Baldwin* [1964] AC 40.
The judgment of Lord Wilberforce in *Malloch* v. *Aberdeen Corp.* [1971] 1 WLR 1578 at 1596 F–H, 1597 F–H shows how, even when the distinction between office-holders and servants is not regarded as absolute, the terminology of 'office' is a strong pointer towards the applicability of natural justice *as a matter of statutory interpretation.*

[4] e.g. *Ridge* v. *Baldwin* [1964] AC 40.

[5] *Fisher* v. *Oldham Corp.* [1930] 2 KB 364.

[6] *Ridge* v. *Baldwin* [1964] AC 40, Lord Reid at 65. It was this fact which made

cases in which the courts issued *certiorari* to quash a dismissal from office concerned offices in the nature of freehold office or life tenure, of which a good example is the office of parish clerk.[1] Employments which were at one time in the nature of freehold offices are today commonly subject to statutory regulation.[2]

Schoolmasters of endowed schools have been held to qualify as officers of charities, in such a way as to enable a wrongful dismissal to be treated as invalid[3] (unless the teacher holds that office only at the pleasure of the governors).[4] The basis of the jurisdiction to grant an injunction in such cases was described as follows by Bowen L.J. in *Rendall* v. *Blair*,[5] a case where the purported dismissal was the act of persons not authorized to dismiss the teacher:

'The Plaintiff's case is really one of contract only or of common law right. He is simply enforcing here, or seeking to enforce, what he considers to be his common law right not to be dismissed by those who have not employed him, and to hold premises [i.e. a school house] which he has received from persons who are authorised to deal with the possession against the unlawful and unauthorised usurpation of those who are strangers altogether in the matter.'

This passage suggests that the courts regarded the employee as having a vested interest in the possession of the school house which took the case outside the ordinary rule relating to the contract of employment.

These are particular examples; it may be suggested, by way of general definition of the distinction between employees and office-holders, that the characteristics of offices are their public nature and the security of tenure which they provide. Thus, for Lord Atkin it was by its permanence that an office was distinguishable from an ordinary employment:

'There is no statutory definition of 'office'. Without adopting the sentence

---

it necessary for s. 48 of the Police Act 1964 to make a subordinate police officer the notional servant of the Chief Constable for the purpose of vicarious liability in tort.

[1] *R.* v. *Gaskin* (1799) 8 TR 209; *R.* v. *Smith* (1844) 5 QB 614. Cf. *Tucker* v. *Trustees of the British Museum* (1968) 112 Sol. Jo. 70.

[2] See Bradley [1965] CLJ 3, 7 (in a note on *Vidyodaya University Council* v. *Silva* [1965] 1 WLR 77).

[3] *Willis* v. *Childe* (1851) 13 Beav. 117; *Fisher* v. *Jackson* [1891] 2 Ch. 84.

[4] *R.* v. *Darlington School Governors* (1844) 6 QB 682.

[5] (1890) 45 Ch. D. 139, 156; quoted with approval by North J. in *Fisher* v. *Jackson* [1891] 2 Ch. 84, 95.

as a complete definition, one may treat the following expression of Rowlatt J. in *Great Western Railway Co.* v. *Bater*[1] as a generally sufficient statement of the meaning of the word: "An office or employment which was a subsisting permanent substantive position which had an existence independent of the person who filled it, which went on and was filled in succession by successive holders." '[2]

Lord Wright also emphasized the public characteristic of 'office': 'The word "office" is of indefinite content. Its various meanings cover four columns of the New English Dictionary but I take as the most relevant for the purposes of this case the following: "a position or place to which certain duties are attached, especially of a more or less public character." '[3] This suggests that it is the responsibilities owed to the community by virtue of certain employments which distinguish the persons engaged upon them as holders of office.

However, these indications of a definition of the term 'office-holder' show that the attempt to decide whether a declaration will lie to invalidate a dismissal, by reference to the question whether the dismissed person holds an office, can very easily become a circular argument. For to distinguish between office-holders and ordinary employees is to pose in another form the very questions which arise in deciding the general issue of when a declaration will lie to hold a wrongful dismissal null and void, namely the questions whether public law principles apply and whether the dismissed person was entitled to a special protection of his security of tenure. It may further be suggested that the distinction between remunerated office-holders and employees is one which has lost much of its meaning by reason of the decline of the freehold office, so that in present-day conditions it tends to confuse rather than to elucidate the general problem of the legal protection of security of employment.

D. *The Effect of Statutory Prohibitions upon Dismissal*

A further exception to the rule against declarations of invalidity of dismissal appears to be constituted by the type of case where there is a prohibition upon dismissal, imposed by statute or by regulation. This type of case is distinguishable from that of a statutory scheme of employment, in the sense previously considered, for there may

---

[1] [1920] 3 KB 266, 274; adopted by Lord Atkinson on appeal in the same case [1922] 2 AC 1, 15. (Both cases were concerned with the meaning of 'public offices or employments of profit' in Schedule E of successive Income Tax Acts.)
[2] *McMillan* v. *Guest* [1942] AC 561, 564.   [3] Ibid. at 566.

be a statutory prohibition upon dismissal in cases of private employment where the employer is not a statutory authority. That there is such an exception to the general rule is illustrated by the decision in *Taylor* v. *Furness Withy Ltd.*,[1] which concerned employment with a private employer, regulated by the provisions of the scheme for the decasualization of dock labour.[2] The Scheme provides that a permanent worker in private employment shall not have his employment terminated, except in accordance with the provisions of the Scheme.[3] Those provisions allow for dismissal only for misconduct or with the permission of the local Dock Labour Board.[4] Upon a dismissal which was neither for misconduct nor with the permission of the Board, but at the insistence of a union concerned with the preservation of a closed shop, a declaration was given that the employment had never been validly terminated. If this decision is upheld, then decasualization will have conferred upon dock workers in permanent private employment a security of tenure as great as that of registered dock workers under the old reserve-pool scheme, and a security of tenure protected by the same remedies as those formerly available to employees of the National Dock Labour Board itself.

Comparison may be made with the effect of other provisions of statute or of regulation which forbid dismissal except with the permission of a third party. Such a provision was made by the Education Acts of 1902 and 1921,[5] whereby teachers in non-provided schools could be dismissed by the governors or managers of those schools only with the consent of the local authority, unless the dismissal was connected with the teaching of religious education, a sphere in which the independence of the school authorities was left intact. There was a conflict of judicial opinion upon the question whether a teacher dismissed without the requisite consent of the local authority could found upon the statutory provision a claim for an injunction restraining the dismissal, or for a declaration declaring it invalid. Buckley J. in *Young* v. *Cuthbert*[6] held that this provision was operative only as between the authority and the

---

[1] (1969) 6 KIR 488.

[2] Dock Workers (Regulation of Employment) (Amendment) Order 1967 (S.I. 1967 No. 1252).

[3] Para 14A(1) of the Scheme.   [4] Paras 14A(2), 17(1)(a).

[5] s. 7(1)(c) of the 1902 Act; s. 29(1)(c) of the 1921 Act (repealed and replaced by s. 24(2)(a) of the Education Act 1944).

[6] [1906] 1 Ch. 451.

school managers, and did not give any right to the teacher—the only consequence of non-compliance being that the local education authority was released from its obligation to maintain the school out of public funds. However, Warrington J. in *Smith* v. *Macnally*[1] took the opposite view, commenting that:

'The plaintiff in this case is not merely in the position of a servant who has contracted with a master, and in whose contract it is a term that she shall not be dismissed except upon compliance with certain conditions, but that she has a statutory right to the position which she has acquired under the Act unless and until the requirements of the Act with regard to dismissal have been complied with.'[2]

In later cases the Court of Appeal and the House of Lords expressly refused to resolve this conflict, deciding the cases before them on other grounds.[3] The question whether the statutes had conferred a special security of tenure upon teachers in non-provided schools was left undecided.[4]

The Essential Work Order[5] made a provision of the same kind, enacting that, in employments to which it applied, the person carrying on the undertaking should not terminate (except for serious misconduct) the employment in the undertaking of any specified person except with the permission in writing of a National Service Officer.[6] It was held that this provision had the effect that an employee could claim that a purported dismissal without the requisite permission was null and void.[7] Thus Goddard L.J. ruled that: 'If a statute says that a person shall not terminate a contract except with the permission of a third person . . . it follows that he is incapable of terminating it

[1] [1912] 1 Ch. 816 at 824. Cf. *Crisp* v. *Holden* (1910) 54 Sol. Jo. 784 (interim injunction given).
[2] This is notably similar to Lord Reid's reason for the decision in *Malloch* v. *Aberdeen Corp.* [1971] 1 WLR 1578, 1582 G–H, see above, p. 284.
[3] *Blanchard* v. *Dunlop* [1917] 1 Ch. 165; *Harries* v. *Crawfurd* [1919] AC 717.
[4] In *Hannam* v. *Bradford City Council* [1970] 1 WLR 937, a teacher at a voluntary school proceeded against the local authority in contract for failing to prohibit his dismissal. It was held that the authority must observe the principles of natural justice in deciding whether to exercise this power; but that the teacher has no direct contract with the authority in such a case.
[5] Essential Work (General Provisions) (No. 2) Order 1942 SR & O 1942 No. 1594.
[6] Article 4(1)(a); Article 4(1)(b) contained a corresponding prohibition upon unauthorized departure by the employee.
[7] *George* v. *Mitchell & King Ltd.* [1943] 1 AER 233; *Woolley* v. *Allen Fairhead Ltd.* [1946] 1 KB 461; so also the leading Australian case of *Automatic Fire Sprinklers Proprietary Ltd.* v. *Watson* (1946) 72 CLR 435.

without that permission. If he refuses to employ that person, he commits an offence, but the contract is not terminated.'¹ Hence it seems that a statutory prohibition upon unauthorized dismissal may be held to create a security of tenure which will cause the unauthorized dismissal to be treated as invalid by the courts.

E. The Effect of Declarations of Invalidity of Dismissal

The reluctance of the judges to grant a declaration that a dismissal is null and void has been due in part to their view that the effect of such a declaration would have the result that wages would be payable as from the date of the purported dismissal onwards. The effect would then be that the rules of mitigation of loss would be circumvented, the employee would have been allowed to 'sit in the sun' at the employer's expense,² and this the judges have regarded as undesirable. It has, on the whole, been taken for granted that this is the effect of a declaration of nullity of dismissal.

In the leading English case on declarations of invalidity of dismissal, the effect of such a declaration upon wages following the purported dismissal is unclear. For in *Vine* v. *National Dock Labour Board*³ the plaintiff was awarded, not remuneration as such, but £250 damages for loss of remuneration.⁴ The awarding of *damages* would suggest that the view was taken that wages were not payable as such; more especially as there was a time lapse of two and a half years between the purported dismissal and the date of the trial, so that the sum awarded did not represent the actual loss of wages since the wrongful dismissal.

In *Francis* v. *Kuala Lumpur Councillors*,⁵ Lord Morris, delivering the advice of the Privy Council, commented, however, that: 'The practical effect [of a declaration of invalidity of dismissal] would be

---

¹ *George* v. *Mitchell & King Ltd.* [1943] 1 All ER 233, 239 E–G. In the Disabled Persons (Employment) Act 1944 it was felt necessary to provide that: 'The fact that the making, termination or variation of a contract involves a contravention of any of the provisions of this Act relating to the duty of employers to give employment to persons registered as handicapped by disablement . . . shall not affect the operation in law of the contract, or of its termination or variation, as the case may be' (s. 13(5)).
² Cf. Salmon L.J. in *Denmark Productions Ltd.* v. *Boscobel Productions Ltd.* [1969] 1 QB 699 at 726 D–E.
³ [1957] AC 488.
⁴ A particular complication in this case is the nature of the payments made by the Dock Labour Board as compensation for lack of employment rather than as wages in respect of employment.
⁵ [1962] 1 WLR 1411, 1418.

to give to the appellant a monetary claim far in excess of any measure of damages to which the appellant appears to the Board to be entitled as flowing from a wrongful dismissal.' This indicates both a view that the declaration would result in a continuance of wages, and also the reluctance of the courts to allow that result. The same view, and the same reluctance, appear in *Ridge* v. *Baldwin*[1] where Lord Devlin says:

'What is unfortunate about the result is that it means that during the whole time taken up in the elucidation of this difficult point of law, the appellant has been legally in office and entitled to the appropriate emoluments.[2] That would be so, I suppose, even if he had been in profitable employment elsewhere, for his claim would be for salary, and not damages for wrongful dismissal.'

The reluctance of the courts to allow such a remedy may be understood if the facts of *Taylor* v. *Furness Withy Ltd.*[3] are considered. It was there held that the declaration of invalidity of dismissal entitled the plaintiff to an account to determine the amount of wages due, and to payment thereof. The plaintiff was dismissed, as the result of union intervention, on the very day on which his work was to begin. The date of the trial was two and a half years later; he thus became entitled to his wages for the entire intervening period.

The possibility of a new and different approach is suggested by *Taylor* v. *National Union of Seamen.*[4] The plaintiff was a member and a paid official of the defendant trade union. He was dismissed from his post as an official and this dismissal rendered him ineligible under the rules of the union for union office. Wishing to stand for office some five years after the dismissal, he sought a declaration of invalidity of dismissal. It was held that a provision in the rule book for an appeal against dismissal from office conferred upon him the right to the implementation of the rules of natural justice in the course of the appeal, and that those rules had not been observed. As to the remedy, Ungoed-Thomas J. held that it would be unreal to make a declaration to the effect that the plaintiff had continued to

[1] [1964] AC 40, 140.

[2] In the settlement which was ultimately reached of this action, the appellant obtained £6,424 arrears of salary from the date of wrongful dismissal to the date of the settlement, and a pension thereafter. *The Guardian*, 30 July 1963. See Ganz, 'Judicial Control over the Exercise of Discretion' [1964] Public Law 367, 382–3.

[3] (1969) 6 KIR 488.   [4] [1967] 1 WLR 532.

be in the employment of the union, because he did in fact obtain other employment and had been in that employment for years, but that his disabilities as a member by reason of the wrongful dismissal seriously affected his position and his prospects of a future career in the union. Accordingly he should have the protection of a declaration that the union should not treat him as if he were dismissed for misconduct.[1] The possibility suggested is that of a declaration which preserves all those prospective rights of the employee which flow from a continuance in employment, without giving him the right to wages between purported dismissal and trial, because the latter might lead to considerable over-compensation of the employee.[2] Occasions might well arise, for example, in which it might be a useful remedy to declare a dismissal invalid for the purpose only of pension rights depending upon the continuity of employment and not for the purpose of continuing remuneration. We now turn to consider the underlying problems of contractual theory raised by wrongful dismissal.

SECTION 5: WRONGFUL DISMISSAL AND THE TERMINATION OF THE CONTRACT

The effect of wrongful dismissal upon the contract of employment presents perhaps the greatest single theoretical problem arising in this branch of the law. The distinction between wrongful dismissal and wrongful repudiation adds further to the problem. The issue is whether wrongful dismissal in itself terminates the contract of employment. The alternative possibility is that the contract will remain in being unless the employee elects to accept a termination, at least until the expiry of a notional period of due notice. The problem arises because the general principles of contract law have, at

---

[1] Ibid. at 553 A–D. In the more recent decision in *Leary* v. *National Union of Vehicle Builders* [1971] Ch. 34 no such compromise was possible, and Megarry J. refused an interlocutory injunction which would have had the effect of restoring a wrongfully expelled union official to office. His refusal was based partly on the ground that such an injunction would be akin to specific performance of a contract of service—ibid. at p. 727 G–H.

[2] Cf. Sir John Donaldson in *Morris* v. *Gestetner Ltd.* [1973] ICR 587 at 592 C–D: 'The power conferred by [the 1971 Act] is to recommend "re-engagement" and not "reinstatement". "Reinstatement" is retroactive in effect. It involves a revocation of the dismissal and payment of wages for the intervening period. "Re-engagement" leaves the dismissal unaffected and an intervening period of unemployment.'

least until recently, dictated that wrongful repudiation of a contract does not in itself terminate a contract, but gives an election to the injured party whether to treat the contract as terminated or still on foot. But wrongful dismissal has always appeared particularly difficult to rationalize in these terms. Wrongful dismissal does terminate the employment in a factual sense, and remedies have not normally been available to challenge this factual termination. In this section we shall examine the state of the law in relation to this problem and conclude by suggesting a possible approach to the theoretical difficulties.

The theory that termination by repudiation requires the acceptance of the injured party is probably still dominant in terms of general contractual principles.[1] This is despite arguments showing the theory to be relatively recent and not conceptually necessary.[2] But this theoretical position has of late been complicated by the recognition that a fundamental breach of contract may inflict such catastrophic damage upon the prospects for the contract as to render an election to terminate otiose and therefore unnecessary.[3] From there it is a short step to regarding certain grave breaches as terminating the contract, not only automatically, but also retroactively at least so far as exception clauses[4] and demurrage clauses[5] are concerned. Furthermore the doctrine in *White & Carter (Councils) Ltd.* v. *McGregor*,[6] of all recent case-law developments, relies most heavily on the elective theory of termination by breach. Yet its doctrine, of avoidance of a duty to mitigate loss by keeping the contract on foot, has been recognized from the outset as applying only where the co-operation of the repudiator is not required for the contract to remain operative.[7] And there are signs of the growth of a body of law to determine when co-operation is regarded as necessary for this purpose.[8] But these imperfections in the theory of elective termination have not

---

[1] See *Decro-Wall International S.A.* v. *Practitioners in Marketing Ltd.* [1971] 1 WLR 361 per Salmon L.J. 369 H–370 G; Sachs L.J. 375 A–H; Buckley L.J. 380 H–381 D.

[2] See Coote, 'The Effect of Discharge by Breach on Exception Clauses' [1970] CLJ 221, 224–7.

[3] Cf. *Harbutt's 'Plasticine' Ltd.* v. *Wayne Tank & Pump Co. Ltd.* [1970] 1 QB 447. See below, pp. 323–4.

[4] As in the *Harbutt's Plasticine Case* (above).

[5] Cf. per Lord Reid in the *Suisse Atlantique* case [1967] 1 AC 361, 398.

[6] [1962] AC 413.   [7] Per Lord Reid, ibid. at 429.

[8] Cf. per Megarry J. in *Hounslow L.B.C.* v. *Twickenham Garden Developments Ltd.* [1971] Ch. 233 at pp. 251 E–254 A.

yet cast serious doubt upon the viability or reality of that theory as far as the law of contracts generally is concerned.

In the law of the contract of employment, however, it has for a long time been clearly perceived that no remedy is normally available to reverse the dismissal, and that as a consequence an elective theory of the effect of wrongful dismissal would be neither realistic nor generally viable. Thus no rule seems better established than the unwillingness of the courts to maintain a contract of employment in force by an injunction or an order for specific performance.[1] And similarly it has long been clear that the courts will not treat the right to remuneration as continuing after wrongful dismissal— another remedy which would, if granted, appear to negate the wrongful dismissal instead of accepting it as a *fait accompli*. The courts for a time contemplated the continuance of remuneration after dismissal under a doctrine of 'constructive service'[2], but later set their faces firmly against such a rule.[3]

However, it is not clear beyond doubt that wrongful dismissal *must* be effective to terminate the contract as a matter of law because no remedy will ever disturb that *de facto* result. Thus in *Hill* v. *C. A. Parsons & Co. Ltd.*,[4] the Court of Appeal felt free to grant an injunction against wrongful dismissal. There was in their eyes no rule of law either forbidding the grant of an injunction in such cases or treating the contract as irreversibly terminated. Equally it is still arguable that there is no special rule of law against the continuance of remuneration after employment has been ended; there is simply the factual objection that the conditions for payment of remuneration will not normally have been fulfilled,[5] coupled with judicial reluctance to impose the effects of a continuation of employment.[6] Nevertheless,

---

[1] See above, pp. 274–8.

[2] See *Gandell* v. *Pontigny* (1816) 4 Camp. 375, 376. (Lord Ellenborough).

[3] *Archard* v. *Hornor* (1823) 3 C & P 349; *Ridgway* v. *Hungerford Market Co.* (1835) 3 A & E 171; *Broxholm* v. *Wagstaff* (1841) 5 Jur. 845; *Smith* v. *Hayward* (1837) 7 A & E 544; *Fewings* v. *Tisdale* (1847) 1 Ex. 295; *Goodman* v. *Pocock* (1850) 15 QB 576; *Wood* v. *Moyes* (1853) 1 WR 166; Crompton J. in *Emmens* v. *Elderton* (1853) 13 CB 495, 509; Lush J. in *National Cash Register Ltd.* v. *Stanley* [1921] 3 KB 292 at 296; Lord Keith in *White & Carter (Councils) Ltd.* v. *McGregor* [1962] AC 413 at 439.

[4] [1972] 1 Ch. 305—see above, pp. 277–8.

[5] See per Winn L.J. in *Denmark Productions Ltd.* v. *Boscobel Productions Ltd.* [1969] 1 QB 699 at 732 B–F.

[6] There are several instances where work under a contract of employment has been wrongfully terminated in circumstances falling short of dismissal, and where the courts felt no difficulty in finding for a continuance of remuneration:

the idea that wrongful dismissal must in principle be effective to terminate the contract has the same persistence as the elective theory of termination by breach in general contractual principles.

The difficulties concerning the theory of wrongful dismissal became more acute when the redundancy payments and unfair dismissal legislation created a new statutory concept of dismissal and defined it by reference to the termination of the contract of employment.[1] The legislation seemed to require the termination of the contract to be the unilateral act of the employer. The courts accorded that effect not only to outright wrongful dismissal but also to wrongful repudiation, where the employer does not terminate the employment outright but seeks to impose changed terms and conditions. This is the concept of 'constructive dismissal' as it emerged from the crucial *Marriott (No. 2)* Case.[2] But it seems even more difficult to rationalize constructive dismissal in terms of orthodox contract theory than to explain ordinary wrongful dismissal. The difficulty seems such that it has been argued that the courts may be giving a special meaning to 'termination of the contract' for the purposes of these statutes, recognizing that ordinary common-law principles may produce quite a different result.[3] In truth, 'constructive dismissal' need not pose a greater theoretical problem than ordinary wrongful dismissal. In both cases the employer is unilaterally terminating employment on the existing contractual terms, i.e. dismissing from the existing employment; it is simply that in the case of 'constructive dismissal' he is also offering to prolong the employment relationship on different contractual terms. But it is understandable that the courts should feel special difficulty about treating the contract as unilaterally terminated by the employer where he is not even insisting on a termination of the employment relationship. And this has brought into question the whole mechanism of termination of the contract by a unilateral and wrongful act of the employer.

Smith v. *Kingsford* (1836) 3 Scott CP 279; *Cook* v. *Sherwood* (1863) 11 WR 595; *O'Neil* v. *Armstrong, Mitchell & Co.* [1895] 2 QB 418; *Lloyd* v. *Sheen* (1905) 93 LT 174; *Sibery* v. *Connelly* (1907) 96 LT 140; cf. *Collins* v. *Price* (1828) 5 Bing. 132 (school fees); *International Correspondence Schools Ltd.* v. *Ayres* (1912) 106 LT 845 (correspondence course).

[1] 1965 Act s. 3(1), 1971 Act s. 23(2); the difference between the two provisions is discussed above, pp. 237–8.

[2] *Marriott* v. *Oxford Co-operative Society Ltd.* (No. 2) [1970] 1 QB 186—see above, pp. 237–8. See also Appendix, para. 3.

[3] See P. L. Davies, 'Law Making in the Industrial Court' (1974) 27 MLR 62, 63–4.

The statutory provisions concerning dismissal have also cast doubt upon the theory of contractual termination in another direction. The problem is whether wrongful dismissal should be allowed to take effect before the date when notice duly given by the employer would have expired. The theory that dismissal is effective to terminate the contract even though it is wrongful would seem to carry with it the consequence that dismissal should have immediate effect upon the contract. Yet this seems to be allowing the employer to profit by his own wrong. The issue is a practical one where the act of dismissal (in the sense of *de facto* termination of employment) occurs before a statutory qualifying date but where notice duly given would have expired or was due to expire within the statutory qualifying period. This is the problem of the 'straddling notice'.[1] The Industrial Tribunals had to consider this issue in relation to the coming into force of the 1965 Act on 5 December 1965. In a number of decisions they at first accepted that the contract of employment continued in force until the date on which a proper notice would have expired.[2]

However, it was shortly recognized that the acceptance of a payment of wages in lieu of notice caused the dismissal to take effect at once;[3] and equally that the period of employment would not be extended on the ground that the employee had been entitled to a paid holiday.[4] Moreover it was later ruled that these early cases had been decided *ex improviso*, and that the dismissal took effect immediately upon the *de facto* termination of employment even where insufficient notice had been given.[5] The reasons given by the Tribunal for so holding were that the employment ended for the purpose of vicarious liability immediately upon dismissal; that the employee had no remedy at common law or in equity to compel the continuance of the contract; and that the Contracts of Employment Act 1963 confirmed that view of the effect of dismissal by providing only for a

---

[1] See per Lord Denning M.R. in *Lees* v. *Arthur Greaves Ltd.* [1974] ICR 501 at 503 B–E.

[2] *Chapman, Blair & Atchinson* v. *Leadley* (1966) 1 ITR 84; *Harris* v. *Wickington Ltd.* (1966) 1 ITR 62; *Johnson* v. *John Thompson Ltd.* (1966) 1 ITR 261; *Reynolds* v. *Groom* (1966) 1 ITR 74; cf. *Ferguson* v. *Telford Grier Ltd.* (1967) 2 ITR 387.

[3] *Taylor's Cater Inns Ltd.* v. *Ministry of Labour* (1966) 1 ITR 242 (Sir Diarmaid Conroy Q.C.); *Ryan* v. *Liverpool Warehousing Co.* (1966) 1 ITR 69—see above, pp. 186–7.

[4] *Aggett* v. *Exter Munitions Ltd.* (1967) 2 ITR 105.

[5] *Nightingale* v. *Biddle Bros. Ltd.* (1967) 2 ITR 624; cf. *X.* v. *Y. Ltd.* (1969) 4 ITR 204, 206.

remedy in damages[1] for failure to give the statutory minimum period of notice. That constituted an important reaffirmation of the view that the contract of employment is effectively terminated by wrongful dismissal; and it enabled certain employers to avoid their new statutory obligations by their own wrongful action.

The Industrial Tribunals and the Courts have had to return to this problem in relation to the date upon which the unfair dismissal provisions of the 1971 Act came into force, 28 February 1972. This time they have treated outright wrongful dismissal as immediately effective.[2] But they have held that once a notice has actually been given, it cannot be cut short by later wrongful dismissal,[3] nor by later pressing payment in lieu of notice upon the employee.[4] But the courts have not yet provided an explanation as a matter of contractual theory why a wrongful dismissal should be treated as immediately effective in some situations but of postponed effect in other cases. Indeed, as with the problem of 'constructive dismissal', they have left it uncertain whether they are achieving their results by means of contractual theory, or whether they admit the limitations imposed by contractual theory and instead arrive at their conclusions by way of statutory interpretation.[5]

In view of these various aspects of the theoretical problem of wrongful dismissal, it is perhaps useful to examine the statements about theory which the courts themselves have made in recent cases. On the whole they have cast increasing doubt upon the view that wrongful dismissal is in principle effective to terminate the contract, and that this is an exception to general contractual principles. In *Denmark Productions Ltd.* v. *Boscobel Productions Ltd.*,[6] the issue was the continuation of remuneration after wrongful dismissal. Harman L.J. held the contract was in principle terminated by wrongful dismissal.[7] Salmon L.J. avoided the theoretical issue.[8] Winn L.J.[9] expressed the view that a contract of employment was not *sui generis*, and was not in principle unilaterally terminated by wrongful dismissal,

---

[1] Now section 1(3) of the 1972 Act.

[2] e.g. *Dedman* v. *British Building Appliances Ltd.* [1974] ICR 53 (wrongful dismissal plus a payment in lieu of salary). See above, pp. 188–9.

[3] *H. W. Smith (Cabinets) Ltd.* v. *Brindle* [1973] ICR 12.

[4] *Lees* v. *Arthur Greaves Ltd.* [1974] ICR 501.

[5] See, for instance, Lord Denning M.R. in *H. W. Smith (Cabinets) Ltd.* v. *Brindle* (above) at 24 E and Megaw L.J., ibid. 24 G.

[6] [1969] 1 QB 699.   [7] Ibid. at 737 E–F.   [8] Ibid. at 726 C–E.

[9] Ibid. at 731 F–732F.

even if the practical consequences made it seem so. In *Decro-Wall International S.A.* v. *Practitioners in Marketing Ltd.*[1] the issue was whether one company could have their contractual right to be sole concessionaires of another company maintained in force by injunction and declaration despite what was in effect a wrongful dismissal. Salmon L.J. now expressed himself as 'doubtful whether a wrongful dismissal brings a contract of service to an end in law, although no doubt in practice it does'.[2] Sachs L.J. expressly left open the question whether 'contracts of personal service do *in strict law* form an exception to the rule that an innocent party has an option when faced with a repudiation'. He favoured the view that they did not form such an exception in strict law but only in practice; but felt it unnecessary to commit himself.[3] Buckley L.J. said that it might be that contracts of service should be regarded as an exception to the general rule about repudiation.[4] In *Hill* v. *C. A. Parsons & Co. Ltd.*[5] the issue was the availability of injunction against a wrongful dismissal. Lord Denning M.R. held that the consequence in law of a wrongful dismissal insisted upon by the employer was that *in the ordinary course of things* the relationship of master and servant thereupon comes to an end, but that the rule was not inflexible and permitted of exceptions.[6] Sachs L.J. now felt convinced that a contract of service was *not* in principle terminated by a wrongful repudiation and was no exception to the general contract rules.[7] Stamp L.J. was prepared to assume, without expressing an opinion, that the contract of service subsisted, the plaintiff not having accepted the defendant's repudiation of their obligations under it.[8] In *GKN (Cwmbran) Ltd.* v. *Lloyd*[9] Sir John Donaldson felt the general rule was that dismissal effectively terminated the contract and that it would be 'rare indeed for an unjustifiable dismissal to be ineffective to terminate the contract'.[10] He explained *Hill* v. *Parsons* as an exception resulting from the fact that the employer did not 'persist in the dismissal' when the employee objected.[11] This is hard to follow. The employer may have acted reluctantly under union pressure, but he nevertheless persisted in the dismissal. There is no such obvious way to reconcile

---

[1] [1971] 1 WLR 361.   [2] Ibid. at 369 H–370 A.   [3] Ibid. at 376 C–D.
[4] Ibid. at 381 E.   [5] [1972] 1 Ch. 305.
[6] Ibid. at 314 B, E. Lord Denning clearly also foresaw the recurrence of the straddling notice problem and the need to adapt existing rules to meet it—ibid. at 313 G–314 A.
[7] Ibid. at 319 C.   [8] Ibid. at 321 F.   [9] [1972] ICR 214.
[10] Ibid. at 221 B–C.   [11] Ibid. at 221 A.

that decision with a theory of effective wrongful termination.[1] But if that theory is discarded, the courts are still left with a sense that elective theory ill accords with the practical effects of wrongful dismissal. They clearly sense that no existing theory satisfactorily explains all the aspects of the problem.

An examination of both the practical and the theoretical aspects of wrongful dismissal shows the absence of a satisfactory treatment of the problem in terms of contract theory. It is worth looking for wider reasons why the theoretical principles operate so unsatisfactorily. Firstly, the theory of repudiation emphasizes the nature of repudiatory conduct as a statement of intention by the wrongdoer— as an offer to terminate the contract, albeit wrongfully. The difficulty arises because wrongful dismissal is rather obviously an offer which cannot be refused. It is hard for an employee meaningfully to defy his employer's intention to exclude him from employment; and the courts feel strong policy objections towards imposing a continuation of employment by the force of legal remedies alone. Nor is it satisfactory for the contractual theory to be deduced from the policy objections to the granting of particular remedies such as injunctions and orders of specific performance. There are many situations where the courts may wish to declare the contract still theoretically in being without actually imposing an employment relationship upon either party. There is no policy objection of the 'enforced employment' kind to holding the employee entitled to a continuance of remuneration (though there may be a rather different policy objection to the employee's being paid without working). There is no policy objection to preventing the employer from avoiding statutory obligations by wrongful dismissal just before statutes come into force. Even where the remedy concerned does impose the fact of employment upon the parties, the courts may sometimes regard the policy objections to doing so as outweighed, as in *Hill* v. *Parsons Ltd.* Hence a theory which tries to arrive at a uniform rule from the availability of remedies is bound to come under continual question.

The attempt to relate wrongful dismissal to contractual theory

[1] In *Sanders* v. *Ernest A. Neale Ltd.* [1974] ICR 565, a case reported too late for full treatment in this work, Sir John Donaldson pronounced himself firmly committed to the effective wrongful termination theory, with the contract of employment as *sui generis* in this respect. He felt that the extent of the *Hill* v. *Parsons* exception would need definition by a higher court, but rightly distinguished the case as special by reason of the survival of mutual confidence between the parties. See a note by the present author at (1975) 4 ILJ 40.

also founders in another sense, related to the concept of contractual termination itself. The theory that wrongful dismissal must be effective to terminate the contract assumes that the contract cannot remain in being after the employment relationship has come to an end. But contracts do not in their nature have to deal in relationships which exist for specific periods of time. We can and do speak of a contract, for instance, of sale being 'in being' or 'in force' without referring to a specific period of time dealt with the contract. And even where the main basis of the contract is a relationship existing for a specific period of time, there may be reasons for regarding the contract as 'in being' after the relationship has ended. This would be true of a contract of employment which provides for pension payments to the employee or subjects the employee to covenants against future competition.[1] The concepts of a contract 'in force' or 'in being', and correspondingly the concept of termination of contract are thus imprecise ones; and this lack of precision undermines this area of contractual theory.

These various considerations may serve to indicate why there is unlikely to be a clear resolution of the theoretical problem in the terms in which the problem is accustomed to be posed. The theory is clearly in the process of becoming more fragmented and complex in general contract law; the growing idea of automatic termination in some cases of fundamental breach shows that. As far as the contract of employment is concerned, it is probably now clear there can be no satisfactory uniform rule. One possibility is that the exceptions to the rule will start to be systematized as a matter of common law. Another possibility is that it will be recognized that the theory is being called upon to serve all kinds of diverse purposes and that it would be better to deal with each of the purposes piecemeal. There are indications of this kind of development in the suggestion that there is a purely statutory concept of termination for the purposes of the 1965 and 1971 legislation. But both legislators and judges have so far been reluctant to concede that the issue is incapable of resolution within the bounds of the common law of contract.

---

[1] Cf. *Robinson & Co.* v. *Heuer* [1898] 2 Ch. 451 where an employee's wrongful departure was treated as ineffective to terminate the contract, with the result that a covenant against competition could be enforced against him. See per Chitty L.J., ibid. at 458.

Chapter Eight

FRUSTRATION

INTRODUCTION

The present chapter is concerned with the termination of the contract of employment as the result of events which are treated by the law as being the fault of neither party. The law concerning the frustration of the contract of employment deals with two different types of case. The one type of case is that where the ability of the employer to continue the employment is affected by a supervening external event. The other is that where it is the ability of the employee to continue to work which is so affected. There may be cases where both situations occur together, as in *Horlock* v. *Beal*,[1] where a ship was detained in enemy harbour upon the outbreak of war and where the seamen employed upon the ship were interned. But it will more commonly be the case that it is one side or the other of the contract which is primarily affected.

It is convenient to consider, firstly, those cases in which the performance of the employee is affected by external events. The most common case in which the ability of the employee to work is affected through no fault of his own is where he is incapacitated by sickness or injury. It is in this situation that many of the problems of the application of the doctrine of frustration to the employment relationship have arisen. Other cases in which the ability of the employee to work has been affected by supervening external events have been those where the employee is conscripted, or interned, during hostilities.

The doctrine of frustration has a relatively narrow application where it is the employer's performance which is affected by an external event. Thus the ability of the employer to continue to employ may be affected by the physical destruction of his plant or premises; but the courts will not readily accept that the contract of employment is thereby terminated under the doctrine of frustration. The contract of employment will, however, be terminated under the

[1] [1916] 1 AC 486.

doctrine of frustration upon the death or supervening incapacity of an employer. A supervening change in, or application of, the law may operate to prevent the continuance of the employment. The effect of this type of event upon the contract of employment varies according to whether it renders performance illegal or impossible. If the wider type of case is considered in which the employment is terminated by the employer for economic reasons, it will be found that the doctrine of frustration cannot generally be invoked to excuse the termination, because the factors producing the termination will be treated as being within the responsibility of the employer.

SECTION 1: FRUSTRATION AS THE RESULT OF EVENTS AFFECTING THE EMPLOYEE

The law concerning the frustration of the contract of employment by reason of events affecting the employee is at once an application of the doctrine of frustration as it affects contracts generally, and the result of developments particular to the employment relationship.

The most significant characteristic of the treatment of the doctrine of frustration by the courts in recent times has been their concern to confine its scope. McNair and Watts define the doctrine as 'the operation of the law in discharging a contract by reason of the occurrence of events or circumstances which were not within the contemplation of the parties when making it, and which are of such a character that to hold the parties to their contract would be to impose a new contract upon them'.[1] Attention has recently been drawn anew to the fact that this doctrine is a departure from the principle of *pacta sunt servanda*, which, although too primitive for a modern system of contract law if treated as an absolute rule, none the less underlies much of the law concerning the performance and termination of contracts.[2] That this very general consideration weighs heavily with the courts is borne out by their reluctance to hold that contracts were frustrated in the latest group of cases in which the issue was raised, the Suez Canal cases.[3]

[1] McNair and Watts, *The Legal Effects of War* (Cambridge, 1966) p. 157.
[2] Aubrey, 'Frustration Reconsidered—some Comparative Aspects' (1963) 12 ICLQ 1165 at 1165, 1169.
[3] *Tsakiroglou & Co. Ltd.* v. *Noblee Thorl G.m.b.H.* [1962] AC 93, overruling *Carapanayoti & Co. Ltd.* v. *E. T. Green Ltd.* [1959] 1 QB 131; *Ocean Tramp Tankers Corporation* v. *V/O Sovfracht (The Eugenia)* [1964] 2 QB 226, overruling *Société Franco-Tunisienne d'Armement* v. *Sidermar SPA (The Massalia)* [1961] 2 QB 278. The cases are reviewed by Aubrey, op. cit. at 1169–74.

It will be shown in the following pages how, in relation to contracts of employment, that general tendency to confine and restrict the doctrine of frustration is accentuated because the operation of the doctrine on too large a scale would result in the widespread loss, on the part of employees, of statutory rights depending upon dismissal.

A. Incapacity due to Sickness or Injury

This is the most obvious and frequent ground upon which frustration of the contract of employment has been claimed. In considering the application of the doctrine of frustration to incapacity due to sickness or injury, it is important to relate the periods of actual or anticipated absence from work to the duration of the contract of employment concerned. It may well be that by losing sight of the importance of that factor, the courts at one time allowed the doctrine of frustration to have too wide an ambit in this context. It is also important to regard the law concerning frustration of the contract of employment by sickness or injury as a fusion of the doctrine of frustration under the general law of contract, and rules peculiar to the employment relationship.

1. Short-term Contracts for a Specific Purpose. It was recognized in a number of cases decided in the latter half of the nineteenth century that a short-term contractual obligation for a specific purpose— such as a theatrical engagement or a contract to paint a picture— could be terminated under the doctrine of frustration by the illness or incapacity of the person employed. The person employed would be relieved of further liability, because he was prevented from fulfilling his contract through no fault of his own. The person employing would be allowed to treat the contract as at an end, and to find a substitute. The combined result was that the contract as a whole was terminated under the doctrine of frustration. This type of case was the source of the development of that doctrine in the context of employment.

Thus in an *obiter dictum* in *Hall* v. *Wright* (1858),[1] Pollock C.B. indicated that in the case of such a contract, illness resulted in a release from liability on the same principle as that whereby death effected a release of liability. This was frustration by reason of physical impossibility:

'A contract by an author to write a book, or by a painter to paint a picture

---

[1] E, B & E 765 at 794.

within a reasonable time, would, in my judgement, be deemed subject to the condition that if the author became insane or the painter paralytic, and so incapable of performing the contract, by the act of God, he would not be liable personally in damages any more than his executors would be if he had been prevented by death.'[1]

It was then made clear in an *obiter dictum* of Bramwell B. in *Jackson* v. *Union Marine Insurance Co.*[2] that incapacity to perform a specific engagement operated to discharge the person employing as well as the person employed, so that the disappointed employer was free to employ a substitute: 'Thus A enters the service of B and is ill and cannot perform his work. *No action will lie against him, but B may hire a fresh servant* and not wait his recovery if his illness would put an end, in a business sense, to their business engagement and would frustrate the object of that engagement; a short illness would not suffice, if consistent with the object they had in view' (emphasis added). This very important dictum marks the emergence of the doctrine of frustration as a single principle operating on both sides of the contract and therefore upon the contract as a whole. The test for frustration which was accepted by Bramwell B. in this case was very closely related to the test for the right to rescind a contract for breach of condition,[3] being that of whether the event in question had produced a fundamental change in the commercial adventure. Bramwell B. indeed regarded the test of whether the disappointed party was discharged from his obligations as being the same whether the failure of performance on the other side was attributable to fault or to an external event.[4]

The same approach to the problem of frustration by sickness could be seen in the case of *Poussard* v. *Spiers*.[5] It was there held that an opera company was entitled to dismiss an opera singer by reason of her absence due to sickness. The issue was treated exactly as if the question was one of the right to rescind for breach of condition; the case was considered from that point of view in previous pages of this work.[6] But Blackburn J. made it clear that there was a

---

[1] Applied in *Robinson* v. *Davison* (1871) LR 6 Ex. 269.

[2] (1874) LR 10 CP 125, 145.

[3] Cf. *Hongkong Fir Shipping Co. Ltd.* v. *Kawasaki* [1962] 2 QB 26 at 69, where Diplock L.J. based himself expressly upon the judgment of Bramwell B. in this case.

[4] See McElroy, *Impossibility of Performance* (ed. Glanville Williams) (Cambridge, 1941) pp. 121 ff., for an account of how 'frustration' was originally the application of the right to rescind in cases of inordinate delay.

[5] (1876) 1 QBD 410.   [6] See above, pp. 212–4.

discharge of obligations on *both* sides of the contract, because the singer's absence was not her fault.[1]

These cases and examples relate to contracts which may well be contracts for services rather than contracts of service. *Poussard* v. *Spiers* is on the borderline between the two types of contract. The other examples quoted in this group of cases and *dicta* are certainly contracts for services—such as the contract to paint a picture or to write a book.[2] But the principles of frustration which were laid down in these cases and *dicta* were seen as applying to the contract of employment too. That is clear from the passage from the judgment of Bramwell B. in *Jackson* v. *Union Marine Insurance Co.* quoted above.[3] However, compared with those examples, it ought in principle to be far less likely that a long fixed-term contract, or a contract for an indefinite period, should be terminated by frustration in the event of illness.

2. *Fixed-term Contracts of Employment.* In the case of a fixed-term contract of employment such as a contract for a year, or a number of years, it seems clear that the *employee* can allege that the contract is frustrated where he is permanently incapacitated by illness. The result of his alleging frustration in such a case is that he cannot be sued for damages for wrongful departure.[4] Where it has been the *employer* who has alleged frustration of a fixed-term contract by reason of the sickness of the employee, the courts at first held that there was frustration only if the employee was incapacitated for the whole remaining part of the fixed term. Thus it was first recognized in an *obiter dictum* in *Cuckson* v. *Stones*[5] that where a person employed under a long fixed-term contract fell ill, the employer might thereupon be entitled to terminate the contract; but it was insisted that this was the case only where the employee was permanently incapacitated, so that he would be unable to work for the remainder of the term.

This right to dismiss for permanent incapacity was seen as an application of the right to dismiss for incompetence which had been recognized in *Harmer* v. *Cornelius*,[6] for in *Cuckson* v. *Stones* Lord

---

[1] Ibid. at 141, basing himself upon the judgment of Bramwell B. in *Jackson* v. *Union Marine Insurance Co.* (1874) LR 10 CP 125 at 141 (above).

[2] See *Hall* v. *Wright* (1858) E, B & E 765, 794.

[3] (1874) LR 10 CP 125 at 145 (see above, p. 304).

[4] Cf. *Boast* v. *Firth* (1868) LR 4 CP 1 (apprenticeship).

[5] (1858) 1 E & E 248, 257 (Lord Campbell C.J.).

[6] (1858) 5 CB (NS) 236.

Campbell C.J. commented thus on the right of the employer to dismiss by reason of sickness. 'We concur in the observation of Willes J. in *Harmer* v. *Cornelius*; and if the plaintiff, from unskilfulness, had been wholly incompetent to brew, or, by the visitation of God, he had become, from paralysis or any other bodily illness, permanently incompetent to act in the capacity of brewer for the defendant, we think that the defendant might have determined the contract.'[1]

In later cases it was decided that an employer could allege the frustration of a fixed-term contract by reason of the incapacity of the employee, not only where the incapacity was of a permanent nature, but also where it was sufficient to frustrate the commercial purpose of the contract. The concept of frustration was extended from complete impossibility to that of fundamental alteration in the contract. However, the courts, while recognizing that this relatively wide test for frustration was applicable, were reluctant to hold that there had been a termination under the doctrine of frustration in particular cases. Thus in one case it was held that the employers of a jockey could not rely upon a purely temporary incapacity as a frustration of a substantial fixed-term contract, even though the incapacity occurred at an important time affecting several particular engagements of the employer.[2]

Wright J. commented,

'I think the matter must be regarded with reference to the nature of the employment and the length of the term for which the agreement was made. I suppose it must be in everyone's knowledge that the profession of a jockey is a dangerous one, and that they frequently meet with accidents, and an agreement to serve for three years . . . must very often be quite an unmeaning and worthless agreement if a temporary incapacity for a week or even a month is to put an end to it.'[3]

Hence in this case the court considered the presumed intentions of the parties concerning the allocation of risk of temporary injury, and decided that this risk was upon the employer.

A similar presumption, that in the case of a long fixed-term contract the risk of temporary incapacity was upon the employer, can be seen in *Storey* v. *Fulham Steel Works Co.*,[4] where the plaintiff

---

[1] (1858) 1 E & E 248, 257. This contrasts with earlier dicta in Poor Law settlement cases placing a high duty upon the master to support the servant in sickness: *R.* v. *Islip (Inhabitants)* (1721) 1 Stra. 423, 244 (Pratt, C.J.); *R* v. *Christchurch (Inhabitants)* (1760) 1 Will. Bl. 214, 215 (Lord Mansfield C.J.).
[2] *Loates* v. *Maple* (1903) 88 LT 288.   [3] Ibid. at 291.
[4] (1907) 23 TLR 306 (affirmed 24 TLR 89).

was employed as a works manager for a fixed term of five years without any provision for termination by notice. Channell J. commented that the agreement was for five years and contained no provision, as was common in such agreements, for putting an end to it by notice, either absolutely or on the happening of a particular event; and that it was clear as a matter of law that if such an agreement was made, and if the servant was absent from time to time through illness, the loss fell upon the employer[1]. The Court of Appeal affirmed his decision, on the ground that he had applied to the facts a correct view of the law. For the more recent development of the doctrine of frustration in this kind of case, it is necessary to look to contracts terminable by notice rather than fixed-term contracts.

3. *Contracts for an Indefinite Period Terminable by Notice.* In the case of contracts of employment for an indefinite period terminable by notice, there would seem to be an especially strong argument for holding that the employer cannot generally allege termination by frustration in the event of the illness of the employee, but must, if he wishes to terminate the employment, do so by giving due notice. On the one hand, it may be said that only permanent incapacity will destroy all prospect of the return of the employee to work within the indefinite period of the contract (unless the employee happens to be close to retirement). On the other hand, it may be said that the parties, by providing for termination by notice, have made their own allocation of risk, so that the employer ought to carry the risk of loss during the period of notice. The courts tended towards this view in earlier cases, and have recently returned to this approach.

Thus in *Carr* v. *Hadrill* (1875)[2] the plaintiff was employed by the defendants as a factory worker in their biscuit factory under a contract for an indefinite period at weekly wages, terminable by a week's notice. The plaintiff was absent for five weeks by reason of illness, during which time he was paid sick pay by the company's own sick club. Upon his return, the employer refused to allow him to resume work and alleged that the contract had terminated by reason of sickness. It was held that the contract had not so terminated, and that the employee was entitled to compensation in respect of a week's notice. Blackburn J. commented[3] that it was always open to the master to give the week's notice and so determine the contract. A similar

[1] 23 TLR 306 at 307.   [2] 39 JP 246.   [3] Ibid. at 247.

result was reached in the case of *Warburton* v. *Co-operative Whole-sale Society Ltd.*[1]

However, this restrictive approach to the doctrine of frustration seemed to have been abandoned by the Divisional Court in the redundancy payments case of *Jones* v. *Wagon Repairs Ltd.*,[2] where an employee who had worked for a number of years as a repairer of steel waggons at weekly wages, apparently under a contract for an indefinite period terminable by notice, was absent from December 1966 onwards as the result of hypertension. In September 1967 the employers notified him that his employment was at an end. They did so in circumstances which suggested that he was redundant, but they successfully contended that there had not been a dismissal by reason of redundancy, on the ground that the contract had been automatically terminated by frustration at an unspecified prior date. The Industrial Tribunal by a majority held that the contract had been so frustrated; and the Divisional Court held that this was a finding of fact with which they could not interfere. This may be regarded as having been a misapplication of the principle of frustration. The employer had the right to give proper notice if he chose to do so. It may well be thought that if the employer keeps the employee on his books during absence, as was done here, he is at least bearing the risk of supervening redundancy for which he is liable to make a redundancy payment.

One result of the vesting in the Industrial Court of appellate jurisdiction over industrial tribunals has been a careful examination of the application of frustration to the contract of employment, and on the whole a restoration of the earlier restrictive approach. The leading decision is now that in *Marshall* v. *Harland & Wolff Ltd.*[3] where there was held to have been no termination under the doctrine of frustration in the circumstances that a shipyard fitter employed since 1946 had been absent by reason of *angina pectoris* from October 1969 until the employers terminated his employment in April 1971, very shortly before the closure of the works at which he was employed. The court treated as decisive against frustration the cumulative effect of the factors that (a) the employer was not paying wages, sick pay, or pension contributions during the employee's absence

---

[1] [1917] 1 KB 663.
[2] (1968) 3 ITR 361. Contrast *Watts & Watts & Co. Ltd.* v. *Steeley* (1968) 3 ITR 363 (sea captain—five weeks' incapacity—no frustration).
[3] [1972] ICR 101.

(i.e. there was no urgent reason to treat the employment as at an end); (b) it was not the policy or practice of the employers to terminate employment upon grounds of sickness; (c) there was no medical evidence that the employee was permanently incapacitated or as to the duration of any incapacity to be expected in the future. The general tenor of the judgment shows an unwillingness to concede a wide scope to the doctrine of frustration in the context of employment.

The court also set out a number of indications as to how to apply the doctrine which were to the effect that the likelihood of frustration was increased by (a) the presence of a relatively short notice period; (b) the fact that an entitlement to sick pay has expired (not, however, at all conclusive as a factor); (c) a short expected duration for the employment in the absence of sickness; (d) the fact that the employee occupies a key post in which he must be replaced on a permanent basis; (e) the fact that the period of past employment is relatively short (i.e. seniority brings about an increasing elasticity in the relationship between employer and employee, so that longer periods of absence due to sickness may be deemed acceptable).[1]

These indications tend to militate against frustration in the case of the reasonably well-established employee employed for an indefinite period terminable by notice. Such an employee is in effect accorded this degree of tenure, that the doctrine of frustration will not readily be applied against him in respect of absence due to sickness.

That approach was followed again by the Industrial Court in *Farmer* v. *Willow Dye Works Ltd.*,[2] where there was held to be no frustration in the case of a dye-house worker employed since 1937 and absent for a series of periods of about four months from 1968 onwards (down to the termination of his employment in July 1971), by reason of generally undermined health caused by wartime hardships suffered as a prisoner of war. That decision does, however, indicate that, as far as his entitlement to redundancy payment is concerned, the employee will have gained nothing by rebutting frustration in that there may still be held to have been a dismissal for ill-health rather than by reason of redundancy. Nevertheless, it is preferable that the issue should be considered in terms of the real

[1] [1972] ICR 101 at 105 B–H.
[2] (1972) 7 ITR 226. A similar approach to the doctrine of frustration was shown in *Hebden* v. *Forsey & Son* [1973] ICR 607.

question, why did the employer dismiss the employee, rather than in terms of the artificial question, had the employment previously been terminated by the operation of a doctrine of law.

B. Unavailability of the Employee as the result of War

The courts have on the whole been willing to treat contracts of employment as frustrated by the internment of the employee, or his absence on military service, provided only that it could be said, at the time at which the contract is alleged to have been frustrated, that the absence of the employee might turn out to be of prolonged duration. The willingness of the courts to hold that there has been frustration in such cases may be criticized on the ground that it ought to be for the employer to decide whether to continue the employment or not; and if not, to give proper notice.

It was nevertheless so held in the First World War in *Marshall* v. *Glanville*,[1] which was the case of a sales representative who joined the Royal Flying Corps, and was later dismissed without notice by his employers. When sued for damages for wrongful dismissal, the employer successfully claimed a declaration that the contract had been frustrated when the plaintiff joined the forces. McCardie J. commented that the question was whether the plaintiff and defendants made their bargain on the footing that a particular state of things should continue to exist: 'If so, a term to that effect is implied, and when that state of things ceases to exist, the bargain itself ceases to exist. Here the parties clearly made their bargain on the footing that it should continue lawful for the plaintiff to render and for the defendants to accept his services.'[2] In order to support this conclusion, that judge invoked a presumption of the perpetual duration of a war, saying: 'A state of war is assumed to be of such prolonged duration as *prima facie* to put an end to contracts which are conditional upon the continuance of a particular state of things which is only consistent with peace.'[3] The earlier decision of the same judge in *Nordman* v. *Rayner & Sturges*,[4] in which a contract of agency

---

[1] [1917] 2 KB 87.

[2] Ibid. at 91 (the supervening illegality resulted from the Military Service Act 1916).

[3] Ibid. at 91.

[4] (1916) 33 TLR 87. It was held also that the contract was not terminated by reason merely of the fact that the plaintiff was upon the outbreak of war registered as an alien enemy. Upon the effect of enemy alien status the decision was followed in *Schostall* v. *Johnson* (1919) 36 TLR 75.

was held not to have been terminated by the internment of the agent for one month, is distinguishable on the ground that the internment was merely temporary. On the special facts 'it was doubtful from first to last whether it would last for any substantial period'[1] and in fact it had come to an end long before the trial of the action.

It was accepted also in cases decided in the Second World War that a contract of employment might be frustrated by the internment or by the conscription of an employee. Thus in *Unger v. Preston Corporation*,[2] it was held that the employer could allege frustration where the employee was interned from June 1940 until March 1941, on the ground that this was more than a temporary interruption, and that it interfered with and frustrated the business purpose of the contract. This decision may be criticized in that the plaintiff's job (as a school medical officer) apparently did not disappear during the war, nor had the employers replaced him. Their aim in alleging frustration was to avoid liability for his salary during his absence.[3]

SECTION 2: FRUSTRATION AS THE RESULT OF EVENTS AFFECTING THE EMPLOYER

The doctrine of frustration has a relatively narrow scope of operation in connection with events affecting the employer. In general, the risk of such events is placed upon the employer, at least to the extent that he cannot allege a termination of the contract by reason of them. More specific considerations will appear from the examination of the main types of supervening events affecting the employer.

A. Physical Destruction of the Enterprise of the Employer

One of the first relaxations of the old rule of strict liability upon contractual obligations was the recognition in *Taylor v. Caldwell*[4] that there might be a release from a particular obligation where its performance had become impossible by reason of the destruction of

[1] Per McCardie J. in *Marshall v. Glanville* [1917] 2 KB 87, 92.

[2] [1942] 1 All ER 200. Comparison may be made with decisions holding employments to have been terminated by entry into the forces for the purposes of bequests to persons 'in the service' of a given employer: *Re Drake* [1921] 2 Ch. 99; *Re Marryat* [1948] Ch. 298. Decisions to the contrary effect in *Re Cole* [1919] 1 Ch. 218, *Re Feather* [1945] Ch. 343 are distinguishable on the ground that the evidence there showed a positive intent on the part of the employers that the contracts of employment should be suspended rather than terminated during war service.

[3] See below, p. 324.   [4] (1863) 3 B & S 826.

the subject-matter of the contract. This exception to liability applies when the fulfilment of the contract depends on the continued existence of the particular physical object.[1] However, the courts show some reluctance to treat a contract as being dependent for its fulfilment upon the continued existence of a given physical object.[2]

So it is also in the case of the contract of employment, where it is made clear by the one reported decision upon the question that the courts will not readily treat such a contract as impossible of performance by reason only of the physical destruction of plant. In *Turner* v. *Goldsmith*,[3] the defendant was a manufacturer of shirts who employed the plaintiff as agent, canvasser, and traveller under a contract for a fixed period of five years and then terminable by notice. The job of the plaintiff was to obtain orders for and to sell the various goods 'manufactured or sold by the defendant'. The factory of the defendant being burned down, he ceased to trade. Upon the issue whether he was excused from liability for not employing the plaintiff by reason of the destruction of the factory, it was held that he was not thereby relieved of liability, because the job of the plaintiff was not defined in such a way that its continuance depended entirely upon the maintenance of an output from the factory. Thus Lindley L.J. commented that, 'Here the parties cannot be taken to have contemplated the continuance of the defendant's manufactory as the foundation of what was to be done; for . . . the plaintiff's employment was not confined to articles manufactured by the defendant.'[4] And Kay L.J. also: 'If it had been shown that not only the manufactory but the business of the defendant had been destroyed by *vis major* without any default of the defendant, . . . the plaintiff could not recover. But there is no proof that it is impossible for the defendant to carry on business in articles of the nature mentioned in the agreement.'[5]

Hence the doctrine of frustration could be invoked in respect of a physical destruction of plant only where that destruction made it impossible to continue any of the work coming within the whole range of the employee's job as contractually defined. It may be that the courts would, where appropriate, go further and say that there

---

[1] Per Blackburn J. at 833. The exception was applied in *Appleby* v. *Myers* (1867) LR 2 CP 651.

[2] Compare, for example, *New System Private Telephones Ltd.* v. *Edward Hughes & Co.* [1939] 2 All ER 844.

[3] [1891] 1 QB 544.   [4] Ibid. at 550.   [5] Ibid.

was no frustration where there was the possibility of offering the employee any suitable employment within a reasonable time.

B. *Death or Incapacity of the Employer*

It is clear that the death of an individual employer will normally result in a termination of the contract of employment under the doctrine of frustration, so that no liability will attach to the estate of the deceased employer for termination of employment consequent upon the death. This result follows from two distinct rules of law, both of which were recognized by the middle of the nineteenth century, at a date substantially earlier than that of the general development of the modern doctrine of frustration.[1]

The first rule is that where the contract is of a personal nature, it will be terminated, without liability, by the death of one party. That this applies to the contract of employment upon the death of the employer is shown by *Farrow* v. *Wilson*,[2] where the contract of employment of a farm-bailiff was held to have been terminated by the death of the landowner who employed him, and Willes J. commented that

'Generally speaking contracts bind the executor or administrator, although not named. Where, however, personal considerations are the foundation of the contract, as in cases of principal and agent and master and servant, the death of either party puts an end to the relation; and, in respect of service after the death, the contract is dissolved, unless there be a stipulation, express or implied, to the contrary.'[3]

It is not clear whether this rule is subject to the further requirement that, for the rule to apply, the personality of the deceased party must be material to the contract, so that if the employer dies, his personality must be material to the employee, and it is not sufficient that the personality of the employee was material to him. The point was expressly left open by Wright J. in *Graves* v. *Cohen*, where he said 'Even if these words, "the death of the party confided in" are a necessary and essential element in the principle, still I think for the reasons I have given that the owner or the employer was a person confided in.'[4] He there held that the personality of the owner of

---

[1] The existence of two distinct rules of law was referred to by Channell B. in *Tasker* v. *Shepherd* (1861) 6 H & N 575, 580 and by Wright J. in *Graves* v. *Cohen* (1930) 46 TLR 121, 123.
[2] (1869) LR 4 CP 744.   [3] Ibid. at 746.   [4] (1930) 46 TLR 121, 123–4.

horses and employer of a jockey was material to the jockey, even though the business of running the race-horses was left to a trainer, because the choice of horses, and of races, was a matter for the owner. It must follow that the personality of an individual employer will, upon that criterion, almost invariably be seen as material to the employee, in the sense that the business acumen, or enterprising personality, or administrative ability of the employer will be important to the employment relationship, even if the employee does not work in personal contact with the employer. There is authority for the view that the personality of a sleeping partner in a partnership of employers may not be material to the employee,[1] but that is quite distinct from the case where there is an individual employer.

The other rule which produces the same result is one whereby a contract may be treated as impliedly limited by the condition that it shall subsist only during the lives of both parties to it.[2] This is a rule closely associated, in a historical sense, with the early recognition of frustration by impossibility resulting from the destruction of a physical object. The basis of this second rule concerning the death of the employer is, not so much a reposing of confidence in the personal qualities of the employer, but rather an implied intention to limit the contract to his lifetime. It would seem to follow that the same principle would apply where the employer is incapacitated from continuing the employment, just as there may be frustration by reason of the incapacity of the employee. But it may well be that if the employer can, as entrepreneur, continue his business by employing a person to manage it instead of himself, then he ought not to be entitled to allege frustration against the employee, if the employee is willing for the employment to continue on those terms.

The question whether it is appropriate for the contract of employment to be treated as frustrated by the death or incapacity of the employer has to be answered in terms of the purpose of the doctrine of frustration in general. If that purpose is seen as being the discharging of liabilities on the ground of the *absence of fault* on the part of the person prevented from contractual performance by supervening events, then it will appear appropriate to apply the doctrine of frustration to this type of case, unless the employer can be held culpable for his death or incapacity, as where he commits suicide

---

[1] *Phillips* v. *Alhambra Palace Co.* [1901] 1 QB 59 (see below, p. 347).
[2] Per Wright J. in *Graves* v. *Cohen* (1930) 46 TLR 121, 124; cf. *Tasker* v. *Shepherd* (1861) 6 H & N 575.

or disregards medical advice. If, on the other hand, the doctrine of frustration is seen as a method of *allocating the risk of loss*, then it may seem that it should not apply where it is appropriate to treat the employer, or his estate, as an insurer against such events, at least to the extent of being obliged to compensate the employee for loss of employment for the period of due notice.[1]

C. Termination of Employment for Economic Reasons

The doctrine of frustration provides for the termination of contracts by reason of supervening events where the occurrence of the event cannot be held to be the responsibility of either party, and where it cannot be said that either party was intended to bear the risk of the continuance of the contract in the events which have occurred. It seems on the whole unlikely that this doctrine will operate in the event of the termination of employment for economic reasons, as it will generally be the case, either that the events leading to that termination will be within the responsibility of the employer, or that the risk of the continuance of the contract will remain with him. There are various types of situation to be considered, in which there may be said to be a termination of employment for economic reasons. The employer may, for instance, allege that the employment is uneconomic by reason of the slowness or inefficiency of the employee. That has not been regarded as a situation to which the doctrine of frustration might apply.[2] A different type of case is that where it ceases to be possible to keep the employee profitably employed, by reason of a general falling-off in demand for goods manufactured or services provided by the enterprise. In other cases, the cancellation or failure of a particular project such as a large commercial contract may produce that result. Alternatively, adverse economic circumstances may result directly in the closure of the business of the employer, or the appointment of a receiver to a company, the liquidation of a company, or the bankruptcy of an individual employer. Could the doctrine of frustration apply to those cases?

It is unlikely that frustration could be alleged in the case where

---

[1] The employer's death will count as a dismissal for redundancy purposes by reason of s. 22 of the 1965 Act. But the estate will not be liable for a redundancy payment where the personal representatives offer suitable re-engagement to the employee within eight weeks of the employer's death (s. 23 & Sched. 4 Part I of the 1965 Act).

[2] Thus at no stage was frustration argued in *Hindle* v. *Percival Boats Ltd.* [1969] 1 WLR 174, which is the most important decision upon this kind of situation.

the employer is unable to continue the employment by reason of generally adverse trading conditions. There is a well-established general principle that the doctrine of frustration cannot be invoked on the ground merely that a contract has become unexpectedly unprofitable to one or other party. The leading case which illustrates this approach is that of *Davis Contractors Ltd.* v. *Fareham U.D.C.*[1] In this case a building contract took longer to complete than had been anticipated by the builder, by reason of an unexpected shortage of labour. As a result, the contract involved the builder in a greater outlay than had been expected. He claimed that the contract had been frustrated, and that he was therefore entitled to claim upon a *quantum meruit* for a higher price. The decision that the contract was not frustrated represents a rejection of the view that the decreased profitability of the contract for the builder could release him from his obligations under the contract.[2]

It might be that frustration could more easily be alleged in a case where a specific project, upon which the employee was specially employed, was cancelled or failed through no fault of the employer. The examples may be considered of an aircraft designer employed by an aircraft-manufacturing corporation, in the event of the cancellation of a government contract with the corporation, or of a research scientist employed by an institute which fails to get the necessary grant for a major project. It may be that such examples could be distinguished from the situation of *Davis Contractors Ltd.* v. *Fareham U.D.C.* and brought within the type of case in which there is held to be frustration by reason of the disappearance of an external circumstance, the continuance of which is essential to the contract as made. The leading authority in favour of frustration in that type of event is the 'Coronation' case of *Krell* v. *Henry*.[3] It is, however, thought by this writer that the courts would view with hesitation the allegation of frustration in these circumstances in the context of employment. They would, on the whole, regard it as the responsibility of the employer to ensure the regular flow of work of the kind contemplated. It may be that if a contract of employment were limited in duration to the period of the specific project in question, so that the

---

[1] [1956] AC 696.

[2] See especially per Lord Reid at 724, Lord Radcliffe at 727, 729; and compare *Tsakiroglou Ltd.* v. *Noblee Thorl G.m.b.H.* [1960] 2 QB 318 per Harman L.J. at 370.

[3] [1903] 2 KB 740. See McElroy and Williams, 'The Coronation Cases' (1940–1) 4 MLR 241, 5 MLR 1.

contract was essentially linked to that particular purpose, then the argument in favour of frustration would be strengthened. But it need not follow, even from an arrangement of that kind, that the employee undertakes to share with his employer the risk that the project in question may not materialize.

It would appear also that those cases where adverse economic conditions compel the employer to cease to trade, or result in insolvency, cannot normally be brought within the ambit of the doctrine of frustration. They are treated as events within the responsibility of the employer. The effect of these events upon the contract of employment is considered in the final chapter of this work. But although various different views have been advanced as to the effect of these events, it has not been asserted that they result in the termination of the contract of employment under the doctrine of frustration. At least one case appears to suggest that a contract of employment may bind an employer only for such time as he continues his business.[1] If it were the case that contracts of employment might be construed in that way, then indeed the same result would be reached as if a closure of the employer's business for economic reasons operated to bring about a frustration of the contract of employment. But these cases in fact deal with agency arrangements which can be distinguished from contracts of employment. The doctrine of frustration is, in general, excluded from the area of termination of employment for economic reasons. In that way, its application to the contract of employment is substantially restricted. That is an example of the approach exemplified in the words of Harman L.J.:[2] 'Frustration is a doctrine only too often invoked by a party to a contract who finds performance difficult or unprofitable, but it is very rarely relied on with success. It is in fact a kind of last ditch, and as Lord Radcliffe says in his speech in the most recent case (*Davis Contractors* v. *Fareham U.D.C.*)[3] it is a conclusion which should be reached rarely and with reluctance.' That exclusion of the doctrine of frustration has since 1965 been the more complete in that the allocation of the risk of termination of employment for economic reasons is now effected by the Redundancy Payments Act.[4] It would be patently

---

[1] *Cowasjee Nanabhoy* v. *Lallbhoy Vullubhoy* (1876) LR 3 Ind. App. 200 (cf. above, pp. 31–2, and below, p. 345 note 3).

[2] In *Tsakiroglou Ltd.* v. *Noblee Thorl G.m.b.H.* [1960] 2 QB 318, 370.

[3] [1956] AC 696, 727 (above).

[4] The concept of redundancy is currently being tested out in relation to questions which could be treated as issues of frustration in the general law of

absurd if the operation of that Act—which depends upon dismissal by the employer—could be defeated by invoking the doctrine of frustration, and there is every reason to suppose that such an argument would have no chance of success.

SECTION 3: SUPERVENING ILLEGALITY

It may occur that a change in existing law will render the further performance of a contract of employment either illegal or impossible. Where that happens, it seems that the contract of employment will generally be terminated as a result. Examples of the situation in which further performance of the contract of employment becomes illegal are to be found in those cases where the employee is conscripted under an Act of Parliament. Such a case was that of *Marshall* v. *Glanville*,[1] considered above.[2] McNair and Watts have commented that supervening illegality results, as a general rule, in a dissolution of the contract, and that the effect is the same as that which occurs when a contract is discharged by supervening impossibility of performance, or by frustration.[3] In particular, they take the view that supervening illegality produces a prospective termination of the contract but not a retroactive cancellation; and that in this respect it operates in the same way as the doctrine of frustration itself. It may, indeed, be that supervening illegality can be regarded as an application of the doctrine of frustration.[4] It seems, at any rate, that the Law Reform (Frustrated Contracts) Act 1943 applies to cases of supervening illegality. Thus Glanville Williams, taking the view that the Act would so apply, commented that, 'Although the law as to supervening illegality may not be quite the same as the law of discharge for impossibility or frustration, every case of subsequent

---

contract, such as what kind of measures the employer is bound to take and entitled to take in order to reduce his (labour) costs for the purpose of preserving the profitability or viability of his enterprise—cf. *Chapman* v. *Goonvean & Rostowrack China Clay Co. Ltd.* [1973] ICR 310; *Johnson* v. *Nottinghamshire Combined Police Authority* [1974] ICR 170.

[1] [1917] 2 KB 87.   [2] See above, p. 310.

[3] McNair and Watts, *The Legal Effects of War* (1966) p. 131.

[4] It is, as such, distinct from *ab initio* illegality, which arises in employment cases chiefly where tax evasion is involved: e.g. *Napier* v. *National Business Agency Ltd.* [1951] 2 All ER 264; *Cole* v. *Fred Stacey Ltd.* [1974] IRLR 73 (IT).

illegality is also a case of discharge for impossibility (by operation of law) or frustration.'[1]

There are cases where a change in the law, or an application of the law (e.g. by statutory instrument), makes the performance of a contract impossible, without making it illegal in the sense considered above. In such cases there will be a straightforward application of the doctrine of frustration by impossibility.

Thus in *Reilly* v. *R.*,[2] the statutory office of member of the Federal Appeal Board, held by the appellant, was abolished by the Canadian Parliament when they repealed the legislation establishing the Board. The advice of the Privy Council was that, although this was not an office terminable at pleasure, the appellant had no claim to damages for breach of contract, because there had been a discharge of the contract by reason of statutory impossibility.

Lord Atkinson said that the case was 'determined by the elementary proposition that if further performance of a contract becomes impossible by legislation having that effect, the contract is discharged'.[3] That decision indicates that where an employment created by public law is abolished by a change in that law, the contract of employment (assuming the employment to be of a contractual nature) becomes impossible of performance, not so much in the sense that the obligation to remunerate cannot be fulfilled, but in the sense that an undertaking to allow the employed person to occupy a particular post, and to exercise a particular function, is frustrated.[4]

It is not expected, however, that the doctrine of frustration would in general be allowed a wide scope in the situation, for instance, of nationalization of an enterprise; and provision for statutory compensation is normally made in statutes which abolish existing employments. In this type of situation, the requirements for the operation of the doctrine of frustration might in principle be satisfied, but there would seem to be strong policy considerations against applying the doctrine, because it would tend to prejudice the position of the employee concerned—a result which the legislators normally feel committed to avoiding.

---

[1] Glanville Williams, *Law Reform* (*Frustrated Contracts*) *Act 1943* (London 1944) p. 23; cf. per McCardie J. in *Marshall* v. *Glanville* [1917] 2 KB 87, 91.

[2] [1934] AC 176.   [3] Ibid. at 180.

[4] Cf. *Studholme* v. *South-Western Gas Board* [1954] 1 WLR 313—solicitor's retainer from private gas corporation frustrated by Gas Act 1948 because although the Act substituted the gas board for the private company, the basis of calculation of the retainer had disappeared.

Where a change in, or application of, the law renders the performance of a contract of employment illegal or impossible, that effect may be of temporary duration—as where an employee is conscripted for a limited period of time, or an employer's premises requisitioned for a limited time. It is not clear how far the law will treat contracts as suspended, rather than terminated, by supervening interruptions of this kind. That question has been considered in an earlier part of this chapter.[1] The rules concerning the effect of changes in, or application of, the law upon the performance of contracts of employment are thus seen, in general, to be somewhat uncertain and obscure. The issue, is, however, one of some importance, especially as the activities and interventions of public authorities constantly increase in their scope. It is the view of this writer that principles are required which allow as far as possible a temporary or partial effect upon the contract of employment, rather than an effect of complete termination. The outright termination of the contract of employment is to be avoided on the ground that many incidental rights of the employee may thereby be prejudiced.

SECTION 4: THE REQUIREMENT OF LACK OF FAULT

Where a party to a contract claims to be discharged from his obligations under the contract by the operation of the doctrine of frustration, it is a requirement of his claim that there is a lack of fault on his part.[2] This rule applies whether he is claiming to be discharged by reason of an event affecting his own performance, or whether he is claiming to be discharged by reason of the non-performance of the other party as the result of an event affecting that other party. (The reader is reminded of the distinction taken in the two preceding sections between events affecting the employer and events affecting the employee.) If a party to a contract alleges termination under the doctrine of frustration by reason of an event affecting his own performance, then it is a requirement of his claim that his own non-performance is not the result of his own fault; for if it is his own fault, he has no claim to be relieved of liability. If that allegation is

---

[1] See above, pp. 310–11, especially p. 311 note 2.

[2] Authority for this proposition is to be found in the decisions discussed in the course of the present section. Cf. Lord Devlin [1966] CLJ 192 at 206: 'We talk about a contract as being frustrated when what we really mean is that the contract has been dissolved by a frustrating event for which neither party is responsible.'

based on an event affecting performance on the other side of the
contract, it is still a requirement of the claim that he himself is not
at fault; the claimant cannot rely upon 'self-induced frustration'.
The principle concerning self-induced frustration was declared in
the judgment of Lord Sumner in *Bank Line Ltd.* v. *Arthur Capel &
Co.*[1] when he commented, 'I think it is now well settled that the
principle of frustration of an adventure assumes that the frustration
arises without blame or fault on either side. Reliance cannot be
placed on a self-induced frustration; indeed, such conduct might
give the other party the option to treat the contract as repudiated.'
That rule was applied in the charter-party case of *Maritime National
Fish Ltd.* v. *Ocean Trawlers Ltd.*[2] and also in a rather unusual employment situation in *Denmark Productions Ltd.* v. *Boscobel Productions Ltd.*[3]

These cases show that there is self-induced frustration in relation
to one who by his deliberate act prevents the performance of the
contract. The concept of self-induced frustration is not, however, a
clearly defined one. The main problem is whether it includes frustration induced by negligence, as well as frustration deliberately induced. That point was expressly left open by Lord Russell in *Joseph
Constantine Steamship Line Ltd.* v. *Imperial Smelting Corporation*[4]
when he said, 'I wish to guard against the supposition that every
destruction of corpus for which a contractor can be said, to some
extent or in some sense, to be responsible, necessarily involves that
the resultant frustration is self-induced within the meaning of the
phrase.' Viscount Simon in his judgment in the same case regarded
that as a problem which might cause particular difficulty in the context of engagements for personal services, in the type of fact situation
which arose in *Poussard* v. *Spiers:*[5]

'Some day it may have to be finally determined whether a *prima donna* is
excused by complete loss of voice from an executory contract to sing if it
is proved that her condition was caused by her carelessness in not changing
her wet clothes after being out in the rain. The implied term in such a
case may turn out to be that the fact of supervening physical incapacity

---

[1] [1919] AC 435, 452.
[2] [1935] AC 524; cf. *Mertens* v. *Home Freeholds Co.* [1921] 2 KB 526; and
Ocean Tramp Tankers Corporation v. *V/O Sovfracht (The Eugenia)* [1964] 2 QB
226 per Lord Denning M.R., at 237.
[3] [1969] 1 QB 699—annotated by the present writer at (1969) 32 MLR 314.
[4] [1942] AC 154, 179.   [5] (1876) 1 QBD 410. See above, pp. 212–14.

dissolves the contract without inquiring further into its cause, provided, of course, that it has not been deliberately induced in order to get out of the engagement.'[1]

The contract in *Poussard* v. *Spiers* may have been a contract of employment, as opposed to a contract with an independent contractor. But even if the case did concern a contract of employment, it can hardly be reproduced realistically in an ordinary industrial setting. If comparable problems arise in the latter context, it would normally be illnesses of a prolonged nature which would have to be considered. If frustration will be treated as self-induced in relation to the employee when it is the result of his negligence, then the problem may be comparable to that of deciding whether there has been contributory negligence when an employee sues in tort in respect of injury, or disease, contracted at work.[2] The issue is the extent to which the employee will be treated as responsible for safeguarding his own health and safety.

The question of the onus of proof of lack of fault was decided in *Joseph Constantine Steamship Line Ltd.* v. *Imperial Smelting Corporation*,[3] where the rule was laid down that once a party alleging termination under the doctrine of frustration has shown that a frustrating event has occurred, then the onus passes to the other side to show that the frustration was the fault of the party relying on the frustrating event.

Thus in that case the owners were unable to perform their obligations under a charter-party by reason of an unexplained explosion aboard their ship. They alleged a termination of the contract by reason of frustration. Their claim succeeded, as the charterers were unable to prove default or negligence on the part of the owners.

It has been convincingly argued that this rule is the result of an illogicality, and that the requirement of lack of fault should be seen as an inherent part of the doctrine of frustration, and not as a separate element requiring to be separately refuted by the party disputing frustration.[4] True, it would be harsh to put the employer to proof of the fact that a fire in his factory was not due to his fault. On the other hand, it might be proper to presume, unless the contrary was shown,

---

[1] [1942] AC 154, 166.
[2] See Munkman, *Employers' Liability* (6th edn. 1966) pp. 518–24.
[3] [1942] AC 154.
[4] Stone, *Legal Systems and Lawyers' Reasonings* (Stanford, Calif., 1964) pp. 244–5.

that he undertook to bear the risk of such destruction to the extent of being obliged, at least, to give his employees due notice of termination. The issue of fault ought not to obscure the wider issue of allocation of risk.

SECTION 5: THE AUTOMATIC OPERATION OF THE DOCTRINE OF FRUSTRATION

It is an accepted general principle of the law of contract that the doctrine of frustration operates to produce an automatic termination of the contract concerned. By that it is meant, firstly, that the contract is terminated as a direct consequence of the frustrating event and independently of the act of either party in treating the contract as terminated; and secondly, that the termination takes effect immediately upon the frustrating event, rather than awaiting the point at which one or other party treats the contract as terminated.[1]

This automatic operation of the doctrine of frustration stands in sharp contrast with the operation upon the contract of a major breach or a wrongful repudiation. These do not result in an automatic termination of the contract but give to the injured party an option to rescind the contract. The contract continues in force unless and until that right is exercised.[2] That contrast was expressly recognized both by Lord Sumner and by Lord Wright in those judgments in which they established the automatic effect of frustration.[3] It should be added that the judgment of Lord Denning M.R. in *Harbutt's 'Plasticine' Ltd.* v. *Wayne Tank & Pump Co. Ltd.*[4] makes the suggestion that where there is a breach of contract whose consequences are of so disastrous a character as to make it immediately apparent that the contract cannot be pursued, there may then be no room for any option in the innocent party; and that there may there-

---

[1] Per Lord Sumner in *Hirji Mulji* v. *Cheong Yue Steamship Co. Ltd.* [1926] AC 497, 505; per Lord Wright in *Maritime National Fish Ltd.* v. *Ocean Trawlers Ltd.* [1935] AC 524 at 525, in *Joseph Constantine Steamship Line Ltd.* v. *Imperial Smelting Corporation Ltd.* [1942] AC 154 at 187, and in *Denny, Mott & Dickson Ltd.* v. *James B. Fraser & Co. Ltd.* [1944] AC 265 at 274.

[2] With wrongful dismissal as, probably, an exception to this general principle—see above, pp. 293 ff.

[3] Lord Sumner in *Hirji Mulji* v. *Cheong Yue Steamship Co. Ltd.* [1926] AC 497 at 509–10; Lord Wright in *Joseph Constantine Steamship Line Ltd.* v. *Imperial Smelting Corporation Ltd.* [1942] AC 154 at 187–8, and in *Denny, Mott & Dickson* v. *James B. Fraser & Co. Ltd.* [1944] AC 265 at 274.

[4] [1970] 1 QB 447 at 464 H–465 B.

fore be an automatic termination of the contract even though that termination is the fault of one of the parties. It is too early to say how far this doctrine will be accepted as eroding the distinction which could previously be maintained, between the automatic operation of the doctrine of frustration and the election to rescind which arises where one party is guilty of a fundamental breach or a wrongful repudiation.[1]

The automatic operation of the doctrine of frustration has the result that when one or other party successfully invokes that doctrine, the termination of the contract is given a partially retroactive effect; it is backdated to the time of the frustrating event. (It is not, however, backdated any *further* than that; the contract is not cancelled *ab initio*. The effect of frustration upon the contractual rights and liabilities arising out of performance which has taken place before the frustration is considered in the next section of this chapter.) In the context of the contract of employment, the backdating of the termination to the frustrating event is well illustrated by the decision in *Unger* v. *Preston Corporation*.[2]

The employee was interned in June 1940. The employers stopped paying his salary, but did nothing else to terminate his contract or to treat it as terminated. In September 1940, they replied to a query from the employee's solicitor that they still needed the employee's services, but would have to give him a new appointment before he could again be employed by them. When in October 1940 he claimed his salary as from June, the employers alleged termination under the doctrine of frustration in June; and their contention was accepted, so that no salary was held to have fallen due to him beyond that date.

However, in the particular case of the supervening incapacity of the employee, the frustrating event has not always been seen as having an automatic operation. It has been seen in an earlier section that incapacitating sickness was originally treated, in the case of *Cuckson* v. *Stones*,[3] as being analogous to incompetence;[4] it was regarded as entitling the employer to dismiss the employee, as if in response to fault. It was not at that time seen as having an automatic

---

[1] See also above, p. 120 note 2 and pp. 293–4. It is now also argued that the principle of automatic termination by frustration may itself be coming into question—see Goldberg (1972) 88 LQR 464, citing *Sainsbury Ltd.* v. *Street* [1972] 1 WLR 834.

[2] [1942] 1 All ER 200.

[3] (1858) 1 E & E 248 per Lord Campbell C.J. at 257.

[4] See above, pp. 305–6.

effect; if the employer did not act upon the incapacitating sickness by dismissing the employee, then the contract would continue in force. But the case of *Cuckson* v. *Stones* was decided before the development of the doctrine of frustration as a distinct principle of law with an automatic effect upon the contract, and the approach of the courts at the present day seems to be one of treating supervening incapacity as having the same automatic operation as other types of event falling within the doctrine of frustration. That was shown by the decision of the Divisional Court in *Jones* v. *Wagon Repairs Ltd.*,[1] where an incapacitating illness was accorded the effect of an automatic termination of the contract of employment operating at a date before the ultimate return of the National Insurance cards and to the overt act of termination by the employer.

An attempt was made to alleviate the harshness of this rule towards the employee in the Industrial Tribunal decision in *Thomas* v. *John Drake & Co. Ltd.*,[2] where Sir John Clayden ruled that, before the doctrine of frustration could be held to have operated in the case of an employee absent by reason of sickness, there must be an act on the part of the employer showing from what date the contract had been terminated (in the absence of some external fact decisively establishing the date of frustration). However, this ruling was expressly declared erroneous by the Industrial Court in *Marshall* v. *Harland & Wolff Ltd.*,[3] the court declaring that 'As a matter of law, it is quite unnecessary to be able to point to a precise point of time at which the relationship was dissolved. Still less is it necessary to be able to point to an act of the employer as marking such a point of time.'

It may be suggested that the automatic operation of the doctrine of frustration has an anomalous effect in the context of the contract of employment. It does not seem correct that the employee should be retroactively deprived of the advantages of being a person employed under a contract of employment. Glanville Williams has criticized the decision in *Unger* v. *Preston Corporation* from this point of view, on the ground that it enables the employer to keep the employee in suspense as to whether he will ultimately be paid wages in respect of a given period of sickness or other unavoidable absence.[4] This is unjust in relation to employees of the kind who would normally be entitled to be paid during absence due to sickness. Moreover,

---

[1] (1968) 3 ITR 361.   [2] (1971) 6 ITR 146.
[3] [1972] ICR 101, 106 E (Sir John Donaldson).
[4] In a note on the case at (1943) 6 MLR 160.

in *Jones* v. *Wagon Repairs Ltd.* the automatic operation of the doctrine of frustration had the result that the employer was able to avoid a finding that he had dismissed his employee by reason of redundancy, and was able to do so without even having to point to any particular date at which he alleged a termination by frustration. It was sufficient that the contract could be said to have been frustrated at some time before the return of the cards by the employer.

It is therefore suggested by this writer that it might be preferable if, in the context of the contract of employment, the doctrine of frustration were held to result in a termination of the contract only from the time at which one or other party treats the contract as terminated. This would avoid a retroactive effect which is capable of having undesirable results. It would seem in particular that if an employer allows an employee to remain on his books during a given period, and retains his cards, he ought not later to be heard to allege that the employment had in fact terminated at an earlier date. On the other hand, the incidence of liability for social security payments already creates an incentive upon the employer expeditiously to dismiss employees who are absent, and it may be that it would be to the ultimate disadvantage of employees to add to that incentive. At all events, the issue depends upon considerations peculiar to the employment relationship, which are not adequately treated by a mere application of general contract principles.

SECTION 6: THE EFFECT UPON THE MUTUAL RIGHTS AND
OBLIGATIONS OF THE EMPLOYER AND THE EMPLOYEE

The termination of the contract of employment under the doctrine of frustration results in an abrupt cessation of the continuing mutual obligations of the parties. The law, however, provides for an adjustment of loss in respect of that which has already been done in pursuance of the contract before the frustrating event occurs. The employee is thereby enabled to recover remuneration in respect of work done before the frustrating event; he can recover upon the frustrated contract itself in respect of sums which have accrued due in respect of services rendered, but have not yet been paid over, at the time of frustration. The effect of termination under the doctrine of frustration is that the contract is treated as coming to an end upon the occurrence of the frustrating event, but it is not cancelled *ab initio*.[1]

Hence upon termination under the doctrine of frustration a contract of employment will survive to the extent of grounding a claim in respect of remuneration already accrued due under it. That is well illustrated by the decision in *Stubbs* v. *Holywell Railway Co.*[2]

The defendants employed S. as a consulting engineer for a period of 15 months for a total sum of £500, payable in five equal quarterly instalments. He was paid for the first quarter and died in the fourth quarter before having been paid for the two intervening quarters. It was held that his personal representative was entitled to recover two quarterly instalments under the contract. It was argued that the death rescinded the contract *ab initio*, but that argument was rejected. Martin B. commented 'The contract, no doubt, is ended by the death of Stubbs, but only in this sense, that the act of God *has made further performance impossible*. The man's life was an implied condition of the contract, but the fact of his death can have nothing whatever to do with the payment due for what has been done—with what has been actually earned by the deceased.'[3]

Hence to the extent that an entire contract has been performed in full, and to the extent that a severable part of a divisible contract[4] has been performed in full, the accrued rights of the employee to remuneration are unaffected by frustration. That rule is preserved by Section 2(4) of the Law Reform (Frustrated Contracts) Act 1943.[5]

To the extent that wages have not accrued due under the contract in respect of services rendered at the time of the frustrating event, the employee is now enabled to recover by Section 1(3) of that Act, whereby it is provided that

Where any party to the contract has, by reason of anything done by any other party thereto in, or for the purpose of, the performance of the contract, obtained a valuable benefit (other than a payment of money to which [s.1 (2)] applies) before the time of discharge, there shall be recoverable from him by the said other party such sum (if any) not exceeding the

---

[1] Per Lord Sumner in the *Hirji Mulji* case [1926] AC 497, 510; per Lord Wright in the *Joseph Constantine* case [1942] AC 154, 183, 187, 191.

[2] (1867) LR 2 Ex 311.

[3] Ibid. at 314 (emphasis added). So also Kelly C.B. at 313–14; Channell B. at 315.

[4] See above, pp. 126 ff.

[5] See Glanville Williams, *Law Reform (Frustrated Contracts) Act 1943* (London, 1944) p. 63.

value of the said benefit to the party obtaining it, as the court considers just, having regard to all the circumstances of the case. . . .

It has been argued that the benefit received must be considered as at the time before the discharge by frustration, so that the fact that the benefit is nullified by the frustrating event is irrelevant.[1] This may, however, be questioned in view of the fact that the sub-section goes on to require the court to have regard, when assessing the value of the benefit, to 'the effect, in relation to the said benefit of the circumstances giving rise to the frustration of the contract'.[2] It is to that extent possible that the employee may be at a disadvantage when seeking recovery under this restitutionary right, by comparison with the contractual rate of remuneration.[3] Goff and Jones have asserted, however, that the courts have adjusted their view of 'benefit' in dealing with restitutionary claims in general, so that the test applied is, in reality, one of what is a reasonable remuneration to be paid for the work done.[4]

With regard to those rights of the employee which are associated with the contract of employment, and which are inchoate at the time when the contract is terminated under the doctrine of frustration, it should be noted that the 1965 Act has made special provision to ensure that the estate of an employee shall not be deprived of the right to a redundancy payment to which a claim was pending at the time of the death of the employee.[5]

However, although the employee is thus enabled by a combination of common law and statute to recover remuneration in respect of services rendered before frustration, and although the right to redundancy payment is protected in the particular case where the contract is terminated by his death, the preservation of the accrued and accruing rights of the employee is in practice likely to be of small consequence when compared with the deprivation involved in the loss of the rights to, and expectations of, prospective employment. Although a termination of the contract of employment under the doctrine of frustration does not prevent the employee from claiming compensation in respect of past services, it results in a sudden disappearance of the asset which is constituted by the job itself.

---

[1] Treitel, *Law of Contract* (4th edn. 1975) p. 607.
[2] Cf. Goff and Jones, *Law of Restitution* (1966) pp. 334–5.
[3] See Glanville Williams, op. cit. pp. 50, 72.
[4] Op. cit. p. 336.
[5] Section 23 and Sched. 4, Part II.

This chapter may therefore be concluded by the general reflection that whereas the doctrine of frustration may provide a necessary method of distribution of loss in the context of large commercial contracts, it effects so abrupt a destruction of the contract concerned that it is not likely to be useful, or appropriate, in a context where extensive continuing factual expectations, and a social relationship, are constructed upon the framework of the contract concerned. That is clearly the position in relation to the contract of employment.

Chapter Nine

CHANGES IN THE EMPLOYING ENTERPRISE

INTRODUCTION

In this chapter we consider the effects of various occurrences affecting the existence, ownership, or legal status of the individual employer or employing enterprise, in particular:

(a) bankruptcy of the individual employer;
(b) change in composition of an employing partnership;
(c) liquidation of the employing company;
(d) appointment of receiver to the employing company;
(e) change in ownership of the business of the employer; transfer of assets of the employer's business; cessation of trading by the employer;
(f) merger, take-over, or amalgamation involving the employing company.[1]

The first of the issues to be considered in relation to these changes in the enterprise of the employer is their effect upon the contracts of employment of persons employed in the enterprise.

The second type of issue raised by these changes in the enterprise of the employer is that of the transferability of the contract of employment. As the result of those occurrences listed above, the employee may be transferred without his consent into an employment which is effectively controlled other than by his original employers; upon the alteration, for example, in the personnel of an employing partnership, the sale and transfer of a business, or the merger or amalgamation of an employing company with another company or with a group of companies. We have perhaps been accustomed to assume that it is necessary, for the protection of the employee, to preserve the principle that the employee cannot be transferred from one employment to another without his consent. In some situa-

---

[1] The case of the death of the individual employer was considered above, pp. 313–5.

tions where a change in the enterprise has produced a *de facto* transfer of employment without the consent of the employee, it may be equally necessary in the interests of the employee to insist that there is a contract of employment still in force.

Each of these changes in the enterprise of the employer raises the further problem of the protection of the rights of the employee based upon his period of past service with the employer. The problem is not simply one of what happens to the employee's right to a continuance of work and wages in these situations, for it is no longer sufficient to conceive of the protection of the employee in terms purely of a right to damages for wrongful dismissal. There is the further problem of whether all the employee's rights and benefits, secured by statute or secured by contract, are protected in these situations. Financially, the most important questions are what happens to the employee's accrued pension rights based upon his period in employment, and to his right to a redundancy payment based upon his years of service.

It will be seen in the course of the discussion of these three issues that each of them has assumed an increased importance in recent years. That is partly the result of changing patterns of commerce and industry which have produced so enormous a number of mergers between enterprises of all kinds. It is also the result of the significance which now attaches to the employee's interest in his job as a species of property. Although changes in the employing enterprise are an aspect of the contract of employment which has received little attention, it is potentially one of the most important parts of the whole of the law of individual employment.

SECTION 1: THE EFFECT UPON THE EXISTING CONTRACT

Changes in the enterprise of the employer may give rise to three different types of fact situation.

(a) Upon a change in the enterprise, the employee may be dismissed, i.e. excluded from further employment either by the original employer or by the person now controlling the enterprise (whether trustee in bankruptcy, liquidator, personal representative, etc.).[1]

(b) Alternatively, upon the change in the enterprise, the employer

---

[1] Compare, for example, *Tasker* v. *Shepherd* (1861) 6 H & N 575—employee employed by two partners. Upon the death of one, the other refused to continue the employee in his employment.

or the person now in control may be willing to continue the employment, but the employee may treat the change as entitling him to terminate the contract.[1]

(c) As a further alternative, upon the change in the enterprise, the employment is in fact continued, either by the original employer, or by the person now in control.[2]

The assessment of the contractual effects of these fact situations involves some principles of company and partnership law, and an examination of transactions such as receivership and bankruptcy. It is at this point that the law of the contract of employment is affected by the law of commercial institutions. Hence we are dealing with a by-product of laws concerned primarily with the protection of investors and creditors. It is not surprising that the rules produced in this way should appear mystifying, irrelevant, and occasionally unjust from the standpoint of the employee caught up in changes in the enterprise employing him.

A. Compulsory Winding-up

We consider first the type of case where a termination of employment follows upon the winding-up order. If the employment of an employee of the company is terminated at the time of the order for compulsory winding-up, then the contract of employment itself is terminated. In the case where it is the company which discontinues the employment, there is a wrongful dismissal. Whereas if it is the employee who refuses to continue in the employment, there will have been a wrongful repudiation by the employer, consisting in the compulsory winding-up order, and an acceptance by the employee of that wrongful repudiation as a termination of the contract. Thus in *Chapman's Case*,[3] the making of a winding-up order, followed by an actual termination of the employment by the company, was held to have resulted in an immediate dismissal of the employee. It was held that the employee's right to remuneration came to an end at the time of the order, by reason of the immediately effective termination of the contract. The later decision in *Re Newman Ltd., Raphael's Claim*[4] shows that in such a case the

---

[1] As in *Brace* v. *Calder* [1895] 2 QB 253 (a partnership case).

[2] Compare, for example, *Re Mack Trucks (Great Britain) Ltd.* [1967] 1 WLR 780—receiver and manager, appointed out of court, continued the employees in his employment. It was held that their contracts of employment with the company continued in force.

[3] (1866) LR 1 Eq. 346.   [4] [1916] 2 Ch. 309.

employee is entitled to arrears of salary down to the date of the order, plus damages for wrongful dismissal.[1]

With this we may compare the treatment of the situation where the employment is continued after the winding-up order. It has been suggested that a compulsory winding-up order effects a termination of the contracts of employment of employees of the company, by wrongful repudiation of those contracts, even where the liquidator continues the employment after the making of the order.[2] The suggestion that the contract of employment is terminated by repudiation upon a compulsory winding-up order, even when the employment continues, is based upon the decision in *MacDowall's Case* (*Re Oriental Bank Corporation Ltd.*)[3] where the employee concerned, a senior clerk, was entitled by his contract of service to three months' notice of dismissal, but it was held that he was entitled to no compensation from the company for loss of employment because the winding-up order had operated as the giving of 'notice to discharge' his contract of employment.

This writer takes the view that the contract of employment was terminated, not by wrongful repudiation, but by proper notice running from the date of the winding-up order. That was made clear by Chitty J. when he said that the case was analogous to that of a domestic servant who is entitled to a month's notice or payment in lieu of notice where notice had been given and the contract of employment terminated with the notice.[4]

The decision in *MacDowall's Case* is nevertheless inconsistent with the earlier decision in *Ex parte Harding*,[5] where employment had continued after the winding-up order, and it had been held that the order had no effect at all upon the contract, so that the employee was entitled to full compensation upon his ultimate summary dismissal. The view taken in *Harding's* case is to be preferred; for the rule in *MacDowall's Case*, that the order operates to terminate the contract of employment by notice even if the employment itself continues, may operate to deprive the employee of compensation

---

[1] Though not damages for loss of commission, it was held in that case, because of the company's cessation of trading—see above, p. 24, n. 6, p. 260, n. 3.

[2] Graham, 'The Effect of Liquidation on Contracts of Service' (1952) 15 MLR 48 at 52.

[3] (1886) 32 Ch. 366. Chitty J. purported to follow *Chapman's Case* (1866) LR 1 Eq. 346, though the facts there were quite different as there had been actual termination of employment at the time of the winding-up order.

[4] LR 32 Ch. 366 at 371.   [5] (1868) LR 3 Eq. 341.

when he is ultimately dismissed. Thus in *Golding and Howard* v. *Fire, Auto and Marine Insurance Co. Ltd. (in liquidation)*,[1] the rule in *MacDowall's Case* was applied to deprive employees of the benefit of all their accrued years of service with the company for the purposes of their claim to redundancy payment. The company was the subject of a winding-up order on 25 July 1966. The two applicants continued to work as before and were paid by the liquidator, one until March 1968, the other until July 1968. It was held, following *MacDowall's Case*, that their contracts of employment with the company had terminated with the winding-up order, and that they had thereafter been employed by the liquidator in his personal capacity and not as agent for the company. Therefore one employee had no right to payment at all, having less than two years' continuous service at the time of termination of employment, and the other lost the benefit of all his prior service.

This matter is clearly one requiring the pronouncement of a superior court, for in *McEwan* v. *Upper Clyde Shipbuilders Ltd (in liquidation)*,[2] a Scottish Industrial Tribunal felt justified in refusing to follow the *Fire, Auto and Marine* decision and in deciding that a liquidator who in the execution of his office retains employees of the company in liquidation does so as the agent of the company. Hence they held that although existing contracts of employment are terminated by the winding-up order, the liquidator's offer of continued employment is made on behalf of the company and prevents this from being a statutory dismissal by the company at the point when the liquidator assumes control. This seems to represent a satisfactory approach to the problem, except perhaps that it should be recognized that where the employment relationship continues after the winding-up order, it does so under the existing contract of employment between the company and the employee, unless the liquidator expressly informs the employee that he is no longer employed by the company. This would not detract from the right of the employee to treat the winding-up order as a wrongful repudiation and to terminate the contract. It would provide a more satisfactory treatment of the case where the employee does not do so, and the employment relationship continues.

---

[1] (1968) 3 ITR 372. A test case for the rights of many employees of the Fire, Auto and Marine Insurance Co.

[2] (1972) 7 ITR 296.

B. Voluntary Winding-Up

Again, it is useful to distinguish the fact situations according to whether or not there is a continuance of employment. Where employment continues after a resolution for voluntary winding-up, it would seem that the resolution has no effect upon the contract of employment. There is no suggestion in the cases that notice of termination starts to run from the resolution. There is authority for the view that the resolution does not effect a dismissal where the employment is continued by the liquidator after the resolution.[1]

Where the resolution for voluntary winding-up is accompanied by dismissal (that is to say, where the liquidator discontinues the employment), this would seem to constitute a wrongful dismissal. Such a case was that of *Reigate* v. *Union Manufacturing Co. Ltd.*[2] This concerned the termination of a commission agency agreement between the plaintiff and the defendant company. The termination took place when the company ceased to trade, upon the passing of a resolution for its voluntary winding-up. The plaintiff was held to be entitled to recover damages for wrongful repudiation by the company. Bankes L.J. pointed out that it was unnecessary for the plaintiff to rely upon the resolution itself; he could found his claim merely on the cessation of business which accompanied it.[3] Pickford L.J. said that 'The voluntary liquidation is only part of the history of the repudiation of the contract by the company.'[4]

In a situation where the liquidator offers a continuance of employment following the resolution for voluntary winding-up, but where the employee wishes to terminate his employment and to claim damages, it is not quite clear whether the employee is entitled to do so. The view has been put forward that he is not necessarily entitled

---

[1] *Gerard* v. *Worth of Paris Ltd.* [1936] 2 All ER 905, Slesser L.J. at 907–9; cf. *Ferguson* v. *Telford Grier, McKay & Co. Ltd.* (1967) 2 ITR 387 (Scottish Tribunal)—held a month's employment after the resolution for voluntary winding-up was employment in the service of the company, and not in that of the liquidator as had been argued; *Bennett* v. *G. W. Thompson Ltd.* (1966) 1 ITR 173 is to like effect. But if, upon the appointment of a liquidator, the business is carried on by a (previously appointed) receiver, the appointment does operate to terminate all subsisting contracts of employment with the company—*Deaway Trading Ltd.* v. *Calverley* [1973] ICR 546, 550 H–551 A.

[2] [1918] 1 KB 592.   [3] Ibid. at 604.

[4] Ibid. at 601. A decision to like effect is that of the Court of Appeal in *Fowler* v. *Commercial Timber Co. Ltd.* [1930] 2 KB 1—where it was held, moreover, that the employee's approval, *qua* managing director, of the resolution for voluntary winding-up did not disentitle him from damages for wrongful dismissal.

to do so; for he is so entitled only if it is clear that the company will not continue to fulfil its obligations, and a resolution for voluntary winding-up is not a conclusive indication to that effect.[1] Gower suggests that if this formulation is correct, a creditors' voluntary winding-up will be more likely to operate as a wrongful repudiation than a members' voluntary winding-up because the intervention by the creditors provides clear evidence of inability by the company to fulfil its obligations.[2]

However, cases upon other types of contract suggest that one party cannot use the passing of a resolution for voluntary winding-up by the other, corporate, party to the contract as an excuse for rescinding the contract.[3] But in such cases it would seem that the obligations of the company in liquidation could validly be discharged by vicarious performance by assignees of the company's contracts. By contrast, it would seem that an employer cannot discharge his obligations to the employee by vicarious performance without the consent of the employee to such delegation.[4] It should follow that where a company in voluntary liquidation purports to assign its contracts of employment without the consent of the employees, the employees are entitled to treat the contract as terminated by reason of wrongful repudiation. However, in *Midland Counties Bank Ltd.* v. *Attwood*[5] it was held that the resolution for voluntary liquidation did not entitle the employee to treat his contractual obligations as ended so that a restrictive covenant could still be enforced against him.[6] Warrington J. distinguished between compulsory winding-up and voluntary winding-up on the basis that the former effected a change in the personality of the company, whilst the latter did not. It followed, in his view, that a winding-up order amounted to wrongful repudiation, whilst a resolution for voluntary winding-up did not. However, in *Reigate* v. *Union Manufacturing Co. Ltd.*[7] Scrutton L.J. rejected the suggestion that a winding-up order effected a change in the personality of the company, pointing out that the company re-

---

[1] Graham, loc. cit. (1952) 15 MLR 48 at 54.

[2] Gower, *Modern Company Law* (3rd edn. 1969) p. 655 n. 8.

[3] *British Waggon Co. Ltd.* v. *Lea* (1880) 5 QBD 149. To similar effect is *Tolhurst* v. *Associated Portland Cement Manufacturers Ltd.* [1902] 2 KB 661— the decision of HL [1903] AC 414 turns upon the further point of the assignability of the benefit of the contract.

[4] See below, pp. 352–4.   [5] [1905] 1 Ch. 357.

[6] Contrast, for example, *General Billposting Co. Ltd.* v. *Atkinson* [1909] AC 118, and cf. above, p. 300 note 1.

[7] [1918] 1 KB 592, 606.

mains in existence until its ultimate dissolution. The decision in *Attwood's* case being therefore based upon a fallacy, it is still open to argue that the employee is always entitled, upon a resolution for voluntary winding-up, to treat his contract of employment as terminated and to claim damages.

C. *Appointment of Receiver*

The effect of the appointment of a receiver and manager upon the contracts of employment of employees of the company depends upon the type of receiver appointed and upon whether the receiver who continues the employment of employees does so as agent of the company, or in his personal capacity, or as agent of the debenture holders. Here, perhaps more than anywhere else, the employee's contractual rights turn upon laws devised without his interests in mind. The employee suffers the arbitrary consequences of the relationship between the company and its debenture holders—itself a matter of considerable complexity and uncertainty.

A receiver and manager appointed by the court cannot continue the employment of the employees of the company in the capacity of agent of the company because he does not generally become the agent of the company.[1] It seems to follow as a necessary result that the contracts of employment are terminated. This is shown by the decision of the Court of Appeal in *Reid* v. *Explosives Co. Ltd.*,[2] where it was held that the appointment of a receiver and manager by the court constituted a wrongful dismissal of the employee even though he continued in his employment under the receiver and manager until the company went into voluntary liquidation. It seems to be in principle correct that such a termination of employment by the company should be regarded as a dismissal of the employee, since there is no person empowered to continue the employment on behalf of the company.[3]

Decisions relating to other types of contract appear to conflict

---

[1] Cf. *Burt, Boulton & Hayward Ltd.* v. *Bell* [1895] 1 QB 276, per Lord Esher M.R. at 279.

[2] (1887) LR 19 QBD 264.

[3] Graham, loc. cit. pp. 49–50, 53–4, places undue emphasis upon the dictum of Fry L.J. in *Reid* v. *Explosives Co. Ltd.* at p. 269: 'I am not prepared to lay down that every entry by a mortgagee is a dismissal of the servants of the mortgagor.' This dictum may refer to entry by the mortgagee in person, or to appointment of a receiver *out of court*. In those cases the entrant *does* act as agent of the company, and there is accordingly no automatic dismissal of employees.

with this view, and to suggest that where a receiver and manager continues their performance the original contracts with the company remain in force.[1] But these cases may be distinguished from the case of the contracts of employment. It could be said of those cases that, although the receiver and manager was not performing the contract as agent of the company, his performance constituted valid vicarious performance by the company. This reasoning cannot be applied to the contract of employment because the obligations of the employer are not susceptible of vicarious performance.[2] The effect of the appointment of a receiver and manager is in this respect analogous to that of the appointment of the liquidator upon a resolution for voluntary winding-up, which was considered above.

Receivers and managers appointed out of court directly by the mortgagees or debenture holders are normally in practice made the agents of the company. It has now been decided that the receiver and manager appointed out of court, acting as agent of the company, is in a different position from that of receivers appointed by the court; where employment is continued by a receiver appointed out of court, it is so continued on behalf of the company, and the previous contract of employment remains in existence.[3] Two possible exceptions to this rule are to be considered.

Firstly, although the receiver and manager appointed out of court will normally be empowered to act as the agent of the company, he may in continuing the employment of employees of the company be

---

[1] *Parsons* v. *Sovereign Bank of Canada* [1913] AC 160—receiver and manager appointed by the court to a company continued to operate contracts made by that company for the sale of paper in bulk. Held the receivers in so doing were acting in continuance of the old contract. Cf. *Re Newdigate Colliery Ltd.* [1912] 1 Ch. 468—receiver and manager appointed by the court sought but was refused permission to discontinue performance of forward contracts for the sale of coal entered into by the company.

[2] The opinion of the Privy Council in *Parson's* case (above) both shows the basis of the reasoning to consist in vicarious performance and distinguishes the contract of employment in that respect: [1913] AC 160 at 167 (Viscount Haldane L.C.).

[3] See the dictum of Plowman J. to that effect in *Re Foster Clark Ltd.'s Indenture Trusts* [1966] 1 WLR 125 (Ch. D) at 123 B–G. (The receiver and manager went on to sell the business and it was held that the sale of the business terminated the contracts of employment of its employees.) Dictum followed and applied in *Re Mack Trucks (Great Britain) Ltd.* [1967] 1 WLR 780 at 786 C–E where Pennycuick J. held that the appointment of a receiver and manager did not in itself terminate contracts of employment with the company (though on the facts the receiver and manager had expressly renewed the contracts of employment, thus making the point unnecessary to the decision).

acting on behalf of the debenture holders and not for the company. If so, the employment with the company will have come to an end. It was so held, for example, in *Hopley-Dodd* v. *Highfield Motors Ltd.*,[1] where the receiver appointed out of court offered a short-term continuation of employment to a particular employee in order to assist him in setting the affairs of the company in order, and where it could be said that the receiver was acting to further the purposes of the debenture holders rather than those of the company.[2] As a result, the employee concerned was not disentitled, by her acceptance of that offer, from treating the appointment of the receiver as a dismissal by the company, attributable to redundancy.

It was also suggested, in *Re Mack Trucks (Great Britain) Ltd.*, by way of an exception to this general rule, that a contract of employment would be terminated by the appointment of a receiver and manager out of court where the employment was of such a nature that its continuance was inconsistent with the appointment of a receiver and manager.[3] This would be so, it was suggested, in the case of the employment of a manager. But there seems no reason why an employee should be placed at an especial disadvantage merely because his function happens to coincide in whole or in part with that of the receiver and manager. It seems wrong to conclude that the contract of employment of the manager of the business of a company, or of a part thereof, is automatically terminated by the appointment of a receiver and manager. Where the employment continues, the appointment ought to be regarded as a repudiation by the employer entitling the employee to terminate his employment,[4] but not as terminating his contract of employment.

---

[1] (1969) 4 ITR 289.

[2] Comparison may be made with the judgment of Sir John Donaldson in *Deaway Trading Ltd.* v. *Calverley* [1973] ICR 546 at 552 D–E, where it is said that a receiver appointed by the debenture holders continued the employment of employees 'for [the Company] and for the debenture holders to the extent of their respective interests'. But elsewhere in the judgment, it appears that the receiver was employing the employees *personally* and as agent *neither* of the company *nor* of the debenture holders (ibid. at 551 B). The court regarded an appeal to a higher court as inevitable and welcome (ibid. at 552 H–553 A).

[3] Per Pennycuick J. [1967] 1 WLR 780 at 786 C. This suggestion originates in the pages of *Kerr on Receivers* (13th edn. 1963) p. 318.

[4] This would seem to follow from *Collier* v. *Sunday Referee Publishing Co. Ltd.* [1940] 2 KB 647—if an employee is employed in a specific post and is deprived of the opportunity to occupy that post, he is entitled to treat his contract as repudiation and to claim damages as for his wrongful dismissal (see above, pp. 241–2.)

D. Company Mergers and Amalgamations, and the Sale of Businesses

Company mergers and amalgamations, and the sale of enterprises to larger commercial concerns, have become the most important type of change in the enterprise as far as the employee is concerned. However, the law of the individual contract of employment has not yet been restated in recognition of this fact. It is for this reason that it is thought useful to state, under one heading, the effects of these changes—effects which follow largely from observations made in other parts of this work in the course of defining wrongful dismissal and wrongful repudiation, and in describing the effect of specific processes such as the winding-up of companies.

The process of take-over of one company by another, or of amalgamation of one company with another, or of merger of one company into a group of companies, may take place by way of a variety of specific transactions.[1] In some cases, the enterprise which has been acquired may remain intact as a corporate entity. This would be the case where its shares are made to vest in the company which takes it over, and it becomes a subsidiary of the taking-over company. Its shareholders will be paid either in cash or in shares in the taking-over company. (The tendency at the present day is towards exchange of shares rather than cash transactions.) The same would be the case where the shares of the company taken over are made to vest in the shareholders of the acquiring company; or where the undertaking, i.e. assets and enterprise, are managed by the taking-over company, but remain nominally the property of the company which has been taken over.

On the other hand, the processes of take-over or amalgamation may involve the destruction of the company taken over, or its cessation to function as an enterprise. This would be the case where the undertaking of the company is acquired, and the company is liquidated, or directly dissolved, and the shareholders get shares in the taking-over company or cash. The same will be the case where the company remains as an empty shell, the shareholders being compensated in cash or shares of the company and the taken-over company becoming a subsidiary without assets. Thus two quite different types of transaction are concerned:

---

[1] See Gower, op. cit. pp. 615 ff. 'Company Reconstructions'; Weinberg, *Take-overs and Mergers* (3rd edn. 1971) Paras 523 ff., 634 ff., 706–11.

(a) transactions involving change in the ownership of the share capital of companies; and

(b) transactions involving change in the ownership of assets, i.e. the undertaking, of companies.

The first type of transaction does not in itself have any direct bearing upon the contractual relationship between the company whose shares change their owner, and its employees. Such transactions are *res inter alios acta* as far as the contract of employment is concerned. Neither the existence of the corporate entity, nor the conduct of its business, is *directly* affected by the change in ownership of its shares. The indirect change in control which is thereby produced may well be followed in practice by great repercussions upon the employment of employees of the company, but does not have any immediate direct effect upon their contracts of employment.[1]

The second type of take-over or amalgamation—that which involves the acquisition of the undertaking (i.e. the assets) of the company—may have a direct effect upon the contracts of employment of the employees of the company. For it may be effected by a method which involves the winding-up or the dissolution of the company. Where the procedure under Section 287 of the Companies Act 1948 is used, the company will be placed in voluntary liquidation and the effect upon the contracts of employment of the employees of the company will be as described above in the event of voluntary winding-up. Where the procedure under Sections 206–8 is followed, the assets and liabilities of the employing company will be transferred to another company by means of a simple vesting order of the court; and the company, having no assets or liabilities, is dissolved by order (without the need for winding-up). Section 208 enables the court to order a statutory novation of the contracts of the company and then to dissolve it.

---

[1] Cf. *Wright* v. *Charlton Concrete Co. Ltd.* (1967) 2 ITR 72 (Industrial Tribunal). The purchase of the entire shareholding of the employing company by a group of companies was held to have had no effect upon the contract of employment of an employee of the company. But a subsequent letter from a director of the employing company who was also chairman of the group was held to have widened the job definition of the employee to include the wider range of activity undertaken by the group as a whole, so that his ultimate dismissal was not attributable to a redundancy. In *Cameron* v. *Finlayson & Co. Ltd.* (1967) 2 ITR 110 (Industrial Tribunal) transfer of share capital of company was held not to constitute a dismissal of employees of the company.

The *ratio* of *Nokes* v. *Doncaster Amalgamated Collieries Ltd.*[1] is that this statutory novation does not operate upon contracts of employment.

The appellant was a coal miner employed by a company which had been amalgamated with the respondent company by the procedure under Section 154 of the Companies Act 1929, the precursor of the present Section 208. The transfer of the employee into the employment of the respondents, following the dissolution of the previous company, had taken place without his knowledge or consent. When the respondent company sought to sue him for absence in breach of his contract of employment under the Employers & Workmen Act 1875, it was held that they were not entitled to do so because there was no contract of employment in force between him and them.

There has been controversy in academic opinion as to whether this is a valuable vindication of the personal nature of the contract of employment[2] or on the other hand a quixotic decision in view of the many means available whereby the control of a company can be made to change hands while the corporate entity remains intact.[3] It would, however, seem that the contract of employment with the company which has been acquired is necessarily terminated by the dissolution of the company, there being no succession by the acquiring company to the contract as a whole.

If the assets of a company are acquired for cash or for shares without a winding-up or dissolution of the company, then the effect on the contracts of employment of the employees of the company does not especially depend upon the corporate nature of the employer. It is just as if the assets of an individual human employer or of an employing partnership had been sold. Just as it was seen that the terms 'take-over' and 'amalgamation' do not connote a single precise type of legal transaction, so the term 'sale of the employer's business assets or undertaking' has no precise significance, and a wide range of transactions may be so described. Legal consequence

---

[1] [1940] AC 1014. Contrast the facts in *Joel* v. *Cammell Laird Ltd.* (1969) 4 ITR 206 where a company was taken over by acquisition of its assets and then wound up. The employees of the company taken over were transferred into the employment of the acquiring company and notified of that transfer by an amendment to the particulars issued to them under Section 4 of the 1963 Act. Under s. 5(4) of the 1972 Act, this kind of change in the name or even the identity of the employer can be notified to the employee as if it were simply a change in the *terms* of employment—there is no need for new particulars to be issued.
[2] Kahn-Freund (1940–1) 4 MLR 221, 224.
[3] Gower, op. cit. pp. 200–1.

has now been attached by the 1965, 1971, and 1972 Acts[1] to the terms 'transfer of a trade or business from one person to another' and 'change in ownership of a business', and these terms have been interpreted as being synonymous.[2] Decisions taken in application of these provisions illustrate the range of transactions which may be described under the general heading of 'sale of the employer's business'.

At one extreme, there is the complete assignment of all the assets and liabilities of a business from one person to another, representing a novation to the extent permitted by the law of all the outstanding contracts of the business.[3] Such a transaction would not effect a novation of the contracts of employment of the assignor company, by reason of the rule in *Nokes* v. *Doncaster Amalgamated Collieries Ltd*. The transfer of a business need not necessarily involve transfer of the liabilities of the transferor, but normally involves the transfer of the premises, stock-in-trade, goodwill, fittings and fixtures of the transferring business, and the benefit of outstanding contracts in so far as allowed by the law.[4] The decisions concerning the concept of the transfer of a business illustrate a wide range of transactions in which the employer disposes of part of his assets without transferring his business as a whole to the purchaser of the assets. Thus there may be a transfer of the premises and machinery of a business but a reservation of the trade marks and goodwill of the business.[5]

[1] The term 'transfer of business' appears in Schedule I para 10 of the 1972 Act, which is used to define the period of continuous employment for the purposes of all three Acts. The term 'change in ownership of a business' appears in s. 13 of the 1965 Act, which limits the employee's claim to a redundancy payment where a business changes its ownership. See below, pp. 363–6.

[2] By the Divisional Court in *Dallow Industrial Properties Ltd*. v. *Else* [1967] 2 QB 449, resolving earlier doubts expressed by Industrial Tribunals in, e.g., *Luckey* v. *Hockley* (1967) 2 ITR 38.

[3] Compare *Chatsworth Investments Ltd*. v. *Cussins (Contractors) Ltd*. [1969] 1 WLR 1 (concerning a building contract).

[4] Compare Diplock L.J. in *Ault (Isle of Wight) Ltd*. v. *Gregory* (1967) 3 KIR 590, 593: 'The agreement which I have read is in any view as plain an example of an agreement for the sale of a business as one could find. It sells the whole of the stock in trade; it sells the plant and equipment; it purports to assign the benefits of all contracts and in effect the vendors part with the goodwill of their business in the Isle of Wight by entering into a covenant not to carry on that business any further'. Quoted with approval by Widgery J. in *Kenmir Ltd*. v. *Frizzell* [1968] 1 WLR 329 at 334 H–335 B.

[5] Compare *Bonser* v. *Patara Ltd*. (1967) 2 ITR 76 (held not to amount to a change in ownership of a business within the Redundancy Payments Act); cf. also *Woodhouse* v. *Peter Brotherhood Ltd*. [1972] ICR 186 where in a similar

Or the apparent transfer of a business from one company to another may turn out upon examination to be nothing more than a transfer of stock-in-trade, the transferee assuming none of the liabilities of the transferor.[1]

In all these situations it is not the sale of the assets as such which terminates the contracts of employment. Further facts must be known in order to decide whether it involves a termination by the employer (by wrongful dismissal or lawful notice) or a termination by agreement between the parties. In *Re Foster Clark Ltd.'s Indenture Trusts*,[2] it was held that the sale of the business of a company as a going concern, which involved all the assets of the company including the goodwill of the business, and whereby it was provided that the company should cease to trade when the sale took effect, operated as a termination of the contracts of employment of employees of the company. But there may be cases where, all these conditions not being present, the sale of assets will not in itself result in a termination of employment. However, even if the sale of assets does not in itself result in a termination of contracts of employment within the enterprise, the decision in *Collier v. Sunday Referee Publishing Co. Ltd.*[3] shows that where an employee is employed in a specific job, and the sale of the employer's assets has the effect that the employer cannot continue to employ him to work in that job, then the employee may treat that failure to employ him in the particular job as a wrongful repudiation of his contract of employment.

There may well arise a situation where the employer disposes of his assets and the working of the business is taken over by the purchaser, but where the employee remains for some purposes in the employment of the original employer. For example, where one company acquires the undertaking of another company in exchange for cash or shares, and where the working of the acquired undertaking

---

case it was held there was no 'transfer of the business' despite the complete continuity of the employee's immediate working environment.

[1] Compare *Austin v. A. R. Clemence & T. J. Clemence (Lanmere) Ltd.* (1966) 1 ITR 370 (held not to amount to transfer of trade or business within the Contracts of Employment Act).

[2] [1966] 1 WLR 125.

[3] [1940] 2 KB 647, following the case of *Driscoll v. Australian Royal Mail S.N. Co.* (1859) 1 F & F 458. (Employee employed as captain of a particular ship. The employers sold that ship and offered him a post as captain of another ship. Held he could nonetheless terminate his employment and sue as upon wrongful dismissal.) See above, pp. 25–7, 241–2 (obligation of the employer to provide actual work).

passes into the control of the acquiring company, the original company (now a mere shell) may be used as the nominal employer of its employees for some time. In this situation, where the company taken over continues to pay the employees and to be responsible for the National Insurance contributions, the employee is then virtually in the position of an employee loaned out by the company taken over. His contract of employment continues in force with the company taken over. The consequences of the transfer of the business upon the contract of employment are then simply postponed until such time as the employee is formally transferred into the employment of the new employer.

E. Change in the Composition of an Employing Partnership

The contract of employment between an employee and a partnership firm is particularly susceptible to termination by reason of a change in the enterprise, because of the non-corporate nature of the partnership. For 'the firm as such has no legal recognition. The law, ignoring the firm, looks to the partnership composing it; any change amongst them destroys the identity of the firm.'[1] The effect of this destruction of the identity of the firm upon the contracts of employment made with the existing partners varies widely according to whether or not the employment is continued with the newly constituted partnership.

The first type of case is that in which a change in the firm occurs and the new partners are not willing to continue the employment. This results in a termination of the contract of employment, but certain decided cases give rise to uncertainty whether this is a wrongful dismissal for which the old firm is liable in damages, or an automatic termination for which the old firm incurs no liability. Those authorities suggest that there may have at one time been a principle of interpretation of contracts between an employee and a partnership, to the effect that such contracts could be construed as being intended to terminate automatically in the event of the death of one of the partners[2] or even in the event of the partners voluntarily deciding to cease to trade as a partnership.[3] It would not seem necessary or desirable that contracts of employment should be so construed today.

[1] *Lindley on the Law of Partnership* (13th edn., London 1971) pp. 25–6.
[2] *Tasker* v. *Shepherd* (1861) 6 H & N 575.
[3] Lord Esher M.R. in *Brace* v. *Calder* [1895] 2 QB 253 at 258–60.

The second type of case to be considered is that in which a change occurs in the composition of the firm, and where the new partners are willing to continue the contract, but the employee is unwilling to work for them. As in the first case, there is necessarily a termina- tion of the contract of employment, since the employee does not continue in employment with the old or with the new firm. However, even if the employee can show that the change in the composition of the firm operates as a wrongful dismissal, it was decided in *Brace* v. *Calder*[1] that the claim for damages for wrongful dismissal is liable to be treated as mitigated in full by the offer of the new partners to continue the employment. It is, none the less, in principle open to the employee to show that he had some valid reason for being unwilling to be employed by the new partners, so that their offer of employ- ment would not operate in mitigation of his claim for damages. To refuse to listen to such arguments would be to put undue pres- sure upon the employee to accept a transfer into the employment of a new and different employer for whom he did not wish to work.

The third type of case is that in which the employment is actually continued with the new firm without a break. One early approach to this situation was to hold that the contract of employment with the old firm continued in force, with the new firm vicariously perform- ing the contract on behalf of the old firm. If the employee was later wrongfully dismissed by the new firm, he could sue the old firm, i.e. the original partners with whom he had contracted, for that wrongful dismissal.[2] But it would now be accepted that the contract of em- ployment is generally not capable of vicarious performance on behalf of the employer.[3] If the original contract of employment is to continue in force despite the change in the composition of the firm, it must therefore be on some basis other than that of vicarious per- formance.[4]

If the employee knows of the change in the firm and agrees to continue in employment with that knowledge, it may be held that the original employment has been terminated by agreement and a new contract of employment formed with the new firm. On this view, there is a lawful termination of the original contract.

---

[1] [1895] 2 QB 253.   [2] *Dobbin* v. *Foster & Others* (1844) 1 C & K 323.
[3] Cf. *Griffith* v. *Tower Publishing Co. Ltd.* [1897] 1 Ch. 21 (contract between author and publisher)—important also as showing that the personality of the employer may be material in the case of a *corporate* employer.
[4] Cf. *Titmus & Titmus* v. *Rose & Watts* [1940] 1 All ER 599 which is a decision to this effect in the case of the employment of an apprentice by a firm of partners.

Moreover, the old firm is subject to no liability for a subsequent wrongful dismissal by the new firm.[1] This would constitute a novation of the contract of employment. Novation takes place where the two contracting parties agree that a third shall stand in the relation of either of them to the other.[2] Opinions differ upon whether novation results in a continuation of a single contract with changed parties, or whether, on the other hand, it results in the termination of one contract and the formation of another.[3] The contractual liabilities of the old firm, the new firm, and the employee are the same on either view. But it could be important where rights are based upon the continuance of a single unbroken contract of employment.[4]

If the employee does not know of the change in the firm, there cannot be a novation by agreement. But the case of *Phillips* v. *Alhambra Palace Co.*[5] suggests that if one partner dies but his personality was not material to the employee, then the contract of employment continues in force with the surviving partners. It seemed necessary to take that view in order to achieve a just result in that case, because the surviving partners sought to rely on the change in the firm as relieving them of liability for wrongful dismissal. It would seem, however, that the contract of employment could not have been enforced *against* the employees by the surviving partners.[6]

It will thus be observed that the law regulating the effect of change in a partnership upon the contract of employment is complex, and depends upon the interplay of rules concerning the duration of

[1] *Hobson* v. *Cowley & Another* (1858) 27 LJ (NS) Ex. 205.
[2] *Chitty on Contracts*, op. cit. Vol. I, Para 1054; cf. *Scarf* v. *Jardine* (1882) 7 App. Cas. 345; *Commercial Bank of Tasmania* v. *Jones* [1893] AC 313 at 316 (Lord Morris).
[3] See Widgery L.J. in *Chatsworth Investments Ltd.* v. *Cussins* [1969] 1 WLR 1 at 7 C–F.
[4] As was, for example, the employee's right to a long-service payment under the Long Service Leave Act 1955 of New South Wales. For the purposes of the British Contracts of Employment Act 1972 and thus the Redundancy Payments Act 1965, a continuous succession of contracts is equivalent to a single continuous contract—Pennycuick J. in *Re Mack Trucks (Great Britain) Ltd.* [1967] 1 WLR 780 at 787 D–H. The 1972 Act also makes provision to ensure that the change of employing partners shall not in itself break continuity—Schedule I Para 9(5). But this fails to cover the case of change from employment by partnership to employment by a sole proprietor who was one of the partners—*Harold Fielding Ltd.* v. *Mansi* [1974] ICR 347.
[5] [1901] 1 QB 59.
[6] See Batt, *Law of Master and Servant* (5th edn. 1967) p. 107. Compare *Nokes* v. *Doncaster Amalgamated Collieries Ltd.* [1940] AC 1014.

such contracts and rules concerning the question whether the personality of the individual partners is material. These complexities arise from the nature of a partnership firm as a non-corporate collection of individuals incurring joint liabilities. The result is a confused body of rules which in some respects fails to provide adequate protection for the employee.

F. *Bankruptcy of the Employer*

The importance of the bankruptcy of the employer for its effect upon the contract of employment is considerably reduced, compared with its importance in the nineteenth century, as the result of the fact that corporate employers have so extensively replaced individual human employers in the area of commercial and industrial employment, and by the fact that full-time domestic employment has undergone so substantial a decline. We consider briefly the effect upon the contract of employment of the main stages in the process of the bankruptcy of the employer. It would seem that the employee might treat various of the successive steps in the process as evidence of the uncreditworthiness of the employer, and that he would accordingly be entitled to treat the contract of employment as wrongfully repudiated, to terminate his employment, and to claim damages as if he had been wrongfully dismissed.[1] His claim for damages will not, however, be a preferential claim, and may as a result be of little value in practice.[2]

The process of the bankruptcy of an employer will normally in practice at some stage involve the dismissal of his employees as part of the winding-up of his business. There is nothing in the law of bankruptcy which entitles the employer to dismiss his employees in the event of his bankruptcy, so that such a dismissal will, as in an ordinary case, be a wrongful dismissal unless proper notice is given. Such a claim will not, however, be a preferential one, any more than that of the employee who terminates his employment himself because of the bankruptcy.

It may indeed be that such contracts of employment are in this situation terminated as a necessary result of the making of the receiving order in bankruptcy against the employer, or at least as a

---

[1] Cf. *Ex parte Pitt* (1923) 40 TLR 5 (making of a receiving order in bankruptcy); Lord Abinger C.B. in *Gibson* v. *Carruthers* (1841) 8 M & W 321 at 343 (adjudication).

[2] See below, pp. 356–7.

result of the adjudication in bankruptcy. These events might be regarded as effecting a wrongful dismissal for which the employee can claim compensation in the bankruptcy. There is no recent authority upon this question, which does not appear to have been an important one in practice. But it would seem that the passing of control in the enterprise to the receiver in bankruptcy[1] or the later vesting of control and assets in the trustee in bankruptcy[2] may be said to be inconsistent with the continuance of former contracts of employment. The early decision in *Thomas v. Williams*[3] appears to be to the contrary effect but may be regarded as decided upon a law of bankruptcy different from that in force today, or otherwise as an unsatisfactory decision.

The most important aspect of the effect of the bankruptcy of the employer upon the contract of employment is, in practice, not so much the remedy of the employee for wrongful dismissal, but the protection accorded to his accrued rights to wages, holiday pay, and other incidental rights of his employment. The adequacy of the provisions for the protection of those rights is considered in later pages.[4]

G. *The General Pattern*

A common pattern emerges from these changes in the enterprise of the employer. They generally result in a change in the person controlling the employment of the employees concerned, i.e.:

(a) liquidation (change to liquidator);
(b) appointment of receiver and manager (change to receiver and manager);
(c) sale of business (change to purchaser of business);
(d) change in constitution of partnership (change to new partners);
(e) bankruptcy (change, first to receiver, later to trustee);
(f) death of employer[5] (change to personal representatives).

The major exception is that of the merger or take-over of a company, which can take place without any formal change of the person in control; that is to say the company remains in existence and in con-

---

[1] See Section 7 of the Bankruptcy Act 1914 and the annotation thereto in *Williams—Law and Practice in Bankruptcy* (18th edn. 1968) pp. 79 ff.

[2] See Sections 53–7 of the 1914 Act and the annotation thereto in *Williams*, op. cit. pp. 423 ff.

[3] (1843) 1 Ad. & E 685.   [4] See below, pp. 355–9.

[5] Discussed (under the heading of frustration) above at pp. 313–15.

trol throughout if the merger or take-over is applied to share capital rather than to assets.

This change of person in control generally entitles the employee to treat the contract of employment as terminated; that is, to leave the employment without liability. Moreover, the employee who does so is generally entitled to sue for damages as upon a wrongful dismissal, except where the change is consequent upon a death, whether of the employer or of one of a partnership of employers. However, the right to claim in damages for wrongful dismissal does not provide a substantial safeguard of the security of the employee in these situations. The advantage to the employee of a right to treat his contract of employment as terminated is more than outweighed by the potential detriment to him from the fact that many of these changes in the enterprise may be held to result in a termination of the contract of employment, regardless of the continuance of the employment after those changes. This will be the case where the person who assumes control of the employment cannot be regarded as the agent of the original employer. Where that occurs, there is a likelihood that the employee may be deprived of his interest in his contract of employment without any, or adequate, compensation for that loss.

In the remaining sections of this chapter, we consider whether a contract of employment comes into force between the employee and the person who assumes control of the employment upon the change in the enterprise, and also other aspects of the protection of the rights and interests of employees in these situations.

SECTION 2: TRANSFER OF CONTRACTS OF EMPLOYMENT[1]

The changes in the enterprise which result in the transfer of the control of the enterprise raise the question, not merely of whether existing contracts of employment are terminated, but also of whether there is a contract of employment in force, after the change, between the existing employees and the person or persons now controlling the enterprise; of whether, and in what circumstances, a contract of employment is transferred from one employer to another. The leading

[1] This is a topic likely to become more prominent in future by reason of the *EEC Draft Directive* concerning the Protection of the Acquired Rights of Employees upon Mergers, Takeovers and Amalgamations, submitted to the Council of Ministers by the EEC Commission in May 1974, which includes a proposal for automatic transfer of employment upon mergers and changes in ownership of enterprises (see below, p. 370 note 2).

case concerning the transfer of contracts of employment is that of *Nokes* v. *Doncaster Amalgamated Collieries Ltd.*[1] It has been pointed out that the victory of the employee in that case was an expensive one.[2] The employee obtained the negative protection of a decision that there was no valid contract of employment in force between him and his apparent employer. It is easy to conceive of a situation in which the employee might seek to claim that he had continued to be employed under a contract of employment throughout his *de facto* transfer from one employer to another. This would be the case, for example, if the employee wished to enforce the right to a minimum period of notice under the 1972 Act, or the right to a redundancy payment under the 1965 Act upon his ultimate dismissal by the new *de facto* employer. In such a case the interests of the employee are protected, rather than jeopardized, by holding that there has been an effective transfer of his contract of employment. In this section, we consider the extent to which it may be possible for the employee to obtain a positive protection of that kind where the situation requires it.

Since English law knows no concept of a contract running with an enterprise, the question of the devolution of contracts of employment upon changes in the legal structure of the enterprise has to be decided by application of the rules concerned with the assignment of contracts. Nor can there, strictly speaking, be such a thing as the transfer of a contract. There may be an assignment of contractual *rights*; there may also be a novation of contractual *obligations*. The question whether the contract as a whole has been assigned is an abstract question with which the courts are not normally troubled. But that abstract issue becomes an important concrete one whenever it is necessary to decide whether there was a contract in existence between given parties at a given time. This is a matter of the utmost importance in the case of the contract of employment. For the various rights of the employee conferred both by common law and by statute are very often conditional upon the existence of a contract of employment in relation to him.

The question of how far the contract of employment as a whole may be assigned from one employer to another depends therefore upon the two questions:

---

[1] [1940] AC 1014 (above).
[2] Kahn-Freund, (1940–1) 4 MLR 221 at 224 (in a contemporary note on the decision).

(a) How far can one employer confer upon another the right to a continuance of the service of the employee? That is to say, how far can one employer assign the benefit of the contract of employment?

(b) How far can one employer transfer to another the obligation to continue the employee in his employment and to pay him for work done? That is to say, how far can one employer assign the burden to him of the contract of employment?

The rule in *Nokes* v. *Doncaster Amalgamated Collieries Ltd.*[1] is that one employer cannot assign the benefit of the contract of employment, i.e. the right to the continuance of the service of the employee, without the consent of the employee. One case suggests that one employer can, on the other hand, confer upon another employer the obligation to continue the employee in his service and pay him for work done.[2] Other cases suggest that the employer cannot, however, effectively divest himself of his own obligations, though those obligations may be rendered purely nominal where another employer does in fact offer continued employment to the employee, or does in fact employ and pay him for work done on terms no less favourable than those of the present employment.[3] The general principle, whereby the obligations of one party under a contract may be discharged by their vicarious performance by a delegate of the contracting party who was under the original obligation,[4] is inapplicable to the contract of employment by reason of the materiality of the personality of the parties.[5]

The reported decisions of Industrial Tribunals provide various instances in which the point has not been taken against the employee that he could be regarded as not having a contract of employment with his employer because a transfer from an earlier employer had

---

[1] [1940] AC 1014 (above); and compare *Denham* v. *Midland Employers Mutual Assurance Ltd* [1955] 2 QB 437. But if the employee expressly contracts to serve his present employer 'or his future co-partner or co-partners, executors, administrators, assignees or successors in business', then the benefit of his obligation to serve *can* effectively be assigned by his employer to another employer taking over that part of the business, and with it also the benefit of a covenant by the employee not to compete with the business: *Benwell* v. *Inns* (1857) 26 LJ (NS) Ch. 663 (an assignment effective in equity before 1873).

[2] *Phillips* v. *Alhambra Palace Co.* [1901] 1 QB 59. See above, p. 347.

[3] *Brace* v. *Calder* [1895] 2 QB 253; compare *Reid* v. *Explosives Co.* (1887) 19 QBD 264.

[4] *British Waggon Co.* v. *Lea* (1880) 5 QBD 149; *Parsons* v. *Sovereign Bank of Canada* [1913] AC 160; cf. *Davies* v. *Collins* [1945] 1 All ER 247 (contract for dry-cleaning of clothing).

[5] Cf. *Griffith* v. *Tower Publishing Co. Ltd.* [1897] 1 Ch. 21.

taken place without his knowledge or assent.[1] It is possible to suggest a method whereby this just solution could be placed upon a more solid theoretical foundation. Legislation would be necessary to provide a complete remedy for the deficiencies of contract theory in this regard, but it may be possible at common law to imply a contract of employment with the new employer in such a situation if the employee has knowledge of the change, even if there is no positive evidence of consent. Furthermore, in the situation where there is neither knowledge nor consent on the part of the employee, it might be possible to hold that where a *de facto* transfer of employment takes place, the new employer ought to be estopped from asserting against the interests of the employee that there was no contract of employment in existence. Kahn-Freund, writing in 1940, thought that in the situation of *Nokes* v. *Doncaster Amalgamated Collieries Ltd.* it would not be easy to construe the conduct of the new company in such a way as to give rise to an estoppel,[2] but perhaps it might now be held that the frontiers of estoppel may be regarded as less firmly fixed than was the case then.[3] It might be necessary to limit such a rule by holding the employee bound by his election whether to proceed, for wrongful dismissal, against his former employer or against his subsequent employer.[4]

However, these suggestions exist in the realm of speculation only. The law as at present established is that there is strong positive

[1] e.g. *Winter* v. *Deepsawin Garages Ltd.* (1969) 4 ITR 162 (various transfers by sale taking place over the head of the employee); *Forrest* v. *Forrest & Co.* (1967) 2 ITR 145 (transfer from employer to trustee for creditors of employer following deed of arrangement treated as not breaking continuity of contract). In certain decisions, Industrial Tribunals have even held the *former* employer liable for redundancy payment upon a dismissal by the *subsequent* employers, where both employers are associated companies. See *Johnson* v. *Drewson's Decor Ltd.* (1966) 1 ITR 267; *Lathey* v. *D.R.B. (Trowbridge) Ltd.* (1966) 1I TR 515.

[2] (1940) 4 MLR 221 at 225.

[3] There is a precedent in *Smith* v. *Blandford Gee Cementation Ltd.* [1970] 3 All ER 154 for an estoppel going the other way—against a denial by the transferor employer of the existence of a contract with him. In redundancy payments cases, an estoppel against the employer might be ineffective against the Department of Employment intervening to protect the Redundancy Fund.

[4] Compare *Ex parte Pitt* (1923) 40 TLR 5. It was contended that the employee, by accepting remuneration from the Sir Thomas Beecham Opera Co. Ltd., following the making of a receiving order in bankruptcy against Sir Thomas Beecham, his original employer, had elected irrevocably not to proceed against Sir Thomas for damages for wrongful dismissal. The Court of Appeal accepted that the doctrine was applicable in principle, but held that it did not apply upon these facts.

authority against the transfer of the right to the services of the employee from one employer to another, and there is little satisfactory precedent for a transfer of the obligations of one employer to another, such as to cause the employee to acquire contractual rights against the new employer. Indeed, the Industrial Court has in two rulings leaned decisively against any notion of automatic transfer of contracts of employment upon the sale and transfer of the business in which the employees were employed. In *Ubsdell* v. *Paterson*[1] and *Cartin* v. *Botley Garages Ltd.*,[2] Sir Samuel Cooke stated (in very similar terms in both judgments) that,

The mere facts that an employee for a short period works hours similar to those which he worked under his contract with the previous employer, and for a short period accepts wages calculated on the same basis as his wages under that contract, are by no means necessarily conclusive evidence that there has been an offer by conduct by the new employer to re-engage the employee on all the terms of the previous contract or that the employee has accepted such an offer.[3]

This is the doctrine of *Marriott* v. *Oxford Co-op. Ltd.* (No. 2)[4] translated into the context of the take-over of a business and the ensuing reorganization of staff. We may see in this a useful protection for the employee against transfer to another employer above his head and without his consent. But if this protection has the result that an employee, who has in fact been transferred into another employment without his knowledge or consent, has no contract of employment with his *de facto* employer, then this protection is dearly bought. And moreover the price is increased by every enactment or contract which accords rights to the employee on the basis of his having the status of an employee under a contract of employment.

SECTION 3: THE PROTECTION OF THE RIGHTS AND INTERESTS OF THE EMPLOYEE

Thus far this chapter has been concerned with the effects of changes in the employing enterprise in purely contractual terms. Those effects have been described fully, as far as the law of the contract of employment concerns itself with them. It will thus be apparent that the law of the contract of employment does remarkably little to protect

---

[1] [1973] ICR 86.   [2] [1973] ICR 144.
[3] [1973] ICR 144 at 147 D; cf. [1973] ICR 86 at 89 C (see above, p. 11).
[4] [1970] 1 QB 186—see above, pp. 60–1.

the employee against the consequences for him of changes in the employing enterprise. The discussion in the preceding sections of this chapter has been concerned not so much with the protection of the employee's rights as with the legal mechanics (in contractual terms) of changes in the employing enterprise as they affect employees. We need to know how the contract of employment operates in this kind of situation, but the answer to that question is very far from being a complete answer to the whole problem of the employee's, position when the situation of his employer (individual or corporate) undergoes a major change. We have found, for instance, that the contract of employment may be differently affected by a compulsory winding-up and by the members' voluntary winding-up of the employing company. We need to know whether there is any case in social and practical terms for differentiating these two events as they affect the employee. Further, we need to know what aspects of the employee's situation fall outside the protection which his contract of employment affords him in either of these events. We should therefore examine the protection accorded to the employee's wider and non-contractual rights upon changes in the employing enterprise. This may enable us to assess the rôle of the contract of employment in the whole problem of the adverse effects upon employees of changes in the employing enterprise. Thus the issue considered in this section is that of what claims and expectations the law should recognize in this area, and how far the contract of employment can be the means of meeting those claims and fulfilling those expectations.

A. Protection where the Employer is Insolvent

Provision is made by the Bankruptcy Act 1914 and by the Companies Act 1948 for preferential payments to employees of an employer adjudicated bankrupt, or an employing company wound up compulsorily by order, or voluntarily by resolution.[1] The provision in respect of bankruptcy is that made by Section 33 of the Bankruptcy Act 1914, as amended by the Companies Act 1947, whereby the wages or salary[2]

[1] The provisions concerning individual bankruptcy apply equally to the bankruptcy of an individual partner in a firm of partners, and to the collective bankruptcy of a firm. See *Lindley on the Law of Partnership* (13th edn.) p. 649.

[2] Interpreted to include amounts deducted from wages in contravention of the Truck Acts: see *Ex parte Cooper* (1884) 26 Ch. D 693 (applied to fund held by employer deducted from wages for the purpose of a 'doctor's fund' and 'reading room fund' which had not yet been paid over to the doctor or to the treasurer of the reading room at the time of bankruptcy). Also extended to include accrued holiday remuneration—by the Companies Act 1947 (ss. 91 and 115).

of any clerk or servant or labourer or workman,[1] not exceeding two hundred pounds, in respect of services rendered during the four months before the receiving order, whether payable for time- or for piece-work, shall be paid in priority to all other debts in the distribution of the property of a bankrupt.[2] The wages which are made into preferential debts by this provision form only one of a number of categories of preferential debts, some other categories being twelve months' rates and income tax due from the bankrupt[3] and twelve months' National Insurance contributions due from the bankrupt as an employer.[4] These preferential debts rank equally between themselves and abate in equal proportions if the property of the bankrupt is insufficient to meet them.[5] An exactly corresponding set of provisions is made in respect of the liquidation (voluntary or compulsory) of a company by Section 319 of the Companies Act 1948, with the additional provision that anyone who has advanced money to the company to pay wages is subrogated to the rights of the employees so paid.[6]

The question arises whether the interests of employees are adequately protected by these provisions. The provisions giving a preferential right to payment of wages and other remuneration accrued due do not give a preferential right to a claim for damages for wrongful dismissal. In making such a claim, the employee ranks *pari passu* with all other non-preferred debts proved in the bank-

---

[1] The Act in its original form made more generous provision in respect of clerks or servants than in respect of labourers or workmen—a distinction which became increasingly difficult to draw. Cf. *Green & Sons* v. *Minister of Health* (No. 2) [1948] 1 KB 34; see *Williams—Law and Practice in Bankruptcy* (18th edn., London 1968) p. 232.

[2] The corresponding provision under the earlier Bankruptcy Law Consolidation Act 1849 was held not to apply in favour of colliers' drawers who were employed, on a labour-only subcontracting system, with an intermediate employer, to whom work was let out at a rate for the task: *Ex parte Ball* (1853) 3 De GM & G 155. The modern parallel, decided in the case of a corporate main contractor under s. 319 of the Companies Act 1948, is *Re C. W. & A. L. Hughes Ltd.* [1966] 1 WLR 1369.

[3] Section 33(1)(a) of the Bankruptcy Act 1914.

[4] Section 33(1)(e) of the 1914 Act as amended by successive National Insurance Acts.

[5] Section 33(2) of the 1914 Act.

[6] By Section 319(4) of the 1948 Act. There is also the additional provision in relation to companies that the employees' preferential rights have priority over the debenture holders' floating charge—1948 Act s. 94(1) and (2)—a provision of some social interest—see Gower, op. cit. p. 424.

ruptcy.[1] Furthermore, the Bankruptcy Law Amendment Committee reporting in 1957[2] disclosed that the preferential claims in bankruptcy proceedings made by the Revenue were often so large as to produce the result that the assets were insufficient even to meet the preferential claims in full. They recommended that in order to provide adequate protection for employees, it would be necessary to grant a specially preferred right to one week's wages or salary.[3] This would enable the trustees in bankruptcy to avoid immediate hardship to employees by enabling them safely to pay one week's wages in full before they knew whether the assets would suffice to meet other preferential claims in full. No action has been taken upon this recommendation.

The additional provision in the case of liquidations (as opposed to bankruptcies), whereby the money advanced by a third party for the purpose of paying current wages ranks as a preferential claim,[4] is intended to protect employees by making banks willing to advance money for that purpose when the company as a whole appears a bad credit risk. But it is extremely difficult to distinguish in practice between advances earmarked for that purpose and other advances, and the attempt to do so has given rise to much litigation and many nice legal problems.[5] The Bankruptcy Law Amendment Committee was of the opinion that the provision was open to abuse, and might operate as an incentive to an employer to carry on his business after he knew he was insolvent.[6]

Moreover, the provisions for preferential wage payments in the event of the insolvency of the employer afford no protection to the employee in respect of his claims against his employer to a pension. This is an area in which the claims of the employee are especially liable to be rendered worthless by the insolvency of the employer. Provision is often made by the rules of an employer's pension fund and the deeds constituting the trusts of the pension fund, for the determination of the trusts of the fund and the distribution of the fund upon the winding-up of the company otherwise than for the purposes of reconstruction.[7] In that case the employee is liable to

---

[1] Despite what is said on this point in Batt, *Law of Master and Servant* (5th edn. 1967) pp. 108-9.
[2] Cmnd. 221 (known, after its chairman, as the Blagdon Committee).
[3] Ibid. at Para. 95.   [4] s. 319(4) of the Companies Act 1948 (above).
[5] Gower, op. cit. p. 659.   [6] Cmnd. 221 at Para. 96.
[7] Compare Phillips, *Pension Scheme Precedents* (London, 1957) s. 960. See Note below, p. 383.

receive the benefits produced by the contributions made to the pension fund on his behalf in a less advantageous form than would have been the case had the fund continued in being.

Worse still, if the employer's pension scheme is not a funded one, i.e. if the employer meets pension liabilities out of current revenue, then the employee has nothing better than a non-preferential claim against the assets of the employer to protect his pension rights in the event of the insolvency of the employer.[1] And if in such a case the employer makes *ex gratia* payments to his employees upon the cessation of his business, those payments are liable to be declared *ultra vires* the company and to be successfully challenged by minority shareholders (though that does not apply to payments made to employees to meet contractual liabilities owed to them).

Thus in *Parke* v. *Daily News Ltd.*,[2] the Daily News, upon sale of its business to another company, proposed to recompense its employees for their loss of pension expectations[3] caused by the fact that the pension scheme was not a funded one. It was proposed to distribute the surplus, following the sale of the company's business and discharge of its debts, to the employees as *ex gratia* payments. But a minority shareholder succeeded in having such a distribution declared *ultra vires* the company on the ground that it could not benefit the interests of the company.

Hence a corporate employer, even if disposed to do so, cannot properly make good to employees the loss of pension expectations where an unfunded pensions scheme ceases to operate.

A quite different kind of protection of the employee's accrued rights upon his employer's insolvency is provided in relation to statutory redundancy payments. The claim of the employee to a redundancy payment receives special statutory protection in the event either that he cannot obtain payment without recourse to a

---

[1] See Hosking, *Pension Schemes* (2nd edn. 1960) Chapter 2 'Unfunded Pensions' pp. 13–20. The Social Security Act 1973 makes provisions directed to ensuring a minimum level of funding of occupational pensions schemes, sufficient to meet the hazards here discussed—see Section 59. At the time of writing, the Government does not intend to bring that part of the Act into effect. See Note below, p. 383.

[2] [1962] Ch. 927. And see Gower, op. cit. pp. 92 and 522; see also Pilch and Wood *New Trends in Pensions* (London 1964) pp. 140 and 147 for a full account of the case as an 'object lesson in the dangers of unfunded pension schemes'.

[3] Pension expectations rather than pension rights. The action of the company in setting aside £500,000 to meet liability for pension rights already recognized as such could not be challenged.

court[1] or that the employer is insolvent.[2] This special protection is made possible by the existence of the Redundancy Fund, to which the employee is given direct recourse in these events. The employer is for this purpose insolvent if he has become bankrupt, or has made a composition with creditors,[3] or if he has died and his estate is ordered to be administered according to the law of bankruptcy,[4] or if, in the case of a company, a winding-up order has been made, a resolution for voluntary winding-up has been passed, a receiver and manager has been appointed, or possession has been taken by debenture holders secured by a floating charge.[5] If the employer is unable to pay his debts, but is not insolvent within this definition, the employee may be able to claim that he cannot obtain payment without recourse to a court.[6] In these events the employee claiming a redundancy payment may apply to the Department of Employment for payment directly from the Redundancy Fund, and the Department is bound to make such a payment once satisfied that the conditions have been met.[7] This provision for recourse to the central fund expresses the dual aspect of the Redundancy Payments Act 1965, whereby it both imposes an obligation upon the employer to compensate the employee in the event of redundancy, and at the same time sets up a state insurance system, whereby to meet part of the cost to the employer of redundancy payments. Hence this statutory right receives better protection in the event of insolvency of the employer than do the contractual rights of the employee to arrears of wages and compensation for wrongful termination.

B. *Protection of Rights based upon Length of Service*

The tendency to base contractual and statutory rights of the employee upon a service qualification, or to increase the value of those rights according to the length of service, is growing fast.[8] There is still a considerable contrast between American and British employment practices, in that contractual seniority rights, in the sense of preferential rights to the opportunity to continue to work when

---

[1] Redundancy Payments Act 1965 s. 32(1)(a).
[2] Ibid. Section 32(1)(b). [3] Ibid. Section 32(5)(a).
[4] Ibid. Section 32(5)(b). [5] Ibid. Section 32(5)(c).
[6] Cf. *Pollard* v. *Teako (Swiss) Ltd.* (1967) 2 ITR 357.
By Section 32(3) of the 1965 Act the Redundancy Fund is subrogated to the rights of an employee to whom a payment is made out of the Fund.
[8] See *Industrial Society Survey No. 146*—'Service recognition and gifts to employee' (February 1968).

there is a reduction in the work force, or to opportunities for promotion, are rarely found in our practice. In so far as seniority rights of this kind exist in Britain, they take the form of expectations created by relatively informal 'first in, last out' collective agreements, and rarely assume the form of defined individual contractual rights.[1] On the other hand, the length of the period of service now commonly affects:

(a) the contractual right to payment during absence due to sickness;
(b) the extent of entitlement to holidays and holiday pay;[2]
(c) the extent of entitlement to notice (this is subject now to the rights to minimum periods of notice under the Contracts of Employment Act 1972. These minimum rights depend themselves upon length of period of service);
(d) the extent of entitlement to severance payment (subject again to the minimum rights to redundancy payments under the 1965 Act in the special case of redundancy, as defined by the Act, these minimum rights again themselves being dependent upon length of service);
(e) the eligibility to participate in profit sharing schemes;
(f) the eligibility for grants upon change in the location of employment and for assistance with house purchase;
(g) the eligibility for, and extent of, entitlement to a pension under an occupational pensions scheme;
(h) the right to increments in remuneration based upon the length of service;
(i) the right to protection against unfair dismissal under the 1971 Act is a right of this kind, to the extent that it is subject to an initial qualifying period of two years' service.[3]

These rights based upon long service may be protected upon the termination of employment, either (a) by enabling the employee to claim immediate payment in respect of those rights or to claim compensation for the loss of them, or (b) by securing to the employee

---

[1] See Seyfarth, Shaw, *Labour Relations and the Law in the United Kingdom and the United States* (Michigan 1968) pp. 489 ff. 'Limitations on transfer and lay-off—seniority systems'.

[2] Cf. the statutory provision to that effect in s. 11(2) of the Wages Councils Act 1959.

[3] s. 28(1) of the 1971 Act. Since the concept of continuous employment, as there used, is not statutorily defined, the right seems to receive no protection upon transfer of employment, except in so far as the transfer itself constitutes an unfair dismissal. See Appendix, para 2.

the same seniority in an equivalent scheme of recognition in his new employment. We proceed to consider the extent to which the various different types of seniority right are protected by either of these methods.

1. The Protection of Pension Rights. The right of the employee which will generally be of the largest financial importance to him upon a transfer of employment is his accruing right to a pension under his employer's occupational pension scheme. Occupational pension rights receive a limited protection by law upon the transfer of employment.[1] They receive a somewhat more effective protection in practice, but that protection is unsystematic and may be regarded as unsatisfactory.

Occupational pension rights are protected by law upon the transfer of employment only to the following extent.[2] If the employee is entitled to treat the termination of his former employment as a wrongful or unfair dismissal, then he may claim loss of pension rights as a head of damages in those actions.[3] If transfer into another employment is alleged by the former employer as a factor mitigating the loss incurred by the employee, the transfer of seniority into the new employer's pension scheme (if any) could be adduced in mitigation too. In that case, any disadvantages of the new scheme as compared with the old could be brought into account in damages, though this would involve complex actuarial calculation. Claims of this kind would in practice probably be made only by managerial and executive employees entitled to very substantial pension rights.

Occupational pension scheme rights receive a more extensive protection in practice than in law upon the transfer of employment. There is generally under the rules of occupational pension schemes a right on the part of the employee to the return of his own contribu-

---

[1] The law is considerably altered in this respect by the Social Security Act 1973, which creates an Occupational Pensions Board responsible for ensuring the preservation of pension benefits upon termination of employment. See generally Gilling-Smith, 'Occupational Pensions and the Social Security Act 1973' (1973) 2 ILJ 197. But the Act was not due to come into force until 1975 and at the time of writing the Government intends to give only partial effect to the Act—see Note, below, p. 382.

[2] There are additional statutory provisions applying where occupational pensions schemes are contracted out of the state graduated pensions scheme— see National Insurance Act 1965 ss. 57–60. These provisions serve the limited purpose of ensuring equivalence with the graduated state pension. See Note, below, p. 384.

[3] *Bold* v. *Brough, Nicholson & Hall Ltd.* [1964] 1 WLR 201. See above, pp. 252 ff., and, for unfair dismissal, p. 256 note 2.

tions upon the termination of his employment, for whatever cause.[1] There is generally also a right to claim the benefit of the employer's contributions upon termination of employment other than by reason of fraud or misconduct.[2] The benefit may be offered in the form of a vested right to a pension upon retirement, the value of which represents the contributions so far made. This is known as a 'vested', 'deferred', or 'frozen' pension right. Or the benefit may be offered in the form of a purchase on behalf of the employee of equivalent rights in the pension scheme of his new employer. This is known as a right to 'transfer-value'.[3] It is felt by many that it is inimical to the long-term interests of the employee to allow him to take a refund of his own contributions upon termination of his employment before retirement. This defeats the objective of the pension scheme, which is to make provision for him at retirement. This is the basis for the view[4] that the employer should be obliged by law to provide full rights either to deferred pensions or to transfer-value upon termination of employment, and perhaps also that employers should be prevented from offering a refund of the employee's contributions as an alternative.

2. *The Protection of Statutory Rights to a Minimum Period of Notice.* The right to a minimum period of notice conferred upon the employee by the Contracts of Employment Act 1972 is a seniority right both in that there is an initial qualifying period of service of thirteen weeks and in that the right is increased after further periods of service.[5] This right is protected upon transfer of employment by the provisions of Section 1 and the First Schedule of the Act, whereby seniority under a former employer is transferred into the employment of the subsequent employer in certain defined cases. In those cases, the period of service under the former employer counts as service with the transferee employer for the purposes of the Act, and the continuity of employment is treated as not having been broken by the transfer.

These cases include the following:

(a) cases where the employee is transferred upon the transfer of

---

[1] See Pilch and Wood, *New Trends in Pensions* (London 1964) p. 153; cf. *Re Foster Clarke's Indenture Trusts* [1966] 1 WLR 125—an example of the application of such a provision in a pension scheme.

[2] Pilch and Wood, op. cit. pp. 72–4.   [3] Ibid. p. 73.

[4] Now reflected in the Social Security Act 1973—see below, Note, pp. 382, 383.

[5] Section 1(1). See Appendix, para 6.

the trade or business or undertaking of his employer (i.e. where the employee follows a transfer of the business).[1] The term 'transfer of a trade or business' has been interpreted as requiring that the transferee be put in possession of an enterprise or a viable unit of an enterprise as a going concern.[2] If there is merely the transfer of the premises or physical assets of a trade or business, there is no 'transfer of a trade or business' for this purpose, even if a particular employee is transferred with the premises.[3]

(b) cases where, on the death of an employer, the employee is taken into the employment of the personal representatives of the deceased;[4]

(c) cases where there is a change in the partners, personal representatives, or trustees who employ any person;[5]

(d) cases where an employee of a company is taken into the employment of another company which, at the time when he is taken into its employment, is an associate of the first company.[6]

Associated companies are defined[7] as companies one of which is a subsidiary of the other, or both of which are subsidiaries of a third company.[8] This provision for transfer of seniority rights between associated companies is an important step towards the protection of seniority rights of employees in the context of a group of companies operating under unified control; which is an increasingly common situation.

3. *The Protection of Statutory Rights to Redundancy Payments.* The statutory right to redundancy payment, upon dismissal by reason of redundancy as defined by the Act of 1965, is, like the right to a minimum period of notice, a seniority right both in that there is an initial qualifying period of service of two years[9] and in that the right

[1] Schedule 1, Para 9(2).
[2] *Kenmir Ltd.* v. *Frizzell* [1968] 1 WLR 329.
[3] *Dallow Industrial Properties Ltd.* v. *Else* [1967] 2 QB 449; *Woodhouse* v. *Peter Brotherhood Ltd.* [1972] ICR 186 (transfer of factory).
[4] Schedule 1, Para 9(4) of the 1972 Act.
[5] Schedule 1, Para 9(5). See above, p. 347 note 4.
[6] Schedule 1, Para 10(1), originally added by Section 48(7) of the Redundancy Payments Act 1965.
[7] By s. 48 of the Redundancy Payments Act 1965, which applies s. 154 of the Companies Act 1948. Contrast the form of definition used by the 1971 Act (s. 167(8)).
[8] The term 'subsidiary company' is defined by s. 48 of the 1965 Act which again applies the (perhaps narrow) definition given by s. 154 of the 1948 Act. See Gower, op. cit. pp. 196–8.
[9] Section 8 of the 1965 Act.

increases in value according to the length of service.[1] There is a series of provisions in the 1965 Act which have the result that upon termination of an employment there is either an immediate right to redundancy payment or a transfer of redundancy protection into the next employment, but not both. The provisions designed to achieve this result are complex and their application is capable of giving rise to anomalies.

Firstly, two provisions of the Redundancy Payments Act 1965 extend the meaning of 'dismissal' for the purposes of the Act beyond the ordinary meaning of the term, in such a way that many of the changes in the enterprise of the employer which have been discussed in this chapter may be treated as a dismissal for the purposes of the Act. Section 22(1) extends the meaning of dismissal by providing that:

where in accordance with any enactment or rule of law, any act on the part of an employer, or any event affecting an employer (including in the case of an individual his death), operates so as to terminate a contract of employment, that act or event shall be treated for the purposes of the Act as a termination by the employer.

Furthermore, as the result of Section 3(1)(c) of the Act, the employee is to be treated as having been dismissed by the employer if the employee terminates his contract without notice in circumstances such that he is entitled so to terminate it by reason of the employer's conduct. It has been shown above that many of the changes in the enterprise of the employer entitle the employee to treat the contract of employment as terminated, e.g. change in partners, winding-up order or resolution, bankruptcy of employer.[2] If the employee does treat the contract as terminated, that should be held to be dismissal for the purposes of the Act.

However, although a change in the employing enterprise may well result in a dismissal of the employee for the purposes of the Redundancy Payments Act, various provisions of the Act exclude the right to redundancy payment where that change is accompanied by a transfer of employment, and in connection with that change the previous owner terminates the employee's contract of employment. The Act provides, in effect, that where there is a change in the ownership of a business, an offer of employment by the new owner, or an actual re-engagement by the new owner, shall operate as if they were

---

[1] S. 1(1) and Schedule 1.   [2] See above pp. 349–50.

an offer or re-engagement by the former owner; that is to say, they will exclude the right to a redundancy payment if the proper conditions are complied with.[1]

In a sense, these provisions represent an encroachment upon the freedom of the employee to choose his employer. In particular, it is provided that no account shall be taken of the substitution of one owner of a business for another in deciding whether the refusal of an offer of employment made by the new owner was unreasonable.[2] Hence although the employee is under no positive obligation to accept employment under the new owner of the business in which he was employed, his refusal to do so may incur the loss of the accrued right to redundancy payment.

Having seen the circumstances in which a change in the enterprise may entitle the employee to an immediate redundancy payment, we consider the circumstances in which the employee may, by contrast, take his seniority for redundancy purposes into the employment of a new employer. The rules for transfer of seniority, that is to say, the rules whereby a period of service with one employer counts as a period of service with the next employer, are the same as those examined above[3] in relation to the 1972 Act.[4] Hence there is a transfer of seniority rights in the case where the employee himself is transferred to the purchaser of the former employer's business or into the employment of a company associated with the former employing company. However, it should be emphasized that this does not occur in every situation of transfer of employment. If an employment is terminated in circumstances *not* entitling the employee to a redundancy payment, it does not automatically follow that he *is* entitled to a transfer of rights into his next employment. He must still satisfy the conditions in Schedule 1 of the Contracts of Employment Act 1972 for transfer of rights, i.e. transfer of trade or business, or transfer into employment of personal representatives of his employer; or transfer into the employment of different partners or

---

[1] S. 13. So also s. 48 (transfer to associated companies), s. 23 and Schedule 4 Part I (transfer to personal representative). See above, p. 315 n. 1.

[2] Section 13(4)(b) of the 1965 Act. Compare Schedule 1 Para 5(b)—no account to be taken of the substitution of the personal representatives of the deceased employer.

[3] See above, pp. 362–3.

[4] With the necessary modification that a period in respect of which a redundancy payment has been made cannot count towards a period of continuous employment for the purposes of any subsequent right to a redundancy payment— s. 24 of the 1965 Act. See also *Lord Advocate* v. *De Rosa* [1974] ICR 480.

different trustees; or transfer into employment of a company associated with the company employing him.[1] The transfer of redundancy rights is restricted, and moreover that restriction depends upon highly legalistic concepts such as 'transfer of trade or business' which have no reference to the working environment of the employee himself.[2] Hence the employee can remain in ignorance of his right to a redundancy payment until that right has been destroyed by a change in the employing enterprise of which he is unaware and whose legal effect he is in no position to assess anyway. The protection of redundancy rights is thus a very imperfect one.

4. Seniority Rights which are not Generally Protected by Law or in Practice. Of the seniority rights listed at the beginning of this subsection,[3] the minor rights do not yet receive general protection either in law or in practice on the transfer of the employee from one employer to another. By transfer of the employee, we mean for this purpose the termination of one contract of employment and the formation of another contract with another employer. In the case of the temporary loan of an employee from one employer to another, the employee remains under contract with his general employer,[4] and his seniority rights are protected by that fact. Hence we refer here to formal transfer, whereby the National Insurance cards are returned to the employee[5] and the income tax form P.45 is issued to him, as upon an outright termination of employment. Upon a complete transfer of this kind, the seniority rights of the employee, to holiday pay, to sick pay, to improved terms of notice, to participation in fringe benefit schemes such as profit-sharing and assistance with house purchase, are not protected by law in the sense that the employee has no right to compensation in respect of that loss of seniority,[6] and has no legal right to equivalent seniority in the employment of his new employer.

---

[1] There is one extension of these conditions. By s. 23 and Para 13 of Schedule 4 of the 1965 Act, a period of service with a deceased employer in the case of a domestic servant in a private household counts as a period of service with any person to whom the management of the household passes in consequence of the death of employer otherwise than by way of sale (e.g. where a relative of the deceased re-engages the employee).

[2] A test based on the continuity of the employee's working environment was specifically rejected by the Court of Appeal in *Woodhouse* v. *Peter Brotherhood Ltd.* [1972] ICR 186.

[3] Above, p. 360.   [4] See Atiyah, *Vicarious Liability* (London, 1967) p. 155.

[5] (Applicable only up till 6 April 1975.)

[6] Unless an unfair dismissal is involved (cf. above, p. 261 note 3).

Moreover, such seniority rights are not protected in practice, in the sense that different employers are so far from maintaining uniform arrangements on these matters that there is little likelihood that the employee can conveniently enjoy a transfer of seniority into an equivalent scheme.[1] Exceptions have been established in some collective agreements regulating transfer of employees upon take-over of one substantial company by another.[2] The decision of the Divisional Court in *Southern Electricity Board* v. *Collins*[3] shows an example of a collective agreement in a public service industry providing that service under any of the Boards constituting that industry shall count as continuous service with any other Board for the purpose of fringe rights of the employee based upon continuous service. Lord Parker C.J. there said of this agreement that it provided that an employee, transferred from the employment of one Board into that of another Board 'carried his accrued benefits with him'.[4] But protection of minor seniority rights in this way is the exception rather than the rule, and it demands a more advanced pattern of industrial relations than is frequently to be found in the context of company take-overs and amalgamations.

C. Protection against the Consequences of Mergers and Take-overs

The aspects of the legal protection of the employee upon changes in the enterprise of the employer which have so far been considered have been based upon the termination of the contract of employment constituted by those changes. But to limit our examination to the immediate contractual consequences of the change in the enterprise of the employer would be to take too narrow a view.[5] Thus a merger between two companies, or the acquisition of one company by another, may have no immediate effect at all upon the contracts of employment of the employees of the company so taken over. That will be the case if the acquiring company takes a controlling interest in the shareholding of the company. Alternatively, the imme-

---

[1] An important exception is the holiday stamps scheme run for the building industry by Building & Civil Engineering Holidays Scheme Management Ltd. A judicial account of this scheme is given by Roskill J. in *Building & Civil Engineering Holidays Scheme Management Ltd.* v. *Post Office* [1964] 2 All ER 25 at 27 E–29A.

[2] The facts of *Joel* v. *Cammell Laird Ltd.* (1969) 4 ITR 206 illustrate such a case, each company agreeing to accept service with the other company as service with itself for the purpose of seniority rights.

[3] [1969] 2 All ER 1166.   [4] Ibid. at 1169 H–I.

[5] See generally Gower, op. cit. p. 634.

diate consequence may be nothing more than a formal transfer of the employee from the employment of one company into that of another. In that situation, the real consequences for the employee in terms of loss of security will consist, not in the immediate effect upon his contract of employment, but in the likelihood that the new controlling company may in the course of time impose a new personnel policy which will result in redundancies, or in changes in the terms and conditions of employment.

In one of its provisions, the Redundancy Payments Act 1965 recognizes this fact and attempts to safeguard employees against it. The definition of redundancy for the purposes of the Act is extended by Section 48(3) so that it may be satisfied by treating a group of associated companies as together constituting one business, and applying the definition to that group. Hence, for example, if a company becomes a subsidiary company in a group of companies and an employee is dismissed, it may be shown that he was dismissed by reason of redundancy by establishing that the group as a whole intends to cease the kind of work concerned, and it is unnecessary to show that intention in the particular subsidiary company.

However, it may be said that the positive protection offered by the law of the contract of employment to employees against the consequences of reorganization following mergers or take-overs is, in other respects, very limited indeed. It is true that the employee cannot be obliged to enter into a contract of employment, nor held to an obligation to work when his employer has been changed above his head and without his knowledge.[1] But that is a purely negative protection to the employee, whose interest is normally not in avoiding the legal consequences of the withdrawal of his labour, but in claiming a right to the continuance of his employment on his existing terms and conditions. And even that negative protection is unavailable where control of a company is altered by the acquisition of its share capital, for that involves no change in the nominal employer. Moreover, employees are especially vulnerable to imposed variations of occupational pensions schemes following merger or amalgamation. Normally, the attempt to impose a variation of terms upon the employee may be regarded as a breach of contract by the employer unless it is preceded by a period of notice as long as that required to terminate the contract of employment. But the rules of

---

[1] *Nokes* v. *Doncaster Amalgamated Collieries Ltd.* [1940] AC 1014; *Denham* v. *Midland Employers' Mutual Assurance Ltd.* [1955] 2 QB 437.

pension schemes normally reserve to employers a discretion to wind up the pension scheme, and in that case the employee has no right to object to the winding-up of one scheme and his transference either into another existing scheme or into a new scheme.[1] In general, if we consider this lack of protection of the employee, in the event of mergers, as a question of the responsibility of the corporate employer to its employees, we may quote the comment of Gower that it represents 'a particularly unfortunate facet of the principle that the interest of the company means only the interest of the members, and not of those whose livelihood is in practice much more closely involved'.[2]

In recent years there have been attempts to move towards legal measures for a more positive protection of the interests of employees affected by take-overs and mergers. The proposals for such legal protection tend to be of the following types:

(a) legal protection by compulsory provision of information concerning mergers;[3]

(b) legal protection by compulsory collective bargaining concerning mergers;[4]

[1] For a discussion of examples of good and bad practice by employers in relation to pensions schemes upon take-overs, see Pilch and Wood, *New Trends in Pensions* (1964), pp. 139–51, discussing the take-over of the *News Chronicle* by Associated Newspapers (which gave rise to the action of *Parke* v. *Daily News Ltd.* [1962] Ch. 927), and the take-over of Commercial Plastics Ltd. by Dominion Tar & Chemical Company. The remark in the text is subject to the provisions of the Social Security Act 1973—see Note, below, p. 383.

[2] Gower, op. cit. p. 634.

[3] Such a proposal was made in the Employees' Security Bill introduced in HC by Mr. Eric Moonman (Bill 55 of 3rd Sess. of 44th Parl.). The Bill was withdrawn upon the undertaking of the Labour Government that their Industrial Relations Bill would include an obligation on managements to supply employees with information about reorganization and its effect—Parliamentary Debates Vol. 780 Col. 1954–90. The Industrial Relations Bill proposed by the Labour Government provided for the production of a Code concerning the disclosure of information by employers to trade union representatives, which it was intended should serve this purpose, among others (Bill 164 of 4th Sess. of 44th Parl. Clauses 20–1). Disclosure of merger and manpower prospects is seen as a specially important aspect of objectives concerning disclosure generally in the *TUC Interim Report on Industrial Democracy* (1973) at Para 78.

[4] Proposals of this kind were made in the *TUC Economic Review* for 1969 at Paras. 157–67, whereby any company contemplating a merger or take-over would be required to negotiate with unions about such matters as union recognition, negotiating machinery, redundancy procedure, and compensation for workers affected by reorganization. The Government reaction was expressed in the NJAC publication 'Dealing with Redundancies' reproduced in the *Guide to Board of Trade Practice on Mergers* (H.M.S.O. 1969) pp. 35 ff., which however

(c) legal protection by representation of workers on supervisory boards of companies, the supervisory board having powers to control or influence the forward planning of the company where manpower requirements are likely to be affected;[1]

(d) (perhaps most important of all) protection of acquired rights by means of an automatic transfer of the employment relationship from the transferring enterprise to the acquiring enterprise—i.e. from the old to the new employer—coupled with protection of employees against dismissal due exclusively to changes in the structure of the enterprise.[2]

In so far as these safeguards relate to union representation and participation by employees in the planning and effecting of reorganization of employment following upon mergers and take-overs, they move outside the scope of this work. They concern the protection of collective interests by collective means. It may be that legal measures will in the future be taken for the better protection of employees affected by mergers. Such protection may consist in these collective safeguards It might on the other hand consist in the importation into private employment of the kind of provisions for compensation which exist in relation to employees of public authorities affected by alterations in the patterns of employment by those authorities.[3]

---

contemplated discussion and consultation with unions, rather than bargaining, about mergers. Extension of the scope of collective bargaining into redundancy and dismissals is stated as a TUC objective in the *Interim Report on Industrial Democracy* (*1973*) at Para. 66; but this is seen as giving insufficient means of controlling the essentially unilateral decisions concerning investment location, closures, take-overs, and mergers which are thought to be matters not readily covered by collective bargaining—ibid. Para. 85; hence the need for co-determination expressed in that report (see below, next note).

[1] Proposals of this kind are made, for instance, by the *TUC Interim Report on Industrial Democracy* (1973) at Para 91; cf. also *Draft Fifth Directive of the EEC Commission on the Harmonisation of Company Law* (*1972*) Article 12.

[2] These are the main points made in an *EEC Draft Directive* concerning the Protection of Acquired Rights of Employees upon Mergers, Take-overs and Amalgamations, submitted to the Council of Ministers by the EEC Commission in May 1974 in implementation of the Programme of Social Action adopted by the Council of Ministers in 1973.

[3] Compare, for example, the Local Government (Compensation) Regulations 1963 (S.I. 1963 No. 999) (as subsequently amended by 1965 Act Sched. 7 and by S.I. 1965 No. 571; S.I. 1968 No. 913; S.I. 1970 No. 1889) which provided for payment of compensation to local authority employees suffering loss of em8 ployment or remuneration by reason or reorganization of local government in England and Wales, these provisions being in various respects more ambitious in their compensatory objectives than the general redundancy payments legislation.

It is not within the scope of the present work to consider in detail how such provisions might be adapted to the needs of private employment. The general reflection may instead be offered that the protection of the employee in merger situations seems to lie partly in the direction of collective labour law, or in the direction of an application of public law principles; and seems in any event to require an enlargement of the scope of the protection which is provided by the law of contract alone. The present chapter, and this topic as a whole, may be concluded by observing that the types of change in the employing enterprise which are assuming so great a practical importance at the present day are at the same time revealing the inherent limitations of the law of the contract of employment, and are illustrating the need for that body of law to be supplemented by recourse to concepts of a different kind—concepts which enable the employment relationship to be seen as a valuable entity extending beyond the confines of the particular contract of employment with the particular employer.

POSTSCRIPT

THE IMPLIED TERMS OF THE CONTRACT OF EMPLOYMENT

It seems appropriate to follow the last chapter of this work with a brief review of the change in the character of the contract of employment which has occurred during the last decade. During that period, the law concerning the termination of the contract has undergone a general re-examination by the courts and has emerged very substantially altered; though it is still in need of further reform, as the last chapter in particular has sought to show. However, for this concluding assessment of the developing nature of the contract, it is preferable not to dwell further upon termination, but to return to our starting-point, namely the formation of the contract and of its terms. Here great changes have occurred which indicate an emerging new rôle for the contract of employment in Labour Law as a whole.

These developments are twofold; but it is useful to identify the starting-point before describing the changes from it. Before 1963, the contract of employment had remained substantially unchanged in character for a long period. It was typically an informal contract in which express terms were often confined to the rates of remuneration and the employer's rules of work. This scanty framework of express terms would be supplemented chiefly by a set of terms implied by law, some of which would provide minimal protection for the employee—such as the right to a 'reasonable' period of notice[1]— and some of which were directed towards protection of unfettered managerial prerogative—such as the prerogative of summary dismissal for disobedience without the obligation to give reasons.[2] Before 1963, the contract of employment could survive in this somewhat anachronistic form more by reason of its disuse than because of its acceptability. Its very archaism, by rendering it of such slight use to the would-be litigant—for instance the dismissed employee—helped to preserve it in an un-reformed condition.

Since that time, two main types of change have occurred. First,

---

[1] See above, pp. 151–4.   [2] See above, pp. 197–200, 221–2.

the contract of employment has become a contract by incorporation rather than a contract by conduct on terms implied by law. Secondly, it has become a vehicle for employees' rights far more extensively than it had been in the past. The contract has come to incorporate a much wider range of terms implied from collective agreements and from formal arrangements made by employers, such as sick-pay schemes[1] and pension schemes, than used to be normal. This is due in part to the development of those kinds of joint regulation and protection of employees during the period concerned. However, it is also the result of the impact of various pieces of legislation producing a response in the case-law. The 1963 Act did much to create the model of the contract as a contract by incorporation when it introduced the new requirements for statutory particulars of certain terms of employment, and allowed that requirement to be satisfied by referring to outside documents.[2] The 1971 Act extended the list of particulars required[3] and caused many employers to issue statutory particulars for the first time. Meanwhile, the 1965 Act had relied upon the contract of employment to provide definitions of employees' hours of work, job specification, and place of work.[4] Industrial Tribunals and the courts relied heavily upon statutory particulars to provide evidence of the contractual terms concerning those matters, and often treated collective agreements as incorporated into individual contracts via those particulars.[5]

While the contract of employment was thus moving towards a pattern of increasing incorporation by reference, it was also becoming increasingly subject to statutory implied terms concerned with the protection of the rights of the employee. The 1963 Act provided rights to minimum periods of notice by statutory amendment of individual contracts of employment,[6] and the Equal Pay Act 1970 added an implied term about equal treatment of men and women.[7] This kind of legislative technique was employed in the 1971 Act,[8] which also used the novel device of making the Section 5 rights and

---

[1] See above, pp. 112–13.   [2] Now 1972 Act s. 4(1), 4(5).
[3] S. 20, now 1972 Act s. 4(1)(d)(i) as repealed in part by TULRA 1974 (see Appendix, para. 4).
[4] See above, pp. 48–53, 47–8, 42–7, respectively.
[5] e.g. *Turriff Construction Co. Ltd.* v. *Bryant* (1967) 2 ITR 292; *Joel* v. *Cammell Laird Ltd.* (1969) 4 ITR 206; *Stevenson* v. *Teesside Bridge & Engineering Ltd.* [1971] 1 All ER 296.
[6] Now 1972 Act, s. 1(3).   [7] Section 1(2).
[8] Section 147 of the Act could be regarded as having this kind of effect, despite its avoidance of the terminology of implied terms. See also p. 374 n. 3.

the grievance procedure resemble contractual rights by requiring employers to give statutory particulars of them as if they were terms and conditions of employment.[1] Moreover, when the TULRA 1974 accorded a degree of legal protection to certain closed shop agreements, it confined this protection to agreements making the closed shop part of the individual terms and conditions of employment for the employees affected.[2] The enforcement of duties to engage in collective bargaining by arbitration awards taking effect as implied terms in individual contracts of employment[3] also contributes to the growing role of the contract as an individual code of employees' rights. In that type of case, regulation of the contract of employment is the ultimate stage of an auxiliary process by which the law promotes or supports collective bargaining. Here, the collective parties control the initiation of a process which culminates in a contractual implied term at the individual level.

What effects have these developments had upon the law concerning the implied terms of the contract of employment? The incorporation of collective agreements via statutory particulars of terms of employment has been a development of great significance with both positive and negative effects. The positive effect has been that reference in statutory particulars has often overridden the difficulties about incorporation of collective agreements—difficulties of evidence of the requisite knowledge of the terms and intention to incorporate them,[4] and about their appropriateness for incorporation.[5] Indeed, sometimes this process seems to go further than the parties are likely to have intended, and the particulars have even tended to create an estoppel against denial of their accuracy.[6] The safeguards of Section

[1] Section 20 (see Appendix, para. 4 for subsequent developments).

[2] Section 30(1), the definition of union membership agreement, and Sched. I para. 6(5). The Trade Union and Labour Relations (Amendment) Bill of 1974, as amended in Committee in the House of Lords, provided that union membership agreements were to be defined as matters of practice not needing to be incorporated into individual contracts of employment (Clause 3(3) of Bill 124 (H.L.) of 1st Session, 47th Parl.).

[3] 1971 Act s. 127(3); Consultative Document on the Employment Protection Bill, Para. 46.

[4] e.g. *Joel* v. *Cammell Laird Ltd.* (1969) 4 ITR 206; *Soutar* v. *Fisher* (1975) 10 ITR 38.

[5] e.g. *Camden Exhibition and Display Ltd.* v. *Lynott* [1966] 1 QB 555 (see above pp. 14, 37); *Bloomfield* v. *Springfield Hosiery Ltd.* [1972] ICR 91; *Soutar* v. *Fisher* (above).

[6] *Soutar* v. *Fisher* (above); *Boyce* v. *Torquay Cemetery Co.* [1975] IRLR 80; contrast *Parkes Classic Confectionery Ltd.* v. *Ashcroft* (1973) 8 ITR 43 where an employer's failure to notify a change of terms did not create an estoppel against him.

18(4) of the TULRA 1974 concerning incorporation of collectively bargained peace obligations were made very necessary by developments of that kind. There is also a negative effect consisting in a growing unwillingness to incorporate the results of collective bargaining where that bargaining is not linked to the contract by reference in statutory particulars. This applies especially to local agreements supplementing or varying national agreements.[1] The same trend is evident in judicial reluctance to regard union representatives as *ad hoc* agents capable of affecting the terms of individual contracts of employment,[2] or to give contractual effect to custom and practice varying the effects of formal agreements.[3] The area of formal and defined contractual terms seems likely to be increased by proposed legislation for notification to employees of works rules and of the title of the employee's job.[4] Where the contract of employment is itself put into writing, the general principles of contract law may operate to exclude evidence of any parol terms or parol variations of the written agreement.[5] This rule may produce unintended and inappropriate consequences by throwing a still deeper gulf between formal and informal bargaining as far as their effect upon individual contracts is concerned.

If we turn from factually implied terms to terms implied by law, we find that the courts are to some extent reflecting the gradual legislative transformation of the contract into a code of employees' rights. Whilst they have been willing to elaborate the employee's duties of co-operation[6] and of fidelity,[7] they have also been prepared

---

[1] *Loman & Henderson* v. *Merseyside Transport Services Ltd.* (1967) 3 KIR 726; *Gascol Conversions Ltd.* v. *Mercer* [1974] ICR 420 (where the particulars had been transformed into an actual contract of employment).

[2] Cf. *Singh* v. *British Steel Corporation* [1974] IRLR 131 (IT) (re-negotiation of terms and conditions of employment) (See Hepple (1974) 3 ILJ 166). (Contrast *Williams* v. *Butlers Ltd.* [1975] ICR 208 where the employee was held to have precluded himself from cancelling a check-off arrangement *except* through the agency of his union, because the agreement for checking-off had become part of his contract of employment.)

[3] e.g. *Graham* v. *Anthony Todd Haulage Ltd.* [1975] IRLR 45 (IT).

[4] Consultative Document on the Employment Protection Bill, Para. 92.

[5] See *Gascol Conversions Ltd.* v. *Mercer* [1974] ICR 420 at 426 F (Lord Denning M.R.).

[6] *Sec. of State for Employment* v. *ASLEF* (No. 2) [1972] 2 ICR 19—see above pp. 30–1.

[7] See, e.g., *Printers & Finishers Ltd.* v. *Holloway* [1964] 3 All ER 731; *Under Water Welders Ltd.* v. *Street* [1968] RPC 498; *United Sterling Corpn. Ltd.* v. *Felton & Mannion* [1974] IRLR 314.

to envisage the development of a contractual right to strike,[1] and a contractual right to work.[2] Moreover, and at least equally significantly, they have resisted arguments for implied terms giving employers the rights to move the employee's place of work,[3] alter his job specification,[4] or transfer him to the employment of an associated company.[5] The overall preference seems to be for an avoidance of judicial law-making via terms implied by law, especially as the factually incorporated and statutory content of the contract tends to increase; though the courts have perhaps been more willing to imply terms in industrial conflict cases than in truly individual employment law cases.

What general conclusions may be drawn from these new trends in implied terms? Is it a welcome development if the contract of employment is to become a more formalized, more fully articulated contract, and if it is to define mutual rights and obligations more sharply and specifically than it previously did? The trend appears to be a constructive one. At the same time it is fair to repeat an argument advanced in the Introduction to this work, that an increase in the legal significance or legal development of the contract of employment does not necessarily involve an increase in its social utility. The contract of employment is still an institution which lends itself very readily to the expression of lawyers' concepts and lawyers' understandings of the employment relationship. Their viewpoints have in the past suffered from archaism and the excessive influence of the patterns of commercial contracting on the one hand, and domestic service on the other. It should not be too lightly assumed that those defects have disappeared from the law of the contract of employment.

---

[1] *Morgan* v. *Fry* [1968] 2 QB 710; see above, pp. 102–5.

[2] *Langston* v. *AUEW* [1974] ICR 180 (subsequent proceedings [1974] ICR 510), see above, p. 27.

[3] *O'Brien* v. *Associated Fire Alarms Ltd.* [1968] 1 WLR 1916; *Rowbotham* v. *Arthur Lee Ltd.* [1974] IRLR 377; cf. *Abernethy* v. *Mott, Hay & Anderson* [1974] ICR 323.

[4] *GKN* (*Cwmbran*) *Ltd.* v. *Lloyd* [1972] ICR 214.

[5] *Kemp* v. *Robin Knitwear Ltd.* [1974] IRLR 69 (IT).

Appendix

THE TRADE UNION AND LABOUR RELATIONS ACT 1974

The purpose of this appendix is to state the effects of the Trade Union and Labour Relations Act 1974,[1] (referred to here as 'the 1974 Act') upon the matters discussed in the present work. The Industrial Relations Act 1971, which was repealed by the 1974 Act, had a marginal rather than a fundamental impact upon the law of the contract of employment. However, where the 1971 Act did have such effects, it produced developments of more than ephemeral interest for the law of the contract of employment. Hence it has been thought desirable to deal with the effects of the 1974 Act in the form of an appendix rather than to eliminate the discussion of the 1971 Act which occurs in the main body of the text.

1. ABOLITION OF THE INDUSTRIAL COURT

Very frequent reference is made in the text of this work to judgments of the National Industrial Relations Court. With the abolition of that court by the 1974 Act with effect from 31 July 1974, the decisions of that court are presumably reduced to persuasive status for the future. Their persuasive force is likely, however, to be considerable, especially as the appellate jurisdiction from Industrial Tribunals in redundancy payment and unfair dismissal cases has not been returned to the Queen's Bench Divisional Court but has been vested in judges of that Division sitting singly,[2] so that the appellate courts will be differently constituted as compared with their equivalents before 1971.

2. RE-ENACTMENT OF THE UNFAIR DISMISSAL PROVISIONS WITH AMENDMENTS

Because the 1974 Act had as an objective the formal repeal of the 1971 Act in its entirety, it was necessary for the 1974 Act to re-enact the unfair dismissal provisions of the 1971 Act, which is done in Schedule 1 Part II

---

[1] For full discussion, see Wedderburn (1974) 37 MLR 527: and for full details of the effects upon individual employment law, see *Chitty on Contracts*, 6th Cumulative Supplement (1975) to 23rd Edition, paras 637–75 *passim*.

[2] This is effected by a combination of s. 25 and Sched. 3 Para. 15 of the 1974 Act together with the Rules of the Supreme Court (Amendment No. 2) Order 1974 (S.I. No. 1115 (L 15)).

of the 1974 Act. The re-enactment also makes some amendments. The most important one from the point of view of the present work is that concerning constructive dismissal—see below, Para. 3.

The law concerning dismissal which is unfair by reason of trade union membership, non-membership, or activity is also changed, and the onus of proof of whether dismissal was reasonable in the circumstances is placed upon the employer (Sched. 1 para. 6).

Other amendments consisted in the reduction of the qualifying period to twelve months in the first instance and eventually to six months; in the increasing of the upper limit of compensation; and in the extension of the basic time limit for applications from four weeks to three months (Sched. 1 paras. 10, 20, 21(4)).

3. EXTENSION OF THE DEFINITION OF UNFAIR DISMISSAL TO INCLUDE CONSTRUCTIVE DISMISSAL

See pp. 237–8.

In the 1974 Act the definition of dismissal for the purpose of the law of unfair dismissal is re-enacted with the addition of the case where the employee terminates the contract of employment with or without notice in circumstances such that he is entitled to terminate it without notice by reason of the employer's conduct (Sched. 1 para. 5(2)(c)). This gives statutory effect to the doctrine of constructive dismissal, whose development in the case-law was examined in the main text of this work. The new provision differs from the corresponding provision of the Redundancy Payments Act 1965 (Section 3(1)(c)) in that it includes termination without notice.

4. THE OBLIGATION TO GIVE STATUTORY PARTICULARS OF GRIEVANCE PROCEDURES AND RIGHTS UNDER SECTION 5 OF THE 1971 ACT

See pp. 14–15.

The 1974 Act repealed without replacement Section 4(2)(a) of the Contracts of Employment Act 1972, which was a re-enactment of a provision first made by Section 20(2)(a) of the 1971 Act. This repeal abolished the obligations to give statutory particulars of rights under Section 5 of the 1971 Act, and no corresponding provision is made by the 1974 Act. However, the obligation to give statutory particulars of grievance procedures which was imposed by Section 20(2)(b) and (c) of the 1971 Act was left unaffected by the 1974 Act, having meanwhile been re-enacted as section 4(2)(b) and (c) of the 1972 Act. In so far as that provision could operate to bring about the incorporation of certain 'no-strike' obligations into contracts of employment (see p. 15, note 2), its effect in that respect will presumably have been curtailed by the new restrictions upon such incorporation contained in section 18(4) of the 1974 Act (see Para. 5 of this Appendix).

5. NEW RESTRICTIONS UPON INCORPORATION OF COLLECTIVE AGREEMENTS INTO INDIVIDUAL CONTRACTS OF EMPLOYMENT

See p. 12 ff., 124, note 6.

An important positive reform of contract law which is carried out by the 1974 Act consists in the placing of elaborate restrictions upon the incorporation of certain terms of collective agreements into individual contracts (Section 18(4)). The effect of this enactment is that provisions in collective agreements placing restrictions upon strikes or other industrial action by workers will not be incorporated into individual contracts of employment unless the collective agreement (a) is in writing, and (b) expressly states that its 'no-strike' provisions are liable to be incorporated into individual contracts of employment, and (c) is reasonably accessible to the workers affected at their place of work and is available during working hours. The union(s) concerned must be independent and the ordinary conditions for express or implied incorporation must also be satisfied. Contracting out of Section 18(4) is expressly declared to be ineffective, whether by collective agreement or individual contract with a worker (Section 18(5)). It is not clear how far the requirement described at '(b)' above may be fulfilled by a general clause as opposed to a clause referring to named terms of the agreement. If a general clause will suffice, the use of it would carry the risk of a wider incorporation of no-strike obligations than all the parties to the collective agreement may have intended.

6. STATUTORY PERIODS OF NOTICE

See pp. 159–161.

The extension of the statutory minimum periods of notice effected by Section 19 of the 1971 Act over and above those provided by Section 1(1) of the Contracts of Employment Act 1963 survives the repeal of the 1971 Act, having meanwhile been re-enacted in Section 1 of the Contracts of Employment Act 1972.

7. THE ABOLITION OF THE LAW OF UNFAIR INDUSTRIAL PRACTICES

See pp. 121 ff. esp. p. 124, note 3.

The total repeal by the 1974 Act of the law of unfair industrial practices affects certain aspects of breach of contract considered in this work. Where the 1971 Act used a concept of 'strike or other irregular industrial action' and defined 'irregular industrial action' by reference to breach of contracts of employment, the 1974 Act makes much more limited use (Sched. I paras. 8, 15) of a concept of 'strike or other industrial action' and refrains from defining these terms at all. Breach of the contract of employment may be treated as a crucial concept in that connection; and retains a significance in the law concerning economic torts and trade disputes, subject to a new provision declaring that a breach of contract in contemplation or furtherance of a trade dispute shall not be regarded as the doing of an unlawful act or as the use of unlawful means for the purpose of establishing liability in tort (1974 Act Section 13(2)(b)).

8. THE REPEAL OF SECTION 147 OF THE 1971 ACT CONCERNING THE CONTRACTUAL EFFECTS OF STRIKE NOTICES AND STRIKES

See pp. 105, 106, 123, 124, 170.

Although the matter is not free from difficulty,[1] the repeal of Section 147 probably restores the relevant law to the position in which it stood immediately before the coming into force of that section. It was unnecessary to re-enact Section 147 in the 1974 Act because of the abolition of unfair industrial practices and the immunities for acts in contemplation or furtherance of trade disputes contained in Section 13 of the 1974 Act.

The judicial comments about the requirements for valid strike notice discussed in the main text of this work,[2] which were made against the background of Section 147, appear to remain equally applicable to the law as it now stands, although their authority may have been diminished by the abolition of the Industrial Court (see Para. 1 of this Appendix).

9. REPEAL AND PARTIAL REPLACEMENT OF SECTION 128 OF THE 1971 ACT (NO COMPULSION TO WORK OR TO TAKE PART IN INDUSTRIAL ACTION)

See p. 276, notes 2 and 5.

That part of Section 128 of the 1971 Act which forbade any court to compel an employee, by an order for specific performance of a contract of employment or by an injunction restraining the breach thereof, to do any work or attend at any place for the doing of work, has been re-enacted by Section 16 of the 1974 Act. It is a provision declaratory of the equitable rule against specific enforcement of contracts of employment as far as the employee's duty to work is concerned.

Applying as it does to any court, this provision could be relevant where orders are sought which have the *effect* of compelling an employee to work or attend for work even though not expressly imposing such a compulsion. The point has not yet been tested in case-law, but could possibly apply to certain injunctions preventing employees from working for any other employer.

The part of Section 128 of the 1971 Act which forbade any court to grant an injunction which, by restraining an employee from working under a contract of employment, would compel him to take part in industrial action, was repealed without replacement by the 1971 Act. This provision of the 1971 Act represented the last vestige of the general prohibition upon enforcement of union rule books by unions against their own

---

[1] See pp. 105 n. 3, 106 n. 1, 169 n. 5.
[2] See pp. 168 n. 1, 169 n. 2.

members which was expressed originally in Section 4 of the Trade Union
Act 1871. Litigation by unions to enforce calls for industrial action has
not been a practical reality, and hence that provision of the 1971 Act
was effectively superfluous.

10. THE POWER TO CONFER JURISDICTION ON INDUSTRIAL TRIBUNALS IN RESPECT OF BREACH OF CONTRACTS OF EMPLOYMENT

See p. 3, note 2.
The power given by Section 113 of the 1971 Act to the Lord Chancellor
to confer on Industrial Tribunals, by affirmative resolution procedure,
jurisdiction in respect of breach of contracts of employment had not been
exercised by the time that the 1971 Act was repealed. The 1974 Act makes
no corresponding provision; but at the time of writing the Government
has indicated its intention to propose the re-enactment of Section 113
in their Employment Protection Bill.

THE SOCIAL SECURITY ACT 1973

This note is concerned with the impact of the Social Security Act 1973 ('the 1973 Act') upon the aspects of occupational pension schemes ('OP schemes') discussed in the main text of this book.

The 1973 Act made three kinds of provisions directly or indirectly affecting OP schemes:

(a) provisions to set up a State Reserve Pension Scheme (Part III of the Act);

(b) provisions for recognition of OP schemes as entitled to exemption from the State Reserve Scheme (Sections 51–62);

(c) provisions concerning preservation of benefit under OP schemes (Section 63 and Sched. 16).

Orders were made for the implementation of these three sets of provisions: Social Security Act 1973 (Commencement) Orders 1973 Nos. 1 and 2, S.I. 1973 Nos. 1249 and 1433.

The Labour Government then decided not to implement the State Reserve Scheme and recognition provisions, but left the preservation of benefit requirements to come into effect on 6 April 1975: Social Security Act 1973 (Commencement) (No. 4) Order 1974, S.I. 1974 No. 823. The preservation requirements have also been the subject of a series of Occupational Pension Schemes (Preservation of Benefit) Regulations: S.I. 1973 No. 1469, S.I. 1973 No. 1784, S.I. 1974 No. 1324. This note tries to state the relevant effects of the preservation requirements and also to draw attention to one or two matters for which provision would have been made by the State Reserve Scheme and the recognition requirements.

1. THE NATURE OF THE PRESERVATION REQUIREMENT

The Occupational Pensions Board has powers to ensure that OP schemes contain rules ensuring that employees who leave their jobs before retirement will retain preserved rights to benefit from the scheme where the employee has been in the scheme for five years or more and is at least twenty-six years old (Sched. 16 para. 6(1)). The preserved benefits must normally be calculated in the same way as the entitlement to benefit upon retirement would have been (Sched. 16 para. 10). These provisions tend to reduce the loss of pension rights which the dismissed employee can suffer; see pp. 247 n. 1; 253 n. 2, n. 3; 361 n. 1; 362 n. 4.

2. REFUND OF CONTRIBUTIONS

The preservation requirements will with effect from April 1980 prevent schemes from making a refund of a member's own contributions as an alternative to preserved benefits where a member has satisfied the qualifying conditions, at least in respect of service from April 1975 onwards (Sched. 16 para. 9). This will tend to increase the effective protection of rights under OP schemes; see pp. 247 n. 1; 362 n. 4.

3. FORFEITURE OF BENEFITS

Apart from exceptions relating to bankruptcy, and certain offences against the state or relating to employment in the public service, the preservation requirements restrict forfeiture provisions in OP schemes to events occurring after the benefits become payable. The preservation requirements also prevent forfeiture rules from discriminating against the holders of preserved benefits—that is, against those leaving employment before retirement as compared with those staying in the employment until retirement (Sched. 16 para. 16). Furthermore, the rules of schemes must not enable the employer to exercise any charge or lien on, or right of set-off against, a member's preserved benefit, except where a debt to the employer arises out of a criminal, negligent, or fraudulent act or omission by the member, and even then only subject to statutory safeguards (Sched. 16 para. 18). More extensive provision against forfeiture of benefits would have been made by the recognition requirements if implemented (Section 60). The provisions which have been made tend to reduce the oppressive effects capable of being produced by forfeiture rules; see pp. 192 n. 3; 230 n. 3; 231 n. 2.

4. WINDING-UP OF PENSION SCHEMES

The preservation requirements have the result that members of a scheme still in service when the scheme is wound up must have entitlement to preserved benefits as though their employment had ended at that date (OP Schemes Preservation of Benefit Regulns. 1973 (S.I. 1973 No. 1469) reg. 12). This will tend to protect employees in general where an OP scheme gives an employer an effective discretion to wind up the scheme, and also where the winding-up of an OP scheme follows as a consequence of the winding-up of a company; see pp. 253 n. 2; 357 n. 7; 369 n. 1.

5. FUNDING OF SCHEMES

The recognition provisions would if implemented have required the Occupational Pensions Board to be satisfied of the adequacy of the funding arrangements of OP schemes to secure the statutory minimum pension benefits (Section 59). These provisions about funding would have tended to protect employees against the adverse effects of insolvency of employers who make unfunded pension provisions; see p. 358 n. 1.

6. STATE RESERVE SCHEME AND NATIONAL INSURANCE GRADUATED PENSIONS SCHEME

The State Reserve Scheme would if implemented have replaced the National Insurance Graduated Pensions Scheme. Despite the non-implementation of the former, the latter has in any event been abolished by the 1973 Act, and the system of contracting out of state graduated contributions disappears with the change to a straightforward earnings-related contribution system with effect from 6 April 1975 (see Part I of the 1973 Act: 'the Basic Scheme'). The references in the main text to the N.I. Graduated Scheme therefore apply with considerably modified effect from 6 April 1975; see pp. 231 n. 1 and 361 n. 2. The 'Basic Scheme' provisions of the 1973 Act relating to contributions have since been embodied in Part I of the Social Security Act 1975, which is a consolidating statute.

BIBLIOGRAPHY

This bibliography contains references to the main literature on the contract of employment in English Law, together with some of the most immediately relevant writings in the fields of industrial relations, industrial sociology, and labour history.

AIKIN, O.   Note on *Report of the Committee on the Truck Acts* (1962) 25 MLR 220.

AIKIN, O. and REID, J.   Labour Law I: Employment Welfare & Safety (Penguin, Harmondsworth, 1971).

ANDERMAN, S. D. Voluntary Dismissal Procedures and the Industrial Relations Act (P.E.P., London, 1972).

AVINS, A.   Employees' Misconduct as a Cause for Discipline and Dismissal in India and the Commonwealth (Allahabad India, 1968).

BAKER, K. H. and ASHDOWN, R. T.   *Disciplinary Procedures; Practice & Law* (1973) 81 Department of Employment Gazette 64.

BAKER, P. V.   Note on *Pepper* v. *Webb* (1969) 85 LQR 325.

BALL, F. N.   Statute Law relating to Employment (3rd edn., Thames Bank, London 1949, 3rd Supp., 1951).

BATT, F. R. (ed. WEBBER, G.)   The Law of Master & Servant (5th edn., Pitman, London, 1967).

BROOKS, D. and SMITH, R.   The Human Effect of Mergers: The Impact on the Shop Floor (III in a series) (Acton Society Trust, London, 1966).

BROWN, W.   *A Consideration of 'Custom and Practice'* (1972) 10 British Journal of Industrial Relations 42.

——   Piecework Bargaining (Warwick Studies in Industrial Relations, Heinemann, London, 1973).

CASEY, J. P.   *Unemployment Benefit and Damages; the Need for a New Approach* [1969] Juridical Review 206.

CHITTY, J. (ed. GUEST, A. G.)   The Law of Contracts (23rd edn. Sweet & Maxwell, London, 1970, and 6th Supp. 1975)—Vol. II Ch. 5—(Employment).

CLARK, G. de N. *Industrial Law and the Labour-only Sub-contract* (1967) 30 MLR 7.

——   Remedies for Unjust Dismissal—Proposals for Legislation (P.E.P. Broadsheet 518, London, 1970).

——   *Unfair Dismissal and Reinstatement* (1969) 32 MLR 532.

Committee of Inquiry under Professor Phelps Brown into certain matters

concerning labour in Building and Civil Engineering—
Report, Cmnd. 3714 (H.M.S.O., London, 1968).

COUNTER, K. N. S.   *Preservation of Pension Rights* [1968] JBL 229.

CRONIN, J. B. and GRIME, R. P.   Labour Law (Butterworths, London, 1970), Chapters 1–5.

DAVIES, J. E.   The Master and Servant Act 1867 (Butterworths, London, 1868).

——   The Labour Laws (Butterworths, London, 1875) (on the Employers and Workmen Act 1875 and contemporary legislation).

DAVIES, P. L.   *Judicial Law-making in the Industrial Court* (1974) 35 MLR 62.

——   Mergers and Other Changes in Structure or Control of Enterprises and their Effects upon Workers (British National Report on Theme II of the 8th International Conference on Labour Law and Social Security Legislation) (Giuffrè, Milan, 1974).

DIAMOND, A. S.   The Law of Master and Servant (2nd edn. Stevens etc. London, 1946).

DIX, D. (ed. CRUMP, D. W.)   Contracts of Employment (on the Contracts of Employment, Redundancy Payments, and Industrial Relations Acts) (4th edn., Butterworths, London, 1972).

DRAKE, C. D.   Labour Mobility and the Law (1969) Bulletin of the Industrial Law Society No. 5 p. 2.

——   *Wage-Slave or Entrepreneur* (1968) 31 MLR 408.

——   Note on *Richardson* v. *Koefod* (1970) 33 MLR 325.

——   Note on *Contracts of Employment Act 1972* (1972) 1 ILJ 242.

EVANS, E. O.   *Works Rule Books in the Engineering Industry* (1971) 2 Industrial Relations Journal 54.

FLANDERS, A.   *Measured Daywork and Collective Bargaining* (1973) 11 British Journal of Industrial Relations 368.

FOSTER, K.   *Strikes and Employment Contracts* (1971) 34 MLR 275.

——   *Strike Notice: Section 147* (1973) 2 ILJ 28.

FOX, A.   Beyond Contract: Work, Power, and Trust Relations (Faber, London, 1974).

FREEDLAND, M. R.   Note on *Denmark Productions Ltd.* v. *Boscobel Productions Ltd.* (*1969*) (1969) 32 MLR 314.

——   Note on *Hill* v. *C. A. Parsons & Company Ltd.* (*1971*) (1972) 1 ILJ 37.

——   Note on *Cyril Leonard & Co.* v. *Simo Securities Trusts Ltd.* (*1972*) (1972) 1 ILJ 101.

——   Note on *H. W. Smith* (*Cabinets*) *Ltd.* v. *Brindle* (*1973*) and *Lees* v. *Arthur Greaves* (*Lees*) *Ltd.* (*1973, NIRC*) (1973) 2 ILJ 96.

—— Note on *Marriott* v. *Oxford and District Co-operative Society Ltd.* (*1969*) (1970) 33 MLR 95.

FRIDMAN, G. H. L. The Modern Law of Employment (Sweet & Maxwell, London, 1963, 2nd Supp. 1967).

GANZ, G. *Public Law Principles Applicable to Dismissal from Employment* (1967) 30 MLR 288.

GARDINER, G. Note on *Report of the Inter-Departmental Committee* on *Lister* v. *Romford Ice & Cold Storage Co. Ltd.* (1959) 22 MLR 652.

GILLING-SMITH, D. The Complete Guide to Pensions and Superannuation (2nd edn. Penguin, Harmondsworth, 1968).

GOODHART, A. L. *Damages and Pensions* (Note on *British Transport Commission* v. *Gourley* (*1956*) (1967) 83 LQR 492.

GRAHAM, G. B. *The Effect of Liquidation on Contracts of Service* (1952) 15 MLR 48.

GRIME, R. P. Note on *Pepper* v. *Webb* (*1969*) (1969) 32 MLR 575.

GRUNFELD, G. Note on the *Contracts of Employment Act 1963* (1964) 27 MLR 70.

HEPPLE, B. A. The Ambit of Natural Justice—Note on (*inter alia*) *Hannan* v. *Bradford Corporation* (*1969*) [1970] CLJ 185.

—— Race, Jobs and the Law in Britain (2nd edn., Penguin, Harmondsworth, 1970).

HEPPLE, B. A. and O'HIGGINS, P. Individual Employment Law (Sweet & Maxwell, London, 1970).

—— *Drafting Employment Terms* (1972) 36 Conveyancer 77.

—— Encyclopedia of Labour Relations Law (Sweet & Maxwell etc., London etc., 1972–), Part I—Individual Employment Law.

HERTSLET, C. J. B. The Law of Master and Servant (Crockford, London, 1850).

HICKLING, M. A. Note on *Report of the Committee on the Truck Acts* (1962) 25 MLR 220.

HOBSBAWM, E. J. Labouring Men (Weidenfeld & Nicholson, London, 1964), Ch. 17—'Custom, Wages and Workload in the 19th Century'.

HOWELLS, R. W. L. *Enforcing the Contract of Employment* (1972) 35 MLR 310.

JOLOWICZ, J. A. *The Right to Indemnity between Master and Servant* [1956] CLJ 101, [1957] CLJ 21.

JONES, G. *Per quod servitium amisit* (1958) 74 LQR 39.

KAHN-FREUND, O. Note on *Nokes* v. *Doncaster Amalgamated Collieries* (*1940*) (1941) 4 MLR 221.

—— *The Tangle of the Truck Acts* (1949) 4 Industrial Law Review 2.

—— The System of Industrial Relations in Great Britain

(ed. Flanders and Clegg) (Blackwells, Oxford, 1954), Ch. II—'The Legal Framework'.

KAHN-FREUND, O.   Note on *National Coal Board* v. *Galley* (*1958*) (1958) 21 MLR 194.

——   *A Note on Status and Contract in British Labour Law* (1967) 30 MLR 635.

KAHN-FREUND, O. and HEPPLE, B. A.   Laws against Strikes (Fabian Research Series 305, London, 1972).

KOH, K. L.   *Restraints against Undertaking Work during Currency of Service* (1970) 4 Journal of the Association of Law Teachers 67.

LEVY, H. M.   *The Role of the Law in the United States and England in Protecting the Worker from Discharge and Discrimination* (1969) 18 ICLQ 558.

LEWIS, N.   Note on *Merchant Shipping Act 1970* (1970) 34 MLR 55.

——   *Strikes and Contracts of Employment* [1968] JBL 24.

LEWIS, R.   Note on *Report of the Committee of Inquiry under Professor Phelps Brown concerning Labour in Building & Civil Engineering* (1969) 32 MLR 75.

LOCKWOOD, D.   The Black-coated Worker—A study in Class Consciousness (Allen & Unwin, London, 1958).

LUPTON, T. (ed.)   Payment Systems—Selected Readings (Penguin, Harmondsworth, 1972).

MACDONALD, A.   Handybook of the Law relative to Masters, Workmen, Servants & Apprentices (Mackenzie, London, etc., 1868).

MCDONNELL, J.   The Law of Master and Servant (3rd edn., Stevens, London, 1908).

MEYERS, F.   Ownership of Jobs—A Comparative Study (University of California, Los Angeles, 1964).

NAPIER, B.   Working to Rule—a Breach of the Contract of Employment? (1972) 1 ILJ 1.

NATIONAL BOARD FOR PRICES AND INCOMES   Report No. 65—Payments by Results Systems (Cmnd. 3627, H.M.S.O., London, 1968). Report No. 132—Salary Structures (Cmnd. 4178, H.M.S.O., London, 1969).

NATIONAL JOINT ADVISORY COUNCIL TO THE DEPARTMENT OF EMPLOYMENT AND PRODUCTIVITY   Report on Sick Pay Schemes (H.M.S.O,. London, 1964).

——   Report on Preservation of Pension Rights (H.M.S.O., London, 1966).

——   Report on Dismissal Procedures (H.M.S.O., London, 1967).

O'HIGGINS, P.   Note on *Contracts of Employment Act 1963* [1964] CLJ 220.

———   *When is an Employee not an Employee?—Inducing Breach of Contract* [1967] CLJ 27.

———   *Legal Effect of Strike Notice* [1968] CLJ 223.

———   *Strike Notices: Another Approach* (1973) 2 ILJ 152.

———   Note on *Sutcliffe* v. *Hawker Siddeley Aviation Ltd.* (*1973*) (1973) 2 ILJ 238.

PILCH, M. and WOOD, V.   New Trends in Pensions (Hutchinson, London, 1964).

———   Pension Scheme Practice (Hutchinson, London, 1967).

PLUMRIDGE, M.   *Disciplinary Practice* (report of a research study) (1966) 48 Personnel Management 138.

REID, J.   Note on *NJAC Report on Dismissal Procedures* (*1967*) (1968) 31 MLR 64.

REID, G. and ROBERTSON, D. J. (eds.)   Fringe Benefits, Labour Costs and Social Security (Allen & Unwin, London, 1965).

RIDEOUT, R. W.   *The Contract of Employment* (1966) 19 Current Legal Problems 111.

———   *The Industrial Tribunals* (1968) 21 Current Legal Probelms 178.

ROBSON, W. A.   *Industrial Law* (1935) 51 LQR 195.

ROYAL COMMISSION ON THE LABOUR LAWS (1873–75)   First Report 1874; Parly. Papers 1874, Vol. XXIV p. 391. Final Report 1875; Parly. Papers 1875, Vol. XXX p. 1.

ROYAL COMMISSION ON TRADE UNIONS & EMPLOYERS' ASSOCIATIONS (1965–68)   Research Paper No. 11 Part 2—changing Wage Payment systems (McKersie, R. S.).

SCHWARZER, W.   *Wages during Temporary Disability—Partial Impossibility in Employment Contracts* (1952) Stanford Law Review 30.

SELECT COMMITTEE OF THE HOUSE OF COMMONS ON THE LAW OF MASTER AND SERVANT   Proceedings & Report—Parly. Papers 1865; Vol. VIII, pp. 1 ff., 1866, Vol. XIII. pp. 1 ff.

SELZNICK, P.   Law, Society & Industrial Justice (Russell Sage Foundation, New York, 1969).

SIMON, D.   Democracy and the Labour Movement (ed. Saville J.), Ch. 2.—'Master and Servant' (on the Master and Servant Statutes) (Lawrence & Wishart, London, 1954).

SMITH, C. M.   The Law of Master and Servant (Sweets, London, 8th edn., 1931).

STOLJAR, S.   *The Great Case of Cutter* v. *Powell* (1956) 34 Canadian Bar Review 288.

TILLYARD, SIR FRANK   The Worker and the State (3rd edn., Routledge, London, 1948). The first (1923) edition is also of special interest.

WEDDERBURN, K. W.   Evidence to the Royal Commission on Trade

Unions and Employers' Associations (1965–68). Minutes of Evidence No. 31 (H.M.S.O., London, 1966).

—— The Legal Force of Plant Bargains (Note on *Loman and Henderson* v. *Merseyside Transport Ltd. (1968)*) (1969) 32 MLR 99.

—— The Worker and the Law (2nd edn., Penguin, Harmondsworth, 1971).

WEDDERBURN, K. W. and DAVIES, P. L. Employment Grievances & Disputes Procedures in Britain (University of California, Berkeley, etc., 1969).

WILLIAMS, G. Note on *Unger* v. *Preston Corporation (1940)* (1943) 6 MLR 160.

—— *Vicarious Liability & the Master's Indemnity* (1957) 20 MLR 200, 437.

WILLIAMS, K. Note on *Lees* v. *Arthur Greaves (Lees) Ltd. (1974, CA)* (1974) 3 ILJ 158.

Index

Employer
  change of, formation of new contract, 10–11
  damages for breach by, *see* Wrongful Dismissal
  death or incapacity of, 313–15
  duties of
    to employ, 21–3, 31–2
    to provide work, 23–7, 86–96
  rights of
    disciplinary suspension, 80–2
    lay-off, 86–96
    lock-out, 102–5
    sickness, suspension during, 108–14
    variation of terms, 376
Employment Relationship
  duty to maintain, 22–3, 31–2
    duty to provide work distinguished from, 23–7
Entire and Divisible Obligations, 126–36
  forfeiture and, 227–9
  frustration and, 327
Equity
  promissory estoppel, 58–60
  reinstatement, doctrine concerning, 272–8
Essential Work Order
  guaranteed wages under, 93
  restriction on dismissal under, 289–90
  right to reinstatement under, 26–7
Estoppel
  promissory, 58–60
  statutory particulars of terms and, 13, 374
  transfer of employment, on, 352–3

Fines
  breach by employee, for, 137–9
Fixed Term Contracts, 193
  frustration and, 305–7
  implied yearly terms, 143–6
  periodic contracts, 146–8
  purpose contracts, 148–9
  statutory treatment of, 162–4, 193
Force Majeure
  guaranteed pay agreements, clauses in, 94–5
Forfeiture
  pension rights, of, 192, 230–1, 383
  summary dismissal and, 227–33

Formation
  contract, of, 8–11
    general contract principles and, 34–9
  terms, of, 11–19, 47–8
    general contract principles and, 32–9
    recent developments in, 372–6
Frustration, 301–29
  automatic operation of, 323–6
  death of employer and, 313–15
  definition of, 302
  economic reasons, for, 315–18
  effect on rights and obligations, 326–9
  fault, requirement of lack of, 320–3
  incapacity
    employee, of, 303–10
    employer, of, 313–15
  redundancy and, 308–10
  self-induced, 320–3
  supervening illegality and, 318–20
  war, caused by, 310–11

Geographical Mobility
  whether presumption of, 44–6
Grievance Procedures,
  particulars of, 14–15, 378
Guaranteed Pay
  lay off, during, 92–6
    industrial action, and, 94
  notice, during, 161–2

Hearing
  dismissal, before, 223–4
Holding Departments
  contractual status of, 114–15
Holiday Pay
  accrual of, 132
Holidays
  suspension of employment during, 77
Hours of Work
  variation of, 48–53

Illegality
  supervening, 318–20
Implied Terms
  co-operation, as to, 29–32
  disciplinary suspension, as to, 80–2
  employees' rights and, 373–6
  fact and law distinguished, 38–9
  incorporation of, 11–19, 37–9, 47–8, 373–5